The Blackwell Encyclopedic Dictionary of Managerial Economics

THE BLACKWELL ENCYCLOPEDIA OF MANAGEMENT

EDITED BY CARY L. COOPER AND CHRIS ARGYRIS

The Blackwell Encyclopedic Dictionary of Accounting
Edited by A. Rashad Abdel-khalik

The Blackwell Encyclopedic Dictionary of Strategic Management
Edited by Derek F. Channon

The Blackwell Encyclopedic Dictionary of Management Information Systems
Edited by Gordon B. Davis

The Blackwell Encyclopedic Dictionary of Marketing
Edited by Barbara R. Lewis and Dale Littler

The Blackwell Encyclopedic Dictionary of Managerial Economics
Edited by Robert McAuliffe

The Blackwell Encyclopedic Dictionary of Organizational Behavior
Edited by Nigel Nicholson

The Blackwell Encyclopedic Dictionary of International Management
Edited by John O'Connell

The Blackwell Encyclopedic Dictionary of Finance
Edited by Dean Paxson and Douglas Wood

The Blackwell Encyclopedic Dictionary of Human Resource Management
Edited by Lawrence H. Peters, Charles R. Greer and Stuart A. Youngblood

The Blackwell Encyclopedic Dictionary of Operations Management
Edited by Nigel Slack

The Blackwell Encyclopedic Dictionary of Business Ethics
Edited by Patricia Werhane and R. Edward Freeman

The Blackwell Encyclopedic Dictionary of Managerial Economics

Edited by Robert McAuliffe

Babson College

BLACKWELL
Business

Copyright © Blackwell Publishers Ltd, 1997, 1999
Editorial Organization © Robert McAuliffe, 1997, 1999

First published 1997
Reprinted 1998

First published in paperback 1999

Blackwell Publishers Inc.
350 Main Street
Malden, Massachusetts 02148, USA

Blackwell Publishers Ltd
108 Cowley Road
Oxford OX4 1JF
UK

Library of Congress Cataloging-in-Publication Data

The Blackwell encyclopedic dictionary of managerial economics /
  edited by Robert McAuliffe.
      p.   cm. – (The Blackwell encyclopedia of management)
  Includes bibliographical references and index.
  ISBN 1–55786–965–0 (alk. paper) — ISBN 0–631–21483–6 (alk. paper: Pbk)
  1. Managerial economics—Dictionaries.   I. McAuliffe, Robert E.
  II. Series.
HD30.22.B55   1996   96–46009
658.15′03—dc20   CIP

British Library Cataloguing in Publication Data
A CIP catalogue record for this book is available from the British Library.

Contents

—— Preface ——

The Blackwell Encyclopedic Dictionary of Managerial Economics provides a valuable, comprehensive, and current resource for business students, practitioners, and researchers. The scope of the entries ranges from basic definitions, such as the *law of demand*, to advanced topics such as *estimating demand* and *time-series forecasting*. Each entry is written clearly and concisely and often includes important reference materials in the bibliography for those who wish to pursue the topics in more detail. In addition, the entries are thoroughly cross-referenced so that the readers may easily find information on related issues for a better understanding of the concepts and their interrelationships.

The dictionary also incorporates new developments in the theory and organization of the firm and the operation of markets. For example, issues such as the *principle-agent problem*, the US Justice Department's *1992 merger guidelines*, and other recent research which has changed economic thinking about the firm and the market are thoroughly discussed. Most of the entries also focus on the application of these ideas in daily operations from a managerial economics perspective.

Another unique feature of this volume is its careful exposition of the statistical and econometric issues that arise in applied work. Statistical tools such as linear regression are now included in spreadsheets and appear in standard texts in managerial economics. Unfortunately, the pitfalls of using these techniques when they are inappropriate are not normally considered. The entries in this volume, such as *simultaneous equations bias*, the *identification problem*, and *estimating demand* address these problems so that practitioners and researchers may better understand and employ these tools.

Robert McAuliffe

—— Contributors ——

Kostas Axarloglou
Babson College

Vickie Bajtelsmit
Colorado State University

Gilbert Becker
St. Anselms College

Alexandra Bernasek
Colorado State University

Roberto Bonifaz
Babson College

Michael D. Curley
Kennesaw State College

John Edmunds
Babson College

Govind Hariharan
University of Buffalo

Sean Hopkins
University of Buffalo

Kent A. Jones
Babson College

Eduardo Ley
Resources for the Future

Wei Li
Fuqua School of Business

Robert McAuliffe
Babson College

Alastair McFarlane
Ecole PolyTechnique Federale de Lausanne

Steven G. Medema
University of Colorado at Denver

Dileep R. Mehta
Georgia State University

Laurence S. Moss
Babson College

Lidija Polutnik
Babson College

Laura Power
Treasury Department, Washington D.C.

Mark Rider
Treasury Department, Washington D.C.

Don Sabbarese
Kennesaw State College

S. Alan Schlacht
Kennesaw State College

James G. Tompkins
Kennesaw State College

Theofanis Tsoulouhas
North Carolina State University

Roger Tutterow
Kennesaw State University

Nikolaos Vettas
Fuqua School of Business

A

accommodation When established firms are threatened by entry, those firms can retaliate against the new firm by cutting prices and increasing advertising, or the firms can accommodate the entrant. Entry will be accommodated when the incumbent firms cannnot maximize profits by deterring entry and they will not react aggressively to the entrant because it would lower their profits to do so. The incumbent firms may have FIRST-MOVER ADVANTAGES since they can take actions before entry which may affect the entrant's profitability and market position. For example, existing firms may under- or overinvest in capital equipment to influence the entrant's choice of its scale of operation even though the existing firms cannot prevent the entry; see Jacquemin (1987) and Tirole (1988).

Whether or not the existing firms over- or underinvest in capital depends on how the investment will affect the existing firms' competitive position in the period(s) after entry has occurred and on the expected reaction of the entering firm if entry were to occur. For example, investment in productive capacity or in producing additional output to experience lower costs from the LEARNING CURVE all make the incumbent firms tougher competitors in the second period. If entry can be deterred, the established firms will then overinvest in the current period. But if the incumbents cannot deter the entrant and the entrant is expected to react aggressively, they should underinvest in these activities to avoid the aggressive response from the entrant in the next period. ADVERTISING, however, can make incumbent firms less likely to respond aggressively to entry since they can enjoy higher profits from the "captive" consumers who have received advertising messages (Schmalensee, 1983). Therefore, in some cases, established firms should underinvest in advertising to indicate their willingness to compete aggressively against an entrant should entry occur.

Bibliography

Fudenberg, D. Tirole, J. (1984). The fat-cat effect, the puppy-dog ploy and the lean and hungry look. *American Economic Review*, 74, 361–6.

Jacquemin, A. (1987). *The New Industrial Organization: Market Forces and Strategic Behavior*. Cambridge, MA: MIT Press.

Schmalensee, R. (1983). Advertising and entry deterrence: an exploratory model. *Journal of Political Economy*, 91, 636–53.

Tirole, J. (1988). *The Theory of Industrial Organization*. Cambridge, MA: MIT Press.

ROBERT E. MCAULIFFE

accounting profit Accounting profit is defined as total revenues from output sold in a given period minus those costs incurred during that period (including DEPRECIATION expenses). The difference between the accounting definition of profits and economic profits lies in how costs and depreciation are calculated (*see* ECONOMIC PROFIT). Under generally accepted accounting practices, all costs incurred by the firm in a given period are expensed in that period (except expenditures on tangible assets, which are depreciated over several periods). This means that expenditures on research and development, training, trademarks, goodwill, and patents (i.e. all sources of intangible capital) are expensed in the current period, even though they may yield benefits well into the future. As a result, accounting profits will overstate economic profits whenever current period profits were generated in part by previous investments in intangible assets because there are no accounting costs applied in the current period for those intangible assets and those assets are not often included in calculations of the firm's total value. In addition, the depreciation expense for tangible assets allowed under accounting rules is not the same as the ECONOMIC DEPRECIATION for those assets.

These problems with accounting measures of economic profits have led some economists to argue that there is no relationship between accounting profits and economic profits (Fisher and McGowan, 1983). This strong assertion has been challenged by several economists and remains controversial; see Long and Ravenscraft (1984) and Martin (1984). Salamon (1985) and Edwards, Kay and Mayer (1987) provide recommendations regarding proper adjustments of accounting profits and those circumstances where they will more reliably approximate economic profits. Salamon suggests using conditional internal rate of return (IRR) estimates from financial statements as a proxy for the economic rate of return which can be used to infer the measurement errors from using accounting profits. He found that accounting rates of return, while strongly correlated with the estimated IRR, nevertheless showed considerable variation that the IRR could not explain. The measurement error from using accounting rates of return was systematically related to firm size and therefore cast doubts on cross-section studies of the relationship between concentration and profitability.

Bibliography

Edwards, J., Kay, J. Mayer, C. (1987). *The Economic Analysis of Accounting Profitability*. Oxford: OUP.

Fisher, F. M. McGowan, J. J. (1983). On the misuse of accounting rates of return to infer monopoly profits. *American Economic Review*, 73, 82–97.

Long, W. F. Ravenscraft, D. J. (1984). The misuse of accounting rates of return: comment. *American Economic Review*, 74, 494–500.

Martin, S. (1984). The misuse of accounting rates of return: comment. *American Economic Review*, 74, 501–506.

Salamon, G. L. (1985). Accounting rates of return. *American Economic Review*, 75, 495–504.

ROBERT E. McAULIFFE

adverse selection   Adverse selection refers to a class of problems that are created by ASYMMETRIC INFORMATION between parties to a transaction. Adverse selection problems arise because the characteristics of products sold in markets differ, and one party (generally the seller) has valuable information about those characteristics which is not available to the other party (generally the buyer). The classic illustration of this kind of problem is Akerlof's (1970) modeling of the used car market (*see* LEMONS MARKET). Adverse selection problems are also a consequence of individuals having different abilities, and there being IMPERFECT INFORMATION about a specific individual's abilities. In those cases, one party to a transaction has valuable information about their own ability, but that information is not available to the other party (or parties). Adverse selection problems often arise in the context of principal–agent problems (*see* PRINCIPAL–AGENT PROBLEM). They are common in insurance markets, financial markets, and labor markets.

Adverse selection has consequences for market EFFICIENCY. In the presence of adverse selection, the allocation of resources is almost always inefficient and, under certain conditions, EQUILIBRIUM may not exist. Rothschild and Stiglitz (1976) establish these effects of adverse selection in insurance markets. The adverse selection problem in insurance markets arises because those with the highest probability of experiencing a negative event are the ones who want to purchase insurance, but they are the least desirable customers from the perspective of the insurance company because of their high probability of becoming claimants. The insurance company's problem is that it has difficulty distinguishing between the different types of individuals.

Stiglitz and Weiss (1981) examine the effects of adverse selection in financial markets. Adverse selection problems arise in credit markets because it is difficult for lenders to distinguish between individuals who have a high probability of default and those who have a low probability. Stiglitz and Weiss find that when banks employ screening devices such as raising interest rates or collateral requirements, these can affect the behavior of borrowers and the distribution of borrowers (for example those who are willing to borrow at high interest rates may be worse risks on average) and can increase the riskiness of the bank's portfolio; thus banks may be more likely to ration credit instead. Their results have implications for landlord–tenant relationships and employer–employee relationships as well.

A classic work on how agents try to overcome problems of adverse selection is Spence's (1974) work on market SIGNALING. He suggests that the more able (higher quality) individuals will want to signal their ability to the other parties in the transaction. In the context of the labor market, for example, those individuals may be willing to incur costly education or training in order to signal their quality to an employer. In the context of the used car market on the other hand, sellers of the "good" cars may be willing to incur the cost of offering a warrantee with the sale of the car.

see also **imperfect information; asymmetric information; principal–agent problem**

Bibliography

Akerlof, G. A. (1970). The market for 'lemons': quality uncertainty and the market mechanism. *Quarterly Journal of Economics*, **84**, 488–500.

Rothschild, M. Stiglitz, J. (1976). Equilibrium in competitive insurance markets: an essay on the economics of imperfect information. *Quarterly Journal of Economics*, **90**, 629–49.

Spence, M. (1974). *Market Signaling*. Cambridge, MA: Harvard University Press.

Stiglitz, J. Weiss, A. (1981). Credit rationing in markets with imperfect information. *American Economic Review*, **71**, 912–27.

ALEXANDRA BERNASEK

advertising Advertising refers to expenditures in various media (such as radio, television, newspapers and magazines) made by firms to increase sales. Firms may often use advertising to differentiate their products from competing brands. If successful, advertising could increase the demand for a product, reduce the price ELASTICITY of demand and allow the firm to charge a higher price and earn higher profits. Advertising has been the subject of some controversy, both in terms of how it affects the demand for a firm's product and whether unregulated markets generate too little or too much advertising. One important issue is whether advertising increases sales by changing consumer tastes (persuasion) or by informing consumers of alternative brands (education). If advertising increases sales merely by persuading consumers, then society is not necessarily better off as a result of advertising expenditures since these outlays have arbitrarily altered tastes in favor of the advertised product. But if advertising provides information, these expenditures may enable consumers to make better choices in the market and reduce their costs of finding appropriate products. When advertising provides information to consumers, the expenditures may increase EFFICIENCY.

Optimal advertising levels

The profit-maximizing level of advertising occurs when the MARGINAL REVENUE from additional advertising expenditures is just equal to the MARGINAL COST. If advertising allows the firm to sell one more unit, then the marginal benefit from the sale is the firm's profit per unit, price minus the MARGINAL COST of production or $(P - MC)$ and this should be equated to the marginal cost of advertising. The additional sales revenue a firm can expect from advertising will depend upon the number of potential consumers exposed to the advertisement and that advertisement's effectiveness in creating a sale. The marginal cost of advertising should be rising as more advertising messages are sent to consumers since additional advertising messages will have decreasing effectiveness as the number of messages increases; see the DORFMAN–STEINER CONDITION.

To maximize profits from a given advertising budget, firms should advertise in different media until the marginal profit per dollar spent on each of the media is equal. If a firm earns a profit of $(P - MC)$ per unit sold, and P_{TV} is the price of an advertising message on television, the marginal profit per dollar spent on television is $(P - MC)/P_{TV}$ for every additional sale brought about by a television advertisement. Similarly, the marginal profit per dollar spent on newspaper advertisements will be $(P - MC)/P_{NEWS}$ and the firm should advertise until it earns the same expected net profits in each of the media. That is:

$$ES_{TV}(P - MC)/P_{TV}$$
$$= ES_{NEWS}(P - MC)/P_{NEWS}$$
$$= \ldots$$
$$= ES_{RADIO}(P - MC)/P_{RADIO}$$

where ES_i represents the expected additional units sold from advertising messages in each of the i media, P_i is the price of an advertising message in each of the media and P_{RADIO} is the price of an advertising message on radio. Following this principle, the firm will maximize expected profits from its advertising budget.

Advertising intensity has often been measured by the advertising–sales ratio, i. e. total advertising expenditures divided by total sales. While the Dorfman-Steiner condition shows that the profit-maximizing level of advertising depends on this ratio, it may not be an appropriate measure of advertising intensity. Consumers do not respond to the dollar amount a company spends on advertising, they respond to the number of messages they see. Therefore the appropriate measure of advertising intensity for managers should be total advertising expenditures deflated by an index of the cost per million viewers in that medium. This adjusted measure will indicate the number of people potentially exposed to an advertising message and could be divided by sales to measure advertising intensity; see Ehrlich and Fisher (1982) and McAuliffe (1987).

Does advertising increase or reduce competition?

If advertising creates a barrier to entry (*see* BARRIERS TO ENTRY), established firms could enjoy long run economic profits (*see* ECONOMIC PROFIT). Advertising could create brand loyalty, for example, and decrease the price elasticity of demand. According to Comanor and Wilson (1974), advertising expenditures could create a barrier to entry by increasing the capital required for entry, creating ECONOMIES OF SCALE, or creating brand loyalty for established brands. If a new entrant has to advertise more to overcome brand loyalty, the entrant could be placed at a disadvantage relative to existing firms. Simon and Arndt (1983) pointed out that it is incorrect to argue that advertising (or any other single input) can create economies of scale because the concept refers to changes in *all* inputs. When costs decline as more of a *single* input is employed, there are increasing returns

to that input. But Simon and Arndt found there are DIMINISHING RETURNS to advertising. Spence (1980) developed a model where advertising is treated as an input in the production of sales revenue for the firm and suggested that advertising could combine with other factors of production to create economies of scale advantages for established firms. He showed that established firms could use these economies of scale to their advantage to deter entry.

Since established firms are already in the market, Cubbin (1981) argued they could have FIRST-MOVER ADVANTAGES. Incumbent firms could use this strategic advantage by increasing their advertising so that potential entrants would have to advertise more as well. But as Schmalensee (1983) and Fudenberg and Tirole (1984) have indicated, advertising to prevent entry, much like LIMIT PRICING, is a reversible decision. The threat to increase advertising or output may not be the profit-maximizing choice once entry has occurred, since established firms may earn higher profits if they accommodate the entrant. In such a case, the threat of higher advertising or higher output is not a credible strategy (*see* CREDIBLE STRATEGIES). When Schmalensee examined the post-entry equilibrium, he found that established firms always advertised less when threatened by entry. This unusual result occurs if the established firm has become a "fat cat" to use Fudenberg and Tirole's terminology. When advertising creates goodwill it will have two effects on potential entry. First, advertising by the incumbent will reduce the market share that remains free to the potential entrant and this reduces the incentive to enter the industry. But as this goodwill increases, the established firm becomes fat and lazy. Since the established firm has a loyal customer base from its past advertising, it is less inclined to react aggressively to a new entrant and will not increase its advertising expenditures or reduce prices. When the latter effect is stronger, the established firm must *underinvest* in advertising to signal to potential entrants that it will aggressively cut prices and increase advertising if entry were to occur. What is important from this literature is that even if established firms have the ability to prevent entry, that does not mean that it is in their best interests to do so. Profits may be higher if the rate of entry is reduced; (*see* ACCOMMODATION; CREDIBLE STRATEGIES; SIGNALING).

Nelson (1974) suggested that the elasticity of demand for a product depended on the number of *known* alternative brands. Since advertising provides information about the existence of competing products, he argued that advertising could increase the elasticity of demand and make entry into an industry less difficult. Furthermore, Nelson argued that the information content of advertising and the best media to choose would differ depending upon whether the product was a search good or an experience good (*see* SEARCH GOODS; EXPERIENCE GOODS). Since consumers can easily determine the characteristics of search goods by inspection, advertising for search goods will tend to be informative and concentrated in more informative media such as newspapers and magazines. But consumers must actually use experience goods to determine their quality, so informational advertising will not be as helpful. Therefore advertising for experience goods relies more on product imagery and seller reputation while being concentrated in more experiential media such as television. Furthermore, Nelson showed that even if advertising for experience goods was not informative, the very fact that the product was advertised conveyed information to consumers about the product's quality. Nelson suggested that only high-quality producers would have the incentive to advertise heavily and this served as a signal of quality to consumers of the good.

Ehrlich and Fisher (1982) agreed that advertising provided information and that it reduced the costs to consumers of finding those products which best fulfilled their needs. They also distinguished between media advertising expenditures and other promotional efforts. Since advertising provides information, both firms and consumers can produce the information, though at different costs. The full price of a product to the consumer is the price paid plus information costs which Ehrlich and Fisher assert are primarily the consumer's time searching for the appropriate product. Firms can reduce these costs through media advertising expenditures or through other promotional efforts such as trade shows, customer services and other selling efforts. They predicted advertising and selling efforts would be greater

the higher are consumer wages and the larger the market for the brand. Higher wages imply higher time costs to consumers from search while a larger market implies a lower cost to the manufacturer of providing information through advertising. Furthermore, media advertising should be less for producer goods since these buyers are very knowledgeable and identifiable relative to buyers of consumer goods. Therefore they predicted that trade shows and other direct selling methods would be more productive for these products. The empirical results using US data from 1946–69, support their hypotheses: advertising and promotional efforts are positively related to wage rates in the economy and advertising–sales ratios are negatively related to the price elasticity of demand. Ehrlich and Fisher also found that advertising expenditures did not have long-lived effects and were completely depreciated within one year, a finding that is also consistent with McAuliffe (1987).

McAuliffe (1987) tested the hypothesis that advertising reduced competition and increased firm profitability. If advertising causes higher profits, then current advertising levels should have significantly positive effects on future profits. Out of 27 firms for which there were data from 1955 until 1983, advertising had significant, consistently positive effects on future profits for only three firms. While there was strong correlation between current advertising and current profits for the firms in the sample, the effects of advertising did not last beyond a year.

There is an important difference between advertising expenditures and other capital expenditures from the entrant's perspective, however. If the attempt to enter the industry does not succeed, the entrant can recover some of its original investment costs by selling its plant and equipment. But advertising costs cannot be recovered and thus represent a sunk cost to the entering firm (*see* SUNK COSTS). When entry requires significant levels of advertising, it is more risky, the costs of failing are that much higher and this could deter entrants; see Kessides (1986) and Sutton (1991). In his study, Sutton suggested that advertising and research and development represent *endogenous* sunk costs because firms can vary the amounts of these expenditures, while the sunk costs of investment in plant and equipment are dictated by technology. This means that, in some industries, firms may engage in ever-escalating expenditures in these areas as they compete to gain advantage.

Bibliography

Comanor, W. S. Wilson, T. A. (1974). *Advertising and Market Power*. Cambridge, MA: Harvard University Press.

Cubbin, J. (1981). Advertising and the theory of entry barriers. *Economica*, 48, 289–99.

Ehrlich, I. Fisher, L. (1982). The derived demand for advertising: a theoretical and empirical investigation. *American Economic Review*, 72, 366–88.

Fudenberg, D. Tirole, J. (1984). The fat-cat effect, the puppy-dog ploy and the lean and hungry look. *American Economic Review*, 74, 361–6.

Kessides, I. N. (1986). Advertising, sunk costs, and barriers to entry. *Review of Economics and Statistics*, 68, 84–95.

McAuliffe, R. E. (1987). *Advertising, Competition, and Public Policy: Theories and New Evidence*. Lexington, MA: DC Heath.

Nelson, P. (1974). Advertising as information. *Journal of Political Economy*, 82, 729–54.

Schmalensee, R. (1983). Advertising and entry deterrence: an exploratory model. *Journal of Political Economy*, 91, 636–53.

Simon, J. L. Arndt, J. (1983). Advertising and economies of scale: critical comments on the evidence. *Journal of Industrial Economics*, 32, 229–42.

Spence, M. A. (1980). Notes on advertising, economies of scale, and entry barriers. *Quarterly Journal of Economics*, 95, 493–507.

Sutton, J. (1991). *Sunk Costs and Market Structure*. Cambridge, MA: MIT.

ROBERT E. MCAULIFFE

antitrust policy   Antitrust policy in the US and Europe (EU) is based on several statutes which identify various forms of business behavior which are deemed to be anticompetitive and therefore illegal. The three main antitrust statutes in the US are the 1890 SHERMAN ACT, the 1914 CLAYTON ACT and the 1914 FEDERAL TRADE COMMISSION ACT. Their counterparts concerning competition policy in the EU lie in Articles 85 and 86 of the 1957 Treaty of Rome. Each of these laws has several sections which are written in language which is open to interpretation. As a result, the implementation of policy is dependent (in part) on the philosophies of the members of the governmental agencies and judiciary who are empowered, at any given point in history, to enforce the law.

Debate in the US has continued for decades as to the original intent of the framers of the Sherman and Clayton Acts. Bork (1966) believes that Senator Sherman was concerned with the reduction of output and DEADWEIGHT LOSS inefficiency resulting from monopoly. Martin (1994) and others believe that their original intent was also to protect consumers from unfair prices yielding excess economic profits (*see* ECONOMIC PROFIT) and in some instances to protect small businesses from unfair practices of their larger rivals. Still others, including Katzman (1984), argue that the original intent, in part, grew out of the concern that economic power, from both large absolute size and large relative size of firms, may translate into political power, to the detriment of democracy and the country's social structure. The interpretation of these statutes and the rigor with which they are enforced has varied over time and likely will continue to do so. In a historical analysis of the first century of antitrust in the US, Schwartz (1990) details cycles of approximately 25 years between peak periods of aggressive antitrust enforcement.

There is also controversy concerning the economic theory supporting these statutes (*see* STRUCTURE-CONDUCT-PERFORMANCE PARADIGM). Kovaleff (1990) has compiled the works of numerous current antitrust scholars who provide an array of studies on the merits of US antitrust law at the conclusion of its first century. Much of this work continues to focus on the perceived tradeoff between abuses of economic power and the benefits of economic EFFICIENCY resulting from large firm size.

EU policy in some respects parallels that of the US in that it prohibits artificial restrictions on competition and proscribes abuses of MARKET POWER. As Martin (1994) points out though, EU policy also has the goal of fostering the economic integration of the Community. Moreover, EU policy more forcefully and directly allows efficiency, *when ultimately used to benefit consumers*, as an exempting factor against charges of violations of the law. Finally,

EU policy specifically allows for small and medium sized firms to fix prices, share markets, and otherwise follow cartel-like activities (*see* CARTELS), in order to better compete with a DOMINANT FIRM, while under US law these activities have been declared illegal in all circumstances. Moreover, the promotion of smaller firms as an end in and of itself appears to be a more prominent goal in the EU than in the US.

Bibliography

Bork, R. (1966). Legislative intent and the policy of the Sherman Act. *Journal of Law and Economics*, 9, 7–48.
Greer, D. (1992). *Industrial Organization and Public Policy*. 3rd edn, New York: Macmillan.
Howard, M. (1983). *Antitrust and Trade Regulation*. Englewood Cliffs, NJ: Prentice-Hall.
Katzman, R. (1984). The attenuation of antitrust. *The Brookings Review*, 2, 23–7.
Kovaleff, T. (1990). A symposium on the 100th anniversary of the Sherman Act. *Antitrust Bulletin*, 35.
Martin, S. (1994). *Industrial Economics*. 2nd edn, New York: Macmillan.
Neale, A. (1977). *The Antitrust Laws of the U.S.A.* 2nd edn, Cambridge: CUP.
Schwartz, L. (1990). Cycles of antitrust zeal: predictability? *Antitrust Bulletin*, 35, 771–800.

GILBERT BECKER

arbitrage Arbitrage is the process of buying goods or assets in one market where the price is lower and selling them in markets where the price is higher for riskless profits. To successfully practice PRICE DISCRIMINATION firms must prevent arbitrage from occurring between the markets in which they sell the product at different prices. The act of arbitrage will tend to equalize prices between the two markets as demand is increased in the market where the price is lower causing its price to rise and supply is increased in the market where the price is higher causing its price to fall. This process may profitably continue until the difference in price between the two markets is equal to the transportation costs of moving the good from one market to the other.

Since arbitrage occurs frequently and easily in financial markets, modern finance theory relies on arbitrage arguments to understand asset pricing; see Varian (1987) and CAPITAL ASSET PRICING MODEL.

Bibliography

Varian, H. R. (1987). The arbitrage principle in financial economics. *Journal of Economic Perspectives*, 1, 55–72.

ROBERT E. MCAULIFFE

arc elasticity Arc elasticity is the measure of ELASTICITY to be used when the effect of a large change in a variable (e.g. price) is examined. Price elasticity of demand, ε_p, defined as the percentage change in quantity demanded for a given percentage change in price, can be calculated as

$$\varepsilon_p = \frac{(Q_2 - Q_1)}{(P_2 - P_1)} \times \frac{P}{Q}$$

where the subscripts indicate (1) initial and (2) final values for price (P) and quantity (Q). When large price changes are used, the value of the second term (P/Q) and thus of ε_p, may vary sharply depending on whether the initial or final price and quantity values are used. Arc elasticity avoids this by using the average price and quantity over the ranges in question. This gives an approximation of the consumer responsiveness for the entire range. As business pricing strategies typically involve discrete changes (for example, a 10 percent off sale) arc elasticity is the appropriate measure for management to examine.

see also **elasticity**

Bibliography

Douglas, E. (1992). *Managerial Economics: Analysis Strategy*. 4th edn, Englewood Cliffs, NJ: Prentice-Hall.

GILBERT BECKER

asset specificity An asset is specific if it has high value only when used in certain applications and does not have much value in alternative uses. Asset specificity is also an attribute of a given transaction and since it represents a greater risk to one party in the transaction, the costs of that transaction will be higher. This can create problems in contracting between firms in cases where, say, a supplier might have to make investments that are specific to its customer. The problem is that such an investment leaves the supplier vulnerable to the whims of its customer and the customer could put the supplier at a disadvantage; this is what the transaction cost literature refers to as the "hold-up problem" (Milgrom and Roberts, 1992). Both parties have an interest in resolving this problem, and economic incentives suggest that they will in those cases where TRANSACTIONS COSTS are not too high. But it is possible that the supplier might avoid making the necessary investments in specific assets if the UNCERTAINTY is too great, and asset specificity is one element that raises transaction costs. All else equal, a transaction will be more easily undertaken when both parties have little to risk. To limit its risk, a supplier might require complex, long-term CONTRACTS with its buyer to safeguard its investments in specific assets (see Joskow, 1987) or the two firms may integrate vertically to internalize these transaction costs and avoid the hold-up problem. In fact, Williamson (1986) has argued that asset specificity provides the major motivation for VERTICAL INTEGRATION.

Williamson identifies four different kinds of asset specificity which affect the decision to organize activities within the firm versus through the market.

(1) Site specificity: when an asset such as a plant must be located at a particular site to meet the requirements of the buyer. This can arise when, for example, railroads provide service to deliver coal to an electric utility. The track investment is not valuable for any other customers other than the utility.

(2) Physical asset specificity: if the rail cars needed to transport the coal to the utility are unique and have little value outside of that purpose, then the railroad's investment in these cars would represent a specific physical asset.

(3) Human-asset specificity: when people acquire skills specific to their work at the firm or in particular teams, their skills may not be as valuable in any other firms or with other teams. In these cases, an employment arrangement rather than a market arrangement would be the expected form of organization because workers are less likely to invest in acquiring skills which are valuable (specific) to only one firm.

(4) Dedicated assets: if a producer must expand capacity to meet the needs of a buyer, that producer now bears more risk and may require contractual assurances from the buyer.

These transaction costs affect the optimal size of the firm, the MINIMUM EFFICIENT SCALE (MES). As Coase (1937) suggested, there are costs to using the market just as there are costs to organizing activities internally within the firm. Decisions made within the firm are made by HIERARCHY and can be less costly than relying on the market. The boundary of the firm is determined at the point where it is less costly to use the market to obtain goods and services than to produce them within the firm. As Williamson (1986) notes, this is essentially a make-or-buy decision for the firm (*see* MAKE OR BUY DECISIONS). Transaction costs are higher from using the market when contracts are difficult to write that will prevent one party from taking advantage of the other or when contracts are incomplete. A well-known example Klein, Crawford and Alchian (1978) discuss is the arrangement between GM and the Fisher Body plant. Fisher was unwilling to make the investments in specific assets required by GM because the plant would be of little use to any company other than GM. Ultimately, GM integrated backward and purchased Fisher Body.

Bibliography

Coase, R. H. (1937). The nature of the firm. *Economica*, 4, 386–405.

Joskow, P. (1987). Contract duration and durable transaction-specific investments: the case of coal. *American Economic Review*, 77, 168–85.

Klein, B., Crawford, R. Alchian, A. (1978). Vertical integration, appropriable rents, and the competitive contracting process. *Journal of Law and Economics*, 21, 297–326.

Milgrom, P. Roberts, J. (1992). *Economics, organization and management*. Englewood Cliffs, NJ: Prentice-Hall.

Williamson, O. E. (1986). Vertical integration and related variations on a transactions–cost economics theme. Stiglitz, J. E. and Mathewson, G. F. *New Developments in the Analysis of Market Structure.* Cambridge, MA: MIT.

ROBERT E. MCAULIFFE

asymmetric information Asymmetric information exists when one party in the market or transaction has more or better information than the other party. Furthermore, the party with less information cannot rely on the other for the necessary information and cannot easily acquire it. For example, Akerlof (1970) noted that sellers of used cars have more information about the quality of the used car than buyers. This asymmetry can place the party with less information at a disadvantage and can interfere with market exchange to the point where market transactions break down. Akerlof showed that if buyers in the used car market considered all cars to be "average" in quality, no sellers of above-average quality cars would want to sell. This would reduce the average quality of the cars remaining in the market until only the worst cars (lemons) were traded; (*see* LEMONS MARKET; IMPERFECT INFORMATION; ADVERSE SELECTION). There is a tendency in these markets for quality levels to fall if consumers cannot discriminate between high-quality and low-quality products. The problem of asymmetric information also arises in employment decisions, insurance markets and credit markets where the person who is applying for a job, insurance or credit knows more about his or her abilities, health or risk than the employer, insurer or creditor. Firms have incentives to acquire more information in these situations while job applicants and consumers have incentives to provide more information, perhaps through SIGNALING.

High-quality producers have incentives for signaling in these markets to convince consumers that their products are better than average. Guarantees or warranties can be provided to assure consumers that a product will perform above the average. Firms also have incentives to invest in their reputation and in brand names to indicate that the product is a high-quality product. The product's price itself may convey information about quality in the appropriate circumstances. For example, Milgrom and Roberts (1986) found that both price

and ADVERTISING could provide signals to consumers for new, EXPERIENCE GOODS that are frequently purchased. High-quality firms have incentives to set a low price because they will benefit more from future repeat purchases than low-quality producers. However, Bagwell and Riordan (1991) suggest that, for a new durable product, the initial price should be high to signal that it is a high-quality product to uninformed consumers. As sales occur and more of the market becomes informed that this is a high-quality product, the firm should decrease price to maximize profits.

Bibliography

Akerlof, G. A. (1970). The market for lemons: quality uncertainty and the market mechanism. *Quarterly Journal of Economics*, **84**, 488–500.
Bagwell, K. Riordan, M. K. (1991). High and declining prices signal product quality. *American Economic Review*, **81**, 224–39.
Milgrom, P. Roberts, J. (1986). Price and advertising signals of product quality. *Journal of Political Economy*, **94**, 796–821.
Shughart, W. F., Chappell, W. F. Cottle, R. L. (1994). *Modern Managerial Economics*. Cincinatti, OH: South-Western Publishing.
Stiglitz, J. E. (1987). The causes and consequences of the dependence of quality on price. *Journal of Economic Literature*, **25**, 1–48.

ROBERT E. MCAULIFFE

auctions These are market institutions where products are purchased or contracts to supply a product are awarded (such as government procurement) through a competitive process, instead of simply posting a price for potential buyers or sellers. The seller of the product to be auctioned has some degree of MARKET POWER as a monopolist or as the buyer of services as a monopsonist (*see* MONOPOLY; AND MONOPSONY). There are four primary types of auctions. Perhaps the best-known is the **English auction** where buyers compete by offering higher bids until the highest offer wins. Since each bidder in such an English auction knows the current highest bid, these auctions provide considerable information to participants. The **Dutch auction** is the reverse of the English auction where the auctioneer calls out a very high bid to begin the process and then lowers the bid price until one buyer accepts the price. For **first-price sealed-bid auctions**, typical of government procurement bids, potential buyers (or suppliers) submit sealed bids and the highest (lowest) bidder wins the good (government contract). The last auction type is the **second-price sealed-bid auction**. Here the bidders submit sealed bids and the highest bidder wins the auction but pays the price of the second highest bid.

Bibliography

Hirschey, M. Pappas, J. L. (1995). *Fundamentals of Managerial Economics*. 5th edn, New York: Dryden.

McAfee, R. P. McMillan, J. (1987). Auctions and bidding. *Journal of Economic Literature*, **25**, 699–738.

ROBERT E. MCAULIFFE

autocorrelation   When estimating a LINEAR REGRESSION with TIME-SERIES DATA the error terms (the residuals in regression analysis) are assumed to be random. A random error is one that, on average, is not related to any preceding errors. When autocorrelation exists, the error term in one period is related to the error terms in previous periods. Such a relation will bias the estimated standard errors of the coefficients in the regression because the EXPECTED VALUE of the error term this period and the error term last period will not be zero. That is,

$$E(\varepsilon_t, \varepsilon_{t-1}) \neq 0$$

where ε_t is the error term for period t, and ε_{t-1} is the error term one period ago.

Autocorrelation can be positive, in which case the error term this period is likely to be above average (zero) if the error term last period was above average (zero). When autocorrelation is negative, the error term this period is likely to be below average (zero) if the error term last period was above average (zero). First-order autocorrelation means that the error term this period is related, on average, to the error term one period ago. Evidence of first-order autocorrelation is provided by the DURBIN–WATSON STATISTIC. An error term with first-order autocorrelation is represented as

$$\varepsilon_t = \rho\varepsilon_{t-1} + u_t$$

where ε_t is the error term for period t, ρ is the autocorrelation coefficient (which may be positive or negative but must be less than one in absolute value) and u_t is a random error. Second-order autocorrelation occurs when the error this period is related to the error last period and the period before that. Higher orders of autocorrelation are also possible.

When the residuals from the regression are autocorrelated, it means that there are persistent errors in explaining the dependent variable with the fitted regression equation. As a result, autocorrelation may indicate that the regression is misspecified and that a significant explanatory variable is missing from the regression equation. Procedures such as the Cochrane–Orcutt method can correct autocorrelation in the regression equation but this should be regarded as a second-best solution if additional explanatory variables have not been considered.

see also **time-series forecasting models**

Bibliography

Gujarati, D. N. (1988). *Basic Econometrics*. 2nd edn, New York: McGraw-Hill.

Maddala, G. S. (1992). *Introduction to Econometrics*. 2nd edn, New York: Macmillan.

ROBERT E. MCAULIFFE

average total cost   This measures the total economic costs of production per unit produced in the short run and is also referred to as short run average cost. Average total costs include the opportunity cost of capital employed (i.e. the normal risk-adjusted rate of return on capital), so a firm operating on its average total cost curve is earning zero ECONOMIC PROFIT; (*see* OPPORTUNITY COSTS). Since economic profits are the signal for ENTRY and EXIT from the industry, the average total cost curve represents a benchmark curve in the short run for predicting whether entry or exit will occur; (*see* SHORT RUN COST CURVES; LONG RUN COST CURVES).

Average total costs in the short run consist of average fixed costs and average variable costs. FIXED COSTS are those costs of production which do not vary with the level of output and are fixed in the short run. Therefore average fixed costs (fixed costs per unit produced) decrease as the quantity produced increases. Variable costs are those costs which vary with the level of output produced such as labor, material inputs, etc. Average variable costs are the variable costs per unit produced and will decrease initially but will eventually increase because of DIMINISHING RETURNS to the variable inputs. Thus the "typical" average total cost curve is U-shaped, representing decreasing per unit costs initially as more units are produced, but reaching a minimum and then rising as output rises per period.

see also **average variable costs; short run cost curves; fixed costs**

Bibliography

Carlton, D. W.   Perloff, J. M. (1994). *Modern Industrial Organization.* 2nd edn, New York: HarperCollins.
Douglas, E. J. (1992). *Managerial Economics.* 4th edn, Englewood Cliffs, NJ: Prentice-Hall.

ROBERT E. MCAULIFFE

average variable costs   Variable costs are those costs which vary with the level of output produced by the firm in the SHORT RUN and average variable costs are total variable costs per unit produced. If the firm did not produce output in a given period, these costs would not be incurred. The variable costs of production will be affected by the per unit cost of each variable input in production (e.g. hourly wage rates for workers), the productivity of the inputs in production, and the production technology available to the firm.

The average variable cost curve is important for short run decisions when the price received for producing output is so low that the firm may choose not to produce. A firm should shutdown its operations when, in the short run, it cannot earn revenues sufficient to pay its average variable costs. The firm has no choice regarding its FIXED COSTS in the short run since these costs must be paid whether or not the firm shuts down. Therefore, fixed costs should have *no* effect on the firm's short run decisions. However, the firm does not have to pay the variable costs of production in the short run, so if operating the plant costs more than the revenues earned, the firm should shutdown and simply pay its fixed costs. For a perfectly competitive firm, the shutdown point occurs where MARGINAL COST equals average variable cost (i.e. when average variable cost is at a minimum). At any price below this point, revenues earned from operations will fail to cover the costs of operations. The firm will have greater losses if it operates and should shutdown.

Bibliography

Carlton, D. W.   Perloff, J. M. (1994). *Modern Industrial Organization.* 2nd edn, New York: HarperCollins.
Douglas, E. J. (1992). *Managerial Economics.* 4th edn, Englewood Cliffs, NJ: Prentice-Hall.

ROBERT E. MCAULIFFE

B

backward integration A firm which buys one of its suppliers or chooses to produce inputs for itself has integrated backward in the production process. Such a decision may be motivated by concerns that supplies might be interrupted or because of ASSET SPECIFICITY problems that prevent successful contractual negotiations with existing, independent suppliers. Firms may also choose to integrate backwards for strategic benefits such as improving product quality or lowering costs. Backward integration gives the acquiring firm more control over its input supplies but it also requires more careful attention from management and coordination with the upstream firm. The upstream firm frequently wants to obtain input supplies at a lower cost, but if the market for these inputs is competitive, the firm's profits will not be maximized by arbitrarily lowering the price of inputs. (*see* OPPORTUNITY COSTS; VERTICAL INTEGRATION, Porter (1980) and Shughart, Chappell and Cottle (1994)).

Bibliography

Porter, M. E. (1980). *Competitive Strategy*. New York: Free Press.
Shughart, W. F., Chappell, W. F. Cottle, R. L. (1994). *Modern Managerial Economics*. Cincinatti, OH: South-Western Publishing.

ROBERT E. MCAULIFFE

bankruptcy A firm or individual which is unable to meet its financial obligations passes into a status called bankruptcy after a court of law issues an order declaring it bankrupt. Bankruptcy may be voluntary, if the firm or individual petitions the court to be placed into bankruptcy status. Or it may be involuntary, if creditors of the firm or individual petition the court to declare the entity bankrupt and place it under the stewardship of a trustee. An entity might seek voluntary bankruptcy to gain time to work out a plan to meet its obligations. Creditors might seek to have an entity declared bankrupt to protect its remaining assets from being squandered, dissipated, or stolen; they might also try to force an entity into bankruptcy because the court and the trustee will pay the claims on the bankrupt in order of priority, not according to the whims or preferences of the entity.

Firms may go bankrupt because of illiquidity, or because of insolvency. A firm suffers from illiquidity if, for example, its only asset is a parcel of land worth $100, and its only liability is a debt of $20 payable immediately. The firm is solvent because its asset is worth more than its liability; but it is bankrupt because it does not have the cash to pay the debt which is due. That firm would probably seek bankruptcy voluntarily, to keep the debtholder from getting the parcel of land, to the detriment of the stockholders. Another firm would be liquid but insolvent if its only asset were $50 in cash and it had debts of $100. That firm might be pushed into bankruptcy by its creditors, so that the creditors would share the $50 in order of priority, and not in the order that the management might choose if it were allowed to continue managing the firm.

The bankruptcy courts have some latitude in settling claims against the bankrupt enterprise. The current practice is to promulgate a settlement that gives every class of claimant something, with only relative priority to the senior claims. Prior to 1978 in the US, the "absolute priority" rule was in effect; that rule gave the senior creditors 100 percent of their principal and interest before giving anything to junior creditors. In recent years, the bankruptcy courts have made settlements that give some payment or future claims to every class of creditors, including stockholders.

Bibliography

Brigham, E. (1995). *Fundamentals of Financial Management.* 7th edn, New York: Dryden.

JOHN EDMUNDS and ROBERTO BONIFAZ

barriers to entry Barriers to entry describe the disadvantages of potential entrants relative to established firms in an industry. Barriers to entry play an important role in determining the structure of an industry, such as the number of firms and the size distribution of firms (*see* MARKET STRUCTURE). There is some controversy regarding the proper definition and consequences of barriers to entry, however. For the purposes of evaluating the likelihood of entry into any specific industry and the basic structure of an industry, these controversies are less significant. As will be clear below, the differences are more important in the areas of social welfare and public policy.

Sources of barriers to entry

As initially described by Joe Bain (1956), barriers to entry allow established firms to raise prices and earn long run economic profits without causing new firms to enter the industry. In perfectly competitive markets, short run economic profits attract entry which, in the long run, causes prices and profits to fall to normal risk-adjusted competitive levels (*see* ECONOMIC PROFIT; ENTRY; PERFECT COMPETITION). If there are barriers to entry in an industry, economic profits will persist even in the long run. For Bain and his followers, higher long run economic profits indicate higher barriers to entry, all else equal. Bain considered ECONOMIES OF SCALE, PRODUCT DIFFERENTIATION, absolute cost advantages of established firms, and capital requirements as sources of barriers to entry.

Established firms in an industry have absolute cost advantages when they can obtain resources at a lower cost than potential entrants. This advantage can occur when established firms have exclusive access to important inputs, or have unique assets (such as a prime location, manufacturing process, etc.) which allow them to produce at a lower cost than potential entrants. Under these conditions, established firms would be able to charge prices above their marginal costs and earn economic profits without attracting entry. If accounting methods valued these superior assets at their true market value (or opportunity cost) the advantages could disappear (*see* OPPORTUNITY COSTS). For example, a firm which enjoys lower costs because of a unique location could sell that location for a higher price. In this case, the firm's location is an asset which is undervalued relative to the true market value of that asset. If the firm properly accounted for the higher value of the asset, the firm's return on assets would correspondingly fall and its costs would be higher.

Bain considered ECONOMIES OF SCALE as a barrier to entry because any potential entrant would have to build a large plant in order to compete with established firms. Bain argued large-scale entry was inherently more risky and difficult to finance and thus reduced the likelihood of entry. Any firms that entered at a scale below the MINIMUM EFFICIENT SCALE (MES) would have higher costs relative to established firms and if entrants chose a plant the size of the MES or larger, they would likely provoke retaliation by the established firms. Economies of scale may also create barriers to entry because they require substantial capital investment. Absolute capital requirements refer to the amount of capital necessary to successfully enter an industry and launch a product. If capital markets are imperfect, entrants may have difficulty obtaining sufficient credit or may have to pay higher interest rates because of the greater risk.

PRODUCT DIFFERENTIATION may also confer advantages to established firms because entrants would have to compete in marketing the product in addition to producing it. Entrants may also need to overcome consumer loyalty to established brands and this would increase the costs and risks of entry. If an entrant must advertise more to make consumers aware of the product, these higher costs increase the risk of entry because they cannot be recovered if the attempt to enter the industry fails. Entrants may also find it difficult to obtain access to distribution channels when competing against established firms offering similar products.

Schmalensee (1982) and Porter (1980) also identified switching costs as a potential barrier to entry. These are the costs incurred by consumers when switching from an established, well-known brand to a new brand. These costs would appear to be particularly important when new products, such as software, require training. Even so, the existence of these costs creates incentives for software companies to ease the transition with special menus and help files for users of competing products. Thus an entrant may be able to reduce these costs to its customers.

Another barrier to entry suggested by Dixit (1979) is actually a barrier to exit: SUNK COSTS. If a firm cannot recover investments when it leaves an industry, then the firm incurs sunk costs and has less incentive to enter that industry. Sunk costs are greater the more specific those assets are to the industry or firm because there are fewer alternative uses for specific assets; (see ASSET SPECIFICITY). Advertising outlays to introduce a product are sunk if an entering firm ultimately fails.

Conceptual questions regarding barriers to entry

George Stigler (1968) disagreed with the notion that economies of scale were a barrier to entry when both the entrant and the established firm have the same costs of production. If the market is not large enough to accommodate two or more firms, we could just as easily argue that insufficient demand is the barrier to entry and not economies of scale. Stigler then defined entry barriers as those costs incurred by any new entrants into an industry that were not incurred by established firms. For Stigler, economies of scale do not represent a barrier to entry when entrants have access to the same technology and costs.

More recent research by von Weisäcker (1980) and Demsetz (1982) has questioned the basic concept of barriers to entry by focusing on the welfare implications of more entry into an industry. Von Weisäcker suggested that Stigler's definition of barriers to entry should apply only when the additional costs borne by an entrant imply a misallocation of resources

from a socially efficient optimum. For example, when there are many firms and economies of scale, society would be better off with *less* entry because additional firms incur more fixed costs and prevent the full exploitation of scale economies. But Demsetz questions the usefulness of the distinction between industry insiders and outsiders altogether. After all, PROPERTY RIGHTS are legal barriers to entry but economists do not consider them to be uniformly anti-competitive. If consumers prefer established products because it is costly for them to experiment with new brands or acquire more information, is that necessarily a barrier to entry?

In a world of imperfect information and transactions costs, Demsetz suggests that society may want to encourage investment in trademarks and advertising. An established firm with a good credit history will be able to borrow more cheaply than a new entrant with no record. Although Stigler might argue that the higher cost of credit to an entrant could be a barrier to entry, does society want to discourage good credit histories? Or consider the case of a product produced by a patented process. The patent grants a legal monopoly to the producer of this product which will likely result in lower output and a higher price than the marginal cost of production. Society would benefit from increased production of this product, but changing the patent laws would not necessarily be beneficial to society since there would now be a reduction in the incentives to invent. In fact, Demsetz argues that there would now be a barrier to entry in the market for inventing new products. According to Demsetz, changing property rights will change the mix and value of resources in society in ways that may not increase social welfare. In Demsetz' view, public policy to eliminate or reduce barriers to entry will have unanticipated effects on property rights that may impose greater costs than benefits.

Gilbert (1989) more recently focused on the advantages enjoyed by established firms. He prefers the term mobility barriers to entry barriers, reflecting the fact that resource allocation will be more or less efficient as capital and other resources are more or less mobile in moving from one industry to another. A mobility barrier exists when an established firm in an industry has economic RENTS (positive or negative) as a result of being in the industry. If a firm earns higher profits in an industry *after accounting for the opportunity cost of the resources employed* than it could earn in another industry, then that firm has an incumbency rent. This definition considers the opportunity costs of scarce factors of production since an incumbent firm could leave the industry by selling its assets. Absolute cost advantages described above would not necessarily create a mobility barrier since established firms must consider the opportunity cost of those resources responsible for their advantage. However, as Gilbert notes, if the value of the asset is specific to the owner, such as investments in human capital, then the market value (opportunity cost) may not reflect the true value to the established firm and the firm could earn an incumbency rent.

Geroski, Gilbert, and Jacquemin (1990) argue that an advantage of using incumbency rents to define barriers to entry is that these rents can be measured. Furthermore, the height of the barrier to entry is measured by the size of the incumbency rent. Unfortunately, it is difficult in practice to determine the opportunity cost of factors of production and this makes incumbency rents difficult to implement. Geroski, Gilbert, and Jacquemin also note that STRATEGIC BEHAVIOR could also create a barrier to entry since established firms can take actions which make entry less appealing to an entrant. For example, a threat to reduce prices if a new firm enters a market may also deter entry; (*see* LIMIT PRICING). They also note that the existence of factors that may impede entry does not imply that these factors reduce efficiency or require policy action.

Fisher and McGowan (1983) questioned the use of accounting profits as a measure of monopoly power in industry studies (*see* ACCOUNTING PROFIT). They asserted the proper measure of economic profitability is the INTERNAL RATE OF RETURN for any investment in an asset. Since firms invest in a number of assets, the internal rate of return will be a weighted average of these internal rates of return, all of which are forward-looking. It is very unlikely that the accounting rate of return will equal the appropriate economic rate of return and, in their simulations, Fisher and

McGowan (1983) showed that the relationship between accounting profits and economic profits was very poor.

For managers attempting to evaluate the conditions of entry into an industry, any of the sources above may represent a barrier to entry (see Porter, 1980) and the controversies in the literature are less important. But for economic policy analysis, such as ANTITRUST POLICY, or for social welfare analysis, the debate in the literature has an important effect on how markets should be evaluated.

Bibliography

Bain, J. S. (1956). *Barriers to New Competition*. Cambridge, MA: Harvard University Press.

Demsetz, H. (1982). Barriers to entry. *American Economic Review*, **72**, 47–57.

Dixit, A. (1979). A model of duopoly suggesting a theory of entry barriers. *Bell Journal of Economics*, **10**, 20–32.

Fisher, F. M. McGowan, J. J. (1983). On the misuse of accounting rates of return to infer monopoly profits. *American Economic Review*, **73**, 82–97.

Geroski, P., Gilbert, R. J. Jacquemin, A. (1990). *Barriers to Entry and Strategic Competition*. New York: Harwood.

Gilbert, R. J. (1989). Mobility barriers and the value of incumbency. Schmalensee, R.   Willig, R. *Handbook of Industrial Organization*. New York: Elsevier.

Porter, M. E. (1980). *Competitive Strategy*. New York: Free Press.

Schmalensee, R. (1982). Product differentiation advantages of pioneering brands. *American Economic Review*, **72**, 349–65.

Stigler, G. J. (1968). *The Organization of Industry*. Chicago: University of Chicago Press.

von Weisäcker, C. C. (1980). A welfare analysis of barriers to entry. *Bell Journal of Economics*, **11**, 399–420.

ROBERT E. MCAULIFFE

basic market structures The basic product market structures in economics are PERFECT COMPETITION, MONOPOLISTIC COMPETITION, OLIGOPOLY, and MONOPOLY. Perfect competition represents the benchmark for welfare analysis where there are numerous buyers and sellers, none of whom is large enough to affect the market price if they leave the market. Any firm that wishes to enter the industry or exit may do so at little cost. The product is homogeneous (no PRODUCT DIFFERENTIATION) and consumers and producers are completely informed. These conditions discipline producers and consumers so that neither has any influence over price. The firm facing a perfectly competitive market sells as much as it can at the market price and cannot compete for consumers other than on price. If the firm were to charge a higher price, consumers would immediately switch to other suppliers whose identical products are perfect substitutes. Thus the demand curve facing a perfectly competitive firm is perfectly (or infinitely) elastic and perfectly competitive firms, unable to affect the market price, are said to be *price takers* (*see* ELASTICITY). In addition, since each firm is so small relative to the market and has so many rivals, there is no advantage from efforts to anticipate competitors' reactions or engage in STRATEGIC BEHAVIOR.

When products are differentiated, information is imperfect, entry or exit is costly, or the number of sellers or buyers is small, markets are imperfectly competitive. Firms in these markets generally have some control over price and therefore face downward sloping demand curves. Prices in these markets may exceed the MARGINAL COST of production and the market may not be efficient in allocating output. Producers may also fail to be technically efficient since they face less pressure to keep costs as low as possible (*see* IMPERFECT INFORMATION; X-EFFICIENCY). Under imperfect competition firms may compete for customers on other dimensions than simply price. Firms may compete through product differentiation, ADVERTISING, strategic behavior and other means.

When firms compete in monopolistic competition, each produces a unique, differentiated product. Entry into the market is free, and firms advertise and pursue research and development to further differentiate their products. Free entry may drive profits down to zero, but recent research in spatial models indicates that long-run economic profits are possible if existing firms can choose their locations and deter entry (Eaton and Lipsey, 1978). EXCESS CAPACITY may exist in monopolistically competitive markets since firms will produce less output than required for minimum average cost. These markets may generate too much or too little product differentiation depending on the

strengths of two opposing effects. When a new firm enters the market with a new brand, it cannot acquire all of the consumer surplus from the new product. Since it is socially optimal to introduce a new product if the social benefits outweigh the social costs, there may be too little product differentiation when each firm cannot appropriate all of the CONSUMER SURPLUS generated by its brand. The opposing effect is that any new product is likely to steal consumers away from existing firms. Since these consumers were already served and stealing them represents a negative externality to the other firms that the entrant does not consider, there may be a tendency for too much product differentiation. The net effect depends on which of these two forces is stronger; see Dixit and Stiglitz (1977), EXTERNALITIES.

In markets where producers are oligopolists, each firm reacts to its rivals' strategies and so STRATEGIC BEHAVIOR becomes important. Profit-maximizing firms must consider how their competitors will respond when determining their best strategy; see GAME THEORY. Since each firm's expectations about the reaction of rivals can be modelled in a variety of ways, predictions about the behavior and performance of oligopolists will depend upon the model. If the oligopolists were to collude on prices, a cartel would exist (*see* CARTELS) and the firms could collectively act as a monopoly. If there is no COLLUSION between the firms, a noncooperative oligopoly exists. In models of noncooperative oligopoly, there may be COURNOT COMPETITION where each firm believes its rivals will keep their production levels (quantities) constant whatever its choice of output, or firms could compete through research and development expenditures, advertising, prices, product differentiation, or other means with varying expectations about competitors' responses in each case; see Lambin (1976).

When there is a single producer of a product, that firm has a monopoly in the market. The monopolist maximizes profits by restricting output and raising prices until marginal revenue equals marginal cost. This normally enables the firm to earn ECONOMIC PROFIT and to maintain its monopoly position, there must be significant BARRIERS TO ENTRY to prevent other firms from entering the market. These entry barriers may be granted by the government through licensing or patents, they may exist because of ECONOMIES OF SCALE (i.e. the firm is a NATURAL MONOPOLY), or they may be created by the firm itself through strategic behavior. Even a natural monopoly may not be sustainable if it can be profitable for entry at some price and cost combinations; see Sharkey (1982).

Bibliography

Carlton, D. W.   Perloff, J. M. (1994). *Modern Industrial Organization.* 2nd edn, New York: HarperCollins.

Dixit, A.   Stiglitz, J. (1977). Monopolistic competition and optimum product diversity. *American Economic Review,* **67,** 297–308.

Douglas, E. J. (1992). *Managerial Economics.* 4th edn, Englewood Cliffs, NJ: Prentice-Hall.

Eaton, B. C.   Lipsey, R. G. (1978). Freedom of entry and the existence of pure profit. *Economic Journal,* **88,** 455–69.

Lambin, J. J. (1976). *Advertising, competition, and market conduct in oligopoly over time.* Amsterdam: North–Holland.

Sharkey, W. W. (1982). *The Theory of Natural Monopoly.* Cambridge: CUP.

ROBERT E. MCAULIFFE

beta coefficient   In portfolio theory, a company's beta coefficient measures the variability of that company's returns relative to the variability of the returns in the market and it helps determine the company's cost of capital within the CAPITAL ASSET PRICING MODEL. An investor who can always receive the risk-free rate of return, r_f, will want to be compensated for additional risk from holding any stock. This is the risk premium for that stock and represents the additional return required by investors over the risk-free rate. If investors have diversified their portfolios, the additional risk incurred by investing in stock j is not the variance of that company's returns (since diversification will reduce some of the risk), but rather how that company's returns relate to the rest of the portfolio. The beta coefficient measures the additional risk a given stock adds to a portfolio and for stock j it is defined as:

$$B_j = (\text{cov}(r_j - r_f, r_m - r_f))/\text{var}(r_m - r_f)$$

where cov() is the COVARIANCE of the risk premium of stock j with the risk premium of the market portfolio, var() is the VARIANCE of the risk premium of the market, r_f is the risk-free rate of return, r_j is the return to stock j and r_m is the return to the market portfolio. The beta coefficient is simply the estimated coefficient from a LINEAR REGRESSION of the risk premium for stock j against the risk premium for the market as a whole.

A company can determine its cost of equity capital by determining the risk premium diversified investors will require to add stock j to their portfolios. This is given by:

$$\text{cost of equity capital} = r_f + \beta_j(r_m - r_f)$$

where β_j is the beta coefficient for company j. Since an average stock will move with the market, an average stock should have a beta coefficient of one. This means that the cost of equity capital for such a company equals the market return: if the market rises or falls by one percent, the company's stock will also rise or fall by one percent. If a company's beta coefficient is 2.5, the stock will rise or fall two and a half times more than any rise or fall in the market. This would be a more risky stock to add to the portfolio and a portfolio comprised of such stocks would be considered aggressive.

Bibliography

Berndt, E. R. (1991). *The Practice of Econometrics.* Reading, MA: Addison-Wesley.

Brigham, E. F.   Gapenski, L. C. (1993). *Intermediate Financial Management.* New York: Dryden.

Shughart, W. F., Chappell, W. F.   Cottle, R. L. (1994). *Modern Managerial Economics.* Cincinatti, OH: South-Western Publishing.

ROBERT E. MCAULIFFE

brand name   An established brand name makes a product easy to identify and can reduce consumers' search costs for their best choice. Firms producing a product may invest in establishing a brand name to assure consumers of the quality of that product. This can be particularly important when there is ASYMMETRIC INFORMATION in the market so that consumers cannot easily determine product quality on inspection (as with EXPERIENCE GOODS and CREDENCE GOODS).

Firms can invest in a brand through ADVERTISING, product improvements and sales efforts. Brand names represent durable investments that show the producer's COMMITMENT to the product over the long term. If consumers were unable to determine product quality and firms could not indicate product quality through SIGNALING, then competition on price could create a LEMONS MARKET where only low-quality producers remained. Brand names provide information to consumers which helps to ensure that quality levels are maintained even in markets when there is IMPERFECT INFORMATION. Consumers are more willing to pay a price premium for brand names the more sensitive they are to quality differences between products and the greater the costs of acquiring information.

Establishing or maintaining a brand name may also be part of a competitive strategy focused on quality leadership in the market; see Douglas, (1992) and Porter (1980). In such a case, the firm tries to achieve competitive advantage and continually earning higher profits by becoming the leading quality producer in the market for the product. The firm's sales efforts, product design and marketing efforts must all be focused on achieving high quality in the eyes of consumers.

Bibliography

Akerlof, G. A. (1970). The market for lemons: quality uncertainty and the market mechanism. *Quarterly Journal of Economics*, **84**, 488–500.

Douglas, E. J. (1992). *Managerial Economics*. 4th edn, Englewood Cliffs, NJ: Prentice-Hall.

Klein, B. Leffler, K. (1981). The role of market forces in assuring contractual performance. *Journal of Political Economy*, **89**, 615–41.

Porter, M. E. (1980). *Competitive Strategy*. New York: Free Press.

Shughart, W. F., Chappell, W. F. Cottle, R. L. (1994). *Modern Managerial Economics*. Cincinatti, OH: South-Western Publishing.

ROBERT E. MCAULIFFE

budget constraint   When choosing the products which will give the consumer the most satisfaction (*see* UTILITY MAXIMIZATION), a consumer's expenditures cannot exceed his or her budget. In practice, this constraint may include the resources available through borrowing and selling assets, but, in most textbook examples, the consumer is limited to this period's income. For example, to illustrate a consumer's decision to buy two products, X and Y, where the consumer's entire income will be exhausted on these two goods, the budget constraint would be:

$$I = P_x^* X + P_y^* Y$$

where I is the consumer's income, P_x is the price of good X, X is the quantity of X consumed. If the consumer spent all of her income on good X, then Y would be zero and the maximum amount of X which could be consumed is $X = (I/P_X)$. The budget constraint shows the combinations of the products the consumer could feasibly buy given market prices and the consumer's income and shows the rate at which a consumer is *able* to substitute purchases of X for Y. Utility maximization requires that the rate at which consumers are able to substitute products just equals the rate that they *desire* to do so given their tastes. The consumer's desired rate of substitution is his or her MARGINAL RATE OF SUBSTITUTION and utility is maximized when the consumer's INDIFFERENCE CURVES are just tangent (equal) to the budget constraint.

When the budget constraint is plotted with good Y on the vertical axis and good X on the horizontal axis, the vertical intercept of the budget constraint will be (I/P_Y) (where the consumer spends all of her income on good Y) and the slope of the budget line will be $-P_X/P_Y$. An increase in P_Y will make the budget constraint flatter, reducing the height of the vertical intercept (since less of Y can be purchased) while an increase in P_X will make the budget line steeper and will reduce the horizontal intercept.

Bibliography

Douglas, E. J. (1992). *Managerial Economics*. 4th edn, Englewood Cliffs, NJ: Prentice-Hall.

Shughart, W. F., Chappell, W. F. Cottle, R. L. (1994). *Modern Managerial Economics*. Cincinatti, OH: South-Western Publishing.

ROBERT E. MCAULIFFE

bundling When firms offer two or more products together at a price below what would be charged for each product separately, the firm is practicing product bundling. Firms will benefit from bundling commodities when they can gain more of the CONSUMER SURPLUS from their customers. In this respect, bundling is a form of PRICE DISCRIMINATION where consumers will sort themselves (or self-select) on the basis of how much they prefer a product. For example, quantity discounts are a form of bundling where additional units cost less when purchased together. Those consumers who value the product the most (i.e. have the highest RESERVATION PRICE) will be willing to buy the larger quantity at a discount although their total expenditures on the good will be higher than if they purchased the smaller size.

The firm profits by raising the prices of the individual products and then choosing the appropriate bundled price to win those consumers who desire both products but are unwilling to pay for both separately. Consumers then self-select by purchasing the individual products or the bundled product according to their total valuation of the good.

Bibliography

Adams, W. J. Yellen, J. L. (1976). Commodity bundling and the burden of monopoly. *Quarterly Journal of Economics*, **90**, 475–98.

Douglas, E. J. (1992). *Managerial Economics*. 4th edn, Englewood Cliffs, NJ: Prentice-Hall.

ROBERT E. McAULIFFE

business entities Various legal entities exist for operating a business enterprise. Each of these has advantages and disadvantages from a legal perspective.

The simplest method of operating a business is the **sole proprietorship**. Any person who engages in business without forming any other entity is a sole proprietor. Since a sole proprietorship is nothing more than the person involved, that person has unlimited liability for all business and personal debts. It does not matter that he may use a tradename to do business; he remains liable. In addition, raising capital depends upon the financial ability of the individual. No state approval is required to start or operate a sole proprietorship, no sharing of profits occurs, and taxation is relatively easy.

A **general partnership** is an association of two or more persons who carry on as co-owners a business for profit. The word "persons" means that any legal entity may be a partner, including corporations. The partnership may be through an express agreement, either oral or written, or it may arise through the acts of the parties showing that they intend a partnership to exist. A sharing of profits is the primary evidence that a partnership is intended. The partnership agreement normally governs the rights and duties of the partners. In the absence of a contract, state law will control. Virtually all states have adopted the Uniform Partnership Act in an attempt to standardize partnership law.

Once formed, a partnership is a legal entity for certain limited purposes. It may enter contracts, sue and be sued, and own property. However, it is not a legal entity for tax purposes since the partners pay tax on the income earned. A partnership is easy to form and operate, can raise capital from each partner, and pays no taxes. The major disadvantage of a partnership is that each partner is jointly and severally liable for the debts of the partnership. Thus, each partner is responsible for acts of the other partners done within the scope of the partnership. Third parties may collect their entire debt from any partner and leave that partner to seek collection from the other partners. In addition, whenever a partner joins or leaves the partnership, whether voluntarily or not, the partnership is dissolved and a new one results. However, the problems of dissolution may be minimized by having a comprehensive agreement.

A **limited partnership** is a variation of the general partnership. The difference is that in addition to the general partner(s) in the firm, limited partners are also present. These partners contribute capital and share in the profits, but they do not participate in the operation of the partnership business. In return, their liability is limited to their contribution. A limited partnership is formed in a manner similar to a corporation. A certificate of limited partnership is obtained from the state and a partnership agreement is entered. The sale of limited partnership interests may require registration with the SEC and each state involved. A limited partnership is operated in the same manner as a general partnership except that the limited partners do not participate for fear of losing their limited liability.

A **corporation** is a legal entity with many of the same legal rights as any person. It can sue and be sued, own property, and enter contracts. It even has many of the same constitutional rights as people, including equal protection, due process, and freedom of speech. A corporation is formed by filing articles of incorporation with the state. A certificate of incorporation is issued showing that the state recognizes the corporation as a person. However, the corporation must then follow all of the laws pertaining to corporations in order to maintain its identity as a separate legal entity apart from its stockholders and employees. This allows the stockholders, who are the owners of the company, to avoid liability for acts of the corporation.

Corporations are owned by stockholders who contribute capital. They in turn elect directors to serve on the board. The board of directors is responsible for setting major corporate policy and hiring the officers. The officers are the corporate agents responsible for the daily operation of the corporation and its business. As long as the corporation maintains a separate identity, it alone is responsible for its debts and liabilities. Although a corporation is more difficult to form and operate, this limited liability is a major factor when choosing a business entity. A disadvantage is the double taxation of corporations. Since a corporation is a person, it must pay tax on its income. The corporation may then distribute profits to its stockholders in the form of dividends, which are then taxed as income to those individuals. One way to avoid this tax burden is to seek IRS approval for the corporation to file as a Subchapter S corporation. This designation allows the company to be treated as a partnership for tax purposes. However, the corporation must meet several requirements, including only one class of stock and no more than thirty five stockholders. In addition, many corporations must register their stock with the SEC since stock is a security.

Many states have enacted corporate codes that allow for different types of corporations. No state allows professionals, such as physicians or attorneys, to avoid professional liability by forming a corporation. Thus, professionals must form **professional corporations** (noted after their names as PC) instead of business corporations. Professional corporations are operated similarly to regular corporations except that the stockholders, who must all be within the same profession, remain liable for their malpractice. In an effort to reduce the administrative burden on small companies, states have also created the close corporation. Since all of the stock is "closely" held by a few stockholders, the close corporation statutes treat these companies more like a general partnership but without the unlimited liability. The IRS continues to treat them as corporations for tax purposes.

Many states have also attempted to attract business by allowing **limited liability** companies (LLC) and limited liability partnerships (LLP). An LLC is very similar to a general partnership except that the owners (who are called members) do not have liability for debts of the LLC. If an LLC is treated by its members as a partnership rather than a corporation, then the IRS will tax it as a partnership and allow it to avoid double taxation. An LLP is designed for professionals who want to limit liability. A few states have crafted their LLP laws to allow professionals to limit liability in certain circumstances. The trend appears to be towards a limitation of liability for professionals in this area.

Other entities exist, although they are utilized less frequently. A **joint venture** is when two or more business entities come together for a single or limited business venture. The parties are treated legally as partners for that venture only. A **cooperative** is an association (which can be incorporated) that is formed to provide a service to its members, such as a farm cooperative. A **syndicate** is when several persons pool their money, usually within a second business entity, in order to finance a business venture. A business **trust**, or sometimes a real estate investment trust, occurs when investors turn over their money or property to a trust which then manages those resources for profit and distributes profits to the members (beneficiaries).

Finally, many business entities choose to operate a **franchise**. A franchise is *not* a legal entity, but rather it is a method of doing business. The franchisor gives the franchisee information, materials, and support for a fee. The Federal Trade Commission regulates franchising (*see* FEDERAL TRADE COMMISSION ACT).

Bibliography

Moye, J. E. (1994). *The Law of Business Organizations.* 4th edn, West Publishing Company.

S. ALAN SCHLACT

C

capital Productive assets which yield benefits over time are called capital or economic capital. Capital can be **tangible** (or physical), such as buildings, plant and equipment, or **intangible** such as the goodwill of a firm or human capital. A firm may invest resources in developing a BRAND NAME which will produce benefits to the firm over time and represents an intangible, goodwill asset to the firm. Training programs a firm might provide to employees will develop their skills and make them more productive. This investment in human capital, if successful, will also yield benefits over time but is not part of the physical assets (or tangible capital) of the firm. It is also important to distinguish capital assets from financial assets. Capital assets are used in the production process while financial assets are paper which may represent the capital assets but are not the capital assets themselves. For example, a company which is in BANK-RUPTCY has all of its capital assets intact. The problem is that the value of the financial assets has declined relative to financial liabilities.

When firms make decisions to invest in capital, the benefits are expected to accrue over a period of time in the future and these are CAPITAL BUDGETING decisions. A firm adds to its capital assets by making decisions to invest in new assets over time. Since a capital investment decision is a forward-looking decision, the expected benefits from such an investment must be estimated and are subject to considerable UNCERTAINTY. Firms use a variety of methods to determine whether a capital investment is worthwhile, but the basic economic principle is that the marginal (expected) benefits from the project should exceed the marginal costs (*see* MAKE OR BUY DECISIONS; NET PRESENT VALUE).

Bibliography

Brigham, E. F. Gapenski, L. C. (1993). *Intermediate Financial Management.* New York: Dryden.
Douglas, E. J. (1992). *Managerial Economics.* 4th edn, Englewood Cliffs, NJ: Prentice-Hall.
Shughart, W. F., Chappell, W. F. Cottle, R. L. (1994). *Modern Managerial Economics.* Cincinatti, OH: South-Western Publishing.

ROBERT E. MCAULIFFE

capital asset pricing model The capital asset pricing model (CAPM) is an equation which specifically links the expected return of a security to its underlying risk. A unique feature of the CAPM is that the risk component is fully reflected in only one parameter: β. The CAPM equation is:

$$\bar{r}_i = r_f + \beta_i(\bar{r}_m - r_f)$$

where

$\bar{r}_i$ = expected return on security i
r_f = return for holding a risk free security
β_i = beta of security i
$\bar{r}_m$ = expected return for holding the market portfolio

Although credit for the CAPM goes to Sharpe (1964), Lintner (1965), and Mossin (1966), the work is considered an extension of the portfolio selection research by Markowitz (1952), and Tobin (1958).

Since CAPM is a model that links expected return and risk, it is important to discuss why β is the parameter that quantifies priced risk in any security. By definition, risk is about unexpected events. For example, if a security's actual return ($\tilde{r}_i$) is always equal to its expected return ($\bar{r}_i$), then it is intuitive that such a security has no risk (since the expected always occurs), and would therefore provide an investor with the risk-free rate of return (r_f). The total risk or VARIANCE (σ_i^2) of a security is therefore calculated as the EXPECTED VALUE of the square of its unexpected returns. Formally, $\sigma_i^2 = E(\tilde{r}_i - \bar{r}_i)^2$ where E denotes mathematical expectation.

If an investor had no choice but to accept the risk of security i, then the variance would capture the relevant risk for pricing purposes. However, Markowitz (1952) had the insight that when a single security is part of a portfolio, there exists the potential for risk cancellation. For example, if you held stock in both an umbrella and ice-cream factory, it is easy to imagine that an unexpectedly hot and dry summer would boost ice-cream sales while depressing umbrella sales. Hence, the risk of unexpected weather would be less if both stocks were held in a portfolio instead of holding them individually. The concept that risks may cancel is known as *diversification*. Thus, if the total risk or variance inherent in a single security can be reduced simply by costlessly holding it as part of a well-diversified portfolio, then the relevant risk for pricing purposes is the risk that the single security contributes to this well-diversified portfolio. By definition, the risk of a single security which may be diversified is known as its *unique* or *non-systematic* or *diversifiable* risk. The risk component of a single security which can not be diversified is known as *market* or *systematic* or *non-diversifiable* risk. Analogous to the variance of a single security quantifying its

total risk, non-diversifiable risk is quantified by the β of the security.

In the set of risky securities, Markowitz (1952) illustrated a frontier of portfolios such that each of them had the greatest return for the given level of portfolio risk. The upper portion of the graph represents the *efficient frontier*. Assuming that investors prefer higher expected returns and less risk, all investors will choose a portfolio somewhere on the efficient frontier. (Other technical assumptions include that each asset is infinitely divisible, and that all investors have common time horizons and common beliefs about the investment opportunity set and their expected returns.)

If we include a riskless security in the above analysis, by definition it will have a portfolio standard deviation of zero. Assuming investors can borrow and buy the riskless asset in unlimited quantities, all investors will choose a convex combination of the riskless asset and the risky portfolio denoted as S in figure 1. This line is known as the *capital market line* and illustrates the investor's *separation principle*. This principle states that investors are able to separate two specific decisions. The first is to calculate the set of efficient assets represented by the efficient frontier as well as the point of tangency between the riskless asset and the efficient frontier (point S). The second decision is to determine which combination of the portfolio S and the riskless asset an investor will choose. If an investor has a low degree of risk tolerance she will invest some of her funds in the riskless asset and some in portfolio S. If

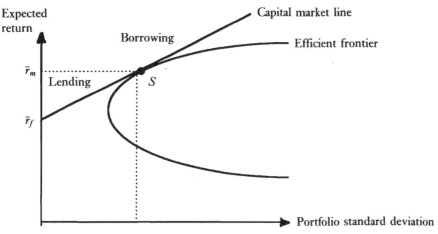

Figure 1   Optimal portfolio selection

Expected return

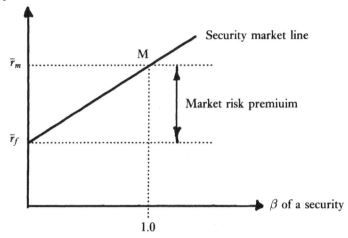

Figure 2   Tradeoff between risk and return for a single security

she has a high degree of risk tolerance, she will borrow at the risk-free rate in addition to using her funds to invest in portfolio S.

In the set of risky assets, if everyone holds portfolio S, then this must also be the market portfolio. To appreciate why β reflects the risk that a single security contributes to a well-diversified portfolio, it is necessary to understand the calculation of portfolio risk. This risk is calculated as a weighted average of the variance of each security in the portfolio plus all the COVARIANCE terms between the securities. Therefore, if w_1 and w_2 are the fractions of your wealth held in stocks 1 and 2 respectively, and the covariance between the two stocks is denoted by σ_{12} then portfolio STANDARD DEVIATION (σ_p) is calculated as the square root of portfolio variance

$$\sigma_p = \sqrt{w_1^2 \sigma_1^2 + w_2^2 \sigma_2^2 + 2w_1 w_2 \sigma_{12}}$$

Notice that with two securities, there are two variance and two covariance terms. Similarly, with three securities, there are three variance and six covariance terms. In short, when there are n securities in a portfolio, there are n variance and $(n^2 - n)$ covariance terms. If we have an infinite number of securities, by definition we hold the market. Hence as n approaches infinity, it can be shown that the covariance of a single security with the market dominates the risk that this security contributes to

a well-diversified portfolio. The covariance that a single security i has with the market standardized by the variance of the market is known as its β. Hence $\beta_i = \frac{\sigma_{im}}{\sigma_m^2}$ where σ_{im} is the covariance between security i and the market. Intuitively, if the β of a stock is 2, this means that when the market rises by 1 percent and the risk-free rate does not change, then the stock will rise by 2 percent.

Conceptually, β is key to the CAPM equation since it quantifies the non-diversifiable risk inherent in any single security. Since it is this risk which can not be costlessly diversified away, and since we assume that investors expect a higher rate of return for higher risk stocks, it must be this non-diversifiable risk that is priced. We are now in a position to understand the intuition behind the CAPM equation.

Whereas the capital market line is derived from the set of risky portfolios and the riskless asset, the security market line shown in figure 2 represents the trade-off between risk and return for a single security.

The security market line illustrates several important points. The first is that the β of the risk-free rate and the market (M) must be zero and one respectively. The second is that this line must be upward sloping since investors require higher returns for higher risk. The third point is that in equilibrium, this must be a straight line. If this were not true, it would mean that the price of risk (ratio of expected return premiums to risk) differed across securities which would provide the motivation to simultaneously buy risk at a low price and sell it at a high price. Hence, if the risk premium of any security is the difference between its expected return and the risk-free rate of return, then it must mean for example that

$$\frac{\bar{r}_A - r_f}{\beta_A} = \frac{\bar{r}_b - r_f}{\beta_B} = \frac{\bar{r}_c - r_f}{\beta_c}$$

The security market line graphically illustrates the CAPM. With the risk free rate as the intercept, the market risk premium $(\bar{r}_m - r_f)$ as the slope, and the expected return and β of a security as the dependent and independent variables respectively, we obtain the CAPM equation:

$$\bar{r}_i = r_f + \beta_i(\bar{r}_m - r_f)$$

It is important to point out that the CAPM is not without its critics. For example, Roll (1977) has argued that the model is impossible to test since it is a prediction about expected returns while an empirical test would have to use actual returns. In addition, there are alternative theories of asset pricing such as ARBITRAGE pricing theory pioneered by Ross (1976). Nevertheless, the CAPM is a model which is widely used today by practitioners throughout the world. For example, a component in the weighted average COST OF CAPITAL calculation includes the cost of equity capital which can be determined using CAPM. Since the cost of capital is key to making major capital budgeting decisions, the CAPM implicitly plays an important role. Another example is that numerous investment reports including *Value Line* show a stock's β to assess its priced risk. In short, the CAPM is an excellent example of theory born in the academic world that has successfully integrated into many practical uses in the business environment.

Bibliography

Lintner, J. (1965). Security prices, risk and maximal gains from diversification. *Journal of Finance*, 20, 587–615.
Markowitz, H. M. (1952). Portfolio selection. *Journal of Finance*, 7, 77–91.
Mossin, J. (1966). Equilibrium in a capital asset market. *Econometrica*, 34, 261–76.
Roll, R. (1977). A critique of the asset pricing theory's tests. Part I: on the past and potential testability of the theory. *Journal of Financial Economics*, 4, 129–76.
Ross, S. A. (1976). The arbitrage theory of asset pricing. *Journal of Economic Theory*, 13, 341–60.
Sharpe, W. F. (1964). Capital asset prices: a theory of market equilibrium under conditions of risk. *Journal of Finance*, 19, 425–42.
Tobin, J. (1958). Liquidity preference as behavior towards risk. *Review of Economic Studies*, 25, 65–86.

JAMES G. TOMPKINS

capital budgeting The process of making investment decisions involving fixed assets is called capital budgeting. Once a particular long-term investment has been identified, the firm's management must estimate the expected cash flows from the project and the timing of those cash flows over the life of the project. The relevant cash flows are the investment outlays that will be required at the outset of the project, including expected increases in net working capital, and the annual net incremental cash inflows, i.e. the difference between the firm's net cash flows with and without taking on the project. Thus, for example, the analysis would not include SUNK COSTS, but would include OPPORTUNITY COSTS and EXTERNALITIES associated with the investment.

The net operating cash flows generally consist of sales revenue minus expenses and taxes plus any tax savings due to the allowable DEPRECIATION deduction. At the end of the project, there may be also be cash flow associated with the salvage value of the used fixed asset. Since it is difficult to make accurate long-term forecasts of sales, expenses, and other associated cash flows, the potential for error in the forecasts may be great, particularly for large, complex investments. Therefore, the next step in the capital budgeting process is to assess the riskiness of the projected cash flows. The management will then determine the appropriate COST OF CAPITAL to be used in determining the NET PRESENT VALUE (NPV) of the project. Alternatively, the management may make their decisions based on INTERNAL RATE OF RETURN (IRR), in which case risk will be incorporated into the analysis by adjusting the "hurdle rate", or minimum acceptable IRR. When the projected cash flows are riskier, the management will increase the hurdle rate to account for the additional risk. The investment opportunity schedule is a graphical depiction of the firm's opportunities in terms of IRR and dollars of new capital raised. Since stockholder value will be maximized by choosing the projects with the greatest return, this schedule will be downward sloping.

When a firm is faced with many different project alternatives, the optimal capital budget is determined by choosing the set of projects that maximizes the net worth of the firm. As the firm increases its total level of new investment, it must raise new capital to support this investment. The intersection of the increasing marginal cost of capital curve and the decreasing investment opportunity schedule will determine the optimal capital budget, i.e. the level of investment and the specific set of projects that will maximize the firm's value.

Although NPV and IRR are the most commonly used decision methods in capital budgeting, there are several alternative techniques that are sometimes used in practice. For example, some managers use payback analysis, in which projects are evaluated based on the time required to recoup initial cash expenditures. This method is generally inferior to NPV and IRR since it ignores cash flows that occur after the break-even point. Another alternative decision tool is the "profitability index" (PI), a ratio of the present value of the cash inflows to the present value of the cash outflows. A PI that is greater than one is equivalent to NPV greater than zero and the criteria is applied similarly.

Bibliography

Brigham, E. F. Gapenski, L. C. (1996). *Intermediate Financial Management*. 5th edn, Fort Worth, TX: Dryden.
Gitman, L. J. (1995). *Foundations of Managerial Finance*. 4th edn, New York: HarperCollins.

VICKIE L. BAJTELSMIT

capital markets   Capital market securities are transferred through a mix of markets and financial intermediaries. The efficient flow of capital market funds is critical for financing real asset growth and economic expansion. Financial securities with maturities greater than one year are traded in capital markets and include debt obligations as well as common and preferred equity. The market for new debt and equity issues is called the primary market. Outstanding debt and equity securities are traded on the secondary market.

Debt securities offer investors interest payments and/or a par or face value payment at maturity. Debt holders can also sell their securities on the secondary market prior to its maturity. Common equity offers investors an expected dividend stream, the potential for capital gains, and voting rights. Preferred stock includes the provision that their dividends must be paid before those to common stock holders.

Various debt and equity securities offer investors a range of features designed to meet individual preferences for risk and return. These securities may differ with respect to default risk, interest rate risk, liquidity and taxability. Callable features, convertible features, sinking funds, adjustable rates, tax exemptions and derivatives are designed to meet changing investor concerns. The capital market infrastructure of intermediaries provides suppliers and demanders of funds with critical decision-making information and facilities necessary for allocating funds based on risk-return preference.

Commercial rating companies provide credit analysis and default risk ratings on corporate debt securities. Moody's Investor Service and Standard Poors are the most widely used bond rating systems. Large institutional investors and investment banks also operate their own credit analysis system.

Investment banks are intermediaries in the primary market for new issues. They collect, assemble, interpret and disseminate information. New issues' prices are set and sometimes guaranteed by investment banks. Brokerage firms and dealers are intermediaries in the secondary market, where outstanding securities are traded. Brokers, through their membership in a central exchange such as the New York Stock Exchange, buy and sell listed stocks for their clientele, to whom they also act as advisors. Unlisted stocks and debt obligations are traded in the over-the-counter markets such as the

National Association of Securities Dealers (NASDAQ). Government securities dealers are specialists who both buy and sell government debt of all maturities.

The capital markets have experienced major changes in the last 30 years. First, innovations in computer technology have led to more sophisticated trading strategies. Other innovations such as pass-throughs and other asset-backed securities evolved along with other securities and related derivatives such as collateralized mortgage obligations and stripped mortgaged backed securities to create new lower risk securities with a broader appeal to investors. Additional concerns over risk management have encouraged the growth of futures and options markets. Finally, small investors' preference for lower risk redirected funds through mutual funds and pensions. As a result, trading systems today are designed to meet the needs of institutional investors rather than those of small investors.

To small investors, institutional investors offer financial services and products, risk reduction and liquidity, as well as reduced costs of contracting. Commercial banks, savings and loans, insurance companies, finance companies, pension funds and mutual funds intermediate billions of small-investor dollars into capital markets based on risk-return preferences and the nature of their business. Commercial banks invest in a wide range of US government securities, federal agency notes and municipal securities so as to meet regulatory restrictions for safety and liquidity. In contrast, savings and loans specialize in mortgages. Life insurance companies select their capital market holdings so that their maturities will match the company's expected policy payouts. Likewise, pension funds tailor their investments to debt securities and equity which match predictable pension payouts. Mutual funds invest in a full range of securities with a special mix of securities in each fund.

Bibliography

Fabozzi, J. F. Modigliani, F. (1992). *Capital Markets, Institutions and Instruments.* Englewood Cliffs, NJ: Prentice-Hall.

DON SABBARESE

cartels When firms make formal agreements to set prices or output levels they may form a cartel to reduce competition between them. Cartels, such as OPEC in oil production and DeBeers in diamonds, are illegal in the US under its ANTITRUST POLICY which prohibits any agreements between firms which have the effect of reducing COMPETITION. Cartel members are cooperating oligopolists who may decide to maximize joint profits, divide the market, or set other goals depending on the number of members and a variety of economic forces. Under US antitrust laws, any agreement to fix prices is illegal *per se* and no defense of the agreement is allowed. The EU prohibits COLLUSION between firms when the sole purpose is to reduce competition, but exemptions may be granted if the agreement satisfies specific public goals; see Martin (1994).

Salop (1986) identified three requirements for firms to successfully collude. First, the firms must agree on the goals the cartel is to achieve; second, the firms must achieve those goals; and third, the firms must maintain the cartel agreement as market conditions change over time. Since firms face different circumstances in terms of their demand and cost conditions, collusive agreements may not be easily achieved. For example, agreements to maximize joint profits would require that output be produced by the lowest-cost producer. This could mean that some members of the cartel produce very little output. The cartel would then need to make side payments to these firms, but they might not be satisfied with the payments they receive or with their status in the cartel. Furthermore, once the cartel is established, all firms have incentives to cheat on the agreement by selling additional output below the cartel price since that price will exceed the MARGINAL COST of production. The incentive to cheat makes it more difficult to maintain the cartel agreement (Stigler, 1968). Successful cartels must be able to detect and punish cheating members, yet punishing cheating firms by increasing output and forcing the price down will punish all members if the product is homogeneous. The incentives to cheat are greater when firms' marginal costs of production do not increase much with increases in output, when the percentage of total costs which are FIXED COSTS is high and when the probability of detection is small. For a given price, the first two conditions mean greater profits for each additional unit produced while the last concerns the likelihood of punishment. Agreements are easier to reach and enforce in industries with a few, large sellers, i.e. industries which are highly concentrated; see MARKET STRUCTURE, Stigler (1968).

Cartel stability is also threatened by potential ENTRY into the market, since the higher prices charged by established firms create incentives for new entrants, so viable cartels must be protected by BARRIERS TO ENTRY. The greater the differences between producers in products, costs or goals, and the more unpredictable are market conditions, the more difficult it will be to agree, achieve and maintain collusive arrangements.

Bibliography

Martin, S. (1994). *Industrial Economics*. 2nd edn, New York: Macmillan.
Salop, S. C. (1986). Factors that (credibly) facilitate oligopoly co-ordination. Stiglitz, J. E. and Mathewson, G. F. *New Developments in the Analysis of Market Structure*. Cambridge, MA: MIT. 265–90.
Stigler, G. J. (1968). *The Organization of Industry*. Chicago: University of Chicago Press.

ROBERT E. MCAULIFFE

cash flow   A firm's cash flow represents the difference between the firm's cash outlays and receipts over a given period of time. Estimates of cash flows for any investment project under consideration are crucial for CAPITAL BUDGETING decisions based on either the NET PRESENT VALUE or INTERNAL RATE OF RETURN criteria. Since future cash flows for an investment are not known with certainty, managers should calculate expected cash flows based on the probability they will occur. In addition, any estimated net present value or internal rate of return should be tested to determine how sensitive the results are to slight changes in the underlying assumptions (such as changes in the probabilities of the cash flows or in the discount or hurdle rate). All cash flows should be estimated on an after-tax basis.

Estimated cash flows should also be adjusted for anticipated INFLATION, particularly since a company's revenues may not adjust to inflation as its costs. For example, a firm in a very competitive market may not be able to raise prices at the same rate as inflation, yet the firm's costs may rise with the inflation rate (due to cost-of-living adjustments in workers' contracts). In such cases, managers may want to separately adjust the revenue and expenditure sides of the estimated cash flows for inflation.

ROBERT E. MCAULIFFE

certainty equivalent   As the term suggests, the certainty equivalent of a risky decision is the amount an investor would require to make her indifferent between accepting that sum (with certainty) or accepting the chance of a risky decision. If an investor is risk averse, then the certainty equivalent will always be less than the expected payoff of a risky decision. The greater a person's RISK AVERSION, the lower the certainty equivalent the person will require for a given risky payoff. For example, an investor who is just indifferent between paying $100 for a stock that could pay $300 or nothing with 50 percent probability for each, has a certainty equivalent of $100.

The certainty equivalent factor is the ratio of the certainty equivalent sum to the expected risky payoff. In the example above, the investor was indifferent between a certain $100 and an expected payoff of $150, so the certainty equivalent factor is 66.67 percent. The cost of one dollar in risky returns is 66 cents of certain returns for this investor. An investor who knows this factor can then adjust the expected future returns from a given investment by this factor to adjust the investment for risk when making CAPITAL BUDGETING decisions, for example. Riskier investments should have lower certainty equivalents and therefore will have lower certainty equivalent factors.

Bibliography

Douglas, E. J. (1992). *Managerial Economics*. 4th edn, Englewood Cliffs, NJ: Prentice-Hall.
Hirschey, M. Pappas, J. L. (1995). *Fundamentals of Managerial Economics*. 5th edn, New York: Dryden.

ROBERT E. MCAULIFFE

ceteris paribus   In economic analysis, many factors can affect a given variable. As an analytical device, economists employ the ceteris paribus assumption (Latin for "all else equal") to isolate the effect of one of the independent variables on the dependent variable. For example, the demand for a product will be affected by the price of that product, the prices of products which are SUBSTITUTES, COMPLEMENTS, and consumers' income among other possible variables. To find the effect of a change in the product's own price on the quantity demanded, the assumption "ceteris paribus" is used to derive a theoretical conclusion. This makes the statement about the relation between the quantity demanded and price a *conditional* statement: *if* no other factors affecting demand are changed, *then* a rise in the product's price should cause the quantity demanded to fall. Clearly, if the conditions are changed (e.g. incomes increase and this is a normal good), then we may not expect to see a decrease in the quantity demanded even if the price is higher because all else was not equal (constant); see NORMAL GOODS.

ROBERT E. McAULIFFE

Clayton Act   The Clayton Act was written in 1914, in part to clarify the legislatures' intentions concerning SHERMAN ACT phrases such as "in restraint of trade". It specifies a number of business practices which are proscribed. The Act includes sections on PRICE DISCRIMINATION, TYING, and mergers, among others. Each type of conduct is identified as a violation of the law, but is not treated as *per se* illegal as the courts had ruled in Sherman Act cases involving behavior such as price fixing. Instead, the Clayton Act considers these competitive strategies as being illegal only if "the effect may be to substantially lessen competition or tend to create a monopoly"; see Stelzer (1986, pp.594–8) for a more complete statement of this Statute. Thus a so-called *rule of reason* approach is used, whereby the adverse consequences (and potential benefits) of the business practices are examined.

Section 2 of the Clayton Act, and its 1936 revision named the Robinson–Patman Act, concerns price discrimination, which is the act of selling the same product to different customers or customer groups for different prices. The law was originally designed to diminish the use of geographic PREDATORY PRICING, where a firm having MARKET POWER in one GEOGRAPHIC MARKET would set an artificially low price (below cost) for its products in another geographic market in an attempt to drive out its rivals and extend its market power to the new area. This could be done by temporarily covering the firm's losses with the economic profits earned in the initial market (*see* ECONOMIC PROFIT). The revised law also focuses on protecting smaller buyers in a market from some of the advantages of large (e.g. chain store) rivals in that market.

Managers should be aware of several legally accepted defenses against charges of price discrimination which have been established. First, price differences are allowed where they exist due to a justifiable difference in costs. Thus differences may be allowed due to service and transportation costs, quality differences in the product and quantity discounts resulting from cost savings. Second, price differences resulting from a good faith effort to meet a competitor's price are allowed. Third, price discrimination may be defended on the basis of the product in question having lost its marketability due to obsolescence or due to its perishable nature. Finally, the lack of a "substantial lessening of competition" or injury to competitors serve as possible defenses. As a result, price discrimination which exists in the airlines, movie, and magazine industries, for example, are not seen as violations of the Act.

Section 3 of the Clayton Act concerns illegal tying arrangements and exclusive dealing contracts. Tying involves a situation in which the seller offers a product (the tying good) to a customer, conditional on the customers' additional purchase of a second (tied) good. The principle concern of the law is the extension of market power from the tying good market into the market for the tied good. For example, the A.B. Dick Company, manufacturer of copier machines, ink, brushes and other accessories, originally tied the purchase of these accessories to that of the machine. The company held patents and therefore some market power in the market for copiers, but the market for the accessories was seen by the courts as being essentially competitive. The courts feared that the tie allowed the company to charge prices above the competitive level for the accessories and thereby inappropriately extend its legally acquired market power in the copier market into the market for accessories.

Here again managers should be aware of the circumstances where tying contracts are allowed. Once again, where competition may not be "substantially lessened" the tie may be allowed. As a result, one defense involves the demonstration of either:

(1) a lack of market power in the market for the tying good or
(2) a limited impact on the market for the tied good.

Second, a tie is allowable where obvious production ECONOMIES OF SCALE are in evidence.

A third defense occurs when the protection of the tying good's quality or the goodwill of the firm necessitates a tie. This precedent was established in a 1960 case involving the Jerrold Electronics Corp., a supplier of community television antenna systems. The firm was allowed by the courts to require the purchasers of the system to also purchase their maintenance contracts, as the systems were new and sophisticated and required specially trained service personnel. In an earlier case though, in which the International Salt Co. tied the purchase of its own rock salt to the sale of its salt dissolving machines, the courts ruled that the tie was illegal, in part because the company's machines were not, as Justice Jackson put it, "allergic to salt of equal quality" produced by another firm; see Stelzer (1986). Finally, the tie between two goods is allowed where it is voluntary or optional to the customer rather than being an absolute requirement.

The practice of exclusive dealing is related to tying in that a customer is "tied" to a particular supplier. Deals between manufacturers and materials suppliers, for example, may connect the two parties via long-term contracts where the former agrees to be exclusively supplied by the latter. Similarly, contracts between manufacturers and retailers may require the latter to purchase a product or set of products exclusively from one manufacturer. The key antitrust concern in both cases here is market foreclosure.

In the first case, an exclusive contract with a large manufacturer may foreclose other suppliers from the market. In the second case, one example of foreclosure involves the practice of "full line forcing" in which a manufacturer of one line of products, for example oil and gasoline, requires retailers to purchase other products such as tires and other accessories exclusively from this seller as well. This contract may foreclose other accessories suppliers from an important retail outlet.

Antitrust enforcement agencies and the courts have also recognized that important benefits may arise for both buyers and suppliers involved in exclusive contracts. A manufacturer may gain from having a guaranteed source of steady supply of materials, which enable better planning, lower backup inventories and a smoother flow of output (and perhaps lower prices for its customers) as a result. The supplier gains from a steady source of demand, which minimizes promotional expenditures, diminishes the uncertainty of long-term capital expenditure planning and also establishes a steady flow of revenues. As a result, the standards applied in the rule of reason approach to resolving these cases have varied over time and across cases.

Section 7 of the Clayton Act focuses on mergers. Here again mergers are outlawed only when their effect "may be to substantially lessen competition or tend to create a monopoly." Perhaps no other area of ANTITRUST POLICY receives as much scrutiny and debate over the proper interpretation of the law. Three times in the last quarter century guidelines concerning merger policy have been written and substantially rewritten by the federal government in an effort to clarify the existing administration's views on the proper interpretation of Section 7 and the circumstances under which the appropriate federal agencies will bring antitrust policy action against merging parties (*see* HORIZONTAL MERGER GUIDELINES; MERGER GUIDELINES, 1992).

There exist three types of mergers for policymakers to consider. These are:

(1) horizontal mergers, involving direct rivals who are producing a similar product in the same geographic market.

(2) vertical mergers, between firms involved at different stages of raw material supply, production or distribution of the same good (*see* VERTICAL INTEGRATION) and

(3) conglomerate mergers, which deal with firms competing in essentially separate product markets.

Of greatest concern to policymakers are horizontal mergers as this type of merger reduces the number of competitors, increases the market share of the acquiring firm in the merger, and thereby potentially changes the MARKET STRUCTURE and increases the firm's market power. Vertical mergers are also of concern when, for example, a firm with market power in the production stage is now able to restrict competition in the distribution stage. Much less, although some, concern has been given to conglomerate mergers, especially when the acquiring firm, in the absence of a merger, may have entered on its own, thereby increasing the number of competitors.

Active antitrust policy concerning mergers was pursued during the 1960s and 1970s during which time the federal government instituted strict guidelines indicating that an antitrust challenge will ordinarily occur against the horizontal merger of firms having relatively small market shares. At the same time, the Supreme Court supported this position by initiating the *incipiency doctrine*, wherein it indicated that a trend (resulting from mergers) toward higher industry concentration would be stopped in its earliest stages. More recently, especially during the 1980s, the extent of antitrust activity against mergers has diminished.

see also **Federal Trade Commission Act; antitrust policy; tying**

Bibliography

Blair, R. Kasserman, D. (1985). *Antitrust Economics.* Homewood: Irwin.
Greer, D. (1992). *Industrial Organization and Public Policy.* 3rd edn, New York: Macmillan.
Howard, M. (1983). *Antitrust and Trade Regulation.* Englewood Cliffs, NJ: Prentice-Hall.
Martin, S. (1994). *Industrial Economics.* 2nd edn, New York: Macmillan.
Neale, A. (1977). *The Antitrust Laws of the U.S.A.* 2nd edn, Cambridge: CUP.
Stelzer, I. (1986). *Selected Antitrust Cases: Landmark Decisions.* 7th edn, Homewood: Irwin.

GILBERT BECKER

Coase theorem The Coase theorem was developed from Ronald Coase's (1960) path-breaking work in *The Problem of Social Cost.* The theorem has been stated in a number of different forms, but its central thrust is that, if rights are well defined and TRANSACTIONS COSTS are zero, the allocation of resources will be efficient regardless of the initial assignment of rights (*see* PROPERTY RIGHTS). Thus, if a power plant emits pollution which harms the operation of a nearby laundry, it does not matter, from an EFFICIENCY perspective, whether the court assigns the power plant the freedom to pollute or the laundry the right to be free from pollution. The ability of the parties to negotiate costlessly will result in the right coming to rest where it is most highly valued.

The Coase theorem is one of the most controversial propositions in modern economics, and understandably so, given its profound implications. For the theorem implies that the structure of law is without effect on the allocation (albeit not the distribution) of resources. Efficiency does not require making the nuisance generator, the tortfeasor, or the contract breacher liable for the harm that they cause. This proposition goes against the grain of a half-century of welfare economics, which has steadfastly argued that the efficient resolution of externalities requires that the government place some type of restraint on those who generate the externalities; against this, the Coase theorem asserts that markets can indeed work to resolve externality problems. Because of this, the theorem has become a weapon in the hands of those who would defend the market against the incursions of government. Rather than tax or regulate polluters, government can simply assign rights and let the market work. Furthermore, there is no reason to hold liable those who generate the harm; efficiency will result in either case.

The linchpin of the theorem is the assumption of zero transaction costs, a concept which has been construed both narrowly and broadly. The theorem tells us that private negotiations, the pricing mechanism, or the market (as the case may be) will allocate rights and resources efficiently if there are no barriers to their working. This has justly been called a tautology. On the other hand, it is an interesting tautology for several reasons. First, it tells us that the market can work in situations (EXTERNALITIES) where it was previously thought to fail, provided that the necessary conditions obtain. Second, it suggests that where markets do fail, one cause may be the presence of transaction costs which are sufficiently high to preclude a negotiated solution. This both adds to our understanding of why inefficient externalities persist and suggests that, where removable impediments to negotiation exist, measures can potentially be implemented to facilitate a market solution. Third, the theorem can be extended to encompass situations where transaction costs are positive: rights will be reallocated through negotiation to higher-valued uses so long as the expected gains from such negotiations make it worthwhile to incur the costs. This is perhaps the most important application of the theorem, for, as Coase recognized, and as numerous subsequent commentators have pointed out, transaction costs are omnipresent – a fact that violates the central assumption of the theorem itself.

The effect of this last point is that the market can, in certain instances, work to resolve externality situations. The issue is one of setting up the proper framework to allow it to do so. The original stimulus for Coase's analysis was his argument that the government should consider setting up a market in broadcast frequencies rather than allocating them by administrative fiat (Coase, 1959). While this idea was roundly rejected for some time after it was made, we have, today, auctions of rights to frequencies upon which new portable telephone technologies will operate. And the current experiments with marketable pollution permits are suggestive of the more general applicability of Coase's contention that the pricing mechanism may be preferable to more traditional externality remedies in certain contexts.

The third point, above, makes particularly clear the link between Coase's analysis in *The Problem of Social Cost* and that in *The Nature of the Firm*. In the latter essay, Coase (1937) undertook to find a rationale for the existence of the integrated firm, including both the hierarchical employer–employee relationship and the decision to make or buy (*see* MAKE OR BUY DECISIONS). Coase suggested that, if market transactions were costless, all production activity would take place through a series of market transactions; the firm would not exist. The firm comes into existence because there are costs associated with transacting through the market, costs which are sometimes higher than those associated with internal organization. The firm, he said, will organize additional transactions internally as long as the cost of doing so is less than the cost of carrying out the same transaction through the market. Thus, while the Coase theorem shows that, from an efficiency perspective, the law has no purpose (apart from some initial assignment of rights), Coase's work in *The Nature of the Firm* suggested that, if market transactions are costless, the firm has no purpose. Of course the import of this comes from the converse: since market transactions are not costless, the institutional structure (the structure of law and the organizational structure of the firm and of firm *vis-a-vis* market) becomes an important part of economic analysis, as these factors play a prominent role in affecting the allocation of resources in society.

This, in turn, brings to the fore the importance of the contracting process and the examination of those factors and forces which influence the process itself and the structure of contracts. The Coase theorem suggests that all contracts will be fully specified against all eventualities. Observed contracts are very different from this, often leaving open a host of potential actions due, at least in part, to the costliness of contracting over these terms (*see* INCOMPLETE CONTRACTS). The result is that, in many instances, the respective rights of the involved parties are not well defined, exposing agents to potentially adverse actions by their counterparts. The effect of this is to induce the expenditure of resources on various types of safeguarding activities or the devising of mechanisms (such as internal organization as against the market, or one type of internal organizational structure as against another) to lessen the potential for or effect of these adverse actions. Consider a situation where A is the sole supplier of an input to B and B does not have readily available alternative sources of supply. B is thus exposed to potentially opportunistic behavior by A. The transaction costs associated with the contracting process may make it difficult or impossible to eliminate this potential within the contract, and A's best response may thus be to produce the input itself (vertically integrate).

Thus, while the Coase theorem is a statement of the virtues of markets, its implications come from the relaxation of its zero transaction costs assumption, which highlights the role that transaction costs play in determining the institutional structure of production and that this institutional structure plays in affecting the costs of transacting.

Bibliography

Barzel, Y. Kochin, L. A. (1992). Ronald Coase on the nature of social cost as a key to the problem of the firm. *Scandinavian Journal of Economics*, **94**, 19–31.

Coase, R. H. (1937). The nature of the firm. *Economica*, n.s., **4**, 386–405.

Coase, R. H. (1959). The Federal Communications Commission. *Journal of Law and Economics*, **2**, 1–40.

Coase, R. H. (1960). The problem of social cost. *Journal of Law and Economics*, **3**, 1–44.

Coase, R. H. (1988). *The Firm, the Market, and the Law*. Chicago: University of Chicago Press.

Coase, R. H. (1992). The institutional structure of production. *American Economic Review*, **82**, 713–19.

Medema, S. G. (1994). *Ronald H. Coase*. London: Macmillan.

Medema, S. G. (ed.) (1995). *The Legacy of Ronald Coase in Economic Analysis*. Aldershot: Edward Elgar Publishing.

STEVEN G. MEDEMA

Cobb–Douglas production function

The Cobb–Douglas production function is frequently employed in the economic analysis of production and costs. This production function relates output produced to the inputs of production (*see* PRODUCTION FUNCTIONS). If labor hours, L, and capital, K, are the only inputs in production, the Cobb–Douglas production function is:

$$q = AL^\alpha K^\beta$$

where A is a coefficient that represents the level of technology and α and β are coefficients indicating how output responds to changes in each of these inputs (additional inputs can be added to the function above in a similar fashion). A convenient feature of the Cobb–Douglas production function above is that ECONOMIES OF SCALE in production can be determined by examining the coefficients α and β. When there are economies of scale in production, doubling all inputs will cause output to increase by more than double. In the case above, if we double the labor and capital inputs, we would have:

$$q = A(2L)^\alpha (2K)^\beta = 2^{(\alpha+\beta)} AL^\alpha K^\beta$$

Doubling the inputs used in production will cause output to rise by $2^{(\alpha+\beta)}$, so the returns to scale in production can be determined by summing the coefficients of the Cobb–Douglas production function. If the sum of $(\alpha + \beta)$ equals one, then there are CONSTANT RETURNS TO SCALE.

Estimates of the Cobb–Douglas production function can be obtained by a LINEAR REGRESSION of the logarithm of output against the logarithm of the relevant inputs in production; see Berndt (1991) and Maddala (1992).

Bibliography

Berndt, E. R. (1991). *The Practice of Econometrics*. Reading, MA: Addison-Wesley.

Cobb, C. Douglas, P. H. (1928). A theory of production. *American Economic Review*, **18**, 139–65.

Maddala, G. S. (1992). *Introduction to Econometrics*. 2nd edn, New York: Macmillan.

ROBERT E. MCAULIFFE

coefficient of variation

When making decisions under risk, the mean and STANDARD DEVIATION provide information about the degree of dispersion, but they are affected by the size and units of measure used. If a company were considering two projects with substantially different EXPECTED PRESENT VALUE, the means and standard deviations are not directly comparable. The coefficient of variation is a measure of relative risk and is defined as the ratio of the standard deviation to the expected present value of the project:

$$\text{coefficient of variation} = \sigma/\text{EPV}$$

where σ is the standard deviation of returns from the project and EPV is the expected present value of the project. Since the expected present value and the standard deviation are measured in the same units, the units will cancel and the coefficient of variation will be unit free. It is a measure of the risk incurred per dollar of expected return. The inverse of the coefficient of variation is EPV/σ which measures the risk-adjusted return.

Bibliography

Douglas, E. J. (1992). *Managerial Economics*. 4th edn, Englewood Cliffs, NJ: Prentice-Hall.
Hirschey, M. Pappas, J. L. (1995). *Fundamentals of Managerial Economics*. 5th edn, New York: Dryden.

ROBERT E. McAULIFFE

established firm to retaliate automatically if another firm in the industry (or a potential entrant) cuts prices and this credible strategy can help maintain the collusive agreement (*see* CREDIBLE STRATEGIES).

Bibliography

Martin, S. (1994). *Industrial Economics*. 2nd edn, New York: Macmillan.
Salop, S. C. (1986). Factors that (credibly) facilitate oligopoly co-ordination. Stiglitz, J. E. and Mathewson, G. F. *New Developments in the Analysis of Market Structure*. Cambridge, MA: MIT. 265–90.
Stigler, G. J. (1968). *The Organization of Industry*. Chicago: University of Chicago Press.

ROBERT E. McAULIFFE

collusion   When firms in a market have formal or informal agreements on pricing, output, or other competitive issues, the firms are in collusion. ANTITRUST POLICY in both the US and the EU prohibits collusion between competing firms in a market. Collusive agreements can be tacit arrangements whereby firms in an industry follow a price leader when it changes price or they may be the formal agreements of a cartel (*see* CARTELS). Collusion is more likely in industries which are highly concentrated (Stigler, 1968; Martin, 1994) and when the costs of organizing firms are lower.

Salop (1986) identified a number of factors which he called facilitating practices that have the effect of promoting information exchange among firms or promoting incentives to adhere to the agreement. Practices which promote information exchange help reduce uncertainty about the actions of competitors and therefore help maintain collusive agreements such as advance notice of price changes. According to Salop, most-favored-nation (MFN) clauses in sales contracts help create incentives for firms to keep to the agreements because if one firm attempts to decrease its price, it must do so to *all* of its customers. This makes price reductions more costly and increases the likelihood that competitors will learn of the discounts. Meet-the-competition clauses have a similar effect in providing pricing information to all competitors. Combining MFN and meet the competition clauses in contracts to buyers commits the

commitment   Commitments that a firm makes can be crucial to the success of its STRATEGIC BEHAVIOR. An established firm may threaten to reduce price if entry occurs, but if the firm cannot commit itself to the price reduction, a potential entrant may not believe the threat, particularly if the established firm would maximize profits by avoiding the price cut. But if a firm invests in capacity to produce, achieves lower costs through the LEARNING CURVE, or includes "meet the competition" clauses in its sales contracts, the irreversible nature of these actions commits the firm to behave aggressively should entry occur. The commitment serves to "back up" the threat of retaliation by the established firm and therefore the behavior of the firm's competitors will be affected. If the firm cannot make commitments, its strategic threats may not be taken seriously (Jacquemin, 1987; Porter, 1980).

Capital expenditures in specialized assets or in brand advertising can have commitment value because these are SUNK COSTS which cannot be recovered. The more specialized the assets of the firm, the greater the sunk costs if the firm fails (*see* ASSET SPECIFICITY). These costs can be a SIGNALING device to competitors that the firm will compete aggressively to defend its market position. Porter (1980) argues that the success or failure of strategic plans, offensive or defensive, depends on the firm's ability to make commitments that are to its advantage. A firm that makes commitments signals its position and likely reaction to competitors and therefore forces them to adjust their decisions. When firms can make commitments before a rival does, those firms may also have FIRST-MOVER ADVANTAGES. Porter lists a number of visible assets which can serve to communicate a firm's commitment: excess cash reserves, excess capacity, and extensive research facilities which can all be used to threaten rival firms.

Commitment may also be necessary to overcome TRANSACTIONS COSTS in the market. A firm may be unwilling to undertake investments in specific assets for a customer unless it can be certain that the customer will purchase the output. CONTRACTS are a formal way of establishing commitment between parties to a transaction when the obligations can be reasonably specified.

Bibliography

Jacquemin, A. (1987). *The New Industrial Organization: Market Forces and Strategic Behavior.* Cambridge, MA: MIT.

Porter, M. E. (1980). *Competitive Strategy.* New York: Free Press.

Tirole, J. (1988). *The Theory of Industrial Organization.* Cambridge, MA: MIT.

ROBERT E. MCAULIFFE

competition   Competition has different interpretations in economics and business. Businessmen regard competition as a process of rivalry where firms try to gain an advantage through pricing decisions, advertising, research and development, product QUALITY and other means. In economics, however, when there is PERFECT COMPETITION firms cannot engage in rivalrous behavior because they are price-takers in the market. This difference in the meaning of competition has created some difficulties in the past.

If a market is perfectly competitive the following conditions hold (Stigler, 1968; Carlton and Perloff, 1994):

(1) The product is homogeneous, i.e. the firms in the industry produce goods which are identical in the eyes of consumers.

(2) Information is perfect, i.e. consumers and suppliers know all offers to buy and sell and

producers also know the returns they could earn if their resources were put to alternative uses.

(3) There are large numbers of buyers and sellers. This condition is necessary to ensure that no single seller or buyer can affect the market price and means that market participants are price-takers.

(4) There is free entry and exit. Resources must be free to move to where they have the highest value. If there are BARRIERS TO ENTRY in an industry, then new firms cannot take advantage of profitable opportunities when they arise.

Since firms in a perfectly competitive industry are price-takers, their only decision is the level of output they produce. Competition under these circumstances is so intense that any firm which tries to charge a price slightly above the market price will have no sales. Therefore perfect competition in economics is more a description of a state of the market than a process. Nevertheless, it has very desirable properties in terms of economic EFFICIENCY and represents a benchmark against which other market structures may be compared. Since the choices of firms in a perfectly competitive market are so constrained, interactions between firms do not matter and difficulties modeling STRATEGIC BEHAVIOR are avoided.

Critics such as Hayek (1948) and High (1990) have argued that the assumptions of perfect competition remove the most essential features of competition in real markets. The dynamic process of rivalry between firms leads to a variety of observed market behavior such as advertising, cost-cutting, quality improvement, and product innovations. These are the weapons of the competitive struggle between firms that create improved standards of living in market economies and better serve consumers. By focusing on perfect competition, these authors argue that economists may miss important features of the market process. While the point is well-made, conventional analysis of markets and competition does include these forms of price and nonprice competition; see, for example, Carlton and Perloff (1994).

When firms compete in markets that are not perfectly competitive, all of the competitive tools described above may be used by firms to improve their market position. Are other forms of competition as effective in eliminating economic profits as price competition? Stigler (1968) showed that price competition would be more effective in reducing profits if the MARGINAL COST of changing the nonprice variable (such as advertising or product quality) is larger than the marginal cost of reducing price.

Bibliography

Carlton, D. W. Perloff, J. M. (1994). *Modern Industrial Organization.* 2nd edn, New York: HarperCollins.
Hayek, F. A. (1948). *Individualism and Economic Order.* Chicago, IL: Chicago University Press.
High, J. (1990). *Maximizing, Action, and Market Adjustment.* Munich, Germany: Philosophia Verlag.
Stigler, G. J. (1968). *The Organization of Industry.* Chicago: University of Chicago Press.

ROBERT E. MCAULIFFE

complements Complements are those products which are consumed together with another product, such as tires or gasoline and an automobile. The services of the automobile cannot be rendered without gasoline, so a consumer's willingness to pay for an automobile will be affected by the cost of gasoline. The prices of complementary goods have a negative effect on the quantity demanded for a product because if the price of a complement (gasoline) rises, the total cost of driving an automobile is now higher and this may reduce the demand for automobiles.

The negative effect of the price of complementary goods on the demand for a product would be observed as a negative cross elasticity of demand (*see* CROSS ELASTICITIES). This means that a given percentage increase (decrease) in the price of a complementary good will cause the demand for the related product to fall (rise) by "Y" percent.

see also **substitutes**

Bibliography

Douglas, E. J. (1992). *Managerial Economics.* 4th edn, Englewood Cliffs, NJ: Prentice-Hall.

Hirschey, M. Pappas, J. L. (1995). *Fundamentals of Managerial Economics.* 5th edn, New York: Dryden.

ROBERT E. MCAULIFFE

concentration indices Concentration indices are summary measures describing elements of MARKET STRUCTURE. Market concentration reflects the number and size distribution of firms in a market. As Stigler (1968) has noted, the measurement of size itself depends upon the purposes for which the measure is to be used. If the goal is to explain deviations of prices or profits from their levels under PERFECT COMPETITION, then measuring firm size by its employment is appropriate when examining the labor market but less so for the product market where sales are a more appropriate measure. Firm size in the capital market may be better measured by its total assets, while in the market for materials, its purchases may better represent the firm's MARKET POWER.

The choice of a concentration measure should also be determined by the purpose for which it is to be used and several measures of concentration have appeared in the literature. The concentration ratio measures the percentage of industry output produced by the largest T firms (usually T is taken as four or eight). If s_i is the market share of firm i, then the T-firm concentration ratio would be:

$$CR_T = \sum_{i=1}^{T} s_i$$

for $T = 4$ or $T = 8$. The Justice department used the four-firm concentration ratio for its 1968 merger guidelines; an industry was considered highly concentrated if the four-firm concentration ratio equaled or exceeded 75 percent. Unfortunately, because it focuses only on the largest firms in the industry, the concentration ratio does not describe the distribution of firm sizes throughout the industry nor does it provide information about the sizes of the individual firms that comprise the top four or eight firms. Concentration ratios are typically reported for *domestic* producers only, so they exclude competition from foreign imports and therefore may overstate the degree of concentration in an industry.

Another frequently used measure is the HERFINDAHL-HIRSCHMAN INDEX, or HHI, which is calculated using the market shares of all n firms in the industry, measured as:

$$HHI = \sum_{i=1}^{n} s_i^2$$

The HHI requires more information to compute relative to the concentration ratio and it is consistent with theories of OLIGOPOLY and COURNOT COMPETITION; see Stigler (1968) and Jacquemin (1987). The HHI has a maximum value of 10,000 in the case of a single firm and a minimum value near zero in the case of a large number of very small firms in the market. The HHI can also be written to represent the number of firms in the industry and the variance of their market shares. Thus:

$$HHI = n\sigma^2 + 1/n$$

where σ^2 is the variance of the firms' market shares in the industry; see Waterson (1984) and Jacquemin (1987).

The entropy index, EI, is less often used as a measure of concentration. It is calculated as the sum of all firm's market shares times the logarithm of their market shares:

$$EI = \sum_{i=1}^{n} s_i \ln(s_i)$$

The entropy index gives greater weight to smaller firms than the HHI. Another index, the Linda index, is based on concentration ratios but reveals differences in the sizes of the large firms. The T-firm Linda index is calculated as:

$$LI = \frac{1}{T(T-1)} \sum_{i=1}^{T-1} \frac{T-i}{i} \frac{CR_i}{CR_T - CR_i}$$

When all T-firms are the same size, this index has the value of $1/T$ and when the $(T+1)$th firm is substantially smaller than the preceding T firms, the value of LI_{T+1} will be much higher than for LI_T (Waterson, 1984). See Encaoua and Jacquemin (1980) for a discussion of the properties of proper measures of concentration.

Bibliography

Encaoua, D.   Jacquemin, A. (1980). Degree of monopoly, indices of concentration and threat of entry. *International Economic Review*, 21, 87–105.

Jacquemin, A. (1987). *The New Industrial Organization: Market Forces and Strategic Behavior*. Cambridge, MA: MIT.

Stigler, G. J. (1968). *The Organization of Industry*. Chicago: University of Chicago Press.

Waterson, M. (1984). *Economic Theory of the Industry*. Cambridge: CUP.

ROBERT E. MCAULIFFE

confidence intervals   In an estimation context, we are often interested in determining a plausible set of values for the unknown parameters rather than to simply rely on single point estimates. Suppose that we want to compute a 95 percent confidence interval, or "an interval with a 95 percent confidence level" for an unknown parameter, β. Then, given our data generation model, we use a rule for constructing an interval for β based on the data such that if the experiment were repeated many times, 95 percent of the time we would expect the interval to indeed include the unknown β. Note that the above is different from the incorrect statement: "there is a 95 percent chance that the confidence interval includes the *true* parameter's value." Once the interval is constructed, it either includes the unknown parameter or it does not. All that we know is that if we were to construct such intervals many times with different samples, we would expect 95 percent of them to include the unknown parameter β.

For instance, suppose that β is a regression coefficient. Then, under fairly general assumptions and when the number of observations is large, the ordinary least squares estimator, $\hat{\beta}$, plus or minus two times its standard error, s, is an approximate 95 percent confidence interval for the unknown coefficient: $\hat{\beta} \pm 2s$. For example, suppose that $\hat{\beta} = 8$ and $s = 2.5$, then the 95 percent confidence interval for $\hat{\beta}$ would be (3,13). Often one divides the OLS estimate over its standard error and compares the result with 2, saying that the estimate is significant (or, significantly different from zero) when it is greater than 2 in absolute value (*see* T-STATISTIC). What is implicitly being done then is checking whether the 95 percent confidence interval contains zero or not. In the previous example, the interval (3,13) does not include 0, or we could calculate the value of the t-statistic for $\hat{\beta} = 8/2.5 = 3.2$ 2 so the estimate is significantly different from zero (at the 5 percent significance level).

Bibliography

Maddala, G. S. (1992). *Introduction to Econometrics.* 2nd edn, New York: Macmillan.

Silvey, S. D. (1975). *Statistical Inference.* London: Chapman Hall.

EDUARDO LEY

constant cost industry A constant cost industry is one whose long run supply curve is horizontal at the constant (average) cost of production. As the industry expands or contracts, the long run average cost of producing output remains the same. It should be noted that this does not necessarily mean that the firms' production technology exhibits CONSTANT RETURNS TO SCALE, the industry could expand through the entry of additional identical firms with U-shaped average cost curves where each firm operates at the minimum point on its AVERAGE TOTAL COST curve.

When demand for a product increases, existing firms produce more output along the SHORT RUN supply curve since it is profitable to do so at a higher price. If this increase in demand occurred in a competitive market when the industry was in long run equilibrium, the higher price will cause existing firms to earn economic profits (*see* ECONOMIC PROFIT) since price will equal MARGINAL COST above AVERAGE TOTAL COST. Managers should note that these economic profits will attract entry into the industry in the long run as long as there are no BARRIERS TO ENTRY, and this entry will cause the short run supply curve to shift out and lower the price of the product. Entry will continue until firms in the industry can only earn the normal, risk-adjusted rate of return. Therefore, in the long run, there will be no economic profits earned. If the costs of inputs in production have not been changed by this expansion of the industry, then the new equilibrium price will be the same as before

the expansion and the long run supply curve will be flat, connecting these two long run equilibrium prices.

Constant cost industries are more likely to be observed in cases where the inputs in production are not highly specialized or when the industry is small relative to the size of its input markets. These conditions make it more likely that the expansion of the industry (and the consequent increase in the demand for inputs in production) will not cause FACTOR PRICES to rise and so the minimum average cost remains the same as ENTRY or EXIT occurs in the industry. Managers in constant cost industries can use this knowledge to anticipate price changes. When the industry expands, prices and costs may initially rise, but they will decrease in the long run as entry occurs and prices and costs return to their original values.

see also **economies of scale; perfect competition**

ROBERT E. MCAULIFFE

constant returns to scale This describes a specific technology of production for the firm. When constant returns in production exist, a firm that doubled all inputs in production would see a doubling of its output. In the case of the COBB–DOUGLAS PRODUCTION FUNCTION, constant returns to scale occur when the of the exponents for the inputs in production sum to one. Since with constant returns to scale there are no penalties to the firm whether it expands or contracts, there is no theoretically unique optimal size plant that minimizes the costs of production. With no theoretical limit on the size of firms in the industry, the theoretical number of firms in the industry is also indeterminate.

see also **economies of scale**

ROBERT E. MCAULIFFE

consumer price index The consumer price index (CPI) measures the changes in the price of a market basket of goods relative to a base year. The basic question to be answered is: what does it cost in today's prices to buy the same goods purchased in the base year? In the US, the Labor Department periodically surveys consumers to determine what they buy and how much. These surveys determine the "market basket" of goods and the weights given to each price in the index. The last US survey was 1982–84. According to economic theory, the demand for a product depends on the relative (or real) price of the product compared with other goods. Therefore to evaluate the demand curve for their product (see DEMAND CURVES), firms should use the CPI to find the relative price of their product, which would be the price the firm charges for its product divided by the CPI. This will give managers a sense of how their product's price compares with the rate of inflation and whether their product is becoming relatively more or less expensive versus other goods.

see also **real prices**

Bibliography

Carlson, K. M. (1989). Do price indices tell us about inflation? *Federal Reserve Bank of St. Louis Review*, 71, 12–30.

ROBERT E. MCAULIFFE

consumer surplus The difference between the maximum amount a consumer is willing to pay to buy a product (also called the consumer's RESERVATION PRICE) and the price actually paid is called the consumer's surplus. This measures how much consumers value a product beyond what they paid for it. In a market, consumer surplus is the area under the demand curve and above the price charged. This measures the benefit to consumers of having this product available and hence the benefits to society from the production of this good if there are no EXTERNALITIES in production or consumption.

When a firm raises its price above the MARGINAL COST of production, those consumers who continue to buy the product pay a higher price and this represents a reduction in their consumer surplus. Since these consumers still purchase the product, it represents a transfer from the consumers to the firm. However, some consumers will not continue to buy the good at the higher price because the new price exceeds their reservation price. Since

these consumers were willing to pay the cost to society of producing the good (the marginal cost) and do not receive it, they have lost consumer surplus. Moreover, the firm does not capture any of this lost surplus as profit because these consumers have left the market. Conceptually, the firm should be willing to produce this good and sell it for the marginal cost of production once the firm has earned its profits in the market. Since this makes the consumers who have left the market better off and the firm no worse off, it is a PARETO OPTIMAL ALLOCATION and so allocative EFFICIENCY would be improved. Because this exchange does not occur, the consumer surplus of those consumers who have left the market is lost and this is called DEAD-WEIGHT LOSS since no one in society recovers those lost benefits.

In a similar vein, when a firm considers introducing a new product, it is concerned about whether it can cover the costs of production, including the OPPORTUNITY COSTS. If the firm is unable to cover these costs, the product will not be produced. Yet, it is possible that the benefits to society from producing the good (as measured by consumers' surplus) exceed the costs. The problem is that the firm cannot capture all the benefits to consumers when it cannot practice PRICE DISCRIMINATION and this can lead to less PRODUCT VARIETY than would be socially optimal.

Bibliography

Dixit, A. K. Stiglitz J. E. (1977). Monopolistic competition and optimum product diversity. *American Economic Review*, 67, 240–59.
Waterson, M. (1984). *Economic Theory of the Industry*. Cambridge: CUP.
Willig, R. D. (1976). Consumers' surplus without apology. *American Economic Review*, 66, 589–97.

ROBERT E. MCAULIFFE

contestable markets As originally presented by Baumol, Panzar and Willig (1982), perfectly contestable markets represented an alternative and more general benchmark for evaluating MARKET STRUCTURE than PERFECT COMPETITION. In perfectly contestable markets, new firms can enter and exit an industry costlessly and at no disadvantage relative to existing firms, and this potential competition severely limits the pricing options of existing firms. Costless entry and exit at no disadvantage imply that factors such as ASYMMETRIC INFORMATION, SUNK COSTS, FIRST-MOVER ADVANTAGES and STRATEGIC BEHAVIOR by existing firms have no effect on the entrant's decision to enter the industry. Since entrants are at no disadvantage relative to incumbent firms, whenever existing firms charge a price sufficient to generate economic profits, entry will occur driving economic profits to zero (see ECONOMIC PROFIT). Costless exit and entry also mean that the entrant can enter the market, earn economic profits, and exit before the incumbent firm can retaliate, sometimes referred to as "hit and run" entry. For hit and run entry to succeed, entrants must be able to enter the market and earn profits before the existing firm retaliates. This means that prices must adjust more slowly than output in the market.

According to Baumol, Panzar and Willig, perfectly contestable markets result in efficient production even in those cases where perfect competition might fail, as in a NATURAL MONOPOLY. A natural monopoly faces ECONOMIES OF SCALE where the average cost of production is falling in the range of output demanded by the market. Since average cost is declining, the MARGINAL COST curve must lie below it and this means that the marginal cost pricing required by perfect competition would not allow the firm to cover its total costs. Perfect contestability requires that the existing firm(s) be able to cover total costs without attracting entry and so a natural monopoly would be forced by potential competition to set its price at its lowest average cost of production.

Perfect competition requires large numbers of small firms producing homogeneous products, among other conditions, to achieve efficiency. Perfectly contestable markets emphasize the importance of *potential* competitors rather than existing competitors and do not require DIMINISHING RETURNS in production. Another important point Baumol, Panzar and Willig raise is that existing firms must produce efficiently or they will be vulnerable to "hit and run" entry by potential entrants. This means that certain inefficiencies attributable to monopoly or oligopoly such as X-EFFICIENCY or

inefficient organization cannot occur in perfectly contestable markets since entry will force these firms to become efficient or drive them out of business.

Some researchers have argued that few markets are perfectly contestable and that this analytical approach is less general than might at first appear. For example, Shepherd (1984) observed that perfect contestability requires *ultra* free entry and no exit barriers (no sunk costs). He asserted this was more restrictive than the requirements of perfect competition because in a sufficiently small interval of time, firms always have sunk costs; see Weitzman (1983). Furthermore, for potential entry to discipline existing firms to the extent Baumol, Panzar and Willig claim, entry must not only be ultra free but *total* in that entrants could replace the existing firms. Yet if entrants can replace existing firms, the assumption employed by Baumol, Panzar and Willig that existing firms do not react to entry is very restrictive and if entrants are small, they cannot discipline existing firms to the extent the theory suggests. For Shepherd, these and other concerns lead him to believe that the traditional industry analysis of industrial organization with its focus on the internal market rivalry and interactions between firms is more appropriate.

Bibliography

Baumol, W. J., Panzar, J. C. Willig, R. D. (1982). *Contestable Markets and the Theory of Industry Structure*. San Diego: Harcourt Brace Jovanovich.

Baumol, W. J. (1982). Contestable markets: an uprising in the theory of industry structure. *American Economic Review*, 72, 1–15.

Schwartz, M. Reynolds, R. J. (1983). Contestable markets: an uprising in the theory of industry structure: comment. *American Economic Review*, 73, 488–90.

Shepherd, W. G. (1984). 'Contestability' vs. competition. *American Economic Review*, 74, 572–87.

Weitzman, M. L. (1983). Contestable markets: an uprising in the theory of industry structure: comment. *American Economic Review*, 73, 486–7.

ROBERT E. MCAULIFFE

contracts Going back to ancient times, contract law has always been a major part of business. Roscoe Pound (1959), a respected legal writer, noted the importance of contracts when he wrote, "The social order rests upon the stability and predictability of conduct, of which keeping promises is a large item." Contract law deals with the formation and keeping of lawful promises. The American legal system is based on the right to enter freely a contract or to not do so. In fact, the US Constitution, Article I, Section 10, provides that "no state shall pass any law impairing the obligations of contracts." As long as the parties to a contract have a lawful purpose and the intent to enter the agreement, a court will enforce its terms. Contract law is primarily determined by state law and varies from state to state. However, certain general principles exist.

A contract is generally defined as an agreement between two or more persons or legal entities regarding the performance or promise to act or the refraining from acting. A contract is determined from the outward manifestation of intent of the parties. Words and actions of the parties as seen from an objective view determine if a contract exists. When the parties have expressly agreed, either verbally or in writing, then the agreement is considered to be an **express contract**. When the parties have shown their intent to be bound by their actions, then the result is an **implied contract**. Courts have even allowed parties to recover compensation when, although a contract does not exist, one of the parties would be unjustly enriched if no compensation was allowed. This principle is known as quasi-contract or **quantum meruit**.

Contracts can also be classified as bilateral or unilateral. A **bilateral contract** involves the promises of one party (the promisor) in exchange for the promises of another (the promisee). These contracts relate to future performance. A **unilateral contract** involves promises in exchange for performance, or vice versa. Thus, some performance is expected for the promise.

Certain elements are required of all contracts in order for a court to enforce the agreement. The first is the meeting of the minds. This element is the **offer** by one party (the offeror) to enter a contract with a corresponding acceptance by the other party (the offeree). An offer is the manifestation of intent by the offeror to enter a binding contact. Expressions of opinion, price quotations, and advertisements are generally considered to be negotiations leading to an offer. In addition, the offer must be reasonably definite. Courts will not supply essential terms that the parties have not agreed upon. Essential terms include at least a description of the subject matter, identification of the parties, the consideration, and in certain situations quantity, location, and time of performance. The offer must also be communicated from the offeror to the offeree in order for a valid acceptance to exist.

An offer may be terminated before acceptance without liability to either party. The death or incompetence of either the offeror or offeree terminates the offer. If the basis of the offer becomes illegal or impossible to perform, then the offer is at an end. The parties may terminate the offer themselves by either revoking the offer (offeror) or rejecting an offer (offeree). Suggesting new terms to an offer by the offeree is a counteroffer and ends the original offer. Last, an offer may terminate due to the expiration of time. If no time is stated in the offer, then it expires after a reasonable amount of time.

A contract is formed when the offeree accepts the offer. Acceptance must be a mirror-image of the offer and must be by some positive act or words of the offeree showing an intent to enter a contract. The acceptance generally must be communicated to the offeror.

The second element of a contract is **consideration**. Consideration is the promise or performance that flows between the parties to a contract. It is also called **legal detriment**. Courts do not require that the exchange between the parties be of comparable value. They only require that something be given up by all parties. Promises made by a party that are not supported by consideration are not enforceable. Thus, a promise to make a gift is generally not enforceable. Consideration states that each party to a contract promise or do an act not otherwise required or refrain from doing an act that is lawfully allowed. The consideration must be bargained for, i.e. present at the time the meeting of the minds occurs. Having performed an act in the past or already being legally obligated to perform an act will not constitute consideration for a current promise. A preexisting duty by law or contract cannot be consideration for a new contract. The only exception is if a promise is made that causes someone to rely on the promise to his detriment. Courts have allowed recovery in this regard under a theory called **promissory estoppel** or detrimental reliance. Moral obligation, however, is not considered to be valid consideration for a contract.

The third element of a contract is **legal capacity**. Courts will not enforce contracts where one or both of the parties do not have the mental or legal competence necessary to engage in such a transaction. The law deems children incompetent to enter contracts due to their age. Thus, minors (generally considered to be persons under the age of 18) have a right to disaffirm a contract for any reason. Once the minor disaffirms, the other contractual party must return all consideration to the minor as long as the minor did not misrepresent his age. Minors cannot disaffirm certain contracts for necessaries, such as medical care or education.

Legal capacity is also lacking when a party has been adjudged incompetent by a court. No contract made by that person thereafter will be enforced. Persons who are intoxicated through alcohol or drug use or persons who are suffering a mental disability are bound to contracts they enter unless they can prove that at the time of contracting they were unable to comprehend the nature and extent of the dealings at hand. If the evidence shows that they could not understand the legal consequences of their actions, then they are released from the contract.

The final element of a contract is **legality**. All contracts must have a lawful purpose. If a contract would violate a criminal or civil statute, then it is void and no court will entertain a case involving the contract. Examples include most gambling agreements and contracts to harm a person or property. Courts have also fashioned common law illegality by determining that certain contracts are bad for society, i.e. violate public policy. Each of these types of contracts must be examined individually to determine if public policy would be offended if the contract was upheld. Examples include non-compete clauses in employment or sale of business contracts, exculpatory clauses, and adhesion contracts. If reasonable under the circumstances, these will be enforced.

In addition to the above elements, certain contracts have to meet further requirements. Under a law passed in England in 1677 and adopted by every state, certain contracts must be ·in writing to be enforceable. Originally entitled, "A Statute to Prevent Frauds and Perjuries", this law is now known as the Statute of Frauds. It requires the following types of contracts to be in writing:

(1) any contract that by its terms takes longer than one year to perform (e.g. a two-year lease),
(2) any agreement relating to the ownership of or liens in real estate,
(3) any promise to pay the debt of another (guarantor),
(4) an executor's or administrator's promise to pay the debt of the deceased from personal funds, and
(5) any promise upon the condition of marriage (e.g. prenuptial agreement).

The Uniform Commercial Code has added certain investment securities and any contract for the sale of goods for $500 or more. Without a writing signed by the other party and containing all the essential terms mentioned above, an aggrieved party is without a remedy. If a contract is found lacking, courts have been willing to award quantum meruit to avoid unjust enrichment. In cases where one party has substantially performed an oral contract, a court may go ahead and enforce the entire contract based on the substantial performance being a substitute for the writing.

Although few contracts are required to be in writing, many are reduced to a writing. Once a contract is put in writing and the document appears to be the entire intent of the parties, no prior or contemporaneous oral statements may be used to vary or contradict the written agreement. Known as the **parol evidence rule**, this principle preserves the integrity of the writing by not allowing a party to attack it using oral evidence. Exceptions do exist, though, including oral evidence to show fraud, mistake, duress, or other reasons to examine the agreement. Also, this rule does not prohibit a subsequent modification of the contract being enforceable.

As discussed above, a contract must be based upon a meeting of the minds of the parties.

However, the meeting of the minds can occur due to a lack of genuine assent. This may happen when one or both of the parties is mistaken as to a material fact in the contract. The mistake must be based on fact, not opinion, prediction, or statements of value. A mutual (or bilateral) mistake of fact occurs when both of the parties are mistaken. In this case, a court will rescind the contract and return the parties to their original position. When only one of the parties is mistaken (unilateral), a court will enforce the contract. An exception to this rule is if the other party knows that a mistake has occurred and takes advantage of the mistaken party. A mistake of law is generally not a basis for rescission since everyone is presumed to know the law.

Duress also removes a party's genuineness of assent. Duress is the use of force or fear of personal harm to induce a party to enter a contract. Threatening to kill or harm a person is duress; threatening to fire an employee if he does not enter a contract is *not* duress. In addition, undue influence cancels a party's assent.

Undue influence requires a party in a fiduciary position who takes advantage of a much weaker party for gain. A classic example is a person who induces an elderly relative in his care to deed property to him. Finally, fraud (also called misrepresentation) will nullify the assent needed to form a contract. Fraud is difficult to prove and requires a party to prove five elements:

(1) a material misrepresentation of fact exists,
(2) it is known to be false,
(3) it is done with the intent to deceive,
(4) the innocent party justifiably relies on the misrepresentation, and
(5) damage occurs.

Courts are reluctant to allow a party to rescind a contract based on fraud if the victim could have exercised reasonable care to avoid the fraud. This defense is known as **caveat emptor**.

Third persons who are not a party to a contract may enforce a contract if the contract specifically contemplates bestowing a benefit on them. An example of such third party beneficiary would be the beneficiary of a life assurance policy. Other parties may have rights in a contract if the contract is assigned to them.

Any contract may be assigned unless the original agreement prohibits assignment or personal services are involved that require the skill or experience of the original party only.

A party can be discharged from further performance on a contract in several different ways. First, the party can complete his performance. Certain contracts require total performance, such as payment of money or performance by a specific time when time is of the essence. Other contracts are deemed complete even though some performance is still lacking, such as construction contracts or performance within a reasonable time. Second, a material breach of contract by the other party relieves a person of continuing to perform, e.g. nonpayment of rent allows the landlord to cancel a lease and evict the tenant.

Third, the occurrence of a condition subsequent in the contract, such as a clause that cancels the contract in the event of war or bankruptcy. Fourth, the failure of a condition precedent, such as the failure of a prospective homebuyer to obtain financing rendering the contract at an end. Fifth, impossibility of performance, such as the destruction of the subject matter or the death or incompetence of a party. Sixth, the parties may agree to end the contract through rescission or settlement. Finally, a party may be discharged due to bankruptcy or the expiration of the statute of limitations.

If a breach of contract occurs, courts will allow the aggrieved party to recover compensatory damages, i.e. the money necessary to put the party in the position he would be in if the contract had been performed as agreed. Courts rarely allow the recovery of attorney fees unless the agreement so stipulated. Virtually no court will allow punitive damages in a contract action. Late fees and other reasonable charges for minor breaches are not considered punitive and are enforceable. When unique goods or real estate are involved in a breach of contract such that money will not adequately compensate a party, a court may grant a decree of specific performance and order the breaching party to perform. In cases where a court can reform a contract to meet the true intent of the parties, it will do so.

Bibliography

Pound, R. (1959). *Jurisprudence, Vol. 3.* West Publishing Company.

Weaver, J. H. (1990). *The Compact Guide to Contract Law.* West Publishing Company.

S. ALAN SCHLACT

cost of capital Firms finance their assets and operations with a variety of types of financial CAPITAL, including debt, preferred stock, and common equity. The providers of these funds would not be willing to invest in the firm unless they expected that their investment would provide them with a return sufficient to offset the risk that they have assumed. Due to the greater certainty of promised cash flows for debt holders, the cost of debt is generally lower than that of equity. Similarly, preferred stockholders require lower rates of return than common stockholders since their dividends have priority over common. Costs of all forms of capital will increase with increasing riskiness of the firm.

In making CAPITAL BUDGETING decisions, firms estimate the NET PRESENT VALUE of projects by discounting future expected cash flows by an appropriate cost of capital to account for the required returns of their investors. Thus, the higher the costs associated with investment capital, the harder it is for firms to find acceptable projects. In general, firms employ several types of capital in their capital structure (*see* FIRM FINANCIAL STRUCTURE). Since these funds are not specifically allocated to particular projects or assets of the firm, the appropriate cost of capital to be used in capital budgeting decisions is the weighted average of the various types of capital used.

The procedure used in developing this weighted average is to:

(1) estimate the marginal after-tax costs of each type of capital; and
(2) calculate the weighted average cost of capital (WACC) by weighting each component cost by the percentage of that type of capital in the firm's target financial structure.

In many cases, the firm is subject to limitations on the amount of capital that it can raise at a particular cost level. For example, retained earnings are a less costly form of equity financing since the firm avoids the transactions costs associated with sales of newly issued securities. However, retained earnings are limited to the dollars remaining from net income after dividends are paid. Similarly, since risk increases with additional debt, the marginal cost of debt financing will increase as new debt obligations are taken on by the firm.

As an example, suppose that a firm estimates that its marginal after-tax cost of new long-term debt is 6 percent, the marginal cost of retained earnings is 10 percent, and the marginal cost of newly issued common stock is 12 percent. If they have no preferred stock in their capital structure and the target capital structure calls for 50 percent debt and 50 percent equity, then the WACC using retained earnings for the equity component is 8 percent, calculated as 0.5 × (6 percent) + 0.5 × (10 percent). However, the firm does not have unlimited retained earnings and may be forced to issue common stock to support a larger capital budget. In that case, the marginal cost of capital, using common stock as the equity component, will be 9 percent. Thus, the marginal cost of capital, defined as the cost of the last dollar of new capital the firm raises in a given period, is an increasing function of new dollars raised in a given period and the appropriate discount rate to be used for NPV analysis will be the WACC that is applicable for the size of capital budget under consideration.

Bibliography

Brigham, E. F. Gapenski, L. C. (1996). *Intermediate Financial Management.* 5th edn, Fort Worth, TX: Dryden.

Gitman, L. J. (1995). *Foundations of Managerial Finance.* 4th edn, New York: HarperCollins.

VICKIE L. BAJTELSMIT

Cournot competition The term Cournot competition refers to a model of OLIGOPOLY which was introduced by the French mathematician and economist Antoine Augustin Cournot in 1838 and is widely used in Industrial Organization economics. The model considers a fixed number of firms which choose their output levels trying to maximize their profits. Given the total output produced, the market demand curve determines the price and the profit for each firm. In the **Cournot equili-**

brium each firm does not want to change its output level given the output of its competitors. The firms have **Cournot conjectures**, i.e. they take the output level of their competitors as given. It is important to recognize that the Cournot EQUILIBRIUM is just the **Nash equilibrium** of the corresponding simultaneous-move game. In a Cournot equilibrium, the prices are higher (respectively, lower), the total output is lower (higher), and the per firm profit is higher (lower) than in PERFECT COMPETITION (MONOPOLY). In fact, as the number of firms increases, the Cournot equilibrium approaches the perfectly competitive outcome.

The Cournot model has to be distinguished from other models of oligopoly competition such as **Stackelberg competition** (with FIRST-MOVER ADVANTAGES instead of simultaneous moves), **Bertrand competition** (where firms compete with prices instead of quantities as the strategic variable) and **Edgeworth competition** (with capacity constraints).

Bibliography

Cournot, A. A. (1927). *Researches into the Mathematical Principles of the Theory of Wealth* (English translation; originally *"Recherches sur les principes mathématiques de la théorie des richesses"*, 1838). 2nd edn, New York: Macmillan.
Daughety, A. F. (ed.) (1988). *Cournot Oligopoly*. Cambridge: CUP.
Vives, X. (1989). Cournot and the oligopoly problem. *European Economic Review*, 33, 503–14.

NIKOLAOS VETTAS

covariance the covariance is a statistical measure of the linear association between two variables, say, X and Y, and is denoted as $\text{cov}(X, Y)$. For T observations on variables X and Y, the sample covariance is calculated as
$$\text{cov}(X, Y) = \frac{1}{T-1} \sum_{i=1}^{T} (X_i - \overline{X}) \times (Y_i - \overline{Y})$$

where $\overline{X}$ is the sample mean for X and $\overline{Y}$ is the sample mean for Y. If there is a positive linear relation between X and Y, the covariance will also be positive and if there is a negative relation between X and Y, covariance will be negative. When there is no linear relationship between the two variables, the covariance will be zero.

Since the covariance measures the extent to which two variables are related, managers can use this information to determine, for example, how sales are related to a new advertising campaign. To determine how much sales will change in response to advertising, a LINEAR REGRESSION should be used. The covariance is a component of the estimated regression coefficient; see Berndt (1991) and Maddala (1992).

Bibliography

Berndt, E. R. (1991). *The Practice of Econometrics*. Reading, MA: Addison-Wesley.
Maddala, G. S. (1992). *Introduction to Econometrics*. 2nd edn, New York: Macmillan.

ROBERT E. MCAULIFFE

credence goods Some EXPERIENCE GOODS are difficult to evaluate before and after purchase and these goods are called credence goods. Medical services, automotive repairs, and investment advice are examples of goods and services where consumers are unlikely to be able to judge product quality. In such cases, it is expensive for consumers to acquire enough information to evaluate product quality. Unfortunately firms have incentives to take advantage of consumers' lack of information and provide a low quality good at a high price. However, established firms have incentives to invest in brand name capital to help to reduce these information costs.

see also **asymmetric information; quality**

Bibliography

Darby, M. R. Karni, E. (1973). Free competition and the optimal amount of fraud. *Journal of Law and Economics*, 16, 67–88.
Shughart, W. F., Chappell, W. F. Cottle, R. L. (1994). *Modern Managerial Economics*. Cincinatti, OH: South-Western Publishing.

ROBERT E. MCAULIFFE

credible strategies Existing firms may try to prevent potential entry by using strategic threats. But for these threats to be believed, they must be the profit maximizing choice the incumbent firm would make should entry occur. For example, an established firm might threaten to lower prices if another firm enters the market.

This threat will not be credible, however, if by lowering prices the existing firm were made worse off. Therefore, for a threat or strategy to be credible, it must be in the best interests of the established firm in the post-entry period. Usually firms can make their threats credible by making commitments in previous periods (*see* COMMITMENT). For example, a firm could invest in additional capacity to make a threat to lower prices in subsequent periods credible.

When entrants do not have perfect information about the established firms, it is possible for established firms to bluff and make threats which would not maximize their profits in the post-entry period. As long as potential entrants believe the threat could occur with a sufficiently high probability, entry can be deterred; see Encaoua, Geroski and Jacquemin (1986). Credible threats represent one element of STRATEGIC BEHAVIOR that incumbent firms can undertake to affect their MARKET STRUCTURE.

see also **first-mover advantages; accommodation**

Bibliography

Encaoua, D., Geroski, P. Jacquemin, A. (1986). Strategic competition and the persistence of dominant firms: a survey. Stiglitz, J. E. Matthewson, G. F. *New Developments in the Analysis of Market Structure*. Cambridge, MA: MIT.

Jacquemin, A. (1987). *The New Industrial Organization: Market Forces and Strategic Behavior*. Cambridge, MA: MIT.

Salop, S. C. (1979). Strategic entry deterrence. *American Economic Review*, **69**, 335–8.

ROBERT E. McAULIFFE

cross elasticities   The quantity demanded (or supplied) of a good depends not only on its own price but on the prices of other goods as well (*see* DEMAND FUNCTION). The cross elasticity of demand is the measure of the effect on the quantity demanded of one product (x) resulting from the change in the price of another (y). It is measured as

$$\epsilon_{xy} = \frac{\Delta Q_x}{Q_x} \bigg/ \frac{\Delta P_y}{P_y} = \frac{\Delta Q_x}{\Delta P_y} \times \frac{P_y}{P_x}$$

where the symbol Δ indicates a change in quantity (Q) or price (P) and the subscripts (x,y) identify the two different goods. For goods which are substitutes, such as imported and domestic beer, the cross elasticity value will be positive since an increase in the price of one good will increase the demand for the other. Goods which are complements, such as hamburgers and hamburger rolls, will have a negative value for cross elasticity. The measurement of cross elasticity is useful to a firm in that it indicates the extent to which consumers perceive a rival product as being a close substitute. A rise in the price of one's own product under circumstances where the cross elasticity with other products is high can lead to significantly diminished unit sales and revenues.

see also **complements; substitutes**

Bibliography

Douglas, E. (1992). *Managerial Economics: Analysis and Strategy*. 4th edn, Englewood Cliffs, NJ: Prentice-Hall.

GILBERT BECKER

cross-advertising elasticity   The cross-advertising elasticity of demand measures the percentage change in the quantity sold of one product given a percentage change in the advertising for another product. For products which are COMPLEMENTS, an increase in advertising for, say, automobiles may also increase the quantity of gasoline sold and so the cross-advertising elasticity would be positive. Products which are SUBSTITUTES would have a negative cross-advertising elasticity since the advertising of one automotive company, Ford, should have a negative effect on the quantity of automobiles sold by General Motors, all else equal. For a company with a product line, the cross-advertising elasticity may also be important since increased advertising of one brand in the product line could reduce sales of a closely related brand.

Bibliography

Douglas, E. J. (1992). *Managerial Economics*. 4th edn, Englewood Cliffs, NJ: Prentice-Hall.

ROBERT E. MCAULIFFE

cross-section analysis   Data which is gathered over a number of households or firms at the same point in time is called cross-section data. Managers can use this source of quantitative information for LINEAR REGRESSION to determine, for example, whether there are ECONOMIES OF SCALE in production. In this case, managers would collect cost data from firms producing the same product at the same point in time, but with different capacities. Economies of scale would exist if firms with larger capacities had lower average total costs of production (*see* AVERAGE TOTAL COST). The econometric tools required for cross-section analysis are sometimes different than those required for time series analysis (*see* TIME-SERIES DATA; TIME-SERIES FORECASTING MODELS). For example, HETERO-SKEDASTICITY arises more frequently in cross-section data than in time series; see Gujarati (1988) and Maddala (1992).

Bibliography

Gujarati, D. N. (1988). *Basic Econometrics*. 2nd edn, New York: McGraw-Hill.
Maddala, G. S. (1992). *Introduction to Econometrics*. 2nd edn, New York: Macmillan.

ROBERT E. MCAULIFFE

— D —

deadweight loss The term "deadweight loss" refers to the welfare loss due to inefficient allocation of resources caused by deviations between market prices and marginal costs. Inefficient allocations of resources can occur in a variety of situations including, for example, the situation where a market is not perfectly competitive or the situation where a sales tax is imposed on a perfectly competitive industry (*see* EFFICIENCY; PERFECT COMPETITION).

When resources are allocated inefficiently (e.g. as a result of a sales tax), there are typically two effects:

(1) welfare transfers that simply redistribute CONSUMER SURPLUS and PRODUCER SURPLUS among consumers, producers and the government; and

(2) net reductions of consumer surplus and/or producer surplus that represent welfare loss.

For example, a higher market price due to a tax will cause some consumers to leave the market and reduce their consumer surplus. However, this reduction in consumer surplus is not captured by producers or by the government. It is pure welfare loss, otherwise known as "deadweight loss."

Bibliography

Bergson, A. (1973). On monopoly welfare losses. *American Economic Review*, **63**, 853–70.
Harberger, A. (1964). Taxation, resource allocation and welfare. Ed. Due, J. *The Role of Direct and Indirect Taxes in the Federal Revenue System.* Princeton, NJ: Princeton University Press.

WEI LI

declining industry This is a mature industry whose sales are decreasing. Such an industry is in the final stage of its life cycle, although industry sales may revive at some point; see INDUSTRY LIFE CYCLE, PRODUCT LIFE CYCLE, Jacquemin (1987) and Porter (1980). When an industry's sales are declining, net rates of EXIT by firms will increase either through failure or through acquisition by other firms. The industry structure may consolidate and industry concentration may rise. In this stage of the industry life cycle, surviving firms often must compete on the basis of costs since many SUBSTITUTES are available to consumers.

If there are exit barriers or if firms are unwilling to leave the industry, competition between the firms that remain in a declining industry may intensify. In the extreme case, firms may engage in a "war of attrition" where no firm wants to be the first to leave the industry since the remaining firm or firms will be able to earn economic profits. Porter (1980) identifies several sources of exit barriers including specialized assets (*see* ASSET SPECIFICITY), fixed costs of exit (such as settling labor and other contracts) and strategic barriers where presence in the declining market may confer advantages for the firm in other markets in which it sells. Whinston (1988) theoretically evaluated the social welfare consequences of exit and observed that firm exits from a declining industry may not be optimal since the "wrong" (lower cost) firm may exit before the higher cost firm. Furthermore, multiplant firms may reduce their capacity when the efficient outcome would require that small firms exit the industry. These welfare effects are similar to the biases from free ENTRY but in reverse; see also Tirole (1988).

Bibliography

Jacquemin, A. (1987). *The New Industrial Organization: Market Forces and Strategic Behavior*. Cambridge, MA: MIT.

Porter, M. E. (1980). *Competitive Strategy*. New York: Free Press.

Tirole, J. (1988). *The Theory of Industrial Organization*. Cambridge, MA: MIT.

Whinston, M. D. (1988). Exit with multiplant firms. *The Rand Journal of Economics*, **19**, 568–88.

ROBERT E. MCAULIFFE

decreasing cost industry A decreasing cost industry is one where costs decrease as the industry expands. In this case, the industry's long run supply curve slopes downward; as the industry produces more output, the minimum average cost of production for each firm decreases with the decrease in costs. Firms in a decreasing cost industry do not necessarily have ECONOMIES OF SCALE in production; the decrease in costs may reflect lower input costs which reduce the minimum point of the AVERAGE TOTAL COST curve as the industry grows.

Input costs may decline as the industry expands if there are economies of scale in the production of an important input. For example, economies of scale in the production of computer chips allow personal computer manufacturers to produce more computers at lower cost as chip prices fall. An industry may also experience decreasing cost if there are "economies of agglomeration." These economies can occur when a number of firms produce in a specific geographic area and as their number grows, supporting services such as transportation can be provided to all firms at lower cost. Again, this lowers each firm's costs as the industry grows and so the minimum point on the average cost curve where there are zero economic profits is lower (*see* ECONOMIC PROFIT). Managers in decreasing cost industries can use this knowledge to anticipate price changes. When the industry expands prices and costs may initially rise, but they will decrease below their original levels in the long run as entry and industry output increase. Decreasing cost industries have long run supply curves which are negatively sloped.

ROBERT E. MCAULIFFE

demand curves For individuals or markets, demand curves show the relationship between the quantity demanded and the price of the good (holding everything else constant). Given the LAW OF DEMAND, the quantity demanded will be inversely related to the relative price of the good. The demand curve will shift whenever any other variables in the DEMAND FUNCTION change (except the price of the product itself). Since TOTAL REVENUE is equal to price, P, times quantity, Q, and the demand curve expresses quantity demanded as a function of price alone, the demand curve is also the average revenue curve. In other words, dividing total revenues (sales) by the number of units sold yields the average revenue (price) per unit sold.

Bibliography

Douglas, E. J. (1992). *Managerial Economics*. 4th edn, Englewood Cliffs, NJ: Prentice-Hall.

Shughart. W.F., Chappell, W. F. Cottle, R. L. (1994). *Modern Managerial Economics*. Cincinatti, OH: South-Western Publishing.

ROBERT E. MCAULIFFE

demand function The demand function shows the relationship between the quantity demanded and *all* variables or factors which affect demand. These variables include the price of the product itself, the prices of related goods (*see* SUBSTITUTES; COMPLEMENTS), consumer income levels, consumer preferences, the information available to consumers, the product's quality, consumer expectations and the advertising and promotional efforts for the product and for competing products. Additional variables may include the population in the market, the weather and other factors specific to a product's market.

Of the variables listed above, firm managers can only control a few. A firm can exert some control over the price it charges, its own advertising outlays, and the quality of its product (including the services offered before and after the sale). Douglas (1992) refers to these variables as strategic variables which the firm can use to enhance its market position.

The specific form the demand function will take depends on the relationship between the quantity demanded and these variables in a given market and time period. For example, the Cobb–Douglas form of the demand function allows the variables to affect demand multiplicatively. In the simplest case where only three variables affect the demand for the product, the Cobb–Douglas demand function is:

$$Q_x^d = P_x^\alpha A_x^\beta I_x^\gamma$$

where Px is the price of product x, Ax is the level of advertising for the product and Ix is the real income of consumers in the market. In this example, the coefficients α, β and γ would measure the ELASTICITY of demand with respect to its own price, advertising and income respectively. Other functional relationships for demand can be specified and estimated; (see Berndt (1991) and LINEAR REGRESSION).

Bibliography

Berndt, E. R. (1991). *The Practice of Econometrics.* Reading, MA: Addison-Wesley.

Douglas, E. J. (1992). *Managerial Economics.* 4th edn, Englewood Cliffs, NJ: Prentice-Hall.

Shughart, W. F., Chappell, W. F. Cottle, R. L. (1994). *Modern Managerial Economics.* Cincinatti, OH: South-Western Publishing.

ROBERT E. MCAULIFFE

depreciation   Depreciation is the decrease in worth of a durable good (often a capital asset used in production) which is associated with use or the passage of time. It is a component of the cost of production for businesses and therefore must be included in the calculation of profit.

Although a capital good is purchased at a single point in time, its use occurs slowly over time. Therefore, some structure must be imposed to determine the decline in the asset's value over time, i.e. the rate at which the asset is depreciated. The two most common measurement methods are **straight line** and **declining balance**. Both distribute the depreciation incrementally over the useful life of the asset. However, the straight line method depreciates it in equal increments over the useful life, whereas the declining balance method depreciates it more rapidly in the initial years after purchase.

Specifically, for an asset which is purchased in period t and has a useful life of T years, $t=1$

to T, the straight line method determines depreciation as:

$$D(t) = B/T$$

where $D(t)$ is the depreciation for period t, B is the initial value of the asset minus the scrap value of the asset. For the declining balance method of depreciation, the relationship is:

$$D(t) = B(t-1) \times R$$

$$B(t) = (B(t-1) - D(t))$$

$$R = DBR/T$$

where $D(t)$ is the depreciation for year t, $B(0)$ is the initial value of the asset minus its scrap value, $B(t)$ is the basis value for t and DBR is the chosen rate of depreciation for the declining balance.

Because depreciation assigns a stream of expenditures to the purchase of a capital asset, it has been used as the value of the tax deductions which have historically been offered for investment. The method applicable for tax purposes is assigned by law; therefore, it can change over time, and is not necessarily identical to the accounting method chosen by a given business. The 1993 Depreciation Guide provides a summary of the measurement methods, assignment of class lives, and history of the depreciation methods utilized for tax purposes. In economic literature, depreciation studies have ranged from vintage capital models (see, for example, Cooper and Haltiwanger, 1993) to estimates of economic depreciation rates.

Bibliography

CCH Tax Law Editors (1993). *1993 Depreciation Guide featuring MACRS.* Chicago, Illinois: Commerce Clearing House.

Cooper, R. Haltiwanger, J. (1993). The macroeconomic implications of machine replacement: theory and evidence. *American Economic Review,* 83, 360–82.

LAURA POWER

diminishing marginal utility   As consumption of any good increases within a specific period of time, additional units of the good will yield less satisfaction (or TOTAL UTILITY). That is, as a person consumes additional glasses of, say, soda, the additional satisfaction from consuming more soda (the MARGINAL UTILITY) will eventually decline. Diminishing marginal utility had been assumed to obtain INDIFFER-ENCE CURVES that were convex to the origin and to obtain downward-sloping demand curves from consumer choice. However, it is not clear that there is diminishing marginal utility for income (the consumption of all goods), so the less restrictive assumption of a diminishing MARGINAL RATE OF SUBSTITUTION between any two goods is now employed; see Douglas (1992) and Stigler (1966).

Bibliography

Douglas, E. J. (1992). *Managerial Economics*. 4th edn, Englewood Cliffs, NJ: Prentice-Hall.
Stigler, G. J. (1966). *The Theory of Price*. 3rd edn, New York: Macmillan.

ROBERT E. MCAULIFFE

diminishing returns   When additional units of a factor of production are added to fixed amounts of other inputs in production, at some point the increase in output which results will decrease. Holding other inputs constant means that the level of technology used to combine inputs in production is also held constant. There may be diminishing total returns where total output actually falls from additional units of an input – as when too many workers in a plant reduce the total output produced by interfering with each other, in which case the TOTAL PRODUCT of labor would be declining. Or there may be diminishing average returns where the average output decreases from additional units of an input. If the input which is increased is labor, the average product of labor would be decreasing in this case.

Diminishing *marginal* returns occur when additional units of an input result in a smaller increase in output or, equivalently, the MAR-GINAL PRODUCT of that input will decline. Since diminishing returns applies when at least one input in production is held constant, it represents a SHORT RUN phenomenon. When all inputs in production are varied, the question is one of returns to scale.

see also **economies of scale; increasing returns; law of variable proportions**

Bibliography

Douglas, E. J. (1992). *Managerial Economics*. 4th edn, Englewood Cliffs, NJ: Prentice-Hall.
Stigler, G. J. (1966). *The Theory of Price*. 3rd edn, New York: Macmillan.

ROBERT E. MCAULIFFE

diseconomies of scale   Diseconomies of scale are said to exist when long run average total costs increase because a firm is too large (*see* AVERAGE TOTAL COST). These diseconomies may arise because of technological factors but are usually attributed to decreasing returns to management. As the size of the firm increases, the firm's planning and coordinating activities become more unwieldy and, as more bureaucratic layers are added to the organization, managers are separated from the market and their customers. If consumer preferences change rapidly or if new products are frequently introduced by rivals, larger firms may be disadvantaged by their lack of flexibility and slow adjustment to the market.

An interesting recent example has been the reorganization of IBM. In the early years of the computer industry, there were no independent suppliers of computer chips and peripheral devices and computer manufacturers had to be vertically integrated to produce those inputs. But, as the industry grew, so did independent suppliers who could specialize and produce components very efficiently. As this occured, changes in technology and factor costs decreased the MINIMUM EFFICIENT SCALE (MES) for computer manufacturing. Even if IBM's separate divisions were as efficient as their competitors, the internal pricing and cost information did not reflect this efficiency. The organization has been restructured so that the divisions operate as separate companies to be closer to the market (*see* VERTICAL INTEGRATION).

Bibliography

Carlton, D. W.   Perloff, J. M. (1994). *Modern Industrial Organization*. 2nd edn, New York: HarperCollins.

Hirschey, M. Pappas, J. L. (1995). *Fundamentals of Managerial Economics*. 5th edn, New York: Dryden.

ROBERT E. MCAULIFFE

dominant firm A dominant firm has significant MARKET POWER which it can exercise over other firms in the industry (often called fringe firms or the competitive fringe). The dominant firm is so much larger than the fringe firms that it does not need to consider their reactions to its decisions (unlike an OLIGOPOLY market structure). It maximizes its profits according to its RESIDUAL DEMAND and the price-taking fringe firms produce along their supply curve at that price. Stigler (1968) suggested a market share of 40 percent or more was required for a firm to be considered dominant and if the second firm in the industry was large, the required market share would be even higher. Other economists have suggested market share thresholds between 30 and 60 percent; see Greer (1992). The dominant firm model may also apply when a group of firms form a cartel in an industry and act as a dominant firm toward non-member firms (*see* CARTELS). In a single period setting where all firms sell identical products, the dominant firm must consider the output which will be supplied by the fringe firms in order to maximize its profits. Attempting to raise price by restricting output will cause fringe firms to produce more output and this will reduce the industry price. Therefore the dominant firm will choose its output level so that given the output of the fringe firms at each price, profits are maximized. That is, the dominant firm should subtract the supply of the fringe firms from market demand and maximize profits by producing until MARGINAL REVENUE equals MARGINAL COST along this new (residual) demand curve. This will determine the profit maximizing output and the industry price, which will also determine the fringe firms' output. As long as the smaller firms charge a price equal to or below that of the dominant firm, they will sell their output. The dominant firm is sometimes said to provide a *price umbrella* under which less-efficient firms can survive, but this will only be true if there are entry barriers which prevent efficient firms from entering the competitive fringe; see Stigler (1968). Dominant firm pricing is also referred to as a PRICE LEADERSHIP model, although there are other forms of price leadership.

The pricing decisions of a dominant firm are constrained by the presence of the fringe firms and this prevents the firm from charging a price as high as the MONOPOLY price. A monopolist has greater market power because it is protected by significant BARRIERS TO ENTRY. When there are no barriers to protect the dominant firm, if it sets its price too high, then it will encourage expansion by the fringe firms through new entry which will reduce prices and will eventually erode the market position of the dominant firm. Gaskins (1971) showed that if the dominant firm had no cost advantages and set its prices optimally over time, it could slow the rate of market penetration by new entrants but would ultimately lose its dominant position.

Dominant firms may increase their market power through STRATEGIC BEHAVIOR aimed at deterring entry. Instead of relying on price adjustments alone to deter entry (as Gaskins assumed), dominant firms can also increase their ADVERTISING, the number of products they produce, they may develop aggressive reputations or maintain excess capacity to threaten potential entrants; see Encaoua, Geroski and Jacquemin (1986). These additional competitive weapons, if successful, would enable dominant firms to maintain their market positions for longer periods of time. In his survey of executives at major American corporations, Smiley (1988) found that managers preferred to use PRODUCT PROLIFERATION and high advertising to discourage potential entry.

see also **limit pricing; price leadership**

Bibliography

Encaoua, D., Geroski, P. Jacquemin, A. (1986). Strategic competition and the persistence of dominant firms: a survey. Stiglitz, J. E. and Matthewson, G. F. *New Developments in the Analysis of Market Structure*. Cambridge, MA: MIT.

Gaskins, D. (1971). Dynamic limit pricing: optimal pricing under threat of entry. *Journal of Economic Theory*, **2**, 306–22.

Greer, D. F. (1992). *Industrial Organization and Public Policy*. 3rd edn, New York: Macmillan.

Smiley, R. (1988). Empirical evidence on strategic entry deterrence. *International Journal of Industrial Organization*, 6, 167–80.

Stigler, G. J. (1968). *The Organization of Industry*. Chicago: University of Chicago Press.

ROBERT E. MCAULIFFE

Dorfman–Steiner condition A firm can increase its unit sales by decreasing price or by increasing ADVERTISING. For a given price, if advertising increases sales by one unit, the revenue from the increased advertising is the profit on that unit sold, or $(P - MC)$ where P is the price of the product and MC is the MARGINAL COST of producing that unit. All else equal, firms should advertise more, the higher the profit margin per unit sold.

Dorfman and Steiner (1954) considered the case where the demand for a monopolist's product is affected by both price and advertising and asked what the optimal (profit-maximizing) combination of price adjustments and advertising might be. Demand for the product depends upon (is a function of) price, P and the number of advertising messages, A:

$$Q^d = f(P, A)$$

Profits for the monopolist will be maximized at the output level where the price-cost margin is equal to the inverse of the absolute value of the price ELASTICITY of demand (*see* MARKUP PRICING). Since advertising can change the price elasticity of demand, the firm will want to advertise until the marginal revenue from advertising equals the marginal cost of advertising. The marginal revenue from advertising is the profit per unit (the price-cost margin) while the marginal cost of advertising is the cost of an advertising message, c_a times the number of advertising messages purchased, A. Therefore, if advertising increases the firm's sales by ΔQ, the condition where marginal revenue is equal to marginal cost is

$$c_a \times \Delta A = \Delta Q \times (P - MC)$$

and this can be rearranged to obtain the Dorfman–Steiner condition:

$$\frac{c_a A}{PQ} = \frac{\epsilon_A}{-\epsilon_p}$$

Since total advertising expenditures are in the numerator of the left-hand side of the equation above and total sales are in the denominator, the left-hand side is the advertising-sales ratio. On the right-hand side, ϵ_A is the elasticity of demand with respect to advertising and it shows the percentage change in unit sales for a given percentage change in advertising messages while the denominator is the price elasticity of demand.

The Dorfman–Steiner condition represents the profit-maximizing level of advertising for a monopolist. When a firm introduces a new product, we would expect demand to be very responsive to advertising, so ϵ_A should be high. This means that the advertising sales ratio will be higher for new products in the early stages of their PRODUCT LIFE CYCLE than for mature products. In a growing market, the elasticity of demand with respect to advertising will be higher and so will the advertising-sales ratio, while the advertising elasticity of demand will be lower in declining markets where each firm's sales will come at the expense of rival firms. The optimal advertising-sales ratio will increase as the (absolute value of the) price elasticity of demand decreases. Firms would rather advertise more than lower prices as the price elasticity of demand decreases. Advertising will be higher the higher the profit per unit sold, so an empirical relationship between advertising and profits would be expected given the Dorfman–Steiner result; see Berndt (1991), McAuliffe (1987) and Schmalensee (1972).

Schmalensee (1972) extends the model to an oligopoly where firms have Cournot expectations about how rival firms will react.

see also **Cournot competition; oligopoly**

Bibliography

Berndt, E. R. (1991). *The Practice of Econometrics*. Reading, MA: Addison-Wesley.

Dortman, R. Steiner, P. O. (1954). Optimal advertising and optimal quality. *American Economic Review*, **44**, 826–36.

McAuliffe, R. E. (1987). *Advertising, Competition, and Public Policy: Theories and New Evidence.* Lexington, MA: DC Heath.

Schmalensee, R. (1972). *The Economics of Advertising.* Amsterdam: North-Holland.

ROBERT E. MCAULIFFE

dumping   According to the traditional definition, dumping is the practice of PRICE DISCRIMINATION in international trade, in which the exporter charges a lower price for a specific product in the export market than in his home market. International trade law, as embodied in the General Agreement on Tariffs and Trade (GATT) article VI, recognizes two additional definitions of dumping, which can be applied if the exporter's home price is deemed inappropriate as a basis for comparison:

(1) charging a lower price for a product in one export market than in another export market; and

(2) charging a price that does not cover the cost of production, including a "reasonable" addition for selling cost and profit.

US international trade law generalizes the definition of dumping as the sale of an imported product at "less than fair value" according to the applicable basis of price comparison. According to GATT rules, if an investigation finds that dumping has taken place and "injures" a domestic industry (see below), the importing country can impose an antidumping duty in the amount of the difference between the export price and the "fair value" price.

Viner (1923) was the first to offer a systematic investigation of dumping. For the purposes of economic analysis, the central questions focus on the motivation for and welfare effects of dumping. If an exporting firm with price-making power has the ability to isolate markets with differing price elasticities of demand, for example, simple profit-maximizing behavior motivates a systematic pricing policy of dumping as an international form of third-degree price discrimination ("persistent" dumping, in Viner's terms). Typically, factors such as transportation cost or import restrictions in the exporter's home country, as well as an international market structure restricting competition, contribute to the exporter's ability to price discriminate. In addition, temporary surpluses may lead to "sporadic" dumping and third-party consignment sales may lead to pricing differentials that can be characterized as "inadvertent" dumping. In these scenarios, dumping generally improves consumer welfare in the importing country while decreasing the welfare of import-competing producers, with a net gain to the importing country as long as competition itself is not significantly reduced.

The main focus of anti-dumping laws, however, is the fear of PREDATORY DUMPING (*see* PREDATORY PRICING), which is presumably motivated by a strategy by the exporter of undercutting prices of domestic producers in the targeted export market in order to drive them out of business and monopolize the market, thus decreasing total welfare in the importing country. Typically, such a strategy would require pricing below the MARGINAL COST of production, which differs significantly from that of simple price discrimination. In addition, the "cost of production" definition of dumping, described above, may merely reflect the loss-minimizing practice of equating MARGINAL REVENUE and MARGINAL COST and then setting price below AVERAGE TOTAL COST but above the shut-down point of the firm (*see* AVERAGE VARIABLE COST) when the firm's demand curve lies below its average total cost curve. In short, dumping may merely reflect traditional profit-maximizing/loss-minimizing behavior by firms in international markets that does not involve predatory motives.

Although the conditions for a successful predatory strategy are difficult to fulfill (see Boltuck and Litan, 1991, chapter 1), antidumping laws are driven principally by the fear of predatory dumping, whether or not there is evidence that the exporter is capable of pursuing such a strategy. According to GATT rules, in order to impose antidumping duties an anti-dumping investigation must establish:

(1) that dumping has taken place and

(2) that the dumping causes or threatens "material" injury to a domestic industry.

see also **profit maximization**

Bibliography

Boltuck, R. Litan, R. E. (1991). *Down in the Dumps: Administration of the Unfair Trade Laws.* Washington: Brookings Institution.

Viner, J. (1923). *Dumping: A Problem in International Trade.* New York: Augustus M. Kelley.

KENT A. JONES

Durbin–Watson statistic One of the most common tests for autocorrelation which is frequently reported in statistical software is the Durbin–Watson statistic. This statistic tests for first-order autocorrelation using the estimated residuals from a LINEAR REGRESSION. The statistic is calculated as

$$DW = \frac{\sum_{t=2}^{T}(e_t - e_{t-1})^2}{\sum_{t=1}^{T}(e_t)^2}$$

where e_t is the estimated residual for observation t and $e_{t,t}$ the estimated residual for observation $t-1$. The numerator measures (approximately) the COVARIANCE between successive observations of the estimated residuals and the denominator measures the VARIANCE. Note that, in order to calculate the covariance in the numerator, the first observation is lost. It can be shown that the Durbin–Watson statistic will lie between 0 and 4; see Durbin and Watson (1951) and Maddala (1992).

When a positive error tends to be followed by another positive error, the covariance in the numerator will be positive and the Durbin–Watson statistic will have a value less than two. If there is no relationship between successive values of the error terms, then the statistic will have a value equal to two, while a negative relation between successive values of the estimated error terms causes the statistic to have a value above two. Since the sampling distribution of the Durbin–Watson statistic is affected by the explanatory variables included in the regression, special tables are used to test the hypothesis of zero first-order autocorrelation. The Durbin–Watson test does have several weaknesses: it only tests for first-order autocorrelation, the test can be inconclusive, and the test is biased when there are lagged dependent variables in the regression. See Berndt (1991) and Maddala (1992).

see also **autocorrelation**

Bibliography

Berndt, E. R. (1991). *The Practice of Econometrics.* Reading, MA: Addison-Wesley.

Durbin, J. Watson, G. S. (1951). Testing for serial correlation in least squares regression. *Biometrika*, 38, 159–77.

Maddala, G. S. (1992). *Introduction to Econometrics.* 2nd edn, New York: Macmillan.

ROBERT E. MCAULIFFE

E

economic depreciation This is sometimes referred to as "Hotelling" depreciation; see Fisher and McGowan (1983) and Edwards, Kay and Mayer (1987). Economic depreciation reflects the change in the value of an asset during a period; this includes physical depreciation and any changes in the market value of the asset. If the PRESENT VALUE of an asset's remaining cash flows (discounted at the asset's INTERNAL RATE OF RETURN) has changed from the beginning of the period to the end, that change represents the economic depreciation. Since accounting standards apply somewhat arbitrary depreciation schedules to physical assets (such as straight line depreciation, sum-of-year's digits and double declining balance), it is unlikely that reported depreciation will be equal to economic depreciation. As a result of this problem and others, accounting profits will not equal economic profits and the accounting rate of return will not equal the economic rate of return (*see* ACCOUNTING PROFIT; DEPRECIATION; ECONOMIC PROFIT).

Bibliography

Edwards, J., Kay, J. Mayer, C. (1987). *The Economic Analysis of Accounting Profitability*. Oxford: OUP.
Fisher, F. M. McGowan, J. J. (1983). On the misuse of accounting rates of return to infer monopoly profits. *American Economic Review*, 73, 82–97.
Shughart, W. F., Chappell, W. F. Cottle, R. L. (1994). *Modern Managerial Economics*. Cincinatti, OH: South-Western Publishing.

ROBERT E. MCAULIFFE

economic profit Economic profits are defined as total revenues in a given period minus *all* costs of production in that period, including the economic costs of tangible and intangible assets and the opportunity cost of those assets employed (*see* OPPORTUNITY COSTS). For example, any costs incurred for training, research and development, and other intangible assets would be depreciated over their expected economic lifetime rather than expensed in the current period. The normal, risk-adjusted rate of return to capital would be included in the calculation of economic costs, so that firms which earned the normal rate of return would have zero economic profits – although they would show positive accounting profits (*see* ACCOUNTING PROFIT). When economic profits are positive, they serve as a signal for ENTRY into the industry, while negative economic profits indicate that firms should EXIT the industry. In the long run, economic profits in competitive markets should be driven to zero by the forces of entry and exit unless there are BARRIERS TO ENTRY or barriers to exit. In fact, Bain (1941) suggested using the accounting profit rate above the competitive return as a measure of the height of entry barriers in an industry. However, this is an appropriate measure only when the accounting rate of return equals the economic rate of return.

Fisher and McGowan (1983) argued that the appropriate theoretical measure of the economic rate of return is the INTERNAL RATE OF RETURN (IRR) and they asserted there was little relation between the accounting rate of return and the economic rate of return. The accounting rate of return is calculated as accounting profits divided by either total assets or owners equity. But accounting statements report assets at their historic costs and not at their current (or replacement) cost, so inflation and the failure to capitalize intangible asset values will cause accounting rates of return to deviate from the economic rate of return. Fisher and McGowan showed that the accounting rate of return will not equal the economic rate of return because:

(1) the depreciation methods used by accountants do not reflect ECONOMIC DEPRECIATION,
(2) the investments made by a firm in any given period will not generally have the same "time shape" (stream of future cash flows), and
(3) the accounting rate of return will vary with the rate of growth of the firm.

From their simulations using the same stream of cash flows from a hypothetical investment but different methods of depreciation, Fisher and McGowan found that the accounting rate of return was a misleading measure and concluded it may provide no information about the economic rate of return.

Not surprisingly, these results generated considerable controversy in the literature. Long and Ravenscraft (1984) and Martin (1984) suggested that other measures of profitability, such as the LERNER INDEX, may serve as better measures of MARKET POWER for economic analysis. Long and Ravenscraft also argued that, in practice, the correlation between accounting profits and economic profits was very high and the examples used by Fisher and McGowan were not representative of industry. Based on these arguments, Long and Ravenscraft concluded accounting data provide useful information about the economic rate of return. Salamon (1985) also found that there was a strong correlation between the accounting rate of return and the estimated *conditional* internal rate of return (IRR) which can be obtained from firms' financial statements. However, he also found systematic errors occurred when the accounting rate of return was employed, so the accounting measure could not simply be treated as a randomly "noisy" proxy for the economic rate of return. In particular, he found that the errors from using the accounting rate of return varied systematically with firm size and therefore jeopardized conclusions from studies relating accounting profits to industry concentration. The problem arose, in part, because the method of depreciation firms choose varies systematically with firm size.

Fisher (1984) noted in his reply that the fundamental problem of accounting rate of return data is that profits in the numerator are measured as an average of *past* investments while total assets in the denominator are based on historic costs and may include recent capital that has been added in the expectation of future profits. The economic rate of return is forward-looking and relates the stream of benefits from an investment to the specific asset that generated them. Because of averaging and a backward-looking perspective, accounting rates of return cannot equal the economic rate of return. Fisher also argued that even a high correlation between accounting rates of return and the economic rate of return would still create measurement errors that were likely to be correlated with other variables used in industry studies (a correlation which Salamon (1985) verified). One of the requirements for estimated coefficients to be unbiased in LINEAR REGRESSION is that the explanatory variables in the regression must not be correlated with the error terms. The systematic measurement error in accounting profits is correlated with variables such as firm size and therefore studies explaining accounting rates of return by economic variables such as firm size will be misleading. In addition, he criticized the use of the rate of return on sales because it fails to properly include economic depreciation which is a cost of production and while it may measure market power, it does not measure the economic rate of return.

Edwards, Kay and Mayer (1987) evaluated several possible adjustments to accounting procedures that might improve the content of accounting information. They suggested that accountants should report several measures of a firm's profits and asset value since there is no single, unambiguous measure of the "true" values and different sources of information are required for different purposes. For example, when an asset or activity has a very long life (such as a going concern) the internal rate of return does not necessarily provide useful information because the IRR is a single value defined for the lifetime of an asset and cannot be used to evaluate performance for a fraction of that asset's life. Other measures of profitability from accounting data may provide investors, economists and others with better information. Among other suggestions they recommend that value-to-the-owner rules should be used by accountants to value company assets and liabilities where assets are valued (in most cases) at replacement cost. Furthermore, all changes in book values should have entries in the profit and loss statement and profits and asset values should be adjusted for inflation.

Bibliography

Bain, J. S. (1941). The profit rate as a measure of monopoly power. *Quarterly Journal of Economics*, 55, 271–93.

Edwards, J., Kay, J. Mayer, C. (1987). *The Economic Analysis of Accounting Profitability*. Oxford: OUP.

Fisher, F. M. (1984). The misuse of accounting rates of return: reply. *American Economic Review*, 74, 509–17.

Fisher, F. M. McGowan, J. J. (1983). On the misuse of accounting rates of return to infer monopoly profits. *American Economic Review*, 73, 82–97.

Long, W. F. Ravenscraft, D. J. (1984). The misuse of accounting rates of return: comment. *American Economic Review*, 74, 494–500.

Martin, S. (1984). The misuse of accounting rates of return: comment. *American Economic Review*, 74, 501–6.

Salamon, G. L. (1985). Accounting rates of return. *American Economic Review*, 75, 495–504.

ROBERT E. MCAULIFFE

economies of scale   Economies of scale exist when increasing all inputs in production causes output to rise by more than the change in inputs. Therefore, if all inputs were doubled (i.e. the scale of the firm's operations doubled) output would more than double. Typically firms vary in terms of *size* and not scale, i. e. large firms do not use all inputs in the same proportion as smaller firms. Expressed in terms of costs for a single product firm, the AVERAGE TOTAL COST of production declines as output increases when there are economies of scale. These economies of scale may occur at the plant level or the firm level of operations. A firm may operate several plants and there may be economies in the management of the firm or in the consolidation of its financial activities. Economies of scale and ECONOMIES OF SCOPE combined with the level of demand in the market have an important effect on the feasible number of firms in an industry; see Panzar (1989), MINIMUM EFFICIENT SCALE (MES), and MARKET STRUCTURE.

The sources of economies of scale at the firm level are not well understood although Sharkey (1982) offers several possibilities. At the level of the plant, economies of scale reflect the technological or engineering aspects of production. For example, if there are fixed setup costs to produce a specific model on an assembly line, then the setup costs per unit will be lower the greater the number of units produced. Furthermore, given the law of large numbers, when unit sales double firms do not have to double their inventories to achieve a given probability of having supplies available to consumers. Firms can also achieve gains from specialization from their labor and capital inputs at higher output levels. In addition, there may be PECUNIARY ECONOMIES of scale when a firm can purchase inputs at lower cost with volume discounts.

For a single product firm, there are economies of scale when average cost per unit is declining. When average costs are declining, then marginal costs must be less than average costs (*see* MARGINAL COST). Therefore one measure of economies of scale is the ratio of average costs to marginal costs:

$$s = AC/MC = \frac{TC}{Q} \times \frac{\Delta Q}{\Delta TC}$$

Here TC is the total cost of production, Q is the quantity of output produced, ΔTC is the change in total costs and ΔQ is the change in output produced. There are economies of scale when s 1 and DISECONOMIES OF SCALE when s 1. Another measure of economies of scale is the cost ELASTICITY which measures the percentage change in TOTAL COSTS for a given percentage change in output. It can be expressed as:

$$\epsilon_{TC} = \frac{\frac{\Delta TC}{TC}}{\frac{\Delta Q}{Q}} = \frac{\Delta TC}{\Delta Q} \times \frac{Q}{TC}$$

which is simply the inverse of the scale economy measure in s. There are economies of scale when $\varepsilon_{TC} < 1$ since costs will increase by less than the increase in output and diseconomies of scale exist when $\varepsilon_{TC} > 1$.

A classic empirical study of economies of scale is due to Nerlove (1963) who examined economies in electricity generation. He found that economies of scale existed in the industry but were exhausted by the largest firms. Sharkey

(1982), and Panzar (1989) provide surveys of both theoretical and empirical issues regarding economies of scale for single product and multiproduct firms. The measurement and estimation of economies of scale for multiproduct firms is much more complicated than for single product firms because firms may vary their output mix among the different products they produce and therefore will have different costs depending on their output mix; see Baumol, Panzar and Willig (1982) and Panzar (1989).

One measure of average costs for a multi-product firm is "ray average cost" where the composition of output (the product mix) is kept constant while the scale of the composite output changes along that ray; see Bailey and Friedlaender (1982). If a firm produced 100 units of good 1 and 200 units of good 2, ray average costs could then be calculated for any scale of output as long as the proportions of output produced remained at 1:2, e.g. 200 units of good 1 to 400 units of good 2. There are economies of scale for a multiproduct firm when ray average costs are declining as the scale of output increases.

Product-specific economies of scale for a multiproduct firm can also be measured and occur when the average incremental cost of producing one product decreases, holding the output of all the other products constant. If a firm produces two products ($q1$ and $q2$), the average incremental cost (AIC) is defined as the difference between the increase in total costs from producing a given product ($q1$) at a specific level of output and the costs incurred if $q1$ is not produced at all divided by the total output of $q1$. Defining total costs of producing both $q1$ and $q2$ as $C(q1,q2)$, this is calculated as:

$$AIC_1 = \frac{C(q_1,q_2) - C(0,q_2)}{q_1}$$

and product-specific economies of scale are then measured as the ratio of the average incremental costs for q_1 to the marginal cost of producing q_1:

$$s_1 = AIC_1/MC_1$$

where MC_1 is the marginal cost of producing good one. Ray scale economies can also be measured as the elasticity of output with respect to costs holding the proportion of the two products constant and represent scale econo-

mies for a multiproduct firm. Bailey and Friedlaender (1982) suggest that mergers in the trucking industry may be motivated by economies of scale and scope once the multiproduct nature of trucking services is recognized.

Bibliography

Bailey, E. E. Friedlaender, A. F. (1982). Market structure and multiproduct industries. *Journal of Economic Literature*, **20**, 1024–48.
Baumol, W. J., Panzar, J. C. Willig, R. D. (1982). *Contestable Markets and the Theory of Industry Structure*. San Diego: Harcourt Brace Jovanovich.
Nerlove, M. (1963). Returns to scale in electricity supply. Christ, C. *Measurement in Economics: Studies in Mathematical Economics and Econometrics*. Stanford: Stanford University Press.
Panzar, J. C. (1989). Technological determinants of firm and industry structure. Schmalensee, R. Willig, R. D. *Handbook of Industrial Organization*. New York: North-Holland.
Sharkey, W. W. (1982). *The Theory of Natural Monopoly*. Cambridge: CUP.

ROBERT E. MCAULIFFE

economies of scope Economies of scope occur when two or more products can be produced together at lower cost than by producing them separately. Rather than increasing the *scale* of the firm's operations (ECONOMIES OF SCALE), costs are changing with changes in the *scope* of the firm's operations (the number of products produced). Economies of scope may arise when two or more products share a common, "public good" input in joint production, where once that common input is acquired it is available to produce other products at no cost; see Bailey and Friedlaender (1982) and Panzar (1989). There may be economies from shared inputs which give rise to economies of scope when costs are reduced in acquiring those inputs in volume or in sharing them (such as sharing overhead, reputation or management). Often knowledge is an important input in production that, once acquired, makes it less costly to produce or sell closely related products. Economies of scale and scope may therefore interact to create advantages for large firms and increase the MINIMUM EFFICIENT SCALE (MES) of operation.

If a firm produces two products ($q1$ and $q2$), the degree of economies of scope can be measured as the difference between the total costs of producing both products separately and the total costs of producing the two products jointly, divided by the total costs of producing the two products jointly. Defining the total costs of producing both q_1 and q_2 jointly as $C(q1,q2)$, this is calculated as:

$$Sc = \frac{C(q_1,0) + C(0,q_2) - C(q_1,q_2)}{C(q_1,q_2)}$$

and economies of scope exist when S_c is greater than zero; see Bailey and Friedlaender (1982) and Baumol, Panzar and Willig (1982).

Friedlaender, Winston and Wang (1983) found there were both economies of scale and economies of scope in US automobile manufacturing for large cars, small cars, and trucks. US producers could share common parts and designs between these products and could exploit pecuniary economies of scale through volume purchases of common parts and materials from suppliers. When the US Department of Justice sought to break up the regional Bell companies from AT&T long distance operations, AT&T initially suggested there were economies of scope in long distance and local phone service and that economic efficiency would be reduced if the NATURAL MONOPOLY in communications were ended. Using Bell system data, Evans and Heckman (1984) tested to determine whether one firm could produce communications output in the US at lower cost than two firms over the period 1958–77. They found that for qualifying data points, costs would be lower if *two* firms produced that output. In other words, the Bell System did not satisfy the necessary cost requirements to be classified as a natural monopoly.

Bibliography

Bailey, E. E. Friedlaender, A. F. (1982). Market structure and multiproduct industries. *Journal of Economic Literature*, **20**, 1024–48.
Baumol, W. J., Panzar, J. C. Willig, R. D. (1982). *Contestable Markets and the Theory of Industry Structure*. San Diego: Harcourt Brace Jovanovich.
Evans, D. S. Heckman, J. J. (1984). A test for subadditivity of the cost function with application to the Bell system. *American Economic Review*, **74**, 615–23.
Friedlaender, A. F., Winston, C. Wang, K. (1983). Costs, technology and productivity in the U.S. automobile industry. *Bell Journal of Economics*, **14**, 1–20.
Panzar, J. C. (1989). Technological determinants of firm and industry structure. Schmalensee, R. Willig, R. D. *Handbook of Industrial Organization*. New York: North-Holland.
Sharkey, W. W. (1982). *The Theory of Natural Monopoly*. Cambridge: CUP.

ROBERT E. MCAULIFFE

efficiency Economists use the criterion of Pareto optimality to determine whether production or consumption decisions are efficient. According to this criterion, an allocation is efficient if in a society no person can be made better off without making someone else worse off. This concept of efficiency treats consumer tastes and the distribution of income as given, and efficiency is achieved when society produces those goods which consumers are willing to pay for at the lowest possible cost. Given the general principle of Pareto optimality, several specific measures of efficiency are provided below for an economy that produces two goods, X and Y, using two inputs in production, labor and capital (L and K respectively) for two consumers, A and B; see Pindyck and Rubinfeld (1995) or Baumol (1977). These efficiency conditions can be generalized for economies with many products, consumers and resources; see Baumol (1977).

Allocative efficiency

Allocative efficiency exists when those consumers who are willing and able to pay the marginal cost to society of producing a product receive it. This requirement is fulfilled when the market price P equals MARGINAL COST (MC) as long as there are no EXTERNALITIES in production or consumption. When a consumer maximizes TOTAL UTILITY, the MARGINAL RATE OF SUBSTITUTION of good Y for good X (MRS_{xy}) is equal to the price ratio, P_x/P_y. If markets are perfectly competitive, then all consumers face the same price ratio and if they also maximize their utility, then the marginal rates of substitution of good Y for good X will be equal across all consumers of the two goods. Thus efficiency in exchange requires:

$$MRS_{XY}^A = MRS_{XY}^B \qquad (1)$$

where MRS_{XY}^j is the marginal rate of substitution of good X for good Y for consumer j. If this condition does not hold, then the consumers could both benefit from exchanging the goods until their marginal rates of substitution were equal (*see* PARETO OPTIMAL ALLOCATION).

Productive efficiency

Productive efficiency requires resources in production to be allocated so that output in the economy is maximized at the lowest cost. As Baumol (1977) has suggested, productive efficiency is simply the application of Pareto optimality to production, where for any arbitrarily selected product, output of that product is maximized subject to the constraint that there is no reduction in the output of all the other goods produced. Productive efficiency is necessary for Pareto optimality but it is not sufficient since society could very efficiently produce products which consumers did not want.

The resources used to produce output will be efficiently employed across different industries in the economy when the MARGINAL RATE OF TECHNICAL SUBSTITUTION of labor for capital ($MRTS_{LK}$) in one industry (X) equals its value in other industries (Y). For the two-good, two-resource economy in this example, the condition for productive efficiency is:

$$MRTS_{LK}^X = MRTS_{LK}^Y \qquad (1)$$

Here resources will be efficiently employed between the two industries when they are equally productive in both. Again, if the markets are perfectly competitive, then firms in both industries will maximize profits by hiring labor and capital until the marginal rate of technical substitution of labor for capital equals the ratio of the labor wage rate to the cost ("rental" rate) for capital. Since all industries face the same wage and capital rental costs in a perfectly competitive economy, the marginal rates of technical substitution will be equal across firms in all industries.

Firms in competitive industries maximize profits by producing until price P equals marginal cost (MC) and this coordinates productive efficiency with allocative efficiency because the price measures the value of a unit of the product to consumers in society (assuming there are no EXTERNALITIES in consumption) while marginal cost reflects the opportunity cost to society (*see* OPPORTUNITY COSTS) of producing that product (if there are no EXTERNALITIES in production). Therefore competitively determined prices coordinate the production and consumption decisions in society so that those consumers who value products the most and are willing and able to pay the costs to society of producing them will receive them. When these efficiency conditions hold, resources cannot be re-allocated to make anyone better off without making someone else worse off.

see also **Pareto optimal allocation; profit maximization; utility maximization**

Bibliography

Bator, F. M. (1957). The simple analytics of welfare maximization. *American Economy Review*, **47**, 22–59.

Baumol, W. J. (1977). *Economic Theory and Operations Analysis*. Englewood Cliffs, NJ: Prentice-Hall.

Pindyck, R. S. Rubinfeld, D. L. (1995). *Microeconomics*. 3rd edn, Englewood Cliffs, NJ: Prentice-Hall.

ROBERT E. McAULIFFE

efficient markets hypothesis   In the most general sense, an efficient financial market is one that allocates funds to their most productive uses, and through competition, results in market prices that are consistent with the underlying value, given the information available at the time (*see* EFFICIENCY). Thus, efficient capital markets are those in which the market price of each security is a good indicator of the firm's future prospects.

In a perfect market, the value of any security will reflect all information that is available to the participants in the marketplace. Therefore, capital market efficiency implies that:

(1) securities are always fairly priced;
(2) their prices react quickly to new information; and
(3) investors cannot make excess returns simply by using strategies based on available information.

As an example, suppose that a firm announces that they have been successful in a bid to buy a company that supplies one of the component parts used in their production process and, as a result, management anticipates increased earnings in the future. If investors believe this announcement, their estimates of the value of the company should rise and the stock price should rise. In an inefficient market, an investor would be able to act on this information to gain excess profits by buying the stock immediately upon hearing the announcement and then selling it when the price has increased as a result of the announcement. In a perfectly efficient market, by the time the investor can call his or her broker, the stock price will already have risen to reflect the new information. Clearly, however, in order for the price to adjust, it must be the case that at least one investor is able to capitalize on the new information. The more efficient the market, therefore, the quicker the information is included in prices and the lower the opportunity to capitalize on new information.

Although the theory of market efficiency as applied to the capital markets has its origins in basic economic theory, Eugene Fama (1970) is often credited as the first to distinguish several levels of efficiency by the *type* of information that is reflected in prices. His analysis of efficiency on this basis has come to be known as the "efficient markets hypothesis" and is subdivided into three levels of efficiency. In the *weak form* of efficiency, prices of securities fully reflect all information contained in historical price movements. In the *semi-strong form* of efficiency, security prices are said to reflect all publicly available information. Finally in a *strong form* efficient capital market, prices fully reflect all information, both public and private. Tests of market efficiency have generally attempted to determine the ability of investors to make excess profits using the sets of information identified by the theory: price data only; all publicly available data; or all information.

Some investors believe that new information is incorporated in stock prices slowly and that they can earn an excess return by trading based on careful analysis of generally available information. Investors that use "technical analysis" – the observation of patterns in past price movements in an attempt to predict future price movements – believe that the market is not even weak form efficient. If seasonal or annual cycles in prices exist or if price changes are correlated over time, an investor might be able to devise a trading rule that produces consistent returns (by buying at the low end of the price cycle and selling at the high end). However, for this to be an effective strategy (and thus proof of market inefficiency), excess returns achieved by the trading rule would have to be sufficient to cover trading costs. Tests of the weak form of efficiency have generally shown that trading rules based on perceived patterns in historical returns do not earn excess returns for investors that are sufficient to cover trading costs.

Although information about past price movements may be instantaneously incorporated in prices, it does not necessarily follow that other information is as well. Therefore, tests of the semi-strong form of efficiency have focused on a variety of types of publicly available information. The methodology, initially introduced by Fama *et al.* (1969) in testing for the effects of stock splits and dividend announcements on security prices, has been applied to many different types of information. Although the techniques have been refined over the years, the conclusions have generally been similar. The market seems to adjust to new information rapidly and much of the impact on price takes place in anticipation of the actual public announcement. Although this supports semi-strong efficiency, it is still possible for investors to make excess profits if they can acquire information that is not widely known and act on it before the information becomes incorporated in prices.

Some investors, such as managers or other insiders, clearly would have an advantage in capitalizing on non-public information. In fact, the only way that all information, both public and private, could be incorporated in market prices (i.e. semi-strong efficiency) would be if insiders were using their private information in trading. In the example above, if the managers purchased shares in their own company prior to making the public announcement and then sold the shares for a gain after the announcement caused stock prices to rise, they would make an excess profit. Insider trading laws make this type of activity illegal, although there is evidence that such fraudulent trading has occurred without detection by the authorities.

Bibliography

Elton, E. J. Gruber, M. J. (1991). *Security Analysis and Portfolio Theory*. 4th edn, New York: Wiley.

Fama, E. (1970). Efficient capital markets: a review of theory and empirical work. *Journal of Finance*, 25(2), 383–417.

Fama, E., Fisher, L., Jensen, M. Roll, R. (1969). The adjustment of stock prices to new information. *International Economic Review*, 10(1), 1–21.

VICKIE L. BAJTELSMIT

elasticity This measure indicates the responsiveness of a buyer or seller to a change in the value of an economic variable. Perhaps the most important type is price elasticity of demand which measures the size of the reaction by consumers of a product to a change in the price of that product. Additional measures including price elasticity of supply, cross elasticity, INCOME ELASTICITY, and CROSS-ADVERTISING ELASTICITY are also important in determining the strategic behavior of firms and outcomes in markets. Price elasticity of demand (ϵ_p) is calculated as the percentage change in quantity demanded resulting from a small percentage change in price. Written in the form of a fraction this becomes

$$\epsilon_p = \frac{\%\Delta Q}{\%\Delta P}$$

where the symbol Δ indicates a change in quantity (Q) or price (P). Where the exact demand curve is already known, an infinitesimally small change in price can be used to calculate what is known as the point elasticity. More commonly, when a manager makes discrete changes in price, the estimation of elasticity involves a range of prices and quantities. Calculating elasticity using the average price and quantity over these ranges yields a useful approximation (see ARC ELASTICITY).

As the LAW OF DEMAND indicates that price and quantity demanded are inversely related, the value of ϵ_p should always be negative. Since the negative sign adds no information about the size of the reaction, by convention it is typically

dropped. Three levels of responsiveness are observable. When a large reaction by consumers occurs (the percentage change in quantity demanded exceeds that of price), ϵ_p has a value greater than 1 and demand is said to be elastic with respect to price. The small reaction case, ϵ_p 1, is that of inelastic demand, while the case where price and quantity reactions exactly offset each other, $\epsilon_p = 1$, is identified as unit elastic demand.

The degree of consumer sensitivity to a price change is influenced by several factors. Switching to alternative products is common when one product's price is changed. Demand for a product thus tends to become more elastic where the number and closeness of available substitutes rises as this switching of products more readily and easily occurs. Nelson (1974) in his study of advertising cautions that elasticity actually depends on the number of alternatives of which the consumer is aware. Managers need to consider this and the appropriate market boundaries (see MARKET DEFINITION) in determining their business strategy. In perfect competition, where large numbers of rivals produce identical products, demand for any one firm's product is perfectly elastic and all firms become price takers. Where a strategy of product differentiation is possible, it can be used to create a more inelastic demand for a product. One well known example is that of 7UP being marketed as the "UNCOLA" in an effort to distinguish itself from its rivals.

Similarly, a product requiring a greater portion of the consumer's budget will tend to have a more elastic demand as a result of the stronger INCOME EFFECT from a price change. Perhaps most apparent is that the greater the extent to which a product is perceived as being a necessity, the more inelastic its demand tends to be with respect to price. Finally, demand tends to become more elastic over longer time periods. This results from the fact that typically a wider array of substitutes become available over time. Also, a consumer simply has more time to react to the price change.

Price elasticity of demand is central to a firm's sales revenues. As a firm's total revenues are dependent on the product's price and the number of units sold, the impact of a price change on revenues depends singularly on the product's elasticity of demand. As the law of demand indicates that price and quantity demanded move in opposite directions, a change in price creates two opposing forces on revenues. The elasticity of demand indicates which force is stronger. A price cut in the face of an elastic demand for the product will increase the total receipts from its sales because of the large and more than offsetting rise in unit sales. Similarly, a price rise where demand is elastic will reduce total revenues.

Price elasticity of demand also plays a vital role in determining optimal prices. For profit maximization, a firm should produce until the MARGINAL REVENUE (MR) equals the MARGINAL COST (MC) of production. For linear demand curves it has been demonstrated that marginal revenue is related to price (P) and elasticity by the equation

$$MR = P \times [1 - (1/\epsilon_p)].$$

As such, if a firm maximizes profits, marginal revenue in the equation above equals marginal cost, and this relation can be used to show that the best price to charge is dependent on both elasticity and cost. Douglas (1992) shows that this relationship can be written as

$$P = MC + [-1/(\epsilon_p + 1)]x\ MC$$

which yields a markup pricing strategy. The profit maximizing markup of price is a percentage of cost and is inversely related to the product's demand elasticity. That is, the more elastic is the demand for the product, the lower will be its profit maximizing markup price.

Bibliography

Douglas, E. (1992). *Managerial Economics: Analysis Strategy*. 4th edn, Englewood Cliffs: Prentice-Hall.

Mansfield, E. (1993). *Managerial Economics: Theory, Applications, and Cases*. 2nd edn, New York: W.W. Norton.

Nelson, P. (1974). Advertising as Information. *Journal of Political Economy*, 82, 729–54.

GILBERT BECKER

entry   Entry occurs when new firms engage in the production of specific goods or services in an industry and represents an important feature of competition in market economies. New firms may enter an industry either as wholly new enterprises or as extensions of existing firms from other markets. Entry is the crucial mechanism which disciplines existing firms within an industry. In the extreme case, where there is a perfectly contestable market, even a monopolist cannot earn economic profits (*see* CONTESTABLE MARKETS; ECONOMIC PROFIT) or incur excessive costs because it will be subjected to hit and run entry that will force the market price down until it equals average cost; see Baumol, Panzar and Willig (1982). However, potential entrants may be prevented from entering the industry when there are SUNK COSTS or other BARRIERS TO ENTRY. Wietzman (1983) argued that, within short periods of time, some costs are always sunk and this has led some to question how much discipline can be imposed on established firms by potential entry; see Shepherd (1984). Barriers to entry may prevent or reduce entry into a market even when economic profits exist. The sources of barriers to entry may also interact and have significant joint effects in deterring entrants although individually each source may not be substantial; see, for example, Geroski, Gilbert and Jacquemin (1990).

Economic theory predicts entry should occur in response to expected economic profits in a given market which are determined by the entrant's costs, the expected response of existing firms to the entrant, and the post-entry price and market share the entrant expects. Porter (1980) discusses several considerations regarding the entry decision, including the anticipated reaction of established firms to the entrant. Among other issues, he mentions several factors that increase the likelihood that existing firms will retaliate such as slow industry growth, high FIXED COSTS, high industry concentration, and products which are not differentiated. When industry concentration is high or when industry sales are slow, an entrant is more likely to take sales from existing firms and trigger a response. High fixed costs and products which are not differentiated raise the probability of a price war because all firms have greater incentives to cut prices. With high fixed costs, any sale will make some contribution to overhead, so firms are motivated to reduce their price to make an additional sale whereas products which are not differentiated have many SUBSTITUTES and consumers are more likely to make purchases based on price.

Entry into an industry may also be motivated by anticipated market growth and technological change in addition to expected economic profits. New products introduced by innovative firms are part of the dynamic process of competition that Schumpeter (1975) called the "gale of creative destruction". Important as it is, the analysis of entry rates is complicated by the fact that existing firms may pursue strategies such as LIMIT PRICING to prevent or reduce the rate of entry. In their survey Geroski, Gilbert and Jacquemin (1990) examined the empirical literature on entry in terms of how quickly it responded to industry profits and how rapidly it reduced those profits. They found that entry rates were low, suggesting high barriers to entry and that even when entry was rapid, industry profits remained high. As they observed, conclusions regarding the relationship between entry and profits are subject to several qualifications. One problem is that accounting profits do not necessarily reflect economic profits (see Fisher and McGowan, 1983) even when the two are highly correlated. Another point they raise is that the threat of entry may force existing firms to eliminate X-inefficiency and reduce costs in production (*see* X-EFFICIENCY). If existing firms reacted this way, then industry profits could remain constant despite the fact that entry had significant effects on firm behavior.

In a careful study of entry and EXIT in US manufacturing over the period from 1963 to 1982, Dunne, Roberts and Samuelson (1988) distinguished three types of entry. Entry into an industry could result from a new entrant constructing a new plant, a diversifying firm from another industry constructing a new plant, or an existing firm changing its product mix. They found that, on average, 38.6 percent of firms in operation in each industry had not produced in that industry in the previous census. Furthermore, new entrants with new plants tended to be small relative to the size of existing firms and accounted for a significant portion of the number of entrants into an industry but their average market share was small. Diversifying firms tended to be larger and were more likely to survive. While single-plant firms accounted for 93.4 percent of the total number of firms in each year, their share of the value of production was only 17.1 percent. On average, most of the value of industry produc-

tion was produced by multiplant firms. One interesting discovery by Dunne, Roberts and Samuelson was that industries with high rates of entry also tended to have high rates of exit. The correlation between the rate of entry into an industry and exit from the industry was very high both in terms of the numbers of entrants and exiters and their market share. In addition, the differences in entry and exit patterns between industries persisted over time, which suggests that industry-specific factors affect both entry and exit.

Bibliography

Baumol, W. J., Panzar, J. C. Willig, R. D. (1982). *Contestable Markets and the Theory of Industry Structure*. San Diego: Harcourt Brace Jovanovich.

Dunne, T., Roberts, M. J. Samuelson, L. (1988). Patterns of entry and exit in U.S. manufacturing industries. *Rand Journal of Economics*, 19, 495–515.

Fisher, F. M. McGowan, J. J. (1983). On the misuse of accounting rates of return to infer monopoly profits. *American Economic Review*, 73, 82–97.

Geroski, P., Gilbert, R. J. Jacquemin, A. (1990). *Barriers to Entry and Strategic Competition*. New York: Harwood.

Porter, M. E. (1980). *Competitive Strategy*. New York: Free Press.

Schumpeter, J. A. (1975). *Capitalism, Socialism, and Democracy*. New York: Harper Row.

Shepherd, W. G. (1984). 'Contestability' vs. competition. *American Economic Review*, 74, 572–87.

Weitzman, M. L. (1983). Contestable markets: an uprising in the theory of industry structure: comment. *American Economic Review*, 73, 486–7.

ROBERT E. McAULIFFE

equilibrium   The concept of equilibrium is fundamental to economic analysis. As with physical systems, an economic system is in equilibrium when it is at rest and exhibits no tendency to change until the underlying market conditions change. Markets are said to be in equilibrium when supply equals demand and this determines the equilibrium price and quantity in the market. Once equilibrium is achieved in a market, consumers are able to purchase the amount they wish to buy at the equilibrium price and firms are able to sell the amount they wish to sell. Since both consumers and firms are able to do what they wish, given the actions of others in the market, they have no reason to change their behavior and so the equilibrium is maintained until cost or demand conditions change. Given this, Hayek (1948, p. 42) suggested that the concept of equilibrium should be extended to require that the plans of economic agents are fulfilled given the behavior of others in the market. High (1990) elaborated Hayek's definition and argued that equilibrium occurs when the various plans made by economic agents are mutually compatible (perhaps intertemporally).

Closely related to the concept of equilibrium is the stability of equilibrium. A stable equilibrium is one to which the economic system will return if, for any reason, it is slightly disturbed from that equilibrium. Fisher (1983) argued that the conclusions reached with equilibrium analysis are only reliable to the extent that it can be shown that markets converge to new, stable equilibrium positions reasonably quickly. However, if consumers and firms trade out of equilibrium, convergence to the equilibrium price may not be achieved. He showed that, with some significant restrictions, markets could converge to equilibrium over time when agents trade out of equilibrium.

Critics of equilibrium analysis in economics have argued that there is no convincing theory describing how markets could achieve equilibrium and that markets may never reach it (Nelson and Winter, 1982; Blaug, 1992; Hausman, 1992). But as High has noted, even if markets never reach equilibrium, it still remains a useful theoretical concept to predict how markets might respond to specific changes. For example, an increase in demand will cause a complex series of adjustments in the market which are not well understood. By focusing on the new equilibrium, economists abstract from the dynamic process of market adjustment altogether to determine where the market process may lead if there are no other changes. High also argues that even if markets do not reach equilibrium, that does not mean that there are no equilibrating forces in the market.

As an alternative to equilibrium analysis, Nelson and Winter (1982) recommend evolutionary modeling where agents in a market develop strategies, react to their environment, learn, and adapt over time. They argue that firms and consumers do not necessarily maximize in new and unfamiliar situations because they have not learned how best to operate in a new environment. Lesourne (1992) developed several simple models where agents learn and adapt to the market environment and he found that, in many cases, when agents had IMPERFECT INFORMATION or there were TRANSACTIONS COSTS, convergence to "the" market equilibrium of neoclassical theory did not occur. He found that markets could reach stable equilibria which were not necessarily optimal and the path taken to reach equilibrium could affect the equilibrium ultimately attained. In this respect, the problems of convergence to equilibrium identified by Lesourne were described in Fisher's (1983) discussion of the behavior of markets in disequilibrium.

Although evolutionary modeling offers an appealing alternative to equilibrium analysis, it also creates additional problems. As Blaug (1992) observes, if the assumption of rational, maximizing agents is abandoned, how can incomplete information and incorrect expectations be modeled? Since firms and consumers can have an infinite variety of incorrect expectations, a Pandora's box of possibilities is opened once the assumption of maximizing behavior in equilibrium is sacrificed.

Several equilibrium concepts which frequently appear in economic applications are discussed below.

Static vs. dynamic equilibrium

A static equilibrium is one which occurs at a single point in time, such as the equality between the quantity supplied and demanded for a good. A dynamic equilibrium is one which occurs over time, such as a predicted increase in the price of a product. If the price increase is correctly anticipated by agents in the market, then no one is surprised as the price increases each period and the market is in a dynamic, though possibly changing, equilibrium from one period to the next.

Short run vs. long run equilibrium

An industry is in short run equilibrium when short run supply (holding the number of firms in the industry fixed) equals demand. In the short run, the number of firms is fixed, so there may be economic profits (see ECONOMIC PROFIT) or losses during this period. However, in the long run, firms may enter or exit the industry, so long run equilibrium occurs when there is no net entry into or exit from the industry. For a perfectly competitive industry, the entry and exit of firms will cause economic profits to be zero in the long run (*see* ENTRY; EXIT; CONTESTABLE MARKETS; PERFECT COMPETITION).

Nash equilibrium

Frequently employed in GAME THEORY, a Nash equilibrium is one where no agent wants to change his or her behavior given the behavior of others in the market. For firms in an oligopoly, a Nash equilibrium in strategy occurs when no firms want to change their strategies (advertising policy, pricing, output, research and development, etc.) given the strategies of the other firms in the industry.

see also **Cournot competition; oligopoly; strategic behavior**

Bibliography

Blaug, M. (1992). *The Methodology of Economics.* 2nd edn, New York: CUP.
Fisher, F. M. (1983). *Disequilibrium Foundations of Equilibrium Economics.* Cambridge, UK: CUP.
Hausman, D. M. (1992). *The Inexact and Separate Science of Economics.* New York: CUP.
Hayek, F. A. (1948). *Individualism and Economic Order.* Chicago, IL: Chicago University Press.
High, J. (1990). *Maximising, Action, and Market Adjustment.* Munich, Germany: Philosophia Verlag.
Lesourne, J. (1992). *The Economics of Order and Disorder.* New York: OUP.
Nelson, R. R. Winter, S. G. (1982). *An Evolutionary Theory of Economic Change.* Cambridge, MA: Harvard University Press.

ROBERT E. MCAULIFFE

error terms in regression   The estimated coefficients from a LINEAR REGRESSION will be the best linear unbiased estimators (BLUE)

when the error terms in the regression have the properties described below. To illustrate, suppose a manager wanted to estimate the relationship between unit sales of a product, Y and advertising, X. The regression relationship is assumed to be linear and is written as

$$Y_i = \beta_0 + \beta_1 \times X_i + \nu_i \qquad (1)$$

where the Y are observations on the *dependent* variable, X are observations on the *independent* or *explanatory* variable, and the ν_i are the error terms. The coefficients β_0 and β_1 are to be estimated and will show how much effect advertising has on sales. If the coefficient for β_1 is not significantly different from zero, then advertising has no effect on this firm's sales. Additional explanatory variables could easily be added, but to simplify the discussion we will assume only one explanatory variable below.

The disturbances in the regression, ν are added to reflect three possible sources of randomness. First is the likely random nature of the relationship between advertising and sales (i.e. the link between these two variables will not be perfect) and so a perfect fit between advertising and sales is unlikely. Second, the effects of other explanatory variables which are missing from the regression are reflected in the error terms. Finally, there may be measurement errors in the observations on the dependent variable which the error term will capture; see Maddala (1992) and Greene (1993).

For linear regression estimates of the coefficients in equation (1) to be BLUE, the error terms must satisfy the following assumptions:

(1) The errors must have zero mean, so their EXPECTED VALUE is zero. $E(\nu) = 0$.
(2) The errors must have a constant VARIANCE: $\text{var}(\nu) = \sigma^2$.
(3) There is no AUTOCORRELATION in the error terms. This means that successive observations of ν are not correlated with each other, so $\text{cov}(\nu, \nu_j) = 0$ for all $i \neq j$.
(4) The error terms are independent of all of the explanatory variables. That is, the COVARIANCE between the explanatory variables and the errors is zero: $\text{cov}(\nu, X) = 0$ for all i and all j. Violation of this assumption will cause the linear regression estimates to be biased.
(5) The error terms are independently and normally distributed. Thus, $\nu \sim \text{IN}(0, \sigma^2)$.

When the error terms in a linear regression satisfy these assumptions, then the least squares estimators will be unbiased and efficient in the class of all linear unbiased estimators. Furthermore, with assumption five statistical hypothesis tests regarding the estimated coefficients can be performed using F-tests and t-statistics (*see* T-STATISTICS) in small samples; see Maddala (1992) and Greene (1993). If the error terms fail to satisfy these assumptions, it may be possible to correct the problem. For example, most regression software allows users to correct for first-order serial correlation (*see* AUTOCORRE-LATION) in the errors and offer procedures to correct for HETEROSKEDASTICITY (the failure of assumption 2).

see also **multicollinearity**

Bibliography

Maddala, G. S. (1992). *Introduction to Econometrics.* 2nd edn, New York: Macmillan.
Greene, W. H. (1993). *Econometric Analysis.* 2nd edn, New York: Macmillan.

ROBERT E. MCAULIFFE

estimating demand   When prices and output in a market reflect the forces of both supply and demand, estimates of the demand (or supply) curve by LINEAR REGRESSION will be biased (*see* SIMULTANEOUS EQUATIONS BIAS). This bias occurs because, in a simultaneous equations system, the regressors will be correlated with the error term (*see* ERROR TERMS IN REGRESSION). For example, consider the system of market supply and demand equations below:

$$Q_t^d = \alpha_1 + \alpha_2 P + \alpha_3 I + \varepsilon_t^d, \qquad (1)$$

$$Q_t^s = \beta_1 + \beta_2 P + \beta_3 C + \varepsilon_t^s, \qquad (2)$$

$$Q_t^d = Q_t^s, \qquad (3)$$

where Q is the quantity supplied or demanded, P is the price of the product, I is the consumers' real income (which is an exogenous variable in this model), C is the resource cost of production (also exogenous), and the ε_t^i are random disturbances to demand and supply. Equations (1)–(3) are referred to as *structural equations* which reflect specific features of the market. These equations are mutually dependent so

random variations in demand or supply will cause random variations in price. But if demand is randomly high (or low) in a given period the price will be higher (lower) in that period as well, and this means there is a correlation between one of the right-hand side variables in the regression (price) and the error term which biases linear regression estimates. The same problem occurs with estimates of the supply curve, or with estimates of any simultaneous relationship in which variables on the right-hand side of the regression are not exogenous. There are several methods for obtaining consistent, unbiased estimates of simultaneous equations.

Indirect Least Squares

One method of estimating demand or supply in a system of equations such as (1)–(3) is to estimate the reduced-form parameters – those parameters derived from the structural equations where the dependent variables are expressed in terms of the exogenous variables only. For the three-equation system above, price and quantity can be expressed solely in terms of the exogenous variables:

$$Q = \pi_1 + \pi_2 I + \pi_3 C + \eta_1, \qquad (4)$$

$$P = \pi_4 + \pi_5 I + \pi_6 C + \eta_2, \qquad (5)$$

where the π_i are the reduced-form parameters and the η_i are error terms. Since the right-hand side variables in equations (4) and (5) are exogenous, a linear regression can be used to estimate the π_i coefficients. If the equations in the system are exactly identified, there is a unique relationship between each of the structural coefficients (the α's and β's) and the reduced-form parameters (the π_i's) which enables the researcher to solve for the structural parameters (*see* IDENTIFICATION PROBLEM). When an equation is over-identified, there may be more than one reduced-form estimate for some of the structural coefficients. Thus the parameters of the structural equations are estimated "indirectly" from the estimates of the reduced-form parameters.

For example, in the system (1)–(3) above, solving for Q and P as functions of the exogenous variables only, we have

$$Q = \frac{\alpha_1\beta_2 - \alpha_2\beta_1}{\beta_2 - \alpha_2} + \frac{\alpha_3\beta_2}{\beta_2 - \alpha_2} \times I$$

$$- \frac{\alpha_2\beta_3}{\beta_2 - \alpha_2} \times C + \text{error term}, \quad (6)$$

$$P = \frac{\alpha_1 - \beta_1}{\beta_2 - \alpha_2} + \frac{\alpha_3}{\beta_2 - \alpha_2} \times I$$

$$- \frac{\beta_3}{\beta_2 - \alpha_2} \times C + \text{error term}, \quad (7)$$

which means that

$$\pi_1 = \frac{\alpha_1\beta_2 - \alpha_2\beta_1}{\beta_2 - \alpha_2}, \quad \pi_2 = \frac{\alpha_3\beta_2}{\beta_2 - \alpha_2},$$

$$\pi_3 = \frac{\alpha_2\beta_3}{\beta_2 - \alpha_2}, \quad (8)$$

and so on. We can solve for the structural parameters using the reduced-form estimates by matching the terms in equations (6) and (7) with those in equations (4) and (5). Thus the "indirect" estimates are

$$\hat{\alpha}_1 = \hat{\pi}_1 - \hat{\alpha}_2\hat{\pi}_4 \quad \text{and} \quad \hat{\alpha}_2 = \frac{\hat{\pi}_3}{\hat{\pi}_6}, \quad \text{etc.}$$

and so on. The indirect least squares method is not widely employed in research but it is useful in demonstrating the identification problem (see Maddala (1992) and Greene (1993) for additional information).

Instrumental Variables and Two-stage Least Squares

The instrumental variables method and two-stage least squares are "limited information" estimation techniques and are more frequently employed to avoid simultaneous equations bias. They are called "limited information" methods because each equation in the system is estimated separately. Full-information methods estimate the entire system of equations and allow interaction between the equations, but are beyond the scope of this entry.

Since the problem in estimating demand or supply is the correlation between one of the regressors (price) and the error term, one

solution is to replace the endogenous variable (price) with a substitute variable which is highly correlated with it, but is not correlated with the error term. The demand or supply equations are then estimated using the substitute variable. This is the essence of the instrumental variables and two-stage least squares techniques.

Given the system of equations (1)–(3), the income and resource cost variables, I and C, are exogenous (uncorrelated with the error term) and should be highly correlated with price because the market price will change whenever these variables change. So I and C are both candidates to serve as instruments. Thus to construct a substitute variable for price in the demand curve, the researcher should regress price on the exogenous variable, C. The resulting fitted values for price, $\hat{P}$, from that regression will then replace price in the original demand curve. These fitted values will be highly correlated with the original price variable but they will also be uncorrelated with the error term in the demand equation by construction. A similar procedure can be used to estimate the supply curve, equation (2) above, using income as the instrument. The demand or supply curve can then be estimated by regressing quantity on the fitted price variable and the exogenous variables. Thus the researcher estimates:

$$Q_t^d = \alpha_1 + \alpha_2\hat{P} + \alpha_3 I + \varepsilon_t^d, \quad (9)$$

$$Q_t^s = \beta_1 + \beta_2\hat{P} + \beta_3 C + \varepsilon_t^s. \quad (10)$$

Although this regression with fitted values is not the same as the original structural model (1) and (2), the structural parameters will be consistently estimated in large samples using this technique. By contrast, estimates from a linear regression will be biased no matter how large the sample is (see Greene, 1993). A number of variables could be used as instruments when an equation is over-identified and the instrumental variable method offers little guidance in such cases.

The two-stage least squares technique also uses instrumental variables for exactly and over-identified equations. However, with two-stage least squares *all* of the exogenous and predetermined variables in the model are used as instruments in the first stage of the regression. The structural parameters are then estimated in the second-stage regression. This procedure is available in most statistical and econometric software programs, and weights each instrument optimally. This can be important when estimating over-identified equations in which several instrumental variables could be used.

Two studies which employed the instrumental variables and two-stage least squares methods to estimate the demand for cigarettes in the U.S.A. were Bishop Yoo (1985) and McAuliffe (1988). In contrast with previous studies which used biased linear regression methods, these authors found that the demand for cigarettes was inelastic with respect to price (see ELASTICITY) and that the 1964 Surgeon General's report on the negative health effects from smoking significantly lowered the demand for cigarettes. However, the 1971 ban on broadcast advertising of cigarettes on radio and television in the U.S.A. had no independent statistical effect.

Bibliography

Bishop, J. A. Yoo, J. H. (1985). Health scare, excise taxes and advertising ban in the cigarette demand and supply. *Southern Economic Journal*, 52, 402–11.

Greene, W. H. (1993). *Econometric analysis* (2nd edn). New York: Macmillan.

Maddala, G. S. (1992). *Introduction to econometrics* (2nd edn). New York: Macmillan.

McAuliffe, R. E. (1988). The FTC and the effectiveness of cigarette advertising regulations. *Journal of Public Policy and Marketing*, 7, 49–64.

ROBERT E. MCAULIFFE

excess capacity   A firm operates with excess capacity when its output is below the level allowed by its invested capacity, i.e. below the level at which all its production inputs are fully employed. Despite the costs involved in this practice (primarily reflecting the opportunity cost of the inputs not utilized), a firm may maintain excess capacity for several reasons. These reasons include demand fluctuations over time (due to either seasonality or the business cycle), and ECONOMIES OF SCALE when demand grows over time. Excess capacity may also be used as a strategic barrier to entry (see BARRIERS TO ENTRY); see Salop (1979). The argument is

that excess capacity makes it less costly for an incumbent firm to increase sales and, thus, increases the credibility of "aggressive" behavior (such as price cutting) after entry occurs. The potential entrants recognize this prospect, and thus entry is deterred (see CREDIBLE STRATEGIES).

Excess capacity has been also studied in the context of MONOPOLISTIC COMPETITION, introduced by Chamberlin (1933). The basic question explored there is whether free entry yields too many firms from a social viewpoint or if firms operate at too low a rate of output to exhaust economies of scale. Chamberlin argued that firms in monopolistically competitive markets would not operate at the minimum of their average cost curve and therefore excess capacity existed in these markets. This issue has been further explored in more recent research; see Dixit and Stiglitz (1977).

Bibliography

Chamberlin, E. (1933). *The Theory of Monopolistic Competition*. Cambridge, MA: Harvard University Press.

Dixit, A. Stiglitz, J. (1977). Monopolistic competition and optimum product diversity. *American Economic Review*, 67, 297–308.

Salop, S. (1979). Strategic entry deterrence. *American Economic Review*, 69, 335–8.

NIKOLAOS VETTAS

exit   Firms exit an industry when they cease production, either voluntarily or through forced BANKRUPTCY proceedings. Exit may occur because an industry is declining or because of intensified competition between existing firms in the industry that forces some firms out of the market. In their study using US Census of Manufacturers' data over the period from 1963 to 1982, Dunne, Roberts and Samuelson (1988) found that industries with high rates of ENTRY also had high rates of exit. This suggests that industry-specific factors may influence both types of behavior. The large numbers of firms entering and exiting manufacturing indicate significant activity and turnover in this sector. Those firms exiting an industry tended to be smaller on average than existing firms and, despite their large number, also tended to account for a small percentage of market output.

Ghemawat and Nalebuff (1985) developed a theoretical model of exit as a strategic game between firms in a market. Given that declining market demand will force reductions in an industry's productive capacity, they questioned whether small firms would be the first to exit or larger firms. When the firms had identical costs, the larger firms were predicted to leave the industry first because the smaller firm could operate profitably at lower output levels for a longer period of time relative to a large firm. Therefore, if both firms know that industry sales will decline, the small firm can wait for the large firm to exit first because the smaller firm can hold out longer knowing that it will be more profitable in a declining industry than the larger firm. Lieberman (1990) called this prediction the "stakeout hypothesis." If the larger firm enjoyed cost advantages over the smaller firm, perhaps through ECONOMIES OF SCALE, this conclusion could be reversed. The interesting prediction from this model was that market concentration would decrease as the market declined.

This theoretical conclusion was later qualified by Whinston (1988) and Londregan (1990). Whinston argued that if a large firm were a multiplant producer, it could reduce its capacity by closing plants without necessarily exiting the industry. From his results, Whinston shows that no general predictions about the order of firm exit can be made when there are multiplant firms since the pattern of exit depends upon the specific characteristics of the industry. He also showed that the exits may not be best from society's perspective: the more efficient firms may exit first and/or the more efficient plants may be shut down first, leaving the market to the less efficient producers. This less efficient outcome could arise because the more efficient firms or plants might be those in the industry that are larger. Since they need more sales to be profitable (relative to smaller firms or plants), they cannot hold out against smaller firms in a declining market because the smaller firms will ultimately be more profitable as industry output falls. Thus the smaller firms can afford to wait and knowing this, the larger firms will choose to exit first. Londregan (1990) showed that when

firms compete over the INDUSTRY LIFE CYCLE and can re-enter a market if they choose, high costs of entry act as a barrier to exit. Once a firm has incurred the startup costs necessary to enter the industry, it is less willing to exit the industry (and possibly have to incur the startup costs again). These entry costs can create advantages for less efficient producers who can preempt the market and keep more efficient firms from entering.

Lieberman (1990) tested the exit models to determine whether large firms were at a disadvantage when markets for particular products declined in the chemical industry. In his sample of declining products, output declined 42 percent on average from the industry production (or capacity) peak, while the number of producers fell 32 percent. The pattern of exit from the industry was consistent with the "shakeout" hypothesis in that smaller firms were much more likely to fail and exit the industry. However, the "stakeout" hypothesis of Ghemawat and Nalebuff (as amended by Whinston) was also supported because when there were steep declines in industry capacity, larger firms tended to reduce their capacity by a greater proportion relative to small firms and, in this respect, larger firms were at a disadvantage when industry demand fell. Lieberman suggests that exit patterns are affected by two offsetting forces: economies of scale which create advantages for larger firms and increase their likelihood of survival versus the strategic liability of being a large firm in competition with smaller firms when the market declines.

see also **declining industry**

Bibliography

Dunne, T., Roberts, M. J. Samuelson, L. (1988). Patterns of entry and exit in U.S. manufacturing industries. *The Rand Journal of Economics*, 19, 495–515.

Ghemawat, P. Nalebuff, B. (1985). Exit. *The Rand Journal of Economics*, 16, 184–94.

Lieberman, M. B. (1990). Exit from declining industries: "shakeout" or "stakeout"?. *The Rand Journal of Economics*, 21, 538–54.

Londregan, J. (1990). Entry and exit over the industry life cycle. *The Rand Journal of Economics*, 21, 446–58.

Whinston, M. D. (1988). Exit with multiplant firms. *The Rand Journal of Economics*, 19, 568–88.

ROBERT E. MCAULIFFE

expected present value   Future cash flows are sometimes known with certainty, for example if they are coming from a portfolio of government bonds. More often, however, there is some uncertainty around exactly what the future cash flows will be. The future cash flows from an investment during the next three years might be $100 each year, but could be lower or higher, depending on how future events develop. The uncertainty can be described in terms of probability distributions, which could be discrete or continuous. For example, there might be a probability of 0.8 that the cash flow for year one will fall between $90 and $110. The probabilities might be symmetric around the most likely outcome, or they might be skewed. Whether the probabilities are symmetric or skewed, the expected value of each year's cash flow can be computed. This is done by assigning a probability to each possible amount of cash flow that might occur, then proceeding to multiply each outcome by its probability of occurring and adding the products together.

In mathematical terms for the discrete case:

$$\text{Expected Cash Flow} = \sum_j x_i p(x_i)$$

where x_i represents each possible cash flow outcome, $p(x)$ is the density function associated with the outcomes and the summation is over all i outcomes.

In the continuous case, the expected cash flow is expressed as:

$$\text{Expected Cash Flow} = \int x f(x) dx$$

where x is the random variable describing future cash flows and $f(x)$ is the corresponding density function.

With the expected future cash flows computed, it is possible to compute expected present value. Each expected future cash flow is discounted, giving its present value. The present values of all the expected future cash flows are summed, yielding the total expected present value. If the initial investment is subtracted from the total expected present value, the resulting number is called expected net present value.

In mathematical terms, for the discrete case:

$$\text{Expected Present Value} =$$

$$\sum_j \left(\sum_i x_i p(x_i) \right) (i + r)^{-j}$$

where j are the time periods and the summation is over all outcomes, i.

In the continuous case:

$$\text{Expected Present Value} =$$

$$\int \int e^{-rt} x f(x) dx dt$$

where t represents the continuous passage of time.

The naive decision rule is that a firm should approve every investment project that offers a positive expected net present value. This rule ignores RISK AVERSION (Friedman and Savage, 1948), and it also excludes the necessity of scrutinizing the distribution of the expected cash flows. An investment with a positive expected net present value has a measurable probability of giving a negative return. It is an essential part of the analysis to compute the probability that the return on investment will be negative. Business managers also calculate the probability that the return on investment will be lower than some minimum acceptable amount. They express this as a rate of return and call it the *hurdle rate*. If each of the annual cash flows comes out in the lower tail of its probability distribution, the final outcome of the investment will be worse than its expected present value.

Bibliography

Brigham, E. F. Gapenski, L. C. (1993). *Intermediate Financial Management*. New York: Dryden.

Friedman, M. Savage L.J. (1948). The utility analysis of choices involving risk. *Journal of Political Economy*, 56, 279–304.

JOHN EDMUNDS AND ROBERTO BONIFAZ

expected value   The mean, or expected value, is a measure of central tendency for a random variable and it is one of the characteristics of probability distributions; the VARIANCE is another common characteristic. If the random variable, X is continuous and has specific values denoted by x, and the probability distribution of the values of X is given by $f(x)$, then the expected value of X, E(X), is calculated as

$$E(X) = \int_x xf(x)dx \qquad (1)$$

where $\int$ is the integral over the complete range of *possible* values for X; see Greene (1993) or Kmenta (1986). When the random variable X is discrete, the expected value is calculated as

$$E(X) = \sum_x xf(x) \qquad (2)$$

where $\sum_x$ indicates the summation is over all possible values of x.

In business analysis, managers work with observed sample data and not necessarily with formal probability distributions. The sample mean, denoted $\overline{X}$ can then be calculated for the observed values of the variable of interest. For example, a firm may want to calculate its average weekly sales in the last quarter from weekly data. In this case, there are twelve weekly observations and the sample mean would be calculated by simply summing the weekly sales figures and dividing by twelve. If a manager randomly selected any single week from the twelve, any single week's sales would be equally likely, so the probability of any specific week's sales being selected would be one-twelfth and this is the value $f(x)$ would take in the summation in equation (2) above. The summation in equation (2) would then be:

$$\overline{S} = \sum_{i=1}^{12} S_i \times \frac{1}{12} = \frac{1}{12} \sum_{i=1}^{12} S_i \qquad (2)$$

where S is the level of sales in each week. It should be noted that the sample mean of sales calculated above may not equal any of the sales figures which occurred but rather it represents the likely value for weekly sales if the company were to have several quarters like the last. Suppose, for example, that sales were 1 million units for the first six weeks of the quarter and 2 million units for the second six weeks. The mean value of sales would then be 1.5 million units, a value which did not occur during the sample period.

For forecasting, a manager will need to assign probabilities based on her best estimate of the likely outcomes since past data will not be available or may not apply. In these cases, it is crucial to perform sensitivity analysis to determine how sensitive the conclusions or forecasts are to changes in the underlying assumptions (or probabilities).

Bibliography

Douglas, E. J. (1992). *Managerial Economics*. 4th edn, Englewood Cliffs, NJ: Prentice-Hall.

Greene, W. H. (1993). *Econometric Analysis*. 2nd edn, New York: Macmillan.

Kmenta, J. (1986). *Elements of Econometrics*. 2nd edn, New York: Macmillan.

ROBERT E. MCAULIFFE

experience goods Experience goods are those products which must be consumed or used by consumers before their quality can be determined, such as autos, food and software. Nelson (1970, 1974) distinguished between these products and SEARCH GOODS and he suggested that the information provided by ADVERTISING would depend upon whether the products were search goods or experience goods. According to Nelson, advertising for experience goods would rely on imagery more than factual information and would advertise proportionately more often in broadcast media rather than print media. Furthermore, since consumers cannot determine the quality of experience goods without purchasing them and advertising cannot convey much direct information about the product, Nelson argued that it is the *volume* of advertising which conveys information about product quality to consumers. Firms that sell higher quality goods or which are more efficient in producing the good have greater incentives to advertise because the profits from additional sales will be greater. Higher quality firms will benefit from repeat purchases in the future if consumers try their products and more efficient firms will earn a greater profit per unit sold than other firms which are less efficient or produce lower quality products. Therefore Nelson claimed that firms which produce higher quality experience goods have greater incentives to advertise and as they do so, consumers will use information about the volume of advertising to infer product quality.

Nelson's model offers several hypotheses: experience goods will be advertised more than search goods; experience goods are likely to be advertised in media which provide "soft" information rather than the "hard" factual information provided for search goods; products which are purchased frequently will be advertised more than products which are purchased less frequently; and durable goods will be advertised less than nondurable goods (whether they are search or experience goods) because they are purchased less frequently. Nelson found search products tended to be advertised more frequently in newspapers and magazines than experience goods. In addition, advertising in local media should provide more relevant information than advertising in national media so experience goods should have a greater proportion of their advertising expenditures in national media, a prediction which was also supported by his data. Nelson (1974) also found a higher advertising–sales ratio for nondurable goods than for durable goods. Ferguson (1974) observed that the distinction between "search" and experience goods can be somewhat arbitrary, yet the distinction is crucial to his theory and tests. Ehrlich and Fisher (1982) extended the model and a survey and tests of the advertising-profitability issue can be found in McAuliffe (1987). Managers can use Nelson's categories to guide their advertising decisions with respect to the volume, content and appropriate media for their products.

Bibliography

Ehrlich, I. Fisher, L. (1982). The derived demand for advertising: a theoretical and empirical investigation. *American Economic Review*, 72, 366–88.

Ferguson, J. M. (1974). *Advertising and Competition: Theory, Measurement, Fact.* Cambridge, MA: Ballinger.

McAuliffe, R. E. (1987). *Advertising, Competition, and Public Policy: Theories and New Evidence.* Lexington, MA: DC Heath.

Nelson, P. (1970). Information and consumer behavior. *Journal of Political Economy*, 78, 311–29.

Nelson, P. (1974). Advertising as information. *Journal of Political Economy*, 81, 729–54.

ROBERT E. McAULIFFE

exponential smoothing models In analyzing TIMES SERIES DATA, exponential smoothing models provide a relatively simple approach. Although the performance of these models is often inferior to more sophisticated econometric techniques, they are quite popular with managers since they have modest data requirements and are simple to implement. The basic idea of exponential smoothing is to remove the irregular component of a time series so that the trend and cyclical components can be better identified.

The simple exponential smoothing model may be derived from the moving average forecasting model (*see* TIME SERIES FORECASTING MODELS). In the moving average model, future values of a time series are estimated as a function of past values. In the exponential smoothing model, each observation of a times series is replaced with a weighted average of its current and past values. The weights on the past values decay exponentially so that observations in the distant past have less influence than more recent observations. Specifically, let y_t and y_t^* denote the actual and smoothed values of the time series. Then the time series may be smoothed according to the following rule:

$$y_t^* = \alpha y_t + \alpha(1 - \alpha) \times y_{t-1} +$$

$$\alpha(1 - \alpha)^2 \times y_{t-2} + \alpha(1 - \alpha)^3 \times y_{t-3} + \ldots$$

It should be noted that in the above equation, the weights on the past values decay exponentially. Further, it can be shown that the weights sum to unity and thus preserve the magnitude of the actual series. By selecting an appropriate α, the manager can control how much weight is placed on current versus past values of the series. If α equals 1, then only the current value of the series matters. If α is less than 1, then past values of the series take on higher weights.

One problem with the above formulation is that it requires information on the entire history of the series. This may be undesirable since it requires considerable computation as well as a burden of storing a large data set. This requirement may be relaxed with an alternative, but equivalent, formulation of the model. Lagging the above equation by one period and multiplying through by $(1 - \alpha)$ we get:

$$(1 - \alpha)y_{t-1}^* = \alpha(1 - \alpha) \times y_{t-1} +$$

$$\alpha(1 - \alpha)^2 \times y_{t-2} + \alpha(1 - \alpha)^3 \times y_{t-3} +$$

$$\alpha(1 - \alpha)^4 \times y_{t-4} + \ldots$$

Subtracting the latter equation from the former and rearranging gives:

$$y_t^* = \alpha y_t + (1 - \alpha) \times y_{t-1}^*.$$

Thus, the current value of the series to be smoothed may be rewritten as a weighted average of the current value and the smoothed value from last period. As such, the computational and data storage requirements become trivial.

One criticism of the above technique is that if there is a trend in the data, smoothed values may consistently lag behind actual values. This weakness is overcome by double exponential smoothing models such as those suggested by Brown or Holt. While the Brown method is simpler in that it requires estimating only one parameter, the Holt method may be preferred since it smooths the trend values separately. Finally, if the series exhibits seasonality, a triple exponential smoothing model, such as Winter's three-parameter method, is appropriate. For a critical survey of these extensions, the reader is referred to Makridakis, Wheelwright and McGee (1983) and the citations contained therein.

Bibliography

Makridakis, Wheelwright & McGee (1983).

ROGER TUTTEROW

externalities Externalities are the costs or benefits from activities engaged in by one set of economic agents that affect other economic agents who are not directly engaged in the activity. For example, the noise from aircraft overhead diminishes the utility (*see* TOTAL UTILITY) or happiness of individuals living in areas surrounding an airport. The diminished utility resulting from noisy aircraft is an external cost of production. Furthermore, external costs or benefits may occur in either the production or consumption of a good or both. An example of an external benefit in consumption is the pleasure enjoyed by the neighbors of an individual who plants a flower bed. Generally goods or activities with external benefits are called public goods (*see* PUBLIC-GOODS PROBLEM) and the term externality typically refers to an external cost. Other common examples of externalities are industrial pollution, automobile emissions, and traffic congestion.

External costs or benefits prevent markets from achieving an efficient allocation of resources (*see* EFFICIENCY). The market will allocate too many resources to the production of goods with external costs and too few to the production of goods with external benefits. For example, ticket prices will not equal the true MARGINAL COST of production if airlines do not take into account the harm imposed on others by their noisy aircraft. Consequently, more resources will be devoted to air travel than in an efficient allocation.

Externalities may require a public sector response in order to remedy the misallocation of resources. There are three tools for controlling externalities: regulation, property rights, and taxes. Frequently, governments issue extensive regulations requiring industry to reduce the external costs associated with certain activities. An important instance of the federal government using regulation to control an externality is the automobile emission standards contained in the Clean Air Act.

Command and control type regulation lacks the necessary flexibility for individuals and companies to find more efficient methods of reducing external costs. But, government can make companies internalize external costs in their decision-making by properly establishing and enforcing property rights (*see* COASE THEOREM). For example, the government could issue vouchers allowing the holder to pollute a given amount. Companies that can reduce emissions relatively inexpensively could sell their vouchers to companies for whom it is more costly to reduce emissions. In this manner, government could achieve the desired reduction in pollution with lower OPPORTUNITY COSTS to society than under a command and control regime.

Furthermore, tradeable vouchers create incentives for firms to strive continuously to lower the cost of reducing pollution. Alternatively, the government could levy taxes on companies equal to the external costs associated with their activities. Again, firms would internalize the externalities and are thereby motivated to reduce the externality in the most cost effective manner.

Bibliography

Baumol, W. J. (1972). On taxation and the control of externalities. *American Economic Review*, **62**, 307–22.

DeSerpa, A. (1978). Congestion, pollution, and impure public goods. *Public Finance*, **33**, 68–83.

Oates, W. E. (1983). The regulation of externalities: efficient behavior by sources and victims. *Public Finance*, **38**, 362–75.

MARK RIDER

F

factor prices Factor prices are the costs (i.e. prices) associated with inputs (i.e. factors) used in production. The primary factors of production include land, labor, and capital. In competitive markets, the price for each of these factors depends on the EQUILIBRIUM between supply and demand. Total demand for a particular factor is determined by the combination of all individual firms' demands for that factor, which in turn are determined by each firm's PROFIT MAXIMIZATION decisions. The determination of total supply is factor specific; for example, the supply of land is relatively fixed, whereas the supply of labor depends on each individual's willingness to work (*see* UTILITY MAXIMIZATION).

The equilibrium pricing of factors serves to allocate resources efficiently (*see* EFFICIENCY). In markets where land is scarce and labor plentiful, the price of land is high, and that of labor is low; whereas in markets where land is plentiful and labor scarce, the reverse is true. At the international level, however, if free trade exists, and if several restrictive assumptions are fulfilled, differences in factor prices across countries hypothetically equalize. This theory is based on the Heckscher Ohlin approach to international trade, and is called factor price equalization.

Bibliography

Albrecht, W. P. (1983). *Economics*. 3rd edn, Englewood Cliffs, NJ: Prentice-Hall.
Samuelson, P. A.   Nordhaus, W. D. (1985). *Economics*. 12th edn, New York: McGraw-Hill.
Varian, H. R. (1992). *Microeconomic Analysis*. 3rd edn, New York: Norton.

LAURA POWER

factor productivity Factor productivity is defined as the output per unit of factor input. The primary factors of production include labor, land, and capital. At the micro level, factor productivities depend on each firm's optimal input combination, which is determined by its PROFIT MAXIMIZATION decision. The level of output associated with the optimal choice of inputs is determined by the production function (*see* PRODUCTION FUNCTIONS), and the ratios of this output to each input are the factor productivities for the firm.

In markets where the price of labor is high relative to that of capital, firms will tend to employ more capital (i.e. will choose high capital-labor ratios), relative to markets in which the price of labor is low relative to that of capital. Firms with such high capital to labor ratios are called capital intensive firms, while firms with high labor to capital ratios are called labor intensive firms. Capital intensive firms have high output per unit of labor input (labor productivity) relative to labor intensive firms.

see also **factor prices; marginal product; efficiency**

Bibliography

Albrecht, W. P. (1983). *Economics*. 3rd edn, Englewood Cliffs, NJ: Prentice-Hall.
Samuelson, P. A.   Nordhaus, W. D. (1985). *Economics*. 12th edn, New York: McGraw-Hill.
Varian, H. R. (1992). *Microeconomic Analysis*. 3rd edn, New York: Norton.

LAURA POWER

Federal Trade Commission Act This is the third principal US antitrust statute (*see* SHERMAN ACT; CLAYTON ACT). This statute created the Federal Trade Commission (FTC) and empowered it to enforce the Clayton and FTC Acts. The primary section of the FTC Act, Section 5, proscribes "unfair methods of competition" and "unfair or deceptive acts or practices in or affecting commerce." This Act may be seen as a pro-active move by the government to create a policing agency empowered to identify and restrict anticompetitive conduct which could not be foreseen by the US Congress or which did not properly fall under the scope of the Sherman or Clayton Acts. Here the Commission's activities range from investigating instances of deceptive ADVERTISING to promulgating trade regulation rules concerning products or industry activities.

Unlike the Antitrust Division of the Department of Justice, which is part of the executive branch of government, the FTC is a largely independent commission made up of five individuals who are appointed for seven-year terms which are staggered to not coincide with national political elections. By giving the Commission's trade regulation rules the full force of law, by enabling it to issue cease-and-desist orders, and by allowing it (in some instances) to require corrective action (e.g. for deceptive advertising), the Act yields considerable power to the FTC to enforce the law. The FTC maintains its own quasi-judicial system, under which an administrative law judge may hand down an initial decision. Any such decision though is subject to appeal to the commissioners, and ultimately to the Federal courts.

As is the case in other antitrust statutes, interpretation of the language used is of central importance. Here, the words "unfair" and "deceptive" have been given great attention by the enforcers of the Act. Many service industries, including automotive and TV repair, funeral services, and the optometry industry, as well as door-to-door sales activities have come under regulation by the FTC as a result of practices which have been identified as "unfair."

As Greer (1992) demonstrates, two standards have been established for the meaning of the term "deceptive." Over the past half century the courts, and for the most part the Commission itself, have required that an act need only to have the *capacity* or *tendency* to deceive a *substantial number* of buyers in some *material*

respect to be declared a violation. Thus, the actual deception, of a buyer, and deliberate intent to deceive, by the seller, need not be proven. During the 1980s the Commission altered its standard by requiring that the action under consideration be *likely* to deceive *reasonable* consumers and achieve *detrimental results* prior to its being declared to be in violation of the law. As Greer further points out, this new standard has not taken hold in the courts nor has it been accepted by individual states, which also have statutes similar to the FTC Act.

Bibliography

Greer, D. (1992). *Industrial Organization and Public Policy*. 3rd edn, New York: Macmillan.

Howard, M. (1983). *Antitrust and Trade Regulation*. Englewood Cliffs, NJ: Prentice-Hall.

Martin, S. (1994). *Industrial Economics*. 2nd edn, New York: Macmillan.

GILBERT BECKER

firm financial structure Business firms acquire resources from lenders, from stockholders, and from other stakeholders including suppliers and employees. By convention, lenders are usually thought to include banks and bondholders, who lend money to the firm; stockholders are the owners of the capital which is permanently invested in the firm. Both are distinguished from trade creditors, employees and other stakeholders who put resources into the firm in the form of merchandise or labor. So the resources the firm uses are classified in three broad categories according to the nature of the resources and terms on which they are placed: equity funds, debt, and inputs which are not in monetary form, e.g. merchandise and labor. The firm's financial structure is the term given to describe the specific composition of these inputs that a firm is using. For example, a firm may be financed in the following way:

Balance Sheet			
Assets		Liabilities and Stockholders' Equity	
Liquid	10	Accounts Payable	20
Accounts Receivable	20	Accrued Wages	10
Inventory	20	Bank Loan Payable	50
Fixed Assets	50	Stockholders' Equity	20
Total	100	Total	100

This firm's financial structure is 50 percent debt, 20 percent equity, and 30 percent other liabilities. Some writers make a distinction between the terms financial structure and capital structure. Financial structure refers to all the resources the firm uses, and is expressed in terms of proportions of the entire amount. Capital structure refers to the mix of resources that come from lenders and stockholders only (*see* CAPITAL MARKETS). Trade creditors, employees and accrued taxes are not taken into account in discussing capital structure, because the resources that come from those sources arise in the routine course of business, and are not the result of financing activities that the firm arranges with its investment bankers to access the capital markets.

Each of the three groups (equity funds, debt and inputs) has different incentives regarding how they would prefer the firm to be managed or how it should be handled in BANKRUPTCY proceedings. These differences in incentives may lead to differences in the management of the firm. For example, workers at a plant on the verge of bankruptcy would prefer that pension obligations receive first priority which might put them at odds with the stockholders or trade creditors. On the other hand, trade creditors might prefer the immediate liquidation of the firm if they thought it likely they would receive full payment, but this short-term focus might conflict with the interests of the firm's stockholders and workers; see Milgrom and Roberts (1992).

Bibliography

Brigham, E. F. Gapenski, L. C. (1993). Intermediate Financial Management. New York: Dryden.

Milgrom, P. Roberts, J. (1992). *Economics, Organization and Management.* Englewood Cliffs, NJ: Prentice-Hall.

JOHN EDMUNDS AND ROBERTO BONIFAZ

first-mover advantages A firm has first-mover advantages when it can act before its rivals and achieve a relatively stronger competitive position. For example, the first firm to introduce a new product may have lower marketing costs because it has no competition or it may be able to accumulate production volume to lower costs along its LEARNING CURVE. Porter (1980) suggests that early entry into an emerging industry can be an appropriate strategic choice when the early firm can develop a reputation in the market, take advantage of the learning curve, or establish brand loyalty among consumers. At the same time, early entry can mean higher risks when the costs of establishing the market are high or when rapid technical advances may make the product obsolete.

Schmalensee (1982) provided a theoretical model showing that the first brand to satisfy consumers in a new market could establish the standard against which all other products were measured and this conferred lasting advantages to those brands. Glazer (1985) examined entry into the Iowa newspaper markets and found that first entrants into a successful market were more likely to survive than second entrants, but when all markets were considered (including those where the first entrant failed) the first firms were not more likely to survive than later entrants. Of course, early entry can be risky and Sutton (1991) argued that being first did not necessarily confer advantages, so markets must be evaluated on a case by case basis. Nevertheless he found evidence of first-mover advantages in the US and UK prepared soups industry, the European margarine market and in the European soft drink market.

Established firms in an industry have first-mover advantages relative to potential entrants which they can use strategically. Existing firms may over-invest in capacity to deter entry, or place the entrant at a relative disadvantage, or they may pursue a PRODUCT PROLIFERATION strategy and crowd the product space; see Tirole (1988). An existing monopolist also has a greater incentive to introduce new products or add to capacity in a growing market before an entrant appears, since monopoly profits will be higher than the duopoly profits a potential entrant might expect. This is known as a market pre-emption strategy; see Tirole (1988).

Bibliography

Glazer, A. (1985). The advantages of being first. *American Economic Review*, 75, 473–80.

Porter, M. E. (1980). *Competitive Strategy.* New York: Free Press.

Schmalensee, R. (1982). Product differentiation advantages of pioneering brands. *American Economic Review*, 72, 349–65.

Sutton, J. (1991). *Sunk Costs and Market Structure.* Cambridge, MA: MIT.

Tirole, J. (1988). *The Theory of Industrial Organization.* Cambridge, MA: MIT.

ROBERT E. MCAULIFFE

fixed costs   Fixed costs are defined to be those costs which are independent of the level of output in the SHORT RUN. As such, these costs often are incurred prior to the actual production of the good in question. Fixed costs include, but are not limited to, the following:

(1) the cost of CAPITAL goods (e.g. buildings, machinery),
(2) the cost of land,
(3) property taxes, and
(4) the cost of various types of insurance.

The total dollar expenditures for any or all of the above costs may change over time, but nonetheless do not vary with the number of units produced on a daily or monthly basis. As such, each of these costs is classified as fixed. Some payments to employees, notably workers or managers who receive a fixed salary which is not tied to production levels, are also fixed costs. In contrast, hourly wages, energy costs and materials costs vary directly with the level of production and are classified as **variable costs**. The term **overhead costs** is often used by managers, but this term holds varying meanings for different managers who sometimes mix fixed and variable costs under this heading.

The importance to managers of the distinction between fixed costs and those which are variable is that the former costs should not be included in the decision as to the proper level of production which a firm should establish in the short run. The rule for PROFIT MAXIMIZATION requires that the firm equate its MARGINAL REVENUE and MARGINAL COST of production in order to find an ideal output. Since the extra cost of producing additional units of output is not influenced by the firm's fixed costs, these fixed costs should not be considered in this decision. Of course, since fixed costs are part of the firm's TOTAL COSTS they will help to

determine the overall level of profits which the firm achieves.

The level of fixed costs may also play a role in determining ENTRY into and EXIT from an industry. Very high fixed costs may deter entry (*see* BARRIERS TO ENTRY). In addition, some fixed costs may not be recoverable by a firm which fails prior to the depreciation of its fixed assets. These fixed costs, classified as SUNK COSTS, may also influence entry and exit as they affect the level of risk facing the owners of the firm.

Bibliography

Hyman, D. (1993). *Modern Microeconomics Analysis and Application.* 3rd edn, Boston: Irwin.

GILBERT BECKER

fragmented industries   Porter (1980) defined a fragmented industry as one comprised of many small firms where the concentration ratio of the four largest firms was 40 percent or less. No firm in such an industry has a significant market share and so there are no "dominant players" which can exert a strong influence on the industry. There are several economic forces at work which can cause a MARKET STRUCTURE to be fragmented and these are primarily cost conditions and demand.

An industry cannot be fragmented when there are significant ECONOMIES OF SCALE in production, or BARRIERS TO ENTRY because these factors lead to market structures which are highly concentrated. Porter also identifies high inventory costs or variable sales as contributing factors since they make it difficult to produce in high volumes to lower costs or invest in capacity which might reduce costs. High transportation costs will also tend to reduce the MINIMUM EFFICIENT SCALE plant and will create isolated geographic markets. Products and services which are highly customized for individual customers do not lend themselves to economies of scale, so the nature of the product plays a role in determining industry structure; see Caves and Williamson (1985).

Consumer preferences on the demand side of the market may also cause an industry to be fragmented. If consumers prefer products which are customized or if they have very diverse tastes, then it will be difficult for any brand to acquire a sizable market share; see Tirole (1988). Diverse consumer tastes are not sufficient for a fragmented industry however, because firms could offer multiple brands (a product line) to increase sales and market share. Additional forces must be at work to cause a fragmented structure, such as DISECONOMIES OF SCALE or the absence of ECONOMIES OF SCOPE. Porter suggests that rapid product and style changes could have these effects and place larger firms at a disadvantage relative to smaller, quicker firms. Finally, an industry structure may be fragmented because the industry is in the early stages of its life cycle, and will become more concentrated as standards emerge (*see* INDUSTRY LIFE CYCLE).

Bibliography

Caves, R. E. Williamson, P. J. (1985). What is product differentiation, really? *Journal of Industrial Economics*, **34**, 113–32.

Porter, M. E. (1980). *Competitive Strategy*. New York: Free Press.

Tirole, J. (1988). *The Theory of Industrial Organization*. Cambridge, MA: MIT Press.

ROBERT E. MCAULIFFE

G

game theory The theory of games is the study of the STRATEGIC BEHAVIOR of rational agents in multiagent decision problems. The term "game" is used in reference to the interactions between a number of decision makers or "players," each one having a set of possible actions or strategies available, with outcomes or payoffs to each player depending on the actions of the other players. Because the payoff to each player depends on the actions of the rest of the players, each player behaves strategically in adopting an action. Formalization of game theory is considered to have begun with the publication of the *Theory of Games and Economic Behavior* (Von Neumann and Morgenstern, 1944) and since then, game theory has become an important analytical tool in economics and other fields.

Games can be either cooperative or noncooperative. In **cooperative games**, players pursue strategies aimed at maximizing joint payoffs, presuming that the players can negotiate agreements with COMMITMENT to playing these strategies. By contrast, in noncooperative games, agents act in their own self-interest. The difference between noncooperation and cooperation is demonstrated by the PRISONER'S DILEMMA, and the COURNOT solution, as opposed to the cartel solution, in OLIGOPOLY (*see* CARTELS). The "core" (*see* PARETO OPTIMAL ALLOCATION) is another example of a cooperative solution.

Noncooperative games can be classified as static games of complete or incomplete information, and dynamic games of complete or incomplete information. Information is complete when every player knows the payoffs of the rest of the players from the possible combinations of actions that can be chosen by the players. An example of a game with incomplete information is an auction where each agent knows the utility he will receive from obtaining the good that is being sold (*see* AUCTIONS), however the payoff that other bidders will receive from obtaining it and their willingness to pay for it may be unknown.

In static games, for example in a Cournot model, players choose their strategies once and for all, and when choosing strategies they are not informed about the strategy choices of other players. In dynamic games, players may move sequentially, or select strategies in repeated play. For instance, in the Stackelberg duopoly model, one leading firm moves first by selecting an output level, and the second firm makes an output choice having observed the leader's output. Primary EQUILIBRIUM solution concepts include *Nash equilibrium* in static games of complete information, Bayes–Nash equilibrium in static games of incomplete information, subgame-perfect equilibrium in dynamic games of complete information and perfect Bayesian equilibrium in dynamic games of incomplete information.

The Nash equilibrium was proposed by the mathematician and economist John Nash in 1950. According to this concept, a strategy profile for all players is a Nash equilibrium if no player benefits by deviating from his strategy given the strategy choice of the other players. As an example, consider the "battle of the sexes" game, where a man and a woman would like to spend the evening together, however, the woman would prefer to go to the opera and the man would prefer to go to a wrestling match. Relevant utility payoffs are given by the following matrix (the first number is the woman's payoff, the second number is the man's payoff):

	Man	
	Opera	Wrestling
Opera	2,1	0,0
Wrestling	0,0	1,2

Woman

This game has two Nash equilibria, (Opera, Opera) and (Wrestling, Wrestling), because neither one of the players benefits by deviating from his strategy, given the strategy choice of the other player. For instance, starting from the (Opera, Opera) equilibrium where the payoff is (2,1), the man would not unilaterally deviate to a wrestling match because he would then receive a zero payoff. An application of the Nash equilibrium is in the Cournot model.

The Bayes–Nash equilibrium concept expands Nash equilibrium to Bayesian games. Bayesian games analyze the strategic behavior of agents in the presence of incomplete information, and were defined and analyzed by the economist Harsanyi (1967). Harsanyi proposed a way for transforming games of incomplete information (which cannot be analyzed) to games of complete but IMPERFECT INFORMATION (which can be analyzed). The "Harsanyi transformation" amounts to the observation that although some players may be incompletely informed about the payoffs to other players from the possible strategy profiles (i.e. some player's may not know the "types" of other players), it is reasonable to assume that they have beliefs about the presence of possible types. A Bayes–Nash equilibrium is a strategy for each type of every player such that each player maximizes his expected payoff by playing this strategy, given the specified strategies for all types of the rest of the players and the player's beliefs about the types of the rest of the players. As an example, the Bayes–Nash equilibrium concept can be used to determine the equilibrium in a market with Cournot quantity competition and imperfect information, in the sense that firms do not know the precise cost structure of other firms but have beliefs about these costs.

In dynamic games of complete information, consider the Stackelberg model presented above as an example. The equilibrium in the Stackelberg model can be obtained by "backward induction." A standard Cournot *reaction function*

can be obtained by starting from the follower's problem that determines the optimal response to each possible output choice of the leader. The leader's problem is then to choose an output level that maximizes his profit, taking the reaction of the follower into account. The equilibrium obtained in this way is the unique credible Nash outcome. This outcome has the property of yielding a profit to the leader that is higher than the profit to the follower, and higher than the Cournot-profit the leader would make if the players moved simultaneously in a Cournot fashion (*see* FIRST-MOVER ADVANTAGES). There is one more candidate outcome. The follower could threaten to produce the Cournot output regardless of the leader's choice, thus forcing the leader to produce the Cournot output as well. This threat, however, is not a credible threat, for if the leader chooses the Stackelberg outcome after all, the follower cannot maximize profits unless it participates in the Stackelberg outcome (*see* CREDIBLE STRATEGIES). Credibility and backward induction were extended to games where players move simultaneously in several periods by Selten (1965) with his concept of a subgame perfect Nash equilibrium, necessitating strategies which are Nash equilibria for the entire game and every subgame of the entire game. The perfect Bayesian equilibrium concept incorporates the intuition behind subgame perfection, and extends the concept of Bayes–Nash equilibrium to dynamic games of incomplete information. For example, the perfect Bayesian equilibrium concept can be used to characterize the equilibria in a model where an incumbent firm engages in LIMIT PRICING to deter the entry of other firms that are incompletely informed about the incumbent firm's MARGINAL COST of production.

Bibliography

Friedman, J. W. (1986). *Game Theory with Applications to Economics*. New York: OUP.
Fudenberg, D. Tirole, J. (1991). *Game Theory*. Cambridge, MA: MIT.
Gibbons, R. (1992). *Game Theory for Applied Economists*. Princeton, NJ: Princeton University Press.
Harsanyi, J. (1967). Games with incomplete information played by Bayesian players Parts I, II, and III. *Management Science*, 14, 159–82, 320–34, 486–502.

Nash, J. (1950). Equilibrium points in n-person games. *Proceedings of the National Academy of Sciences*, 36, 48–9.

Rasmusen, E. (1990). *Games and Information: An Introduction to Game Theory*. Cambridge, MA: Blackwell.

Selten, R. (1965). Spieltheoretische behandlung eines oligopolmodells mit nachfrageträgheit. *Zeitschrift für Gesamte Staatswissenschaft*, 121, 301–24, 667–89.

Shubik, M. (1982). *Game Theory in the Social Sciences*. Cambridge, MA: MIT.

Von Neumann, J. Morgenstern, O. (1944). *Theory of Games and Economic Behavior*. Princeton, NJ: Princeton University Press.

THEOFANIS TSOULOUHAS

geographic market   One of the two boundaries which establish the scope of a market in an economic sense is the relevant geographic area of the market in question. Since not all markets are national in scope, it is often difficult to properly define the geographic area in which a group of rivals compete. This area, ideally defined, must be broad enough to encompass all rivals which are reasonably seen as being in competition with one another while not being so broad as to include firms which are in some sense not actual or potential competitors. Moreover, it should include all sources of supply of this product which could or do impact market outcomes, especially price.

The importance of accurately defining the geographic market lies primarily in the application of ANTITRUST POLICY. For example, Section 2 of the SHERMAN ACT deals with attempts to monopolize a market while Section 7 of the CLAYTON ACT places restrictions against mergers which lessen competition in any section of the country. The structure of a market and its degree of competition depend, in part, on the number of rivals competing with one another. Hence, the determination of whether an antitrust law violation has occurred depends in part on a proper count of the number of rivals existing in the market in question, and this requires the delineation of an appropriate geographic area to be considered.

While the courts are often guided in their determination of a relevant geographic market by legal boundaries, such as interstate differences in commercial practice laws, or topographical boundaries, such as mountains or rivers, economic analysis has also been of assistance in this effort. Elzinga and Hogarty (1973) developed the "20 percent rule" which remains to date perhaps the most practical guide. The rule holds that a reasonable boundary has been established if less than 20 percent of the product which is consumed within the area under consideration is imported from outside of that area, and less than 20 percent of the product which is produced within this same area is shipped outside of that area for consumption in a different region.

The logic here is that when the conditions of the rule hold, the great majority of the firms affecting the market supply and demand, and therefore price, have been identified. If the actual figure in the first instance exceeds 20 percent then rivals whose output may significantly impact the market price are erroneously being ignored and the geographic boundary should be expanded to include them. If the second part of the rule is being violated and a significant portion of the supply of the product is being shipped beyond the geographic area being considered, this offers another indication that suppliers are not facing transportation and distribution costs sufficiently great so as to be considered prohibitive. Here again the geographic boundary under consideration should be expanded.

While the courts have used the 20 percent rule for some time, Boyer (1979) developed the basis of a theoretically more advanced measure which recently has come to be used by the federal antitrust enforcement agencies. This method, known as SSNIP (*see* MARKET DEFINITION), can be used for both product market and geographic market definitions. The method involves examining a hypothetical monopolist in the geographic area in question and its ability to raise prices above the current level. It is currently part of the 1992 merger guidelines established by the government, but has not, as yet, been widely accepted by the courts (*see* MARKET DEFINITION; MERGER GUIDELINES, 1992).

see also **Clayton Act; Sherman Act**

Bibliography

Boyer, K. (1979). Industry boundaries. Calvani, T. Siegfried, J. *Economic Analysis and Antitrust Law.* Boston: Little, Brown.

Elzinga, K. Hogarty, T. (1973). The problem of geographic market delineation in antimerger suits. *Antitrust Bulletin*, **45**, 45–81.

Greer, D. (1992). *Industrial Organization and Public Policy.* 3rd edn, New York: Macmillan.

Howard, M. (1983). *Antitrust and Trade Regulation.* Englewood Cliffs, NJ: Prentice-Hall.

GILBERT BECKER

gross domestic product Gross domestic product (GDP) is a measure of a country's output and is the current dollar value of all final goods and services produced for the market by those resources within the country's borders per period of time. GDP does not include the DEPRECIATION of capital equipment used to produce output over the period. Since GDP is measured in current dollars, it may rise either because current output increased or because the general level of prices increased (INFLATION). To compensate for the effects of changes in the purchasing power of the domestic currency, a measure of general price change is used to translate current dollars into constant purchasing power (or base-year) dollars. When current dollar figures (nominal values) are adjusted by the appropriate price index, such as the GDP deflator or the consumer price index (CPI), the result is an inflation-adjusted figure, i.e. a real value. Thus when real GDP has increased, a nation has produced more output.

For example, nominal GDP in the US grew from 5.54 trillion dollars in the second quarter of 1990 to 5.58 trillion dollars in the third quarter. But, after adjusting for changes in the price level, real GDP fell from 4.917 trillion 1987 dollars to 4.906 trillion 1987 dollars, reflecting the recession that occurred during that period. Managers in industries whose products follow the business cycle, such as automobiles, housing construction and durable goods, can use GDP figures to forecast business conditions and sales.

see also **nominal income and prices; real prices**

Bibliography

Douglas, E. J. (1992). *Managerial Economics.* 4th edn, Englewood Cliffs, NJ: Prentice-Hall.

Sommers, A. T. (1985). *The U.S. Economy Demystified.* Lexington, MA: DC Heath.

ROBERT E. MCAULIFFE

—— H ——

Herfindahl-Hirschman index While a complete analysis of market structure may require information on the market share of each competitor, industrial concentration is frequently measured with a single summary index. Such indices are desirable for both econometric research and in establishing anti-trust guidelines. The Herfindahl-Hirschman index (HHI) is among the most widely accepted measures of market concentration. The index is defined as

$$HHI = \sum_{i=1}^{n} S_i^2$$

where S denotes the market share of the ith firm in an industry composed of n firms. The HHI ranges between negligible values for perfectly competitive industries and a maximum value of 1.0 for a pure monopoly.

Considerable theoretical work has related the HHI to industrial behavior. Stigler (1964) related the HHI to the pricing behavior of oligopolies. Adelman (1969) suggested that the HHI has an intuitive "numbers equivalent" interpretation in that 1/HHI is the number of equal-sized firms which will produce a given HHI. Cowling and Waterson (1976) demonstrated that the HHI may be related to profitability in industries with constant marginal cost.

Since the 1980s, the Department of Justice has utilized the HHI as a primary measure of market concentration. For the calculations used in their merger guidelines, the decimal point in the firms' market shares is ignored, thus producing a HHI which is larger by a multiple of 10,000. Accepting this modification, current guidelines specify that markets in which the HHI exceeds 1800 are said to be highly concentrated. Thus, mergers raising an HHI by more than 50 and resulting in an HHI above 1800 are likely to attract in antitrust litigation. Mergers producing an HHI between 1000 and 1800, are likely challenged only if the HHI increases in excess of 100 units. Mergers resulting in an HHI of less than 1000 are unlikely to meet objection.

Bibliography

Adelman, M. (1969). Comment on the "H" concentration measure as a numbers equivalent. *Review of Economics and Statistics*, **51**, 99–101.

Cowling, K. Waterson, M. (1976). Price–cost margins and market structure. *Economica*, **43**, 267–74.

Stigler, G. (1964). The theory of oligopoly. *Journal of Political Economy*, **72**, 44–61.

ROGER TUTTEROW

heteroskedasticity Heteroskedasticity is present when the VARIANCE of the error terms in a LINEAR REGRESSION is not identical for all observations. This violation of the homoskedastic assumption underlying the classical regression model is common in CROSS-SECTION ANALYSIS of microeconomic data where the variance of the explained variable is often correlated with the size of an explanatory variable. An example is the consumption function of a family where there is a greater variation in expenditures as family income rises.

Under heteroskedasticity, the ordinary least squares estimator is not efficient, i.e. there exist other estimators that possess a lower variance. Another implication of heteroskedasticity is that although the ordinary least squares estimator of the regression coefficient will be unbiased, the estimator of the STANDARD ERROR OF THE

COEFFICIENT will be biased. This bias causes hypothesis tests to be invalid (*see* STANDARD ERROR OF THE COEFFICIENT; T-STATISTIC).

One method of detecting heteroskedasticity is to examine the residuals plotted against particular explanatory variables. A more formal approach is the Glesjer test which involves regressing the absolute value of the residual on a selected independent variable (or some function of that variable). Other frequently used tests are the White Test, the Goldfeld-Quandt test, and the Breusch-Pagan test; see Maddala (1988).

One solution to the problem of heteroskedasticity is to specify the variables in a manner that reduces the error variance. Common practices are to deflate all variables by some measure of size or to transform the data to logs. A second approach is to use a regression technique known as weighted least squares where observations with smaller variances receive a larger weight in the computation of the regression coefficients.

Bibliography

Greene, W. H. (1990). *Econometric Analysis*. 1st edn, New York: Macmillan.
Kennedy, P. (1985). *A Guide to Econometrics*. 2nd edn, Oxford, UK: Blackwell.
Maddala, G. S. (1988). *Introduction to Econometrics*. New York: Macmillan.

ALASTAIR MCFARLANE

hierarchy   As Coase (1937) observed, markets and firms are alternative methods of organizing production and allocating resources. Given the prevalence of large business organizations in market economies, it is important to analyze how corporations operate and make decisions. The term hierarchy refers to the hierarchical structure of business organizations and Williamson (1975) examined the factors which affect the decision to produce inputs internally within the firm rather than purchase them externally from the market. Coase (1937) argued that it was costly for firms to use the market because of TRANSACTIONS COSTS. Therefore firms would expand the scope of their operations to reduce these costs. But as the firm increases in size, the costs of coordinating decisions within the firm

increase. The optimal size of the firm is the size which minimizes the total transactions costs of using the market and internal production.

Williamson (1985) stressed that transactions costs are affected by UNCERTAINTY, the frequency of the transaction, and the specificity of assets in which the parties must invest (*see* ASSET SPECIFICITY). When a firm contracts in the market and requires a supplier to purchase specific equipment which has few alternative uses, the supplier could be vulnerable if the purchasing firm decides to purchase its inputs elsewhere. Detailed, long-term contracts could be written to reduce the supplier's risk, but all future contingencies cannot be specified and so uncertainty and INCOMPLETE CONTRACTS may prevent the transaction from occurring. In such a case, VERTICAL INTEGRATION may solve the problem by internalizing the transaction. The governance of the market is then replaced by the hierarchical governance of the firm.

Hierarchies perform a variety of functions in the market. For example, a hierarchy can be viewed as an information system, since the structure of an organization affects the flow of information within the firm. As Radner (1992) suggests, economic EFFICIENCY requires specialization but specialization requires decentralized decision-making which introduces additional coordination problems within the firm. Another interesting feature of hierarchies is the internal labor market they create. It is important for any economic organization to properly match labor skills with job requirements. Holmstrom and Tirole (1989) suggest that when there is uncertainty about the job characteristics or the worker's skills, the hierarchy can act as a filter providing information about worker's abilities and matching them with the appropriate current position and providing a learning environment for future positions. In fact, Holmstrom and Tirole suggest that when a mismatch between the worker and the job is too costly, long career paths with assignments throughout the hierarchy provide more information about the worker's abilities (as with doctors and airline pilots).

Bibliography

Coase, R. H. (1937). The nature of the firm. *Economica*, **4**, 386–405.

Holmstrom, B. R. Tirole, J. (1989). The theory of the firm. Schmalensee, R. Willig, R. D. *The Handbook of Industrial Organization.* Amsterdam: North-Holland.

Radner, R. (1992). Hierarchy: the economics of managing. *Journal of Economic Literature*, 30, 1382–415.

Shughart, W. F. (1990). *The Organization of Industry.* Boston, MA: Irwin.

Williamson, O. E. (1975). *Markets and Hierarchies: Analysis and Antitrust Implications.* New York: Free Press.

Williamson, O. E. (1985). *The Economic Institutions of Capitalism: Firms, Markets, Relational Contracting.* New York: Free Press.

ROBERT E. MCAULIFFE

horizontal merger guidelines Section 7 of the US CLAYTON ACT proscribes mergers which may substantially lessen competition. The language of the Act leaves open to interpretation, by the courts and the antitrust enforcement agencies, the exact nature of the circumstances under which there exists a violation, and varying interpretations have been offered (*see* ANTITRUST POLICY). On three occasions since the late 1960s the federal government, in an effort to clarify the antitrust enforcement philosophy of the existing administration, has issued guidelines indicating the conditions under which the challenge of a merger will be likely.

The first set of guidelines was presented by the Department of Justice (DOJ) in 1968. These guidelines followed a strict *structuralist* approach (*see* STRUCTURE-CONDUCT-PERFORMANCE PARADIGM) whereby markets were classified as "highly concentrated" or "less highly concentrated" and the decision to challenge a merger between rival firms was essentially based on one criterion, that being whether the market shares of the firms in question were unacceptably high. Specific rules were established by the guidelines. For example, in a highly concentrated industry, one in which the 4–firm concentration ratio (CR4) was above 75 percent, a merger between an acquiring firm holding a market share in excess of 10 percent and a firm to be acquired having a market share in excess of 2 percent was to be challenged (see *Antitrust Bulletin* (1982) for a complete statement of these

guidelines and those developed in 1982; see also CONCENTRATION INDICES). These guidelines offered a possible exemption in the case where the acquired firm was failing and no other more suitable purchaser was forthcoming, but little else by way of a defense was to be allowed for mergers not falling within these rules. Moreover the guidelines indicated a willingness by the government to challenge an acquisition, even when the market shares were acceptably low, if the firm to be acquired had shown to be an aggressive, competitive force, or if the merger was part of a trend toward increasing concentration in a market.

The revised 1982–84 guidelines and those, written in 1992, which are currently in force, present a substantial change from the first set of guidelines in terms of the level of economic analysis generated and in terms of their economic philosophy. The prevailing criticism of the first set of guidelines is that they were too simplistic, and too rigid and that the long evidentiary record of the link between MARKET STRUCTURE and MARKET PERFORMANCE was weak and not sufficiently compelling to justify the strict rules which had been used. Thus, while both of the new sets of guidelines maintain an analysis of market structure as part of their approach, they replace the rigid rules approach with a case-by-case approach which uses additional economic factors, beyond market shares, in order to help indicate the *probability* of a challenge.

The new guidelines since 1982 replace the CR4 with the use of the HERFINDAHL-HIRSCHMAN INDEX, HHI, as the preferred measure of industry concentration. In addition, three levels of concentration are identified and used in the first step of the evaluation process:

(1) low concentration (where the post merger HHI 1000), in which a challenge is *unlikely*,
(2) moderate concentration (where after the merger 1000 HHI 1800), in which a challenge is *more likely than not* if the proposed merger increases the HHI by more than 100 points, and
(3) high concentration (where the post merger HHI 1800), in which a challenge is *likely* if the HHI increases by more than 50 points.

From there, the new guidelines significantly expand the use of economic analysis relative to their earlier counterparts. For example, a principle concern of antitrust enforcers dealing with horizontal mergers is the possibility that the declining number of rivals may facilitate the abuse of MARKET POWER through COLLUSION. As a result, the new guidelines investigate other factors which are known to influence the possibility of collusion. Since economic theory indicates that collusion is easier to achieve in a market where the good in question is homogeneous, and where information on rivals' prices and sales are readily available to competitors, these factors will also be considered in evaluating the merger. Once all such factors are considered, if the evidence indicates that the market in question is one in which collusion is easy, the merger in question will be *more likely* to be challenged, all else being equal, than one involving a market where collusion is seen as being difficult.

Similarly the new guidelines call for increased emphasis being placed on the condition of ENTRY into the market, under the theory that potential entrants may be able to discipline firms which attempt to abuse market power resulting from a merger. The guidelines detail a number of factors which are to be used in defining markets. In addition they offer a new approach (SSNIP) to defining markets (*see* MARKET DEFINITION).

Finally, the latest two sets of guidelines offer significant changes concerning the question of ENTRY. It has long been recognized that mergers may promote competition by allowing ECONOMIES OF SCALE and other cost saving efficiencies to take place. Williamson (1968) developed a framework for analyzing the merits of a horizontal merger in which such efficiencies occur. Using a simple cost-benefit approach (*see* PROFIT MAXIMIZATION), he argued that a merger should be approved if the potential gains to society from the lower costs of production exceed the potential cost to society from the DEADWEIGHT LOSS resulting from increased market power. Moreover, his model indicates that a relatively small gain in efficiency was necessary to offset the social loss and as a result the efficiency resulting from a merger should be considered as an important factor. Although neither the earlier (1968) guidelines nor the courts nor the Clayton Act itself has accepted efficiency considerations as a defense

of a merger, the newer guidelines treat efficiency much more favorably than in the past.

One of the areas of greatest debate concerning antitrust policy has been that of the merger guidelines. The first of many issues debated is that of the merits of a more strict "rules" approach as offered in the first guidelines, in comparison with the more open "case" approach used during the last decade. Meehan (1977), in a survey of the early literature defending the rules approach, cites several arguments. The first is that it is a much less costly method since the case approach requires gathering a great deal of information, much of which comes from the firms in question and therefore must be verified due to the incentives of these firms to provide biased information. Second, the difficulty in the case approach of evaluating the social loss is recognized as a problem.

Third, and perhaps most importantly, significant problems arise using Williamson's model to defend the efficiency argument. Meehan cites two studies which find that economies are often not a primary goal cited by managers involved in mergers and, more importantly, that in nearly half of the cases of mergers examined, no attempt was made to achieve potential economies. Moreover, evidence is offered that the gain in market power accrued from these mergers was a primary cause for the diminished desire to achieve the efficiencies which were available. In addition, although mergers may offer cost savings through multiplant operations or through the rationalization (removal) of excess capacity, the denial of such mergers may only delay these cost savings as competition will induce the individual firms to expand or contract on their own. Finally, the argument has been made that since mergers may increase ECONOMIC PROFIT, firms may misallocate (from society's point of view) a significant amount of resources in an effort to achieve these profits, and that this misallocation should be included in any cost-benefit analysis.

Meehan's solution to the efficiency defense question called for a modification of the 1968 guidelines to ignore mergers in which CR4 is less than 50 percent, as the threat of market power is minimal. This would also allow for significant economies to be achieved where they are most likely to occur, i.e. in mergers among small and medium sized firms (*see* MINIMUM EFFICIENT SCALE (MES)).

In evaluating merger policy following the introduction of the 1982–84 guidelines, several scholars have offered policy solutions concerning efficiency which paralleled those cited in Meehan, while generally approving of the new approach. Fisher (1987) argued for a very high standard of proof for firms claiming efficiencies and a refusal of the claims if an alternative method is available for achieving the economies. Schmalensee (1987) argued that efficiency should only be used as a tiebreaker of last resort, and should not save an otherwise objectionable merger. In general, these and other scholars favor the new case approach in its treatment of market definition and entry, while disagreement arises as to the rewriting of the Clayton Act to specifically allow an efficiency defense. Miller (1984) takes the strong stance that the 1984 revision of the 1982–84 guidelines, by evolving to a cost-benefit approach wherein efficiency is considered, "borders on executive legislation" as courts are unlikely to be able to test this doctrine since the government is not bringing cases where efficiencies are great.

The 1992 guidelines, closely following the letter and spirit of those developed a decade earlier, nonetheless offer some revisions. First, the new guidelines more forcefully indicate that a merger can be challenged because of an anticipated transfer of wealth from consumers to producers, i.e. economic profit. While the earlier guidelines had focused primarily on the misallocation of resources, the current guidelines clearly offer both issues as a reason for governmental action against a proposed merger. This, in theory, may substantially tip the cost-benefit scales used in Williamson's model. To the extent that the current and future administrations measure and include excess profits as a cost of a proposed merger, this will, as suggested in Meehan (1977), dramatically increase the efficiency gains needed to justify most mergers.

A second change in the 1992 guidelines is that the language dealing with the likelihood of a challenge is, by the government's own assessment, weaker than in the past. This is particularly true in the moderately and highly concentrated industry categories. For example,

in the latter category, the 1984 guidelines indicated that a challenge would occur "except in extraordinary cases" while the current guidelines, while presuming anticompetitive effects of such concentration, indicate that the demonstration of the importance of other effects may overcome the initial presumption; see FTC (1992, pp.1–7). Other changes clarify and modify the analysis of market definition and entry, but largely leave the 1982–84 guidelines intact.

In a sharp critique of both the 1982–84 and 1992 guidelines Mueller (1993) argues that they have lost focus of their original intent, which was to clarify the government's position on Section 7 of the Clayton Act. The 1968 guidelines were simple and clear rules under which mergers would be evaluated. The new guidelines, from Mueller's point of view, delineate much of the current economic knowledge concerning markets and develop numerous tests and screens in the process of evaluating a merger, and no longer reduce the uncertainty on the part of business in the US as to which mergers will be challenged.

Moreover, Mueller argues that the proliferation of the factors identified in the new guidelines deliberately furthers a bias, held by the government in the 1980s, toward favoring big business. The potential time and cost to small firms of a court challenge would be prohibitive, while large firms wishing to merge could impose significant costs on the government agency opposing the merger by forcing them to develop the extensive evidence required by the new guidelines. In addition, Mueller argues that the bias toward bigness is enhanced by the efficiency criteria in the guidelines, which are biased in that they do not block mergers where the effect is likely to reduce efficiency. He cites the example of the LTV-Republic Steel merger, allowed by the government, as a result where the bias toward big business enabled a merger to occur although losses in efficiency were predictable from the records of past acquisitions of LTV.

In sum, the horizontal merger guidelines of the past 25 years have continued to develop in terms of their economic content and analysis. As sharp differences in economic philosophies exist, these guidelines continue to be a source of contention among antitrust policymakers, scholars and industry leaders.

Bibliography

Fisher, F. (1987). Horizontal mergers: triage and treatment. *Economic Perspectives*, 1, 23–40.

Greer, D. (1992). *Industrial Organization and Public Policy*. 3rd edn, New York: Macmillan.

Meehan, J. (1977). Rules vs. discretion: a reevaluation of the merger guidelines for horizontal mergers. *Antitrust Bulletin*, 20, 769–95.

Miller, R. (1984). Notes on the 1984 merger guidelines: clarification of the policy or repeal of the Celler-Kefauver Act? *Antitrust Bulletin*, 29, 653–62.

Mueller, D. (1993). US merger policy and the 1992 merger guidelines. *Review of Industrial Organization*, 8, 151–62.

Schmalensee, R. (1987). Horizontal merger policy: problems and changes. *Economic Perspectives*, 1, 41–54.

US Department of Justice   Federal Trade Commission (1992). *Horizontal Merger Guidelines*. Washington, DC: US Government Printing Office.

US Department of Justice (1982). Merger guidelines, 1966 1982. *Antitrust Bulletin*, 27, 633–83.

US Federal Trade Commission Bureau of Competition (1992). *How 1992 Guidelines Differ from prior Agency Standards*. Washington, DC: US Federal Trade Commission.

Williamson, O. (1968). Economies as an antitrust defense: the welfare tradeoffs. *American Economic Review*, 58, 18–36.

GILBERT BECKER

identification problem Two econometric issues arise whenever a researcher attempts to estimate simultaneous relationships: the identification problem and SIMULTANEOUS EQUATIONS BIAS. When an equation is not identified, the researcher cannot estimate the underlying equation (such as the demand or supply curve). When an equation is part of a simultaneous system of equations, such as the supply and demand for a product, direct estimates obtained from a LINEAR REGRESSION will be biased and other estimation methods must be employed.

To understand the basic nature of the identification problem, consider a competitive market in which the prices and quantities observed result from the interaction of *both* supply and demand. Given that both supply and demand determine observed data for prices and quantities, how can a researcher know whether the resulting EQUILIBRIUM data points reflect the underlying demand curve or supply curve? This is the issue of identification. Without any additional information beyond observed data on prices and quantities, a researcher cannot know whether the observed points reveal a demand or supply relation, or a weighted average of both. However, if additional information is available, it may be possible to identify either the DEMAND CURVE or the supply curve, or both.

Consider the following system of supply and demand curves for any competitive market:

$$Q_t^d = \alpha_1 + \alpha_2 P + \varepsilon_t^d, \qquad (1)$$

$$Q_t^s = \beta_1 + \beta_2 P + \varepsilon_t^s, \qquad (2)$$

$$Q_t^d = Q_t^s, \qquad (3)$$

where Q is the quantity supplied or demanded, P is the price of the product, and the ε_t' are random disturbances to demand and supply. Equations (1)–(3) are referred to as *structural equations*, which reflect specific features of the market. These equations are mutually dependent, since price and quantity cannot be determined without all of them. Even when a researcher is only interested in estimating one of these equations (such as demand), if price and quantity are determined by both supply and demand, the demand curve must be regarded as part of a system of equations (see Maddala, 1992; Greene, 1993).

As written, neither demand nor supply is identified above without additional information, since each curve contains identical information relating quantity to price. Because neither equation is identified, their underlying parameters (the α's and β's) cannot be estimated from the data. However, if a researcher knew that there was no disturbance to demand (or very little random variation in demand), this additional information would serve to identify the demand curve. The reason is that in this case the researcher would know that demand was given by

$$Q_t^d = \alpha_1 + \alpha_2 P, \qquad (1')$$

which would mean that the observed fluctuations in price and output in the market were due to variations in supply. That is, if the demand curve had little or no variation, then the researcher would know that observed movements in prices and quantities were caused by shifts in supply along a (relatively) constant demand curve. The resulting data on prices and quantities would thus trace out the demand curve, as shown in figure 1.

Price

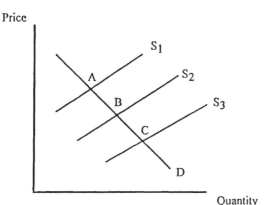

Quantity

Figure 1   Shifts in supply identify the demand curve

This example illustrates the identification problem and how it may be solved. To state the requirement loosely at the moment, for a given equation to be identified, that equation must *exclude* variables which are included in other equations in the model, or other restrictions must be imposed on the data. In the above example, the demand curve (1′) would be identified, but the supply curve is not identified because the disturbance term is excluded from the demand curve; there are no variables excluded from the supply curve which are included in demand. It should also be noted that identification is a property of the data that is available: a researcher could not simply assume that there was no variation in demand to identify the demand curve if it were not the case, because the observed data would reflect shifts in both demand and supply.

Consider the following system of supply and demand equations:

$$Q_t^d = \alpha_1 + \alpha_2 P + \alpha_3 I + \varepsilon_t^d, \qquad \text{(1a)}$$

$$Q_t^s = \beta_1 + \beta_2 P + \beta_3 C + \varepsilon_t^s, \qquad \text{(2a)}$$

$$Q_t^d = Q_t^s, \qquad \text{(3)}$$

where I is consumer income (an exogenous variable) and C is the cost of resources in production (also an exogenous variable in this system). In this case, both supply and demand are identified. The demand curve is identified because resource costs which shift supply are excluded from the demand curve. Supply is identified because variations in consumer

income will shift demand without changing supply. As long as the parameters α_3 and β_3 are not equal to zero, then changes in income and costs will serve to identify supply and demand respectively.

More generally, a single equation in a system of simultaneous equations may be *exactly identified*, *over-identified*, or *under-identified* depending (in part) on whether the exclusion restrictions necessary to identify the equation are met. In the modified example above, the demand curve (1a) is exactly identified, as is the supply curve (2a). To be identified, any given equation must meet the *order* and *rank* conditions described below (see Maddala, 1992; Greene, 1993).

Consider a system of equations with N *endogenous* variables (that is, variables which are to be explained by the model, such as price and quantity in the above examples) and K *exogenous* or *predetermined* variables. Exogenous variables are those which are not explained by the model and which are not correlated with the disturbance terms in each equation, such as income and resource costs in the above example (*see* ERROR TERMS IN REGRESSION), while predetermined variables are past values of the endogenous variables. For linear systems the order condition requires that the total number of endogenous, exogenous, and predetermined variables *excluded* from the equation must equal the number of endogenous variables *included* in that equation minus 1. So if there are J endogenous, exogenous, and predetermined variables excluded from an equation in a system of N endogenous variables, then:

1. The equation is exactly identified when $J = N - 1$.
2. The equation is over-identified when J $N - 1$.
3. The equation is under-identified when J $N - 1$.

When an equation is under-identified, its parameters cannot be estimated. The order condition is necessary for identification but is not sufficient. In most cases, the rank condition for identification will be satisfied when the order condition is satisfied, but exceptions can occur.

The rank condition for identification is both necessary and sufficient for identification, and refers to the rank of largest number of linearly independent rows or columns of a matrix (the system of equations). Maddala (1992) provides a convenient summary of the requirements for identification: consider a system of three equations with three endogenous variables, y_1, y_2, and y_3, and three exogenous variables, x_1, x_2, and x_3, (this method easily generalizes to systems with different numbers of equations and variables than those used in this example). Consider the rows and columns for the equations as if in a spreadsheet, and place a cross when a variable appears in the equation and a zero when it does not appear. For a system such as the one below, we can check each equation to see if it is identified:

Equation	y1	y2	y3	x1	x2	x3
1	X	0	0	0	0	X
2	X	0	X	0	0	X
3	0	X	X	X	X	0

The rules that Maddala provides for identifying any equation are as follows:

1. Delete the row of the equation being considered.
2. Take the columns with the zero entries for that row.
3. Given these remaining columns, there must be $N - 1$ rows and columns which do not have only zeros, and no row (or column) can be proportional to any other row (or column) for all parameter values. If these requirements are fulfilled, then the equation is identified.

This version of the rank condition is both necessary and sufficient for an equation to be identified. Consider the above table. There are three endogenous variables ($N = 3$), so the order condition requires that at least two variables are excluded from each equation. The first equation has four variables missing and is over-identified, and the second equation has three variables excluded and is also over-identified, while the third equation has two variables excluded and is exactly identified. Therefore all three equations meet the order condition for identification.

For the rank condition we require that there be $N - 1 = 2$ nonzero rows and columns. For equation (1), delete that row and take those columns where zeros appear in the equation. The columns with zeros for equation (1) are

$$\begin{matrix} 0 & X & 0 & 0 \\ X & X & X & X \end{matrix}$$

Since we have two rows (and two columns) which are not completely filled with zeros, the equation is identified. To apply the rank condition to equation (2), delete that row and take those columns in which zeros appear, to obtain

$$\begin{matrix} 0 & 0 & 0 \\ X & X & X \end{matrix}$$

Since an entire row contains zeros and only one row does not, equation (2) does not meet the rank condition of having $N - 1$ rows and columns that are not all zeros. Thus equation (2) is not identified, despite the fact that the order condition was fulfilled, and so its parameters cannot be estimated. As the reader can verify, the third equation also meets the rank condition for identification. The identification problem can also be expressed in terms of the relationship between the structural equations of the model and the *reduced form equations* (see ESTIMATING DEMAND, and Fisher (1966) and Hsiao (1983) for more advanced treatments).

Bibliography

Fisher, F. M. (1966). *The identification problem in econometrics*. New York: McGraw-Hill.
Greene, W. H. (1993). *Econometric analysis*, **2nd edn**, New York: Macmillan.
Hsiao, C. (1983). Identification. in Griliches, Z. Intriligator, M. D. (eds), *The handbook of econometrics*. Amsterdam: North-Holland.
Maddala, G. S. (1992). *Introduction to econometrics*, **2nd edn**, New York: Macmillan

ROBERT E. MCAULIFFE

imperfect information Perfect information is the strongest information requirement that can be assumed in an economic model. Traditionally, it has been a standard assumption in economic theory. Even though many of the real world markets being modeled (e.g. insurance markets, financial markets, and labor markets) were recognized as having important information imperfections, it was not subject to debate until fairly recently. Stigler's (1961) article, "The economics of information," is recognized as a path-breaking article on the formal modeling of imperfect information.

Incomplete information is a type of imperfect information. For example, one or more parties to a transaction may lack knowledge of some aspect of the transaction that affects their payoffs. When consumers have incomplete information, markets which would be perfectly competitive otherwise have the features of MONOPOLISTIC COMPETITION and firms have some degree of MARKET POWER. ASYMMETRIC INFORMATION is another type of imperfect information. For example, one party to a transaction may have valuable knowledge of some aspect of the transaction that another party does not. Information asymmetries are an important source of information imperfections which may in turn create problems of MORAL HAZARD and ADVERSE SELECTION.

An early article on the effects of imperfect information on the standard conclusions of economic theory is Rothschild and Stiglitz (1976). They examined the effects of imperfect information on competitive insurance markets and found that under plausible conditions an EQUILIBRIUM did not exist in those markets in the presence of imperfect information. Although their focus was on insurance markets their results also had implications for financial markets and labor markets. In the context of credit markets, Stiglitz and Weiss (1981) show how equilibrium in credit markets can be characterized by rationing in the presence of imperfect information.

One of the implications of Rothschild and Stiglitz (1976) was recognizing imperfect information as a source of market inefficiency. Another was recognizing that specific institutions in markets may be responses to the difficulties of handling problems of imperfect information. This second implication has had a profound influence on recent developments in what has come to be called the "new institutional economics." The approach taken by the imperfect information strand of the new institutional economics is associated primarily with the work of Akerlof and Stiglitz. It is rigorous, specifying assumptions and equilibrium solutions, and making sharp distinctions between different types of information problems. Stiglitz (1986) utilizes the imperfect

information theory of institutions to provide an explanation of the existence of certain agrarian institutions as substitutes for incomplete insurance markets, credit markets, and futures markets.

Screening and SIGNALING are two methods individuals use in attempting to overcome problems of imperfect information that arise due to ADVERSE SELECTION. Stiglitz (1975) develops a theory of screening which he uses to analyze the allocation of resources to education. Screening serves to sort individuals on the basis of their qualities. Stiglitz finds that screening in education has productivity returns but it increases inequality, creating a trade-off between distributional and efficiency considerations. Leland and Pyle (1977) develop a signaling model where entrepreneurs seek financing for projects whose true qualities are known only to them. An entrepreneur's willingness to invest in their own project is seen as a signal of the project's quality. They conclude that the value of the firm increases with the share of the firm owned by the entrepreneur, and suggest that financial intermediation is a natural response to asymmetric information.

see also **asymmetric information; adverse selection; moral hazard**

Bibliography

Leland, H. Pyle, D. (1977). Informational asymmetries, financial structure and financial intermediation. *Journal of Finance*, **32**, 371–87.

Rothschild, M. Stiglitz, J. (1976). Equilibrium in competitive insurance markets: an essay on the economics of imperfect information. *Quarterly Journal of Economics*, **90**, 629–50.

Stigler, G. J. (1961). The economics of information. *Journal of Political Economy*, **69**, 213–25.

Stiglitz, J. (1975). The theory of "screening", education and the distribution of income. *American Economic Review*, **65**, 283–300.

Stiglitz, J. (1986). The new development economics. *World Development*, **14**, 257–65.

Stiglitz, J. Weiss, A. (1981). Credit rationing in markets with imperfect information. *American Economic Review*, **71**, 393–410.

ALEXANDRA BERNASEK

income effect   The income effect refers to the change in a consumer's real income (or purchasing power) when the price of a product changes.

When the price of a product increases, those consumers who purchase the product have lost purchasing power and will tend to buy less of all goods – including the good whose price rose. The strength of this income effect depends on the importance of the product in the consumer's budget and the availability of substitutes. Thus an increase in the price of a specific manufacturer's product, of say chicken, will have less effect on consumers than an increase in the price of all chicken and this will have less effect than an increase in the price of all food products.

Just as consumers are worse off from a price increase, a price decrease will make consumers better off by increasing their purchasing power. For most products, the income effect is positive – i.e. consumers tend to purchase more of the good as their incomes rise. This holds for NORMAL GOODS and for luxury goods, but the income effect is negative for INFERIOR GOODS. The income effect normally reinforces the SUBSTITUTION EFFECT causing DEMAND CURVES to slope downward.

see also **law of demand**

Bibliography

Douglas, E. J. (1992). *Managerial Economics.* 4th edn, Englewood Cliffs, NJ: Prentice-Hall.

ROBERT E. MCAULIFFE

income elasticity Income elasticity is defined as the percentage change in quantity demanded given a small percentage change in income, and is calculated by the ratio

$$\varepsilon_I = \frac{\Delta Q}{Q} \bigg/ \frac{\Delta I}{I} = \frac{\Delta Q}{\Delta I} \times \frac{I}{Q}$$

where the symbol Δ indicates a change in quantity (Q) or income (I). Its measure may take on a positive or negative value and is of considerable importance to managers. For most goods, an increase in income raises demand and thus ε_I has a value greater than zero. For some of these goods, formally classified as luxury goods, the change in demand is greater than the income change and ε_I takes on a value greater than one. For a few goods, such as bus transportation, increased income causes substi-

tution to alternative goods and the value of ε_I is negative. These goods are identified as INFERIOR GOODS. The degree of consumer sensitivity to income changes is important in anticipating the periodic growth and decline in demand for a good. Products with a large positive value for income elasticity will find demand growth exceeding the growth rate of income in the economy. These products are also more susceptible to sharp declines in demand during recessions. Suppliers of inferior goods on the other hand should expect a decline in demand for their product in the long run as consumer income grows.

see also **elasticity**

Bibliography

Douglas, E. (1992). *Managerial Economics: Analysis Strategy.* 4th edn, Englewood Cliffs, NJ: Prentice-Hall.
Mansfield, E. (1993). *Managerial Economics: Theory, Applications, and Cases.* 2nd edn, New York: Norton.

GILBERT BECKER

incomplete contracts Incomplete contracts are a response to bounded rationality which results from the inability of people to exactly foresee and articulate all possible contingencies or because the cost minimization requires the contract to be incomplete (*see* TRANSACTIONS COSTS). Simon (1951) analyzed the consequences of bounded rationality for the employment relationship. A complex long-term relationship between the employee and the employer is most commonly defined as an incomplete contract and is a rational response to human limits of bounded rationality and uncertainty. When contracts are incomplete, a possibility for opportunistic behavior exists because incentives are not properly aligned and this leads to problems of imperfect commitment.

Imperfect commitment can lead to an incentive for one of the parties of the contract to prefer renegotiation of the contract *ex post*. For example, when the contract fails to specify how the price should change over time as a result of a change in costs, the buyer may refuse to take the supplier's word for the change in costs and a risk-averse buyer will find a contract that does not specify prices with certainty unattractive. Fear of reneging may make contracting parties engage in costly behavior aimed at protecting themselves to assure completion of a contract or decide not to enter into a contract in the first place.

As a result of contractual incompleteness a hold-up problem may occur. Certain transactions may necessitate that specific investments be made. When this investment is made, the value of the input in its present use is much higher than in its next best use which creates a basis for opportunistic behavior. One of the parties may refuse to abide by the contractual terms after the specific investment has been made. The party whose contract terms have worsened as a result of contractual incompleteness is said to be held-up. This inability to commit parties to postcontractual behavior may result in fewer asset-specific investments being made (*see* ASSET SPECIFICITY).

Williamson (1979) showed that the problem of commitment and opportunistic behavior is lessened when firms engage in long-run relationships with frequent interaction and the degree of asset specificity of the investment made by the parties is low. There is a variety of contractual means for reaching a commitment when parties engage in complex transactions that last over a period of time and contracts are incomplete. A hold-up problem may be avoided and opportunism mitigated if a single firm owns highly specialized assets (*see* VERTICAL INTEGRATION). Relational contracts are a common way of trying to resolve unspecified contingencies should they occur. They are abstract in nature but do necessitate specification of an authority or governance structure. For example, a supervisor has discretionary power over an employee's assignment of tasks. Also important in practice are "implicit contracts." These are defined by a set of shared expectations about the behavior or a relationship. They are not enforceable in a court of law but are designed to be self-enforcing. Rosen (1985) provides a nice survey of studies pertaining to the implicit nature of employment contracts and explanations for different phenomena, such as wage rigidity, human resource policies in a firm and their objectives for employment security, recruiting, etc.

A noncontractual way of achieving commitments and aligning incentives when contracts are incomplete is with reputations. Reputational effects can sustain contracts until the near end and save the firm the costs of writing a complete contract. In the employment relationship, the firm reneging on a promise of a wage increase damages its reputation and reduces the future possibility of an equally profitable relationship with its employees. Kreps (1990) provides numerous examples of corporate culture being employed to enforce expected behaviors in a corporation.

see also **asset specificity; Coase Theorem; game theory; transactions costs**

Bibliography

Carlton, D. W. Perloff, J. M. (1994). *Modern Industrial Organization*. 2nd edn, New York: Harper Collins.

Kreps, D. (1990). Corporate culture and economic theory. Alt, J. Shepsle, K. *Perspectives on Positive Political Economy*. Cambridge, MA: CUP. 90–143.

Milgrom, P. Roberts, J. (1992). *Economics, Organization and Management*. Englewood Cliffs, NJ: Prentice-Hall.

Rosen, S. (1985). Implicit contracts: a survey. *Journal of Economic Literature*, 23, 1144–75.

Simon, H. A. (1951). A formal theory of the employment relationship. *Econometrica*, 19, 293–305.

Williamson, O. (1979). Transaction-cost economics: the governance of contractual relations. *Journal of Law and Economics*, 22, 233–61.

Williamson, O. (1985). *The Economic Institutions of Capitalism: Firms, Markets, Relational Contracting*. New York: Free Press.

LIDIJA POLUTNIK

increasing returns There are increasing returns to an input in production when as incremental units of that input are added, the resulting increases in output are rising. Increasing returns typically occur in the early stages of production as the first units of a variable input are added but, as more units are added, diminishing returns set in (*see* LAW OF VARIABLE PROPORTIONS). For example, the increases in output from adding the first workers to a plant should rise as those workers assist each other in production, so the MARGINAL PRODUCT of labor would be rising. Eventually, additional workers will not be as productive and their marginal product will be falling. As with diminishing returns, increasing returns refer to the short run when other factors of production are held constant. When all factors of production are changed, the issue is one of ECONOMIES OF SCALE (or of returns to scale).

ROBERT E. MCAULIFFE

indifference curves These curves are used to describe the preferences of a consumer who is faced with an array of market baskets, or sets of goods, from which to choose. One indifference curve represents all of the different combinations of goods which give the consumer equal TOTAL UTILITY. Typically, market baskets containing different quantities of two goods are examined. Ordinarily, as the amount of either of the goods is reduced, utility is lost. As a result, the quantity of the second good must be increased in order to compensate for the loss and to leave the consumer indifferent between the initial and new position. For example, a consumer may indicate that a combination of four pairs of sneakers and one warm-up suit per year gives the same overall satisfaction as does three pairs of sneakers and two warm-up suits or one pair of sneakers and four warm-up outfits. These three combinations would be part of the same indifference curve for that consumer.

As it is generally assumed that more is preferred to less, any combination having more of at least one of the goods and no less of the second good would generate more total utility. Thus, for example, four pairs of sneakers in combination with three outfits would yield more total utility than the first combination identified above (and, by transitivity, more than the other two combinations as well). When other combinations having the same total utility as this new point are identified, a second indifference curve is created. The complete set of such curves is known as an **indifference map**.

It is important to recognize that the indifference curve represents the consumer's evaluation of these combinations without regard to income or the prices of the two goods. As such, the indifference map identifies a complete ranking of these combinations of goods solely on the basis of the consumer's tastes. The various combinations of goods which the consumer can afford and that set which leads to UTILITY MAXIMIZATION requires the analysis of the consumer's BUDGET CONSTRAINT as well.

A diagram of an indifference curve is drawn with the y-axis measuring the quantities of one good (Y) and the x-axis measuring the quantities of the second good (X). The different combinations which are equivalent in the eyes of the consumer are combined to form a curve which ordinarily is negatively sloped. The slope of the indifference curve indicates the amount of good Y which the consumer is willing to trade in order to receive one extra unit of good X. This is identified as the MARGINAL RATE OF SUBSTITUTION of X for Y. Each indifference curve is typically bowed inward toward the origin due to the law of DIMINISHING MARGINAL UTILITY which causes the marginal rate of substitution between the two goods to decline. Indifference curves which are farther from the origin represent higher levels of overall utility and are thus more desirable.

Indifference curve analysis can be used to demonstrate how an advertising campaign for a product works to alter consumers' marginal rates of substitution and thus favorably alter their choices toward greater purchases of the good being promoted. Alternatively, the analysis can be used to show how a pricing strategy which lowers the price of one good causes greater consumption of that good through the choice of a new combination on the consumer's indifference map.

Moreover, both the INCOME EFFECT and the SUBSTITUTION EFFECT of the price change can be demonstrated. In addition, indifference curves can be used to examine investment decisions by managers. Combinations of risk and rates of return (in the place of goods X and Y) can be used to create indifference curves which describe varying degrees of RISK AVERSION. The cost of financing capital expenditures can also be examined using this approach (*see* CAPITAL ASSET PRICING MODEL).

Finally, important advances have been made by Lancaster (1971) who used indifference curves to describe consumer preferences in terms of product characteristics. By identifying consumers tastes towards combinations of features which a product may hold, *target markets* can be established and marketing strategies concerning PRODUCT DIFFERENTIATION can be developed (*see* PRODUCT ATTRIBUTES MODEL).

Bibliography

Douglas, E. (1992). *Managerial Economics*. 4th edn, Englewood Cliffs, NJ: Prentice-Hall.
Lancaster, K. (1971). *Consumer Demand: A New Approach*. New York: Columbia University Press.

GILBERT BECKER

industry life cycle   This is the extension of the PRODUCT LIFE CYCLE concept to the industry. When a new product (or product category) has been created, the industry is in the **introduction phase** of the cycle where the market is small but growing and risk is high because the market is not yet fully established. Firms tend to have high ADVERTISING expenditures in this stage as they inform consumers about the new product. In addition, firms may be more vertically integrated if markets for supporting services and parts have not developed. For example, in the early years of the computer industry, there were few independent producers of peripherals such as disk drives or software, so companies such as IBM and later Digital had to produce these products themselves. During the **growth phase** of the cycle, the market grows rapidly as new firms enter the industry (*see* ENTRY). New product development, innovations and marketing methods occur during this period as firms compete for higher profits and market share. Eventually as the market becomes saturated, growth slows and the industry reaches the **maturity phase** of the cycle where profits stabilize and firms tend to compete more on price rather than through PRODUCT DIFFERENTIATION. Following this phase, the industry enters the **decline phase** with a contracting market and higher EXIT rates among firms. The industry structure tends to consolidate as larger firms acquire weaker rivals, competition focuses on price and costs and industry profits are falling.

As Porter (1980) observed, there are several criticisms of the life cycle approach. Every industry or product will not necessarily pass through each stage of the cycle, nor is it always clear where a specific industry may be in the life cycle. The evolution of the industry and competition between firms may vary between industries rather than follow the course predicted by the life cycle. However, the industry life cycle does offer interesting dynamic predictions regarding ENTRY, EXIT, competition and profits over time; see Greer (1992) and DECLINING INDUSTRY.

Bibliography

Greer, D. F. (1992). *Industrial Organization and Public Policy*. 3rd edn, New York: Macmillan.
Jacquemin, A. (1987). *The New Industrial Organization: Market Forces and Strategic Behavior*. Cambridge, MA: MIT.
Porter, M. E. (1980). *Competitive Strategy*. New York: Free Press.

ROBERT E. MCAULIFFE

inelastic demand   Inelastic demand is the situation where consumer reaction to a change in price is small. Specifically, it is defined as the case where the percentage change in quantity demanded is less than the percentage change in price, or $|\,\varepsilon p\,| < 1$ (*see* ELASTICITY). When a class of products has few or no SUBSTITUTES, such as gasoline, market demand tends to be inelastic. As the product is more narrowly defined though, and a specific brand of gasoline is considered, more substitutes are available and its demand becomes more elastic. In addition, goods considered to be necessities, such as food or prescription medications, and goods which play a small role in consumers budgets, such as salt, also tend to have demands which are inelastic. In all cases of inelastic demand, price increases will increase TOTAL REVENUE and price decreases will lower revenues. Moreover, in cases where consumers of the same product (e.g. movie tickets) can be separated into different groups (e.g. children, adults, senior citizens) and charged different prices, elasticity plays a critical role in the pricing strategy. In order to maximize profits, managers should charge the highest price to the group with the most inelastic demand, and lower prices to groups whose demand is more elastic (*see* PRICE DISCRIMINATION).

Bibliography

Mansfield, E. (1993). *Managerial Economics: Theory, Applications, and Cases.* 2nd edn, New York: Norton.

GILBERT BECKER

inferior goods A good is called inferior if consumers choose to buy less of this good when their REAL INCOME is higher. An example that is often used to illustrate this behavior is potatoes: as people's income rises, they may choose to consume fewer potatoes (and more of some other food). Goods which are not inferior are called NORMAL GOODS. Of course, a good may be normal at some income levels and inferior at other levels of income.

For a demand curve to have positive slope, it is necessary (but not sufficient) that the good is inferior (*see* DEMAND CURVES). The demand curve for an inferior good may be either increasing in price ("Giffen good") or decreasing in price, depending on whether the INCOME EFFECT or the SUBSTITUTION EFFECT dominates.

NIKOLAOS VETTAS

inflation Inflation measures the rate of change in the general level of prices in the economy. The inflation rate is calculated as the percentage change in a price index (such as the CONSUMER PRICE INDEX, the producer price index, or the GDP deflator) over a given period of time. For example, if the consumer price index at the end of May 1995 is 100 and its value for the end of June 1995 is 101, then the inflation rate for the month would be

$$\text{Inflation} = \left[\frac{(\text{CPI}_{June} - \text{CPI}_{May})}{\text{CPI}_{May}} \right] \times 100\%$$

$$= \left[\frac{(101 - 100)}{100} \right] \times 100\% = 1\%$$

Since a company's revenues and costs may adjust differently when inflation occurs, managers should consider the effects inflation may have on profits and may need to estimate its effects on costs and revenues separately for accurate forecasts. A firm might use the producer price index to measure inflation changes in its costs and the consumer price index to measure inflation in revenues. A subset of either price index may be preferred if specific elements of price change in the company's costs or revenues were more suitable. Thus a clothing retailer might be more interested in the price changes in clothing specifically than in changes in the overall index of consumer or producer prices and would choose that specific category of items in the price index.

ROBERT E. MCAULIFFE

internal organization of the firm Coordination of tasks and a division of work can be organized quite differently among different firms. One of the first methods of organizing activities within a firm was the **functional organization**. Firms were organized in a centralized fashion according to the functions they performed; for example, separate departments for finance, marketing, production, purchasing, etc. were formed. This type of internal organization of the firm permitted specialization of labor and the guiding principle for the formation of departments was technical efficiency. However, functional organizations were not very capable of accommodating the needs of large, multiproduct corporations that performed their activities in several geographic regions.

The expansion of product-lines in the 1920s and increasing multiproduct production by firms led to a new organizational form of a firm: the **multidivisional** (or **M-form**) organization. Du Pont was the first company to introduce this new form as a result of difficulties in producing goods as diverse as paints, fertilizers, and vegetable oils. New divisions were created within companies, each of which was responsible for a product, geographical location, market, or technology. These divisions may then be organized functionally. Multidivisional organization permits less specialization but it makes each division and its management responsible for profit maximization. Multidivisional organization evolved as a result of not only minimizing production costs but TRANSACTIONS COSTS as well. For example, this type of organization allows for better coordination of activities: division managers are more knowledgeable and better informed about their particular product lines and their incentives are better aligned with the overall performance objectives of the company than under functional organizations.

see also **principal–agent problem**

Bibliography

Carlton, D. W. Perloff, J. M. (1994). *Modern Industrial Organization*. 2nd edn, New York: HarperCollins.
Milgrom, P. Roberts, J. (1992). *Economics, Organization and Management*. Englewood Cliffs, NJ: Prentice-Hall.

LIDIJA POLUTNIK

internal rate of return   The internal rate of return is the discount rate which makes the NET PRESENT VALUE of an asset equal to its current cost. Formally, if an asset which costs P_0 today will generate cash flows of C in each period i for T periods in the future, then the internal rate of return is that value of r^* which solves

$$\sum_{i=1}^{T} \left[\frac{C_i}{(1 + r^*)^i} \right] - P_0 = 0$$

The internal rate of return essentially measures the expected rate of return from an investment and this can be compared with some hurdle rate for CAPITAL BUDGETING decisions. Based on this criterion, an investment should be made if its internal rate of return exceeds the cost of capital. The internal rate of return may not be unique if future cash flows alternate between positive and negative values and the ranking of alternative investments by this criterion may not correspond with rankings from the net present value method; see Edwards, Kay and Mayer (1987) and Brigham and Gapenski (1993). Fisher and McGowan (1983) assert that the internal rate of return is the appropriate measure of the economic rate of return, but Edwards, Kay and Mayer (1987) suggest that adjusted accounting data could be used in economic analysis.

see also **economic profit**

Bibliography

Brigham, E. F. Gapenski, L. C. (1993). *Intermediate Financial Management*. New York: Dryden.
Edwards, J., Kay, J. Mayer, C. (1987). *The Economic Analysis of Accounting Profitability*. Oxford: OUP.
Fisher, F. M. McGowan, J. J. (1983). On the misuse of accounting rates of return to infer monopoly profits. *American Economic Review*, 73, 82–97.

ROBERT E. MCAULIFFE

isoquant-isocost curves   These curves form the basis for the analysis of the choice of the optimal combination of inputs to be used in the production of any good. An isoquant curve identifies the set of all combinations of inputs which yield the same level of total output. As such, it is the production analysis counterpart to consumption INDIFFERENCE CURVES. Since less of any one input typically decreases total output, more of the second input is needed as compensation in order to maintain constant total output (see MARGINAL RATE OF TECHNICAL SUBSTITUTION). Because of this, isoquant curves are ordinarily negatively sloped, although in circumstances where too much of one input is used the result may be a negative marginal productivity from that input (see DIMINISHING RETURNS). At this point, the isoquant curve's slope becomes positively sloped.

One example comes from agricultural production where it has been demonstrated by Heady (1957) that various combinations of different per acre amounts of two fertilizers lead to an equal per acre yield of a given crop. For any one isoquant, greater amounts of 1 input (phosphate) will require lesser amounts of the second (nitrogen). Increases in both inputs will, up to some level, cause greater total output. A series of isoquant curves, each identifying different levels of output, can be identified and an isoquant map can be constructed.

An isocost line identifies the financial constraint which the firm faces in terms of purchasing inputs to be used in the production process. It includes both the prices (P) of the inputs in question and the total dollar amount of funds (F) available for inputs. This is described in the following equation for the case of two inputs:

$$F = P_a \times Q_a + P_b \times Q_b$$

where Q designates the quantity of each input (a,b) used; (*see* BUDGET CONSTRAINT) for a description of the equivalent limitation facing the consumer.

The isocost line identifies the different possible maximum combinations of inputs which the firm is able to buy with a fixed amount of available funds. Its slope, measured by the ratio of the input prices, represents the trade-off which the market requires of the firm in that it indicates the amount of one input which must be sacrificed in order to purchase an extra unit of the second input.

The tangency point between the firm's isocost line and the highest achievable isoquant curve indicates the optimal combination of the two inputs to be selected. This combination maximizes the total output which can be produced from a given expenditure level on inputs. Equivalently, the combination minimizes the TOTAL COST of producing a given level of output. Since a firm's profits are equal to its TOTAL REVENUE minus its TOTAL COST, cost minimization through the selection of an ideal combination of inputs is essential for a firm striving to achieve PROFIT MAXIMIZATION.

Bibliography

Heady, E. (1957). An econometric investigation of the technology of agricultural production functions. *Econometrica.*

Hirschey, M. (1995). *Fundamentals of Managerial Economics.* 5th edn, Fort Worth: Dryden.

GILBERT BECKER

J

junk bonds Junk bonds are high risk debt securities that are rated Ba (or lower) by Moody's Investment Services, Inc. and BB (or lower) by Standard and Poor's Corporation. Standard and Poor's Bond Guide defines this rating as "predominantly speculative with respect to capacity to pay interest and repay principal in accordance with the terms of the obligation." Because many institutional investors have restrictions against investing in speculative securities, low rated bonds are termed "below investment grade." To offset the greater risk exposure to investors, low grade bonds carry yields that are at least 3 percent greater than that of high quality corporate debt.

Prior to the 1970s, publicly traded bonds were not issued with below investment grade ratings, although they could be subsequently downgraded. During the 1980s, Drexel Burnham Lambert (DBL), a large investment banking firm, increased interest in this type of investment by pioneering the use of newly issued junk bonds as a source of financing for takeovers and mergers. DBL convinced investors that junk bonds offered a high return without commensurate risk and also offered to provide liquidity to the market by promising to buy back bonds from their customers on demand. However, the economic environment of the late 1980s and early 1990s resulted in many defaults and, ultimately, the failure of DBL. The result has been reduced investor interest in this type of security.

Bibliography

Gruber, M. J. (1991). *Modern Portfolio Theory and Investment Analysis.* 4th edn, New York: Wiley.
Kolb, R. W. (1992). *Investments.* 3rd edn, Miami, FL: Kolb.

VICKIE L. BAJTELSMIT

K

kinked demand curves These DEMAND CURVES demonstrate the relation between the price of a firm's product and its quantity demanded when taking into account specific reactions by rival firms. The LAW OF DEMAND indicates that, all else constant, as the price of one firm's product is reduced, its quantity demanded will rise. This generates a demand curve which typically is assumed to be continuous. Under the CETERIS PARIBUS condition though, rival firms' reactions to the price change are not allowed and thus are not considered.

Numerous models have been developed which apply different assumptions concerning rivals' reactions to a price change by one firm. One of the most widely known models is that developed by Sweezy (1939) in which rivals are expected to react to a firm's price increase by not changing their own price, but are expected to match any price decrease made by the first firm. The strategy by the rivals here is designed to increase their market share (for the case of price increases by the first firm) and protect their market share (for the case of a price decrease). If the first firm expects such asymmetry in the reactions by its rivals it would anticipate a sharp drop in unit sales for any price increase which it initiated. That is, it expects the demand for its product to be *elastic* for a price rise. At the same time, a price cut by this firm would be expected to bring a small increase in unit sales, that is, a more INELASTIC DEMAND for a decrease in price. Hence, the complete demand curve for such a firm contains a distinct kink at its current price level.

Kinked demand curves were first proposed as models of OLIGOPOLY. They attempted to explain a perceived inflexibility in oligopoly pricing relative to that which occurred in more competitive markets. As the firm which considers initiating a price change anticipates a harmful response from its rivals, these expectations may deter it from in fact changing price. The theory has maintained its popularity in part through its ability to explain, at times, the pricing behavior in some markets, especially those for homogeneous goods where price becomes a very important strategic variable. Evidence by Stigler (1947), Primeaux and Bomball (1974) and others rejects the existence of a kink in the demand curves of firms in several oligopoly markets. Another considered failure is the inability of the model to explain the current price of the firm. These and other shortcomings indicate that kinked demand curve models, while useful, do not form a general theory for oligopoly.

Bibliography

Douglas, E. (1992). *Managerial Economics Analysis and Strategy*. 4th edn, Englewood Cliffs, NJ: Prentice-Hall.
Primeaux, W. Bomball, M. (1974). A reexamination of the kinky oligopoly demand curve. *Journal of Political Economy*, **82**, 851–62.
Stigler, G. (1947). The kinky oligopoly demand curve and rigid prices. *Journal of Political Economy*, **55**, 432–49.
Sweezy, P. (1939). Demand under conditions of oligopoly. *Journal of Political Economy*, **47**, 568–73.

GILBERT BECKER

L

law of demand A fundamental principle of economics states that an inverse relationship exists between a change in the price of any product and the resulting change in its quantity demanded in the market. More formally the law of demand states that, CETERIS PARIBUS, as the price of a good rises its quantity demanded falls and as the price of a good falls its quantity demanded rises in the market. It is important to note that the motivating force behind the change in consumer behavior here is a change of price rather than, and without any other, change occurring in variables such as consumer tastes and income, which also make up the DEMAND FUNCTION.

The price change influences the adjustment in quantity demanded through two separate effects. The INCOME EFFECT is that portion of the change in quantity demanded which is due to the change in consumer purchasing power resulting from the price change. For example, when the price of a product decreases, the existing (and unchanged) level of consumer income now has greater real purchasing power. This makes consumers of the good in question richer and induces an increase in the number of units purchased. The SUBSTITUTION EFFECT recognizes that in the calculus of consumer decision making, individuals are also concerned with the price of a product relative to the prices of any SUBSTITUTES which are available. Since the ceteris paribus condition in the law holds these other prices constant, a fall in the absolute price of a good causes a decrease in its price relative to all others. This makes the good in question more attractive to consumers who then substitute away from other goods toward this good. Both effects normally reinforce the inverse relationship between price and quantity demanded.

The near universal applicability of this consumer behavior to a wide array of goods has elevated the principle to the status of an economic law. Even the demand for goods which are absolute necessities, such as water, tends to follow this law. Studies have shown that when faced with higher water prices, while people do not necessarily drink less water they will economize on its other uses. Also, what often appears to be a counter example to the law is actually a situation in which one or more of the other variables in the demand function have changed and the ceteris paribus condition has been broken.

Economic laws are not always obeyed and thus the law of demand is not without exceptions. Individuals sometimes violate the law, for example when a "snob effect" occurs and a higher price induces increased purchases. Here the individual's demand shows a positive relation between the product's price and the quantity demanded. The market demand for this product sometimes, but not always, continues to maintain the inverse relation indicated by the law. A second example where the law of demand may be violated concerns markets where new goods are involved. Bagwell and Riordon (1991) indicate that a higher price for a new product may induce increased sales as it sometimes acts as a signal of higher quality in markets where information is imperfect (*see* ASYMMETRIC INFORMATION).

Managers should be aware that the law indicates that a price change will ordinarily have an important impact on a firm's sales volume and TOTAL REVENUE, and thus its profitability. Although the law identifies the direction of the change in quantity demanded resulting from a price change, it does not indicate the size of the change. This size change is central to the overall impact of the price change on revenues (*see* ELASTICITY; INELASTIC DEMAND).

Bibliography

Bagwell, K. Riordon, M. (1991). High and declining prices signal product quality. *American Economic Review*, 81, 224–39.

Douglas, E. (1992). *Managerial Economics: Analysis and Strategy*. 4th edn, Englewood Cliffs, NJ: Prentice-Hall.

Miller, R. (1994). *Economics Today*. 8th edn, New York: HarperCollins.

GILBERT BECKER

law of variable proportions   Sometimes referred to as the law of diminishing returns, the law of variable proportions is concerned with the effect of changes in the proportion of the factors of production used to produce output. As the proportion of one input increases relative to all other inputs, at some point there will be decreasing marginal returns from that input. Adding more units of an input, holding all other inputs constant, will at some point cause the resulting increases in production to decrease, or equivalently, the MARGINAL PRODUCT of that input will decline. Among the inputs held constant is the level of technology used to produce that output. This is an empirical law and is therefore a generalization about the nature of the production process and cannot be proven theoretically; see Friedman (1976), Stigler (1966) and DIMINISHING RETURNS. Applied to management, Friedman argues that the law of variable proportions requires firms to produce by using inputs in such proportions that there are diminishing average returns to each input in production.

Bibliography

Douglas, E. J. (1992). *Managerial Economics*. 4th edn, Englewood Cliffs, NJ: Prentice-Hall.

Friedman, M. (1976). *Price Theory*. 2nd edn, Chicago: Aldine.

Stigler, G. J. (1966). *The Theory of Price*. 3rd edn, New York: Macmillan.

ROBERT E. MCAULIFFE

learning curve   The learning curve refers to the reduction in AVERAGE TOTAL COST which occurs as workers gain experience from producing a product over time and for this reason it is also called the **experience curve**. Unlike ECONOMIES OF SCALE where long run average costs decrease when more output is produced per period of time, the learning curve shows the reduction in average costs arising from the total accumulated volume of production to date. Therefore if a firm produced 2 million units per month at MINIMUM EFFICIENT SCALE (MES) and the average cost per unit was $10, if there were learning effects in production, they would cause the average cost curve to shift down over time. In this example, the firm might find that its average costs of production fell to $8 per unit once the firm had produced 24 million units over a year, even though production remained at 2 million units each month.

One of the first theoretical treatments of learning effects was provided by Arrow (1962) and learning curves have been estimated for a variety of industries; see Ghemawat (1985) for a survey. When significant learning effects exist, they can confer strategic advantages (*see* FIRST-MOVER ADVANTAGES) to those established firms which increase their production volumes quickly to reduce their costs; see Porter (1980). To take advantage of the learning curve managers should set prices for new products below the level which would only maximize current period profits recognizing that future costs will be lower and profits higher.

This aspect of pricing with a learning curve makes it difficult to establish whether a firm has engaged in PREDATORY PRICING, because a firm may price below AVERAGE TOTAL COST anticipating lower costs in the future from learning effects. Since this form of pricing is a legitimate business practice and leads to more efficient production, it is difficult to determine whether pricing below average cost is actually predatory in nature; see Carlton and Perloff (1994).

Some care is required when estimating learning curves because the effects occur over time but as time passes other factors (such as FACTOR PRICES) which affect average costs will also change. A simple but common representation of the learning curve would be:

$$AC_t = AC_0 \times CV_t^\lambda \times e^{u_t} \qquad (1)$$

where AC_t is the *real* average cost per unit of production in period t, AC_0 is the real average cost in the initial period of production, CV_t represents the cumulative volume of output produced up to period t, λ is the ELASTICITY of average costs with respect to volume, and u_t is an error term (with e the natural exponent). Since equation (1) relates current real average costs of production to the initial cost and the total volume produced, it omits the costs of factors of production which, if they have changed during the sample period, will cause estimates of the learning curve to be biased; see Berndt (1991). In fact, Berndt shows that unless the effects of changes in input prices can be captured by an appropriate deflator and there are constant returns to scale, estimates of the learning curve based on equation (1) will be biased.

If we ignore the biases mention above, how would a manager estimate the learning curve? Taking logarithms of both sides of equation (1) yields:

$$\ln(AC_t) = \ln(AC_0) + \lambda \times \ln(CV_t) + u_t \qquad (2)$$

which can be estimated by LINEAR REGRESSION. As Berndt observed, it is important to use general price deflators to obtain real unit average costs, since a price deflator for the industry will already include learning effects and will therefore mask the cost reductions we wish to estimate. Once λ has been estimated, average real costs will decrease according to

$$AC_{new} = (2^\lambda) \times AC_{old} \qquad (3)$$

when total volume doubles. For example, if the estimated value of λ were -0.25, then costs would decrease by 25 percent of their previous level when production volume doubled and the learning curve would have a 75 percent slope.

Bibliography

Arrow, K. J. (1962). The economic implications of learning by doing. *Review of Economic Studies*, **29**, 153–73.

Berndt, E. R. (1991). *The Practice of Econometrics*. Reading, MA: Addison-Wesley.

Carlton, D. W. Perloff, J. M. (1994). *Modern Industrial Organization*. 2nd edn, New York: HarperCollins.

Douglas, E. J. (1992). *Managerial Economics*. 4th edn, Englewood Cliffs, NJ: Prentice-Hall.

Ghemawat, P. (1985). Building strategy on the experience curve. *Harvard Business Review*, 63, 143–49.

Porter, M. E. (1980). *Competitive Strategy*. New York: Free Press.

ROBERT E. MCAULIFFE

lemons market In information theory, a "lemons market" is a market in which the degree of ASYMMETRIC INFORMATION between buyers and sellers is very high, and, in the extreme, may result in market failure. Akerlof (1970) provided an intuitive and logical explanation of this theoretical result by reference to a used car market. In a used car market, there may be cars that are of good quality and those that are "lemons." Since sellers are generally better informed than buyers regarding the quality of the car and buyers are not easily able to discern car quality, buyers will be unwilling to pay the "good car" price for a car of uncertain quality, so they value a car at the average price. In the extreme, owners of good cars will be unwilling to sell their cars at the prevailing price and ultimately, the only cars in the market will be those that no one wants and the market will fail.

The solution to this problem requires that market participants act to reduce the level of information asymmetry. For example, buyers might invest in additional information by hiring experts or gaining expertise themselves. Sellers may attempt to better convey information, although they will have to bear some costs to make their claims of value believable to potential buyers (*see* SIGNALING).

The logic and intuition used in the used car example has been extended to several other markets that exhibit imperfections due to information asymmetry. Spence (1974) suggests that the willingness of a potential employee to incur the costs of education and training is a reliable signal of quality that can be used to overcome the information asymmetries in the labor market. In insurance markets, the inability of insurers to accurately identify the risk class of potential policyholders creates the potential for market failure. If premiums are set at a rate based on the risk of the pool of potential policyholders, the good risks will choose to forgo insurance and the pool of policies will make losses for the insurer. However, Rothschild and Stiglitz (1976) suggest that the willingness of good risks to forgo full insurance (e.g. through deductibles and co-insurance) may provide a reliable signal that will allow the insurer to charge them appropriate premium rates. The result is that there will be two kinds of policies in the market: partial insurance policies at lower rates for the good risks, and full insurance at higher rates for the higher risks.

In the context of financial markets, information asymmetry exists between managers and shareholders. In addition, incentive conflicts make managers' favorable public announcements regarding the firm's future prospects less credible. Therefore, it is necessary that managers signal information to investors in a credible way, e.g. their willingness to accept compensation in the form of stock options. The high degree of regulation of information in the financial markets is, in part, designed to reduce information asymmetry that could lead to reduced investor confidence and market failure.

Bibliography

Akerlof, G. A. (1970). The market for 'lemons': quality uncertainty and the market mechanism. *Quarterly Journal of Economics*, **August**, 488–500.

Brigham, E. F. Gapenski, L. C. (1996). *Intermediate Financial Management*. 5th edn, Fort Worth, TX: Dryden.

Rothschild, M. Stiglitz, J. (1976). Equilibrium in competitive insurance markets: an essay on the economics of imperfect information. *Quarterly Journal of Economics*, **November**, 629–49.

Spence, M. (1974). *Market Signalling*. Cambridge, MA: Harvard University Press.

VICKIE L. BAJTELSMIT

Lerner index   This is one of several measures developed by economists to establish the extent of MARKET POWER held by firms in a market. Lerner (1934) devised this measure which is calculated as

$$L = \frac{(P - MC)}{P}$$

where P is the price of a firm's product and MC is the MARGINAL COST of its production.

In theory, values for L can range from zero to one, with larger values indicating greater market power. Under PERFECT COMPETITION a firm's MARGINAL REVENUE (MR) from additional sales is constant and equal to price, which is determined by the market. Following the rule for PROFIT MAXIMIZATION, the firm finds the output where MR (and thus P) is equal to MC. As a result the Lerner index for such firms, which have no ability to influence the market, has a value of zero.

For MONOPOLY and other imperfectly competitive markets, price typically is greater than marginal cost and thus L 0. In general, the ability of a firm to set its price above marginal cost and sustain the given differential over time is indicative of market power. To the extent that MC approximates the firm's average total cost, the Lerner index indicates the existence of positive ECONOMIC PROFIT resulting from this power. One difficulty with this index is that of measuring marginal cost. Often, to make the index operational, constant costs are assumed wherein marginal and average costs are equal. When this is done, the value of the index must be examined over time in order to identify market power since even perfectly competitive firms can earn positive economic profits in the short run.

The Lerner index is also a measure of MARKET PERFORMANCE. The social loss arising from the allocative inefficiency of imperfectly competitive markets depends directly on the extent of the divergence between price and marginal cost in the market (*see* DEADWEIGHT LOSS).

Bibliography

Greer, W. (1992). *Industrial Organization and Public Policy*. 3rd edn, New York: Macmillan.

Lerner, A. (1934). The concept of monopoly and the measurement of monopoly power. *Review of Economic Studies*, 1, 157–75.

GILBERT BECKER

limit pricing   When a firm practices limit pricing it chooses its price (and therefore output) in such a way that the remaining market demand (RESIDUAL DEMAND) is insufficient for an entrant to cover its AVERAGE TOTAL COST. As originally described by Modigliani (1958), if an established firm were threatened by entry in a single-period, the limit price was the highest price it could charge without allowing entry to occur. Naturally, the limit price which would accomplish this objective depended on the expectations of potential entrants. Modigliani assumed that entrants would expect the established firm to continue producing at the entry-limiting output even if entry occurred, equivalent to the assumption of COURNOT COMPETITION where each firm believes its rivals will continue to produce at current levels. If there are ECONOMIES OF SCALE in production, limit pricing would allow established firms to earn economic profits while preventing entry, even when entrants have the same costs as incumbent firms (see ECONOMIC PROFIT). Gilbert (1989) refers to this pricing policy as "classic limit pricing."

Gaskins (1971) extended this model to consider dynamic limit pricing where a firm is threatened by potential COMPETITION in the current period and in future periods and where the rate of entry by new firms depended on the difference between the current price and their marginal costs. If the established firm set a high price, it would earn high profits initially but would also encourage more entry and would decrease the price (and profits) in the future. A lower price set by the established firm would slow the rate of entry into the industry but would also lower profits. If the established firm had no cost or other advantages over entrants, ultimately it would lose its dominant position and the market would become perfectly competitive (see DOMINANT FIRM). But, as Jacquemin (1987) notes, if an existing firm has no cost advantages over entrants and is only able to use price as its strategic weapon, a competitive outcome is not surprising.

In the classic limit pricing model and the dynamic limit pricing model, potential competition constrains the MARKET POWER of existing firms who are forced to set prices below the monopoly level. However, the assumption about the entrant's expectations in these cases is restrictive. Why should an entrant expect the established firm to maintain its output level after entry has occurred if that is not the profit-maximizing choice? In the post-entry period, both firms would earn higher profits by restricting output and raising price, so a threat by established firms to keep output constant after entry has occurred is not credible and an entrant should not believe it. For such a threat to be credible, the established firm must make commitments in the current period which make high output levels profitable in subsequent periods. Dixit (1980) showed that investments in EXCESS CAPACITY or in other SUNK COSTS could commit the established firm to maintain high output in subsequent periods. These sunk costs represent a signal to potential entrants that the established firm would respond aggressively to entry and make entry deterrence credible.

Limit pricing is an element of firm conduct in a market which, if successful, can affect MARKET STRUCTURE. In his survey of research in the area, Gilbert (1989) found weak evidence in support of the classic limit pricing theory and the dynamic limit pricing theory. Established firms do not appear to set prices at the MONOPOLY level, nor do they set prices so low that entry is deterred; see Masson and Shaanan (1982) and Greer (1992). However, in his survey of executives, Smiley (1988) found that managers of major American companies preferred higher ADVERTISING expenditures and PRODUCT PROLIFERATION as strategic weapons to deter entry and were less likely to rely on excess capacity and limit pricing.

see also accommodation; credible strategies; signaling

Bibliography

Dixit, A. (1980). The role of investment in entry deterrence. *Economic Journal*, **90**, 95–106.

Encaoua, D., Geroski, P. Jacquemin, A. (1986). Strategic competition and the persistence of dominant firms: a survey. Stiglitz, J. E. Matthewson, G. F. *New Developments in the Analysis of Market Structure.* Cambridge, MA: MIT.

Gaskins, D. (1971). Dynamic limit pricing: optimal pricing under threat of entry. *Journal of Economic Theory*, **2**, 306–22.

Gilbert, R. J. (1989). The role of potential competition in industrial organization. *Journal of Economic Perspectives*, **3**, 107–28.

Greer, D. F. (1992). *Industrial Organization and Public Policy.* 3rd edn, New York: Macmillan.

Jacquemin, A. (1987). *The New Industrial Organization: Market Forces and Strategic Behavior.* Cambridge, MA: MIT.

Masson, R. Shaanan, J. (1982). Stochastic dynamic limit pricing: an empirical test. *Review of Economics and Statistics*, **64**, 413–23.

Modigliani, F. (1958). New elements on the oligopoly front. *Journal of Political Economy*, **66**, 215–32.

Smiley, R. (1988). Empirical evidence on strategic entry deterrence. *International Journal of Industrial Organization*, 6, 167–80.

ROBERT E. MCAULIFFE

linear regression Linear regression allows managers and researchers to estimate (or quantify) how much a particular variable is affected by another and to determine whether the relationship is statistically significant. Although nonlinear models and techniques are also available (Greene, 1993), a wide class of models can be estimated with linear regression methods, which may explain their popularity. Even so, linear regression techniques are appropriate only when the *true* underlying relationship between the dependent variable and the independent variable(s) is in fact linear or can be transformed into a linear relationship. If the model is misspecified then the resulting estimates are likely to be biased.

In a linear regression, also referred to as **ordinary least squares**, the true population relationship between the dependent variable, Y, and the independent variable, X is assumed to be linear. For example, in the simplest case with only one independent variable, the relation to be estimated is:

$$Y_i = \beta_0 + \beta_1 \times X_i + \nu_i \qquad (1)$$

where the Y are observations on the *dependent* variable, the X are observations on the *independent* or *explanatory* variable, and the ν are the error terms. The coefficients β_0 and β_1 are the population parameters to be estimated and reflect the effect of the variable X on Y. For example, a manager or researcher might be interested in the effect of advertising on sales, and the expected relationship might be given as in equation (1). The least squares estimators of β_0 and β_1 are obtained by minimizing the sum of the square of the estimated sample errors. If we let $\hat{\beta}_0$ and $\hat{\beta}_1$ represent the least squares estimators of β_0 and β_1 in equation (1), then the estimated sample error, $\hat{\nu}_i$ can be defined as

$$\hat{\nu}_i = Y_i - \hat{\beta}_0 - \hat{\beta}_1 \times X_i \qquad (2)$$

Given equation (2), the least squares estimators are obtained by minimizing the sum of the squared sample errors below with respect to $\hat{\beta}_0$ and $\hat{\beta}_1$. Thus we minimize

$$\sum_{i=1}^{n} \hat{\nu}_i^2 \qquad (3)$$

by choosing the best values for $\hat{\beta}_0$ and $\hat{\beta}_1$ where the summation is over all n observations. It can be shown that the least squares estimators, $\hat{\beta}_0$ and $\hat{\beta}_1$, are given by:

$$\hat{\beta}_1 = \frac{\sum (Y_i - \overline{Y})^2 \times (X_i - \overline{X})^2}{\sum (X_i - \overline{X})^2}$$
$$= \frac{\text{Cov}(Y, X)}{\text{Var}(X)}$$

$$\text{and } \hat{\beta}_0 = \overline{Y} - \hat{\beta}_1 \times \overline{X} \qquad (4)$$

where $\text{cov}(Y, X)$ is the COVARIANCE of the dependent variable, Y, with the independent variable, X; $\text{var}(X)$ is the VARIANCE of the independent variable; $\overline{Y}$ and $\overline{X}$ are the sample means of Y and X. Therefore, if the goal is to choose linear estimators to make the sum of the squared estimated errors as small as possible, the estimators in equation (4) will satisfy this requirement. In fact, it can be shown that the ordinary least squares estimators are the *best* in the class of unbiased linear estimators (Maddala, 1992; Greene, 1993) if the assumptions regarding the error terms hold (*see* ERROR TERMS IN REGRESSION).

It can be shown that the least squares estimators in equation (4) have expected values equal to the population parameters when the assumptions regarding the ERROR TERMS IN REGRESSION hold. The standard errors of these estimators are calculated by most statistical programs (*see* STANDARD ERROR OF THE COEFFICIENT; STANDARD ERROR OF ESTIMATE) and CONFIDENCE INTERVALS and T-STATISTIC can then be calculated to determine whether the independent variable significantly affects the dependent variable. One measure of how well the estimated model fits the data is the coefficient of determination, or R^2, which measures the percentage of the variation in the dependent variable explained by the independent variable. A high value of the R^2; (i.e. a value close to one) indicates that most of the variation in the dependent variable is explained by the independent variable.

In many cases, the underlying relationship between the dependent and independent variables is nonlinear, but can be transformed into a linear relation. For example, the COBB–DOUGLAS PRODUCTION FUNCTION is:

$$q = AL^{\alpha}K^{\beta} \qquad (5)$$

where q is the output produced and L and K are the labor and capital inputs respectively. This production function can be transformed by taking logarithms of both sides to obtain:

$$\log(q) = \log(A) + \alpha \times \log(L) + \beta \times \log(K) \qquad (6)$$

which is now a linear relationship and can be estimated by least squares. A convenient feature of a logarithmic regression as above is that the estimated coefficients are elasticities. The coefficient α above is the ELASTICITY of output with respect to a change in labor input.

Another possibility when the underlying relationship is nonlinear is to create additional explanatory variables which are simply higher powers of X:

$$Y_i = \hat{\beta}_0 + \hat{\beta}_1 \times X_i + \hat{\beta}_2 \times (X_i)^2 + \hat{\beta}_3 \times (X_i)^3$$

This transformation allows a researcher to estimate a cubic relationship between the independent variable and the dependent variable, although MULTICOLLINEARITY might occur.

When there are several explanatory variables in the regression equation (multiple regression), the basic features of the least squares estimators remain but some additional problems are created. First, the estimated coefficient in a multiple regression represents the additional or incremental effect of the independent variable *holding the other independent variables constant*. The multiple regression would be written as:

$$q_i = \hat{\beta}_0 + \hat{\beta}_1 \times X_{1,i} + \hat{\beta}_2 \times X_{2,i} + \hat{\beta}_3 \times X_{3,i} + \nu_i$$

where the $X_{k,i}$ represent the i observations on the different explanatory variables. For example, the Cobb–Douglas production function might specify X_2, as observations of the units of labor employed to produce output, X_2, as the units of capital employed and X_3, as the units of some other input, such as energy or materials. The coefficient $\hat{\beta}_0$ would then be an estimate of the logarithm of technical change while the coefficient $\hat{\beta}_1$ would be the estimated elasticity of output given a change in labor input, holding all other variables constant.

A problem in multiple regression is multicollinearity, where there is correlation between the explanatory variables. When one of the independent variables is correlated with one or more of the remaining explanatory variables, the data make it difficult to determine the independent contributions of each of the X_k variables. As a result, the estimated standard error of the coefficients will be larger and this will make it appear as though one or more of the independent variables have no significant effect on the dependent variable when in fact they may.

When estimating a multiple regression, it is important to avoid specification errors in the model. A researcher may, for example, include irrelevant explanatory variables in the regression or may omit variables which should be included. Generally, including irrelevant explanatory variables will not bias the estimated coefficients, but omitting variables which should be included in the regression will cause the least squares estimators to be biased; see Maddala (1992) or Greene (1993). One indication that relevant variables may have been omitted from the regression is the presence of AUTOCORRELATION in the estimated residuals.

Bibliography

Douglas, E. J. (1992). *Managerial Economics*. 4th edn, Englewood Cliffs, NJ: Prentice-Hall.

Greene, W. H. (1993). *Econometric Analysis*. 2nd edn, New York: Macmillan.

Maddala, G. S. (1992). *Introduction to Econometrics*. 2nd edn, New York: Macmillan.

Hirschey, M. Pappas, J. L. (1995). *Fundamentals of Managerial Economics*. 5th edn, New York: Dryden.

ROBERT E. MCAULIFFE

long run cost curves   For the firm, the long run refers to the length of time required so that all inputs in production are variable. There are no fixed costs in the long run. Since the firm is free to choose its capacity level in the long run, this is also considered the planning horizon. The long run is not fixed in calendar time but may vary across industries and even between firms within the same industry if their contractual commitments differ. From the perspective of the industry, Stigler (1966) suggested that the long run was the time required for a market or industry to fully adjust to "new conditions" and the period of adjustment required would depend upon the questions under consideration.

The long run average cost (LRAC) curve is the planning curve for the firm because it shows the minimum average cost of production using plants of varying sizes. As such it envelopes the short run average cost (SRAC) curves for different capacity levels and is typically assumed to be U-shaped. Associated with the long run average cost curve is a long run marginal cost (LRMC) curve which lies below the LRAC curve when the LRAC is falling (due to ECONOMIES OF SCALE), intersects the LRAC curve at its minimum, and lies above the LRAC curve when the LRAC curve is rising (when DISECONOMIES OF SCALE occur) as in figure 1 below.

The LRMC curve reflects the change in total costs when an additional unit of output is produced, given that all inputs are adjusted optimally (including capital). When capital expenditures are discrete and cannot be adjusted to produce one additional unit, such as when the scale of the plant is changed, the LRMC curve shows the changes in total costs moving to the next scale of operation; see Sexton (1995). In these cases, the LRAC curve will not be as smooth as in figure 1 and will follow the individual short run average cost curves more closely. If a manager anticipated sales of 1 million units per period, then she would choose capacity level $SRAC_1$ above. However, if sales were expected to be 1.5 million units per period, $SRAC_2$ would be the best capacity choice and in this example, it is also the MINIMUM EFFICIENT SCALE. For this plant, both the LRAC and SRAC curves are at their minimum points at 1.5 million units of output per period and so the LRMC curve intersects the short run marginal cost ($SRMC_2$) curve at this point as well. It should also be noted that for each point on the long run marginal cost curve, a short run marginal cost curve passes through it. Since some factors of production are fixed in the short run, the short run marginal cost curve should be steeper than the long run marginal cost curve where all

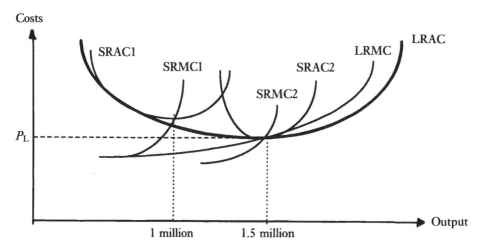

Figure 1   Long run and short run cost curves

factors of production can be adjusted optimally; (*see* Friedman (1976), Shughart, Chappell and Cottle (1994) and SHORT RUN COST CURVES).

The output level of 1.5 million units at a price P_L represents the long run EQUILIBRIUM for a firm in a competitive industry, where the representative firm earns zero ECONOMIC PROFIT and operates a plant at the minimum efficient scale. At this price, there will be no net ENTRY into or net EXIT from the industry unless the conditions of supply or demand change.

Bibliography

Friedman, M. (1976). *Price Theory*. 2nd edn, Chicago: Aldine.

Sexton, R. L. (1995). *Microeconomics*. Englewood Cliffs, NJ: Prentice-Hall.

Shughart, W. F., Chappell, W. F. Cottle, R. L. (1994). *Modern Managerial Economics*. Cincinatti, OH: South-Western Publishing.

Stigler, G. J. (1966). *The Theory of Price*. 3rd edn, New York: Macmillan.

ROBERT E. MCAULIFFE

M

make or buy decisions A firm's decision to make an input in production rather than buy that input in the market is an important one that firms frequently fail to reconsider. What a firm chooses to produce is one of the most fundamental decisions it can make. But if markets are so efficient in providing resources, why should firms even exist? Coase (1937) answered that there were costs from using the market to obtain resources just as there are costs of producing them within the firm. The TRANSACTIONS COSTS of using the market must then be weighed against the coordination costs of producing the input internally.

Williamson (1985) argued that internal production requires additional bureaucracy to manage the new activity along with higher production costs. But if the firm obtained the input in the market, it would be costly (in terms of time) to locate suitable suppliers, monitor quality levels, and ensure that supplies will be delivered on time. When the part is unique and very specialized, it is costly to use the market because there may only be one or two suppliers. In this case, the firm may decide to produce the part internally.

Porter (1980) suggests that VERTICAL INTEGRATION may also achieve strategic goals for the firm. For example, a firm may want to improve the quality or lower the production costs of its product but would need closer coordination with its suppliers to accomplish this goal. Another possibility is that internal production will improve the firm's flexibility to produce new products.

Bibliography

Coase, R. H. (1937). The nature of the firm. *Economica*, **4**, 386–405.

Porter, M. E. (1980). *Competitive Strategy*. New York: Free Press.

Shughart, W. F. (1990). *The Organization of Industry*. Boston, MA: Irwin.

Williamson, O. E. (1985). *The Economic Institutions of Capitalism: Firms, Markets, Relational Contracting*. New York: Free Press.

ROBERT E. MCAULIFFE

marginal cost The marginal cost is the change in total costs due to a unit (or incremental) change in output. For discrete changes in output, marginal cost is given by:

$$MC = \frac{\Delta TC}{\Delta q} \qquad (1)$$

where MC is the marginal cost, ΔTC is the change in total costs, and Δq is the change in output. In the short run, fixed costs do not vary with output so marginal costs can also be written as:

$$MC = \frac{\Delta TVC}{\Delta q} \qquad (2)$$

where ΔTVC is the change in TOTAL VARIABLE COST. If the total cost function is known or has been estimated, marginal cost would be the derivative of total costs with respect to output. Therefore, if total costs are:

$$TC = 1000 + 5 \times q + 8 \times q^2 \qquad (3)$$

marginal costs would be:

$$MC = \frac{dTC}{dq} = 5 + 16 \times q \qquad (4)$$

Understanding marginal costs is crucial for optimal decision making because, unless there are resource constraints, any activity should be continued as long as the additional (or marginal) benefits exceed the marginal costs. If two or more activities have marginal benefits which exceed their marginal costs but a manager cannot fully fund all of them, then each activity should be funded until each provides the same marginal benefits per dollar (*see* PROFIT MAXIMIZATION; UTILITY MAXIMIZATION). For any *change* in an activity (production, pricing, advertising, etc.) a manager must compare the marginal benefits of the change against the marginal costs to make the best decision.

For example, consider a manager whose only variable input is labor. The change in total costs will then be the change in labor input (ΔL) multiplied by the wage rate (w), and since marginal costs are the change in total variable costs divided by the change in quantity (Δq), from equation (2) we have:

$$MC = \frac{\Delta TVC}{\Delta q} = \frac{w \times \Delta L}{\Delta q} = w \times \left\{ \frac{\Delta L}{\Delta q} \right\}$$

(5)

The term in braces is the inverse of the MARGINAL PRODUCT of labor, so (5) shows the relationship between marginal costs, variable input costs (the wage rate, w) and productivity (the marginal product of labor). An increase in the cost of variable inputs, w, will increase the marginal cost of production while an increase in productivity (a rise in the marginal product of labor) will reduce marginal costs, as would be expected; see Shughart, Chappell and Cottle (1994) and Friedman (1976).

As Baumol (1977) notes, managers frequently use average values rather than marginal values when making decisions, and this can lead to incorrect conclusions. This occurs because much of the accounting information provided to managers is in the form of average or total figures. In addition, marginal calculations may require information a company does not yet have, such as the marginal benefits and costs of an increase in advertising. The important issue is not whether past advertising expenditures have generated net revenues which exceeded the costs, but whether any increase (or decrease) in advertising is justified. Finally, because marginal costs reflect the change in total costs for the last unit(s) produced, they reflect changes more quickly than average total costs which are based on the costs for all units produced to that point (*see* AVERAGE TOTAL COST). Thus even if the average increase in net revenues from advertising fell by a small amount, the *marginal* change could be substantial and profits could be increased by reducing advertising expenditures.

Bibliography

Baumol, W. J. (1977). *Economic Theory and Operations Analysis.* Englewood Cliffs, NJ: Prentice-Hall.

Douglas, E. J. (1992). *Managerial Economics.* 4th edn, Englewood Cliffs, NJ: Prentice-Hall.

Friedman, M. (1976). *Price Theory.* 2nd edn, Chicago: Aldine.

Shughart, W. F., Chappell, W. F. Cottle, R. L. (1994). *Modern Managerial Economics.* Cincinatti, OH: South-Western Publishing.

ROBERT E. MCAULIFFE

marginal product The marginal product of any input, such as labor or capital, measures the change in TOTAL PRODUCT as a result of a small change in the usage of that input, holding all other inputs constant. For example, the marginal product of labor or capital is the additional output from using one more labor or machine hour.

The marginal product of an input that is infinitely divisible can be obtained by taking the partial derivative of the production function with respect to that input (*see* PRODUCTION FUNCTIONS). In the relevant range of production, marginal product is positive. An increase in the marginal product (or an increase in productivity) of an input means that through better technology, more efficient management, or an increase in work effort, the company is able to obtain more output from the same amount of inputs. Alternatively, marginal product can be improved through the restructuring of the company by decreasing the number of work hours while holding the addition to total output constant.

The total product and marginal product curves demonstrate the LAW OF VARIABLE PROPORTIONS which states that as the quantity of a variable input increases, holding the amount of other productive factors constant, beyond some point the marginal product of the variable input begins to decrease; total product continues to increase though at a decreasing rate. DIMINISHING RETURNS arise because the fixed amount of plant and equipment is gradually spread among an even greater number of workers, leaving a smaller amount of capital for each one.

By enabling us to measure the change in total product as a result of a change in a variable input, marginal product permits comparisons with the short run cost of production (*see* SHORT RUN COST CURVES). If the costs of labor and machine hours are known, we can calculate the MARGINAL COST by dividing an input's cost by the marginal product of the input. Therefore, marginal costs are inversely related to the marginal product of the variable inputs. For example, when the marginal product of labor is falling, the marginal cost of output is increasing, and vice versa. When the marginal product of labor is constant, additional units can be produced with constant marginal cost.

Knowledge of the marginal products of inputs enables managers to determine the short-run optimal level of employment of capital and labor in the production process. To maximize total profit inputs should be hired up to the point where the marginal input cost equals the marginal revenue product of labor. Marginal input cost is defined as the amount that an additional unit of the variable input adds to total cost. Marginal revenue product is defined as the amount that an additional unit of the variable unit adds to total revenue and equals the marginal product of the variable input times the marginal revenue resulting from the increase in output produced.

Bibliography

Douglas, E. J. (1992). *Managerial Economics.* 4th edn, Englewood Cliffs, NJ: Prentice-Hall.
Shughart, W. F., Chappell, W. F. Cottle, R. L. (1994). *Modern Managerial Economics.* Cincinatti, OH: South-Western Publishing.

LIDIJA POLUTNIK

marginal rate of substitution   The marginal rate of substitution of good X for good Y (MRS$_{xy}$) is defined as the amount of good Y which the consumer is willing to give up in exchange for one additional unit of good X, in order to maintain the same level of TOTAL UTILITY. Since the same total utility is achieved

from the two choices, MRS$_{xy}$ concerns the movement along a consumer's indifference curve (*see* INDIFFERENCE CURVES). Specifically, it measures the slope of the indifference curve between any two points. This identifies the tradeoff of one good for another which the consumer is *willing* to make, independent of the prices of the two goods which indicate the tradeoff conditions *required* by the market.

The marginal rate of substitution between two goods describes the relative importance of the two goods to the consumer and it is defined as the ratio of the marginal utilities of the two goods. For example, a MRS$_{xy}$ with the value of 3 to 1 indicates that the consumer is currently willing to give up 3 units of good Y in order to receive 1 extra unit of good X. Here, the MARGINAL UTILITY of good X (MU$_x$) is three times that of good Y. This can be formally expressed as:

$$\mathrm{MRS}_{x,y} = -\frac{\Delta Y}{\Delta X} = \frac{\mathrm{MU}_x}{\mathrm{MU}_y} = 3$$

where Δ indicates the change in the quantity of the good in question.

Since the marginal utility of either good will typically decrease with greater consumption of that good, the marginal rate of substitution and therefore the slope of the indifference curve is typically not constant. One exception is the case where the two goods in question are perfect SUBSTITUTES. Here the marginal rate of substitution will be constant, e.g. 2 aspirin may be substituted for every 1 acetaminophen tablet.

The rate at which consumers are willing to trade off one product for another can be altered by changing their tastes. Here, ADVERTISING and other forms of promotion can be useful.

see also **diminishing marginal utility; utility maximization**

Bibliography

Hirschey, M. Pappas, J. (1995). *Fundamentals of Managerial Economics.* 5th edn, Fort Worth: Dryden.

GILBERT BECKER

marginal rate of technical substitution The production of virtually every good requires the use of two or more inputs such as labor, capital or raw materials. Typically, these inputs can be used in varying proportions to generate the same level of output. For example, in agriculture varying amounts of labor and capital can be used to plant or harvest the same number of acres of land per day. Modern farming techniques in the US and other developed nations use large harvesting combines requiring relatively few workers, while less sophisticated farming operations often use a highly labor intensive approach. Since reducing the amount of any one input generally tends to reduce total output, a greater quantity of a second input is needed to compensate for the lost output. The marginal rate of technical substitution measures the rate at which any one input must be substituted for one unit of another input in order to maintain a constant level of output.

Formally, the production of varying levels of output using different combinations of inputs is described using an isoquant map (see ISO-QUANT-ISOCOST CURVES). The marginal rate of technical substitution is measured by the slope of a given isoquant curve between any two points on that curve. Since increased use of any one input tends to reduce that input's marginal productivity, the marginal rate of technical substitution tends to decrease with greater substitution towards an input. That is, the isoquant curve tends to be convex.

The marginal rate of technical substitution between inputs is important information for managers selecting the optimal combination of inputs. Cost minimization requires that the marginal rate of technical substitution between inputs be equal to the ratio of the prices of those inputs.

see also **marginal rate of substitution**

Bibliography

Hirschey, M. Pappas, J. (1995). *Fundamentals of Managerial Economics.* 5th edn, Fort Worth: Dryden.

GILBERT BECKER

marginal revenue   Marginal revenue is the change in the total revenue resulting from a one unit increase in the sales of a product. It is important to a firm because PROFIT MAXIMIZA-TION requires the firm's managers to find the output level where this extra revenue equals the MARGINAL COST of production. While greater sales resulting from price reductions generally cause marginal revenue to fall, marginal cost eventually rises with greater output. Thus, any output below the level where the two are equal leaves the possibility for additional profits to be made, but output beyond that level costs more to produce than the gain in revenues from the additional sale.

The nature of the relation between marginal revenue and the level of output sold varies with the basic market structure under consideration (see BASIC MARKET STRUCTURES). Under PERFECT COMPETITION the firm, being too small to influence market outcomes, can sell as much output as it desires without changing the market price. As such, for any additional sales, the marginal revenue is constant at the level of the market generated price. In other words, the firm faces a demand which is perfectly elastic for its own product.

Under OLIGOPOLY and other forms of imperfect competition, additional sales may occur as a result of a change in the quality of the product or a change in advertising (see DORFMAN-STEINER CONDITION), or they may be brought about by a change in the product's price. The LAW OF DEMAND indicates that, all else being equal, an increase in the number of units sold requires a reduction in price. In the absence of PRICE DISCRIMINATION, the marginal revenue from an additional unit sold tends to decline as the lower price needed to generate a larger number of unit sales tends to more or less offset the gains from the increased quantity sold (see ELASTICITY). Moreover, the estimation of marginal revenue becomes more difficult in oligopoly since the amount of additional sales resulting from a price reduction depends in part on the reaction of rivals, who may or may not respond with price cuts of their own.

see also **kinked demand curves; profit maximization; perfect competition**

Bibliography

Carlton, D. W. Perloff, J. M. (1994). *Modern Industrial Organization.* 2nd edn, New York: HarperCollins.

Douglas, E. (1992). *Managerial Economics: Analysis and Strategy*. 4th edn, Englewood Cliffs, NJ: Prentice-Hall.

GILBERT BECKER

marginal utility   Marginal utility is defined as the change in the TOTAL UTILITY resulting from the consumption of one additional unit of a good by a consumer. For any individual good, consumer behavior typically follows the law of DIMINISHING MARGINAL UTILITY which states that in any given time period, as the rate of consumption of a good rises, the additional utility, or satisfaction, acquired by the consumer eventually declines.

It can be shown that for an individual who is purchasing several goods simultaneously, the maximization of total utility requires equating the marginal utility per dollar spent on each good. More formally, this ideal combination of goods occurs when

$$MU_1/P_1 = MU_2/P_2 = \ldots = MU_i/P_i \quad (1)$$

where MU and P indicate the marginal utility and price of the ith good. An imbalance between any two of these ratios, for example

$$MU_2/P_2 > MU_1/P_1 \quad (2)$$

would result in a situation where a reallocation of the consumer's income toward purchasing more of good 2 would cause a net increase in total utility. This is because the additional satisfaction gained from consumption of an extra unit of good 2 would more than offset the loss of utility from the decreased consumption of good 1. An inequality such as in equation (2) would occur if, for example, the price of the second good, P_2, was decreased. The equation demonstrates why a decrease in the price of this good would lead to a shifting away from good 1 and an increase in the purchase of good 2 (*see* SUBSTITUTION EFFECT). This helps to generate the negative relationship between the price of good 2 and its quantity demanded, which is the foundation of the LAW OF DEMAND. Similarly, equation (2) can be used to demonstrate how a manager may create a more favorable position for a product by using increased advertising. This strategy, when successful, creates imbalances between the ratios by altering the marginal utility of one good relative to the others.

The marginal utility of income, to a gambler, or profit, to an investor, can be used to identify the three categories of risk behavior which individuals may portray. An individual is identified as a **risk lover** if his marginal utility of income grows as his level of income rises. An individual is said to show RISK AVERSION if the marginal utility of an extra dollar of income falls as income rises, and RISK NEUTRALITY if the marginal utility of an extra dollar of income is constant. A **risk averter** typically sees risk as being undesirable and is only willing to tolerate greater uncertainty in an outcome if rewarded with a greater expected return. A risk lover is a gambler who prefers the increased uncertainty.

Bibliography

Douglas, E. (1992). *Managerial Economics: Analysis and Strategy*. 4th edn, Englewood Cliffs, NJ: Prentice-Hall.
Mansfield, E. (1993). *Managerial Economics: Theory, Applications, and Cases*. 2nd edn, New York: Norton.

GILBERT BECKER

market definition   An economic definition of the term "market" is the group of all firms willing and able to sell a similar product or service to the same potential buyers. As such, the market definition for a given product is the identification of the relevant group of sellers which may be seen as being in competition with one another for the sale of a particular product. Two boundaries are used to define a market:

(1) the product boundary and
(2) the geographic boundary.

Properly identifying these boundaries for a particular market will result in a more accurate count of the number and size distribution of firms in that market. This information is useful for a firm in developing its competitive strategy. The information is essential for the government and the courts in developing ANTITRUST POL-ICY and in deliberating antitrust cases. For example, the CLAYTON ACT proscribes mergers which substantially lessen competition "in any line of commerce" (i.e. product market) and "in any section of the country" (i.e. GEOGRAPHIC MARKET).

The central issues in market definition are where and how these boundaries are to be drawn. Various theoretical and practical tests have been developed. The relevant product market boundary determines a set of competitors in terms of the substitutability of the product. For markets under PERFECT COMPETITION the product boundary is relatively easy to establish since the product is homogeneous across firms. Where PRODUCT DIFFERENTIATION exists, this boundary becomes blurred. Here, CROSS ELASTICITIES are tools which have been used for decades.

The cross elasticity of demand between two goods measures the percentage change in unit sales of one firm's product given a 1 percent change in the price of a rival's product. As such it measures the degree to which the two goods are substitutes in the eyes of consumers. A high cross elasticity measure indicates close substitutability and thus the firms in question should be counted as being in the same market. Similarly, cross elasticities of supply must be considered. High values for this measure indicate a firm's willingness and ability to produce more of their own good in reaction to a rival's price increase. It may also indicate a similarity in technological process between firms and the potential to switch product lines and readily and easily enter a product market where price has been increased above the competitive level. For antitrust purposes, the condition of ENTRY is important to evaluate as potential entry often can diminish the effectiveness of existing firms' attempts to abuse MARKET POWER. As a result, both measures of cross elasticities are needed to properly define the relevant product market.

Scherer and Ross (1990), and others have identified several difficulties arising in the application of these measures. First, what constitutes a "high" value for cross elasticity is necessarily an arbitrary decision. Second, two different estimates for the cross elasticity of demand between two goods A and B will be generated for the relatively similar cases of a 1 percent price increase in product A and a 1 percent price decrease in product B. Third, the correct estimation of elasticities requires using price changes originating from the competitive price level. As a result, the courts have also attempted to generate "common sense" product market definitions by identifying product groups in terms of their different product attributes.

One theoretically appealing new method for market boundary delineation, developed by Boyer (1979), has recently been put to use by the federal government. Boyer argues that a market can be identified, from the point of view of a single firm, as the smallest group of rivals necessary to organize in order to successfully act as a cartel (see CARTELS). If this group of firms could raise prices without bringing about reaction by other firms which was sufficient to force a retreat in the cartel price hike, then these other firms can correctly be seen as being outside of the market. This may be due to their producing a sufficiently different (non-substitutable) product, or because of the fact that their business takes place in a geographically distinct location. If, on the other hand, the initial group of firms in question could not successfully collude for a significant period of time without feeling the disciplinary effects of the other rivals increasing their supply, then the relevant market should be expanded to include these firms. One nice feature of this method is that it can be used to define the relevant GEOGRAPHIC MARKET as well as the product market boundary.

In revising its guidelines for mergers in 1982, the Department of Justice introduced a variation of Boyer's method to define markets. The method uses what is known as the 5 percent rule, or SSNIP (a small but significant nontransitory increase in prices). This involves examining a hypothetical monopolist existing at the site of the proposed merger and evaluating its ability to raise price (by 5 percent) above the current level for a sustained period. If the potential SSNIP would not be successful in the eyes of antitrust officials because of the reactions of rivals outside of the area being considered, the definition of the market will be expanded. This method, with modest revisions, was retained in the most recent 1992 merger guidelines.

The proper definition of the relevant market can be crucial in these and other antitrust cases. An expanded market definition which includes a greater number of rivals will naturally tend, for example, to diminish the market share of the merging firms and thus make the merger less potentially onerous in the eyes of the antitrust enforcers. Boyer's work recognized that problems similar to those involved in the use of cross elasticities still exist with the new approach. Moreover Scherer and Ross argue that the use of the 5 percent rule in a market in which market power already exists will tend to yield biased market definitions which could increase the likelihood of allowing mergers which are being examined.

see also **geographic market; horizontal merger guidelines; merger guidelines, 1992**

Bibliography

Boyer, K. (1979). Industry boundaries. Calvani, T. Siegfried, J. *Economic Analysis and Antitrust Law.* Boston: Little, Brown.

Greer, D. (1992). *Industrial Organization and Public Policy.* 3rd edn, New York: Macmillan.

Howard, M. (1983). *Antitrust and Trade Regulation.* Englewood Cliffs, NJ: Prentice-Hall.

Scherer, F. Ross, D. (1990). *Industrial Market Structure and Economic Performance.* 3rd edn, Boston: Houghton Mifflin.

US Department of Justice, Federal Trade Commission (1992). *Horizontal Merger Guidelines.* Washington DC: US Government Printing Office.

GILBERT BECKER

market performance Market performance is the ability of firms in a market to achieve certain socially desirable goals, including EFFICIENCY and equity. Several types of efficiency have been identified. The first, **production efficiency**, occurs when suppliers minimize the AVERAGE TOTAL COST of production of a good, in both the SHORT RUN and the long run. By choosing the optimal combination of labor and other variable inputs, managers can minimize the short run per unit cost of production. By achieving MINIMUM EFFICIENT SCALE, long run costs of production can also be minimized. As a result, production efficiency enhances firms' profitability. In addition, lower production costs and competition lead to lower prices, which benefit consumers. Moreover, this type of efficiency benefits society on the whole by minimizing the amount of its scarce resources which are needed to produce the product.

A second type of efficiency is **dynamic efficiency**, which focuses on technological progress. Here efficiency is achieved if market conditions induce a socially optimal amount of research and development, leading to a maximum level of innovation and invention. Schumpeter (1942) first proposed that large firm size and high industry concentration enhanced innovation. Many explanations, from the existence of ECONOMIES OF SCALE in research and development, to the disproportionate availability of funds for large firms in imperfect CAPITAL MARKETS, to the existence of economic profits in concentrated markets (*see* ECONOMIC PROFIT), have been advanced in favor of this hypothesis. Other arguments conflict with Schumpeter, maintaining that the incentive to innovate is diminished in markets where competition is imperfect. Cohen and Levin (1989) survey this literature and find that although there is a wealth of empirical studies of these hypotheses, the results are inconclusive. They suggest that other variables which affect dynamic efficiency, such as the demand for innovation and the technological opportunity for innovation, need additional investigation.

A third type of efficiency is that of **allocative efficiency**. This is achieved when the amount of resources allocated to (and thus the number of goods produced in) each market maximizes society's welfare by reducing the DEADWEIGHT LOSS associated with MARKET POWER. This type of efficiency is achieved when price is determined by the MARGINAL COST of production, as is the case in PERFECT COMPETITION.

The final performance criterion, **equity**, involves a question of fairness of the levels of prices and profits which are established in markets. The topic is quite controversial. By one definition, zero long run economic profits constitutes a fair result, since the buyers pay only for the economic costs of production, and the sellers have all of their costs covered, including the owners' OPPORTUNITY COSTS. An alternative definition of fairness establishes that any level of economic profits are acceptable as long as there is a voluntary exchange between buyers and sellers in a market which is reasonably competitive. Martin (1994) indicates that this divergence of opinion as to an appropriate definition of fairness has resulted in differences in state and federal government policies concerning antitrust enforcement during the 1980s. As one example of this, the National Association of Attorneys General, fearing that market power would increase the likelihood of unfair transfers of wealth from consumers to producers, established more stringent standards for mergers than those introduced by the federal government.

Measurement

Most empirical studies investigating issues concerning market performance have used one of two measures. Perhaps most prominent are studies using measures of firm and industry **profit rates**. If long run rates of return on assets or owner's equity are derived in part from the existence of market power, such profits may indicate a lack of market fairness. Moreover, these profits may be indicative of inefficiency resulting from this power if BARRIERS TO ENTRY or other factors foster an environment wherein maximum efficiency is not forced by competition.

Unfortunately, the use of profit rate data suffers from a number of measurement problems. Fisher and McGowan (1983) point out several of these flaws. For example, if the value of the firm's capital, or the depreciation thereof, is measured using accounting as opposed to economic definitions, the correct profit levels will not be measured. Similarly, the value of advertising and research and development can not be correctly associated with only the year in which the expenditure takes place and thus the measure of economic profit for that year may diverge from that of the reported ACCOUNTING PROFIT. In addition, profit rates for different industries need to be adjusted for differences in risk which occur across industries if a correct evaluation of the extent of excessive profit is to be made. Finally, profit rates suffer conceptually as a measure of performance since high profits may indicate economic efficiency and thus good performance.

A second tool used to measure performance is the **price–cost margin**. One theoretically appealing example is the LERNER INDEX, which measures the difference between price and marginal cost as a percentage of price. While also indicating profitability, the extent of allocative inefficiency is directly measured in

this index since the deadweight loss to society depends on the size of the gap between the marginal value which consumers give to the last unit consumed (price) and its marginal cost of production. Unfortunately, data on marginal cost is also difficult to obtain. These and other issues continue to make the evaluation of market performance difficult.

see also **structure-conduct-performance paradigm; market power; efficiency**

Bibliography

Carlton, D. Perloff, J. (1994). *Modern Industrial Organization*. 2nd edn, New York: HarperCollins.
Cohen, W. Levin, R. (1989). Empirical studies of innovation and market structure. Schmalensee, R. Willig, R. *Handbook of Industrial Organization*. Amsterdam: Elsevier Science.
Fisher, F. McGowan, J. (1983). On the misuse of accounting rates of return to infer monopoly profits. *American Economic Review*, 73, 82–97.
Martin, S. (1994). *Industrial Economics*. 2nd edn, New York: Macmillan.
Schumpeter, J. (1942). *Capitalism, Socialism, and Democracy*. New York: Harper.

GILBERT BECKER

market power   Market power is generally defined as the ability of one or more firms to influence price. Greer (1992) broadens the definition somewhat to include "the ability to subdue rivals," including suppliers and potential entrants as well as customers. This power may arise from firms involved in either single or multiple markets. Market power stems from a variety of possible sources and has a number of potential consequences. It has been examined theoretically and estimated empirically by an ever growing number of authors.

The principal source of market power is size – that of the single firm alone, or a group of firms – relative to the overall size of the market. This size, in theory, generates power through its effect on market supply. For the individual firm in the case of MONOPOLY, the firm's size is equal to that of the market. As such the firm enjoys the ability to influence the market price since it supplies the entire market and can choose the point along the market demand curve where it wishes to operate. In contrast, in

PERFECT COMPETITION the individual firm's size is so small that its output has no noticeable impact on the market supply and thus it becomes a *price taker*. For groups of firms, as the collective market share of a small group rises, the potential for (and perhaps likelihood of) collusion increases, again raising the ability to influence price (*see* OLIGOPOLY).

Several measures have been constructed which examine market power. One of the first theoretical models developed was the **Rothschild index**. This index is defined as the ratio of the slope of the individual firm's demand curve to that of the market demand. Following the analysis presented above, the ratio for a monopolist will have a value of one as the demand for its product is equal to the market demand. Overall the value of the index ranges between zero (for perfect competition) and one, with higher values being associated with greater market power. The practical application of this index has been limited by the difficulty of estimating demand curves.

Three other measures have been more widely used in measuring market power. Each goes beyond the ability of a firm(s) to influence the market and instead focuses on the outcome of using that power which typically manifests itself in some measure of increased profit. The first of these three is the LERNER INDEX, measuring the extent of the divergence between price (P) and MARGINAL COST (MC). It is calculated as

$$L = \frac{(P - \mathrm{MC})}{P}$$

and, as was true of the Rothschild index, may range in value from zero for perfectly competitive firms to one in the case of monopoly. Once again greater values for L indicate the presence of more market power. One of the difficulties in using this measure lies in the measurement of marginal cost, the data for which is not readily available. As a result, early studies used average variable cost as an estimate for marginal cost. More recent studies estimate the value of MC econometrically; see Bresnahan (1989) and Carlton and Perloff (1994).

A third measure of market power, presented by Bain (1941), involves a direct measure of **excess profits**. Under perfect competition economic profits should equal zero in the long run (*see* ECONOMIC PROFIT) while the existence

of market power in some imperfectly competitive markets should provide positive profits. Although ACCOUNTING PROFIT data are readily available and have been used in numerous studies following Bain's work, several difficulties arise in properly adjusting this data to reach a value for economic profits; see MARKET PERFORMANCE for details on measurement problems of this and other variables. In addition, positive economic profits may occur in the short run even in the absence of market power. For example, exogenous shocks to market demand may temporarily increase price and result in short term profit even in the case of perfect competition. Consequently, in order to correctly use this measure of market power these profits should not be examined with a single static estimate. Instead, a long term trend of sustained economic profits is necessary to establish the existence of market power.

A final measure of market power which has been used in some studies is **Tobin's q**. This measure, calculated as the ratio of the current market value of a firm's assets relative to the replacement cost of those assets is an alternative method for measuring excess profits. Values of this ratio which exceed 1 indicate the existence of such profits. This measure has the advantage of not requiring an estimate of economic profits, as in Bain's measure, but does require the estimation of replacement cost, which in some instances may be quite difficult.

A great number of studies investigating the existence of market power have been undertaken over the past half century. In a recent survey of this literature, Bresnahan (1989) identifies two classes of studies. The early studies followed Bain (1951) and the structuralist school. Tests of this school of thought commonly involved CROSS-SECTION ANALYSIS, across several industries, of the effects of MARKET STRUCTURE on MARKET PERFORMANCE. Here market power, arising from various structural factors, was expected to manifest itself in terms of firm and industry profitability, which was used as an indicator of performance. As noted above, the primary source of market power is firm(s) size. As such, these tests examined the effects of single firm market shares and/or industry concentration (sources of power) on the value of the Lerner index or profit rates (the outcome of the use of power).

These studies found a consistently positive but weak link between size (market power) and profitability. Their conclusion that size caused profitability was hampered by the argument that the efficiency of large size may also be driving this profitability. Because of this, Bresnahan argues, a new class of studies identifiable as industry specific econometric case studies has arisen. In surveying the results of these studies he concludes that:

(1) some concentrated industries possess significant amounts of market power; and
(2) anticompetitive conduct is a significant cause of market power.

Numerous consequences may arise from the existence of market power. First, positive economic profits which result from the use of this power indicate a transfer of income from consumers to producers. Second, poor market performance, ranging from allocative inefficiency to a reduced rate of product innovation are alleged to result from this power. Third, following Greer's definition, market structure can be changed if suppliers, and rivals can be "subdued." The use of PRICE DISCRIMINATION, exclusive dealing, PREDATORY PRICING, and other forms of conduct often requires the existence of some power, but also may enable the further extension of that power across markets and over time.

see also **structure–conduct–performance paradigm**

Bibliography

Bain, J. (1941). The profit rate as a measure of monopoly power. *Quarterly Journal of Economics*, 55, 271–93.

Bain, J. (1951). Relation of profit rate to industry concentration: American manufacturing, 1936–1940. *Quarterly Journal of Economics*, 65, 293–324.

Bresnahan, T. (1989). Empirical studies of industries with market power. Schmalensee, R. Willig, R. *Handbook of Industrial Organization*. Amsterdam: Elsevier Science.

Carlton, D. Perloff, J. (1994). *Modern Industrial Organization*. 2nd edn, New York: HarperCollins.

Greer, D. (1992). *Industrial Organization and Public Policy*. 3rd edn, New York: Macmillan.

Martin, S. (1994). *Industrial Economics*. 2nd edn, New York: Macmillan.

GILBERT BECKER

market structure Market structure consists of those relatively fixed features of a firm's environment which identify the competitive nature of the industry. As such it is related to MARKET POWER, MARKET PERFORMANCE and ANTITRUST POLICY. Its first element is the number and size distribution of the sellers in the market. As the number of sellers increases, the market moves toward PERFECT COMPETITION and market power tends to diminish. Several measures of the size distribution of firms, including various CONCENTRATION INDICES and the HERFINDAHL-HIRSCHMAN INDEX emphasize the collective market shares of an industry's leading firms. High values in these indices indicate a potential for market power. The market share of a single firm may also help to explain the market's structure and competitive conditions (*see* PRICE LEADERSHIP). The second element of market structure is the number and size distribution of buyers, which is important as it offers an indication of the extent of their countervailing power which exists.

A third vital element of market structure is the condition of ENTRY. High BARRIERS TO ENTRY are a central feature of MONOPOLY and are common to OLIGOPOLY. The condition of entry is important in understanding the competitive process in two ways. First, it helps to explain the number and size distribution of firms currently in the market. Second, it helps to evaluate the potential for new competitors. Some researchers cite this element of structure as being uniquely important. Baumol, Panzar and Willig (1982) maintain that in the absence of any barriers to entry or exit (*see* SUNK COSTS) markets become contestable and the number of rivals, their size and other structural variables become irrelevant in determining the outcome of market performance (*see* CONTESTABLE MARKETS). Their research cites examples such as the airline industry where high resource mobility and low barriers to entry into new geographic markets assures market EFFICIENCY (*see* GEOGRAPHIC MARKET). Despite this, Shepherd (1984) and others have argued that the number of truly contestable markets is extremely limited and that the level of competition already in existence in a market is of far greater importance than the degree of potential competition.

Two other elements of market structure are the degree of PRODUCT DIFFERENTIATION and the extent of X-EFFICIENCY existing in the market. Both influence the nature of industry costs and the strategic behavior among the rivals within the market. Both may also play a role in determining the condition of entry by increasing the costs and risk of entry.

The structure of a market is dependent on several factors, the two most basic of which are the underlying consumer demand and the industry's production cost conditions. Industry technology which offers substantial ECONOMIES OF SCALE relative to market demand may require large firm size and greater market concentration and thus limit the room for and number of existing rivals. In addition, these circumstances may limit the number of potential new entrants, which may face cost disadvantages stemming from an inability to produce at MINIMUM EFFICIENT SCALE (see BARRIERS TO ENTRY; ENTRY).

Market structure may also be influenced by government policy ranging from patent laws and licensing requirements, which influence entry, to antitrust policy such as restrictions on mergers (see HORIZONTAL MERGER GUIDELINES), which may influence the number and size distribution of existing rivals. Finally, LIMIT PRICING and other forms of STRATEGIC BEHAVIOR can be used by rival firms to alter the structure of a market.

The work by Porter (1980) on competitive strategy emphasizes the importance of market structure to successful business management. Five basic forces (including potential entrants, substitute goods industries and the rivalry of materials suppliers) which exist in every market are identified. Porter demonstrates that from these forces evolve the competitive strategies which firms must adopt to be profitable. He argues that a sound evaluation of market structure and MARKET DEFINITION is essential for managers in order to properly develop offensive and defensive strategies, assess the company's strengths and weaknesses, and examine its ability to cause changes in market structure.

Analysis of market structure is also important in the development of industrial policy. Shepherd (1982) uses an analysis of market structure to investigate the extent to which goods in the US economy are produced in competitive markets. He uses structural elements to create categories such as "effective competition" (wherein industries have low concentration ratios, unstable market shares and low entry barriers) and "tight oligopoly" (where concentration ratios exceed 60 percent, and barriers are medium or high). He finds that more than 75 percent of the economy's national income in 1980 is generated in markets which were competitive. Moreover, this percentage has increased sharply (from somewhat more than 50 percent) since the 1950s. Shepherd cites active government antitrust policy as the primary explanatory variable and imports as a secondary variable causing this shift. The policy implications here, and surrounding market structure in general, are controversial (see STRUCTURE-CONDUCT-PERFORMANCE PARADIGM).

Bibliography

Bain, J. (1956). *Barriers to New Competition.* Cambridge: Harvard University Press.
Baumol, W., Panzar, J. Willig, R. (1982). *Contestable Markets and the Theory of Industry Structure.* New York: Harcourt Brace Jovanovich.
Carlton, D. Perloff, J. (1994). *Modern Industrial Organization.* 2nd edn, New York: HarperCollins.
Porter, M. (1980). *Competitive Strategy: Techniques for Analyzing Industries and Competitors.* New York: Free Press.
Shepherd, W. (1982). Causes of increased competition in the U.S. Economy, 1939–1980. *The Review of Economics and Statistics,* **64,** 613–26.
Shepherd, W. (1984). 'Contestability' vs. competition. *American Economic Review,* **74,** 572–87.

GILBERT BECKER

markup pricing This can be an optimal pricing policy where prices are set to cover all direct costs plus a percentage markup for profit contribution. It applies only for market structures where companies have some MARKET POWER and, therefore, are able to set the prices of their products. In other words, it is used by *price-setting* companies, as opposed to *price-taking* ones in a perfectly competitive market (*see* PERFECT COMPETITION).

Markup pricing is one of several different pricing policies companies use to price their products. For that, they calculate the cost per unit of output, to which they add a profit margin, or a price markup to determine the final price of their product. The cost per unit is the variable production and marketing cost per unit of output plus the average overhead cost. Then, the final price is determined by adding a certain percentage margin to the unit cost.

The price markup is usually expressed as the difference between the final price and the MARGINAL COST of production, as a percentage of either the price or the marginal cost. Here, the marginal cost represents the per unit cost of production. The former method gives the markup on price, while the latter gives the markup on cost. If P represents the final price of the product, and MC its marginal cost, then the markup on price equals

$$\frac{P - MC}{P}$$

and the markup on cost is

$$\frac{P - MC}{MC}$$

Although the markup pricing policy is relatively easy to apply, there are some problems associated with its use. First, the overhead cost per unit is calculated based on the expected overhead cost divided by the "normal" amount of the product the company expects to produce. However, in many cases, the actual production deviates from the expected volume of production, and this becomes a source for cost miscalculations. Also, in calculating the per unit cost of production, companies usually use only actual expenses, and they ignore the opportunity cost of their resources (*see* OPPORTUNITY COSTS). Consequently, they may underestimate their cost of production. Finally, since companies do not change their prices very frequently, they need to determine the optimal price which will cover the period of time until the next price adjustment.

Economic theory suggests that the pricing rule, which allows companies to maximize their profits, is

$$P = \frac{1}{1 + \frac{1}{e_p}} MC$$

where e_p is the price ELASTICITY of the firm's demand for its product (when there is no strategic interaction between firms, see OLIGOPOLY). Obviously, the profit maximizing price depends on the marginal cost, and it is inversely related to e_p, the price elasticity of demand (notice that e_p is always a negative value). In other words, companies with very elastic market demand (large absolute value of e_p), and, therefore, a market demand very sensitive to changes in prices, will charge a price close to their marginal cost. Their price markup will be low, since high prices might result to a significant decline in their sales. In a perfectly competitive market, where e_p is a very large number (in extreme cases it approaches ∞), P is very close to MC, or the price markup is close to zero. From the optimal pricing equation above, the price to cost markup can be derived as

$$\frac{P - MC}{P} = -\frac{1}{e_p}$$

which is called the LERNER INDEX, introduced by Abba Lerner in 1934. Obviously, the price markup is inversely related to the price elasticity of market demand. High e_p makes the company very aggressive in pricing its products and willing to accept a low price markup as a way to stay competitive and preserve its market share. On the other hand, low e_p (demand is relatively price inelastic) implies large profit maximizing price markups. In such a case, the company has some market power and, for that reason, it can charge a rather large price markup over its marginal cost. (For the factors which influence e_p, see the discussion in the entry on elasticity.)

The above discussion suggests that the price markup is closely related to the degree of market power a company can exercise. More competitive market structures are usually characterized by lower price markups. Domowitz, Hubbard and Petersen (1986), by using data from US industries and between 1958 and 1981, found that those industries with high concentration (with a four-firm concentration ratio in the range of 80 to 100) show a markup on cost ratio of 0.32, while those industries with low concentration (with four-firm concentration ratio in the range of 0 to 20) show a lower markup on cost ratio of about 0.23, as expected. Also, Hall (1986), using data from 48 US industries in manufacturing and for durable and non-durable products, shows that in most of these industries price markups are significantly different from zero, or that in US manufacturing overall, companies seem to have significant market power.

Rotemberg and Saloner (1986), and Rotemberg and Woodford (1991, 1992), present evidence that price markups are correlated with the changes of economic activity during the different phases of the business cycle. They usually increase during economic recessions and decline during economic booms. Finally, Axarloglou (1994) finds some evidence of the same behavior in the publishing industry.

Bibliography

Axarloglou, K. (1994). Product variety and counter-cyclical price markups: an empirical assessment. *The Fuqua School of Business, Duke University Working Paper*.

Domowitz, I., Hubbard, R. G. Petersen, B. C. (1986). The intertemporal stability of the concentration-margins relationship. *Journal of Industrial Economics*, 17, 1–17.

Hall, R. (1986). Market structure and macroeconomic fluctuations. *Brookings Papers on Economic Activity*, 2, 285–322.

Greer, D. (1992). *Industrial Organization and Public Policy*. 3rd edn, New York: Macmillan.

Lerner, A. (1934). The concept of monopoly and the measurement of monopoly power. *Review of Economic Studies*, 1, 157–75.

Rotemberg, J. Saloner, G. (1986). A supergame-theoretic model of price wars during booms. *American Economic Review*, 76, 390–407.

Rotemberg, J. Woodford, M. (1991). Markups and the business cycle. *NBER Macroeconomic Annual* 63–129.

Rotemberg, J. Woodford, M. (1992). Oligopolistic pricing and the effects of aggregate demand on economic activity. *Journal of Political Economy*, 100, 1153–207.

KOSTAS AXARLOGLOU

maximin criterion Suppose that, when a manager is faced with a decision, the payoffs from choosing any of the different strategies available will depend on circumstances beyond her control, e.g. stochastic events, other people's strategies, etc., which we shall refer to as "states of the world." If we rank the strategies available by each strategy's payoff in the worst-case scenario, then the highest ranked is a maximin strategy. A maximin strategy has the property that the worst that can happen with it is no worse than the worst that could happen with any of the other strategies available. In other words, this is a conservative criterion for choosing a strategy which is the best in the worst possible scenario. As an example, suppose that there are two available decisions, d_j, and three possible states of the world, ω_i with the probabilities and payoffs shown in the following table:

	d_1	d_2	Prob(ω_i)
ω_1	25	1	0.50
ω_2	10	15	0.35
ω_3	−5	5	0.15

The worst scenario for decision 1 has payoff −5, while the worst payoff with decision 2 is 1. Since 1 −5, decision 2 would be chosen by the Maximin criterion despite the fact that decision 1 has a higher expected payoff (*see* EXPECTED VALUE). Note that the maximin criterion does not take into account the probabilities of the different states of the world. (In public economics, the maximin criterion refers to the welfare criterion which mandates maximizing the utility of the individual who is worst off.)

Bibliography

Raiffa, H. (1968). *Decision Analysis: Introductory Lectures on Choices under Uncertainty*. Reading, MA: Addison-Wesley.

EDUARDO LEY

merger guidelines, 1992 These guidelines are the third set of guidelines offered to the business community in the past quarter century. They are an effort to clarify the circumstances under which the current administration will challenge a merger which it believes to be in violation of the CLAYTON ACT. The guidelines offer a five-step approach to the analysis of a merger:

(1) the definition of the market and measure of industry concentration,

(2) the evaluation of the potential adverse effects of the proposed merger,

(3) the analysis of the condition of entry into the market (*see* BARRIERS TO ENTRY),

(4) the existence of potential EFFICIENCY from the merger and

(5) the examination of the circumstances in the case where one of the merging firms is failing.

Once the market boundaries are defined using the method known as the five percent rule, or SSNIP (*see* MARKET DEFINITION), the market is classified as being highly concentrated (if the post merger HERFINDAHL-HIRSCHMAN INDEX, HHI, has a value greater than 1800), moderately concentrated (if, after the merger, 1000 HHI 1800), or unconcentrated (if the post merger HHI 1000). While a challenge in the latter case is unlikely, in general the likelihood of a challenge increases, all else constant, for higher levels of concentration and for larger changes in the level of concentration.

The second and third steps involve numerous tests and screens which evaluate factors inherent in the industry which facilitate or limit collusion which could arise as a result of the merger.

Evidence indicating a diminished capacity for the abuse of MARKET POWER will tend to lessen the likelihood of a challenge. When the reverse is true, the likelihood of a challenge is enhanced. In addition, the extent to which the proposed merger may offer a unique method for achieving ECONOMIES OF SCALE or other cost savings is considered as a possible defense in cases which might otherwise be challenged. Finally, the guidelines recognize that the threat of increased market power is minimized in cases where one of the merging firms is in imminent danger of failure. As such, a challenge is not likely as long as the failing firm has made a good faith effort to find an alternative partner with which there exists a decreased potential danger to competition arising from a merger.

These guidelines are largely an extension of those presented in 1982–84. Both sets of guidelines are generally accepted as being more lenient toward firms which wish to merge than those introduced in 1968. In an examination of recent antitrust activity Lande (1994) finds that of 61 mergers challenged by the Federal Trade Commission between 1987 and 1992 only one involved a merger with a post merger HHI value less than 2000. In addition, only four challenges involved mergers where the change in the HHI was less than 400 points. He cites this and other evidence as indicative of the attenuation of aggressiveness in antitrust enforcement.

Heightened concerns by business over increasing foreign competition during the past decade may have fueled the discussion of a need for greater leniency in the guidelines, but foreign competition's effect on the leniency of the new guidelines appears to be limited. While the two most recent sets of guidelines specifically recognize the need to include foreign imports in the definition of the market, they also clearly recognize that trade restrictions may limit the ability of foreign firms to respond to domestic price increases.

see also **horizontal merger guidelines; geographic market; antitrust policy**

Bibliography

Lande, R. (1994). Beyond Chicago: will activist antitrust arise again? *Antitrust Bulletin*, 39, 1–25.

Mueller, W. O'Connor, K. (1993). The 1992 horizontal merger guidelines: a brief critique. *Review of Industrial Organization*, 8, 163–72.

Ordover, J. Willig, R. (1993). Economics and the 1992 merger guidelines: a brief survey. *Review of Industrial Organization*, 8, 139–50.

US Department of Justice (1992). *Horizontal Merger Guidelines*. Washington, DC: US Government Printing Office.

US Federal Trade Commission Bureau of Competition (1992). *How 1992 Guidelines Differ from Prior Agency Standards*. Washington, DC: US Federal Trade Commission.

GILBERT BECKER

minimum efficient scale (MES)   The MES represents the smallest output level for a firm at which long run average costs are at a minimum (*see* LONG RUN COST CURVES). If the long run average cost curve were U-shaped and continuous, then the MES firm size would be unique. However, statistical estimates of cost curves for various industries suggest that long run average cost curves are L-shaped where there are significant ECONOMIES OF SCALE at low levels of output which are exhausted relatively quickly, then average costs remain constant; see Johnston (1960) and Scherer, Beckenstein and Kaufer (1975). This means that the MES represents a lower bound on firm size but not an upper bound.

Estimates of the MES have also been obtained using engineering surveys and survivor studies. With engineering surveys, industrial engineers and other experts provide information concerning the expected changes in costs as the scale of operations increases and from this the MES is determined. Recognizing the difficulties in estimating the MES, Stigler (1958) suggested that those firms which survived in the competitive environment should be the most efficient. Survivor studies examine the changes in the number of firms in different size classes over time to determine the optimum size plant (or, as Stigler suggested, optimum range of sizes). In the short run, firms may not be operating at the optimal scale, so reliable survivor estimates must be based on industries in long run equilibrium. Unlike engineering studies, these studies use data from operating firms, but those firm sizes which survive could have done so through anti-competitive behavior or because of BARRIERS TO ENTRY which would not reflect efficiency. Nevertheless, survivor studies tend to confirm the results obtained from the engineering and statistical cost studies: there appears to be a wide range of optimum plant sizes suggesting a range of output levels where long run average costs are constant.

Knowledge of the plant-level MES in an industry is important to understand the feasible number of firms which could operate in the industry. Scherer, Beckenstein and Kaufer (1975) concluded from their estimates of MES that actual concentration ratios in US industries are much higher than required by the estimated minimum efficient scale. If correct, these estimates indicate that antitrust policies which would break up large firms might not cause inefficiency. However ECONOMIES OF SCOPE are also important in industry and estimates of economies of scale and the MES may fail to detect these additional causes of larger firm size, so any policy actions must be carefully considered. (See Gold (1981) for a critical survey of the theoretical issues regarding firm size.)

The behavior of costs for plants operating at less than MES is also important. If costs increase significantly when plants are smaller than the MES, then the disadvantages of small size are much greater and this could deter entry into the industry.

Bibliography

Gold, B. (1981). Changing perspectives on size, scale, and returns: an interpretive survey. *Journal of Economic Literature*, **19**, 5–33.

Johnston, J. (1960). *Statistical Cost Analysis*. New York: McGraw-Hill.

Scherer, F. M., Beckenstein, A. Kaufer, E. (1975). *The Economics of Multi-plant Operation: An International Comparisons Study*. Cambridge, MA: Harvard University Press.

Stigler, G. J. (1958). The economies of scale. *Journal of Law and Economics*, **1**, 54–71.

ROBERT E. MCAULIFFE

monopolistic competition   This is a MARKET STRUCTURE characterized by a large number of firms where every firm has some MARKET POWER with respect to its products. The concept was introduced by Edward Chamberlin (1933) to study deviations in terms of prices and the number of firms in the market from the perfectly competitive market structure (*see* PERFECT COMPETITION).

The basic market characteristics of a monopolistically competitive industry are the following:

• There is a large number of firms, and every firm has a small market share.

• Every firm sells a differentiated product (*see* PRODUCT DIFFERENTIATION) from its competitors, and therefore it has some market power (downward-sloping market demand schedule).

- There is free ENTRY and EXIT of companies into and from the industry in the long run, which usually leads to lower market share and zero economic profits (*see* ECONOMIC PROFIT).

- Because of the large number of firms in the industry, each firm does not consider the reactions of its rivals in its own decisions (*see* OLIGOPOLY).

The market structure of monopolistic competition is suitable to study several different questions which cannot be easily addressed in the context of other market structures. First, since every firm in the industry sells a different variety, the level of product variety in the market can be assessed (*see* PRODUCT VARIETY) along with its social welfare implications (*see* OPTIMAL VARIETY). Second, this market structure allows economists to explore the reasoning behind companies' decisions on the type, the design, and the selection of the varieties (brands) they offer in the market. Finally, the implications of brand selection on companies' pricing policies can be also assessed.

In analyzing the monopolistically competitive market structure, two major families of models have been developed: **Chamberlinian-type models**, sometimes also called the *representative consumer* models, and **Hotelling-type models**, also known as *location* or *address* models.

Chamberlinian models

Introduced by Chamberlin (1933) and extended by Dixit and Stiglitz (1977), the Chamberlinian model is a representative consumer model with a large number of firms, each one of which offers a distinct product variety in the market. In the model, consumers have an insatiable desire for product variety and perceive every brand as an equally good substitute for every other brand available in the market. The elasticity of substitution between different brands is exogenously given and constant, and is not related to market entry or exit. In other words, the representative consumer does not have an "ideal" variety, i.e. one he prefers the most. Firms produce one variety each and compete only in terms of prices so they do not compete in terms of the design and the particular characteristics of their products.

The number of different varieties in the market is equal to the number of firms in the industry. Firms will enter in the market until all profitable opportunities are exhausted (zero economic profits). Overall, the model predicts that monopolistically competitive industries will have a large number of varieties when there are low fixed costs in production, and/or a low elasticity of substitution between different varieties, and/or a large market demand.

However, the free entry of firms has some significant welfare implications on the economy (*see* OPTIMAL VARIETY). Overall, these models predict that the product variety provided in the market can be either greater or less than optimal because of two contradicting forces. On the one hand, a firm will enter the market with a new brand if it believes entry will be profitable, but the new brand may take business from other firms already in the market. Since the entrant does not worry about the negative effect it will have on established firms, there tends to be too much entry and too many varieties. Offsetting this force is the fact that society may benefit more from a new brand than it costs to produce, but if the firm cannot practice PRICE DISCRIMINATION, it cannot capture all the benefits to society from introducing a new brand and this force tends to reduce the number of brands.

The main criticism against these models, aside of the fact that they are based on a representative consumer, is the fact that they can not explain how companies choose the attributes of their brands. There is no basis for a theory of product *choice* and product *design*. Also, the assumption that the representative consumer does not have an "ideal" variety is rather simplistic and not very appealing. Finally, the fact that the degree of substitution between different varieties is exogenously given, and is independent from the number of varieties in the market, does not allow economists to study the implications of the level of product variety on companies' pricing policies.

Recently, there have been some efforts in improving the basic Chamberlinian model, while preserving some of its fundamental characteristics. Perloff and Salop (1985) introduce a model where every consumer places a different relative value on each available brand. The consumer's preferences, along with the price of a brand, results in CONSUMER SUR-

PLUS, and the consumer buys the brand which gives the highest surplus *(the "best buy")*. However, in their structure, all brands compete symmetrically with all the others (a Chamberlinian element).

Hotelling-type models

In this family of models, product variety is due to the large number of consumers in the market with diverse preferences. In fact, it is usually assumed that consumers have an "ideal" variety for every product they consume. In other words, consumers can be "located" along the product characteristics space, a space where each point represents a different product variety. The consumer's location in this space indicates his ideal variety.

Introduced by Hotelling (1929), the model assumes that consumers are uniformly distributed along the product characteristics space and each one has an ideal product variety. The product characteristics space is linear (a straight line), and bounded, and can be considered equivalent to the market for the product. There are also many firms in the market, and each one produces one brand of the product. Firms decide about the particular attributes of these brands by choosing the location of their brands along the product characteristics space. Brands compete with only their neighboring products on either side of their location in the product characteristics space. Hence, the degree of substitution between different brands is not the same for all brands.

Based on this structure, Hotelling showed that in a case of a *duopoly* (a market with just two firms), when companies do not compete in terms of price, it is optimal for them to locate next to each other in the middle of the product characteristics space. In other words, firms choose varieties which are very close substitutes, since that way they can achieve maximum market share. The reason for this is that consumers will purchase from the store which is closest to them in the market. If consumers were located along a one-mile stretch of road, the first firm in this market would want to locate in the middle – one half mile down the road – because this location allows the firm to attract the greatest number of consumers. Given this, the next firm would want to locate next to the first because it will also attract the greatest

number of consumers and since the firms do not compete on price, only their location matters to customers. This result, known as *minimum* PRODUCT DIFFERENTIATION, depends on specific assumptions of the model, as it will be discussed later. High market demand, low fixed costs (weak ECONOMIES OF SCALE), and weak substitution between different varieties, lead to high product variety in the market. Overall, this model predicts a larger number of varieties in the market than the Chamberlinian models do, because there is weaker competition among brands, since varieties compete only against their neighbors and not against all the other varieties in the market.

As mentioned, Hotelling's result of minimum product differentiation is a special one. It depends on the assumptions that companies do not compete in terms of price, and that the market is bounded. Generalizing Hotelling's results, Eaton and Lipsey (1975) show that in a case of a large number of firms, there is an equilibrium where firms locate in pairs along the product characteristics space with some space between the pairs. In other words, there is some *clustering* of varieties in the market.

Other researchers derive Hotelling's result of minimum product differentiation by assuming instead that consumers are not uniformly distributed along the product characteristics space, but instead, that they are clustered around certain points (in some cases in the middle of the product characteristics space). In other words, consumers tend to prefer varieties relative to others. Then, companies have incentives to locate in those areas of high demand (*thick markets*). This is one of the causes of geographic concentration of economic activity in large metropolitan areas (*spatial agglomeration*).

Finally, Lancaster (1979), introduces a model where consumers perceive products as bundles of characteristics, and have preferences over different collections of characteristics and not necessarily over individual products. Therefore, by combining different products in their consumption, they can end up with the set of characteristics and qualities they find most desirable. Called the **characteristics approach**, this model allows formalization of different situations like whether products can or cannot be combined in consumption, or whether such combinations preserve the characteristics of the separate products.

Monopolistic competition and price markups

Recent research has studied how the entry and exit of firms in a monopolistically competitive market influences the pricing policy of companies and especially their MARKUP PRICING. In the context of the Chamberlinian models, price markups are constant and not related to entry and exit because the degree of substitution between different varieties is constant and not influenced by the number of brands in the market. In terms of Hotelling-type models though, price markups are inversely related to the entry of firms since market entry implies a larger number of brands, stronger competition, a higher price elasticity of demand and lower price markups. The conclusion is that periods of high market demand and therefore high market entry (e.g. an economic boom or a seasonal increase in market demand during Christmas), are associated with lower price markups. Weitzman (1982) and others, present theoretical justification for this result, while Barsky and Warner (1995) offer some empirical support.

Bibliography

Barsky, R. B. Warner, E. J. (1995). The timing and magnitude of retail store markdowns: evidence from weekends and holidays. *The Quarterly Journal of Economics*, CX, 321–52.

Chamberlin, E. (1933). *The Theory of Monopolistic Competition*. Cambridge, MA: Harvard University Press.

Dixit, A. K. Stiglitz, J. E. (1977). Monopolistic competition and optimum product diversity. *American Economic Review*, 67, 297–308.

Eaton, B. C. Lipsey, R. G. (1975). The principle of minimum differentiation reconsidered: some new developments in the theory of spatial competition. *Review of Economic Studies*, 42, 27–49.

Hotelling, H. (1929). Stability in competition. *Economic Journal*, 39, 41–57.

Lancaster, K. J. (1979). *Variety, Equity, and Efficiency*. New York: Columbia University Press.

Perloff, J. M. Salop, S. C. (1985). Equilibrium with product differentiation. *The Review of Economic Studies*, 52, 107–20.

Salop, S. C. (1979). Monopolistic competition with outside goods. *The Bell Journal of Economics*, 10, 141–56.

Weitzman, M. (1982). Increasing returns and the foundation of unemployment theory. *The Economic Journal*, 92, 787–804.

KOSTAS AXARLOGLOU

monopoly   A monopoly exists when there is a single seller of a product in the industry. As a consequence, the monopolist's demand curve is the same as industry demand and is thus downward sloping (*see* DEMAND CURVES). A monopolist must be protected by BARRIERS TO ENTRY to remain a single seller while earning ECONOMIC PROFIT. The monopolist may be protected by licensing requirements, patents, its own strategic behavior, or ECONOMIES OF SCALE which prevent entry into the industry.

Since the industry demand curve facing the monopolist is the *average revenue curve*, when it is decreasing the MARGINAL REVENUE curve must lie below it. To maximize profits the monopolist will produce until marginal revenue equals MARGINAL COST, a condition all profit-maximizing firms must fulfill regardless of MARKET STRUCTURE (*see* PROFIT MAXIMIZATION). Suppose the monopolist sells a single, nondurable product and market demand is

$$P = f(Q) \qquad (1)$$

where P is the market price of the product, Q is the quantity sold and $f(Q)$ is the inverse demand function. Then the marginal revenue for the monopolist is

$$\text{MR} = \frac{\Delta \text{TR}}{\Delta Q} = P + Q \times \frac{\Delta P}{\Delta Q} P \qquad (2)$$

where ΔTR is the change in total revenues and ΔQ is the change in the quantity sold; see Martin (1994). The marginal revenue curve slopes downward because in the absence of PRICE DISCRIMINATION, the monopolist must lower the price to all consumers of the product in order to sell an additional (marginal) unit and this is why the third term on the right in equation (2) above is less than P. Multiplying and dividing the penultimate term in equation (2) by P yields

$$\text{MR} = P \times \left(1 + \frac{Q \Delta P}{P \Delta Q} \right) = P \left(1 + \frac{1}{e_p} \right)$$

where e_p is the price ELASTICITY of market demand for the product. Since the elasticity of demand is always negative, the marginal revenue in (3) above will be negative whenever market demand is inelastic (when $| e_p | < 1$). This means that the monopolist could increase revenues (and profits) by selling fewer units and raising price, so an unregulated, profit-maximizing monopolist should never operate on the inelastic portion of its demand curve. Setting marginal revenue in equation (3) above equal to marginal cost (MC) yields the profit-maximizing markup for the monopolist (*see* MARKUP PRICING):

$$MC - P = \frac{P}{e_p}$$

$$\frac{P - MC}{P} = -\frac{1}{e_p} \qquad (4)$$

Thus the optimal markup for a monopolist is inversely related to the absolute value of the elasticity of demand. The term on the left-hand side is the LERNER INDEX of monopoly power and shows that the monopolist will charge a higher price markup over marginal cost when consumers have fewer substitutes (market demand is less elastic).

The social costs of monopoly

In the preceding discussion, it was shown that a monopolist will set its price above marginal cost, while in perfectly competitive markets, price

equals marginal cost (*see* PERFECT COMPETITION). This means that some consumers who are willing to pay the cost to society of producing this product do not receive it and this is called DEADWEIGHT LOSS. Consider an example where, for simplicity, there are no fixed costs in production, so that the long run marginal cost (LRMC) is equal to long run average cost (LRAC) in figure 1 below. To maximize profits the monopolist will produce Q_m units of output (where MR = MC) and the market price for Q_m units will be P_m. If this industry were perfectly competitive it would produce until $P = MC$ which would be Q_c units sold at price P_c above. Compared with a perfectly competitive industry, the monopolist produces less output and charges a higher price. In the figure above, the rectangle P_m, M, B, P_c is the monopolist's profit which is a transfer from consumers (who lose this amount in CONSUMER SURPLUS) to the monopolist. Since this transfer makes consumers worse off and the monopolist better off, the welfare consequences cannot be judged on the grounds of Pareto optimality (*see* PARETO OPTIMAL ALLOCATION). However the triangle M, B, C is lost consumer surplus which is not gained by the monopolist. This is the deadweight (efficiency) loss to society from a monopoly. Once the monopolist has earned its profits, hypothetically it should be willing to produce additional units for those consumers who are willing to pay the marginal cost of

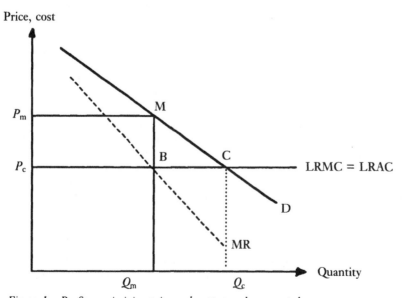

Figure 1   Profit-maximizing price and output under monopoly

production (i.e. those consumers along the demand curve between points M and C). This production would make consumers (and therefore society) better off and leave the monopolist no worse off, so it is a more efficient (Pareto optimal) allocation. Since the monopolist does not produce and sell these additional units, this loss in allocative efficiency is one of the costs to society from monopoly.

Another potential cost of monopoly is what Leibenstein (1966) termed X-inefficiency (see X-EFFICIENCY), the failure to minimize production costs. Without the pressure of competition, a monopolist has less incentive to be efficient and may waste resources in production. Therefore the monopolist's costs would not be equal to those achievable under perfect competition and so the social costs of monopoly would include the monopolist's higher costs of production in addition to the deadweight loss.

Potential monopoly profits may encourage firms or individuals to expend resources attempting to acquire or maintain a monopoly. Such behavior is called RENT SEEKING and if these expenditures do not create benefits to society, then the effort to monopolize is costly to society. Posner (1975) argued that if firms compete for these monopoly profits, they would expend resources until the net expected profit was zero, and this meant that the social cost of monopoly was all of the monopolist's profits. Although this represents an extreme upper bound, some resources are wasted in rent-seeking behavior and this increases the costs to society from a monopoly; see Tirole (1988).

An interesting issue considered by Arrow (1962) was the effect of MARKET STRUCTURE on the incentives to innovate. In his model, firms could innovate to reduce their marginal costs of production, and he examined the returns from this innovation under perfect competition and monopoly. Arrow found that the monopolist had *less* incentive to innovate because it was already earning monopoly profits and the innovation would replace its existing position. On the other hand, a competitive firm could become a monopoly and would earn higher profits. Therefore monopolies may also be costly to society in terms of dynamic efficiency; these firms may fail to innovate or introduce new products. However, if the monopolist is threatened by entry, it has a greater strategic incentive to innovate and preempt potential entrants because in doing so it will remain a monopolist, while an entrant will have to share the market with the monopolist; see Tirole (1988) for a survey.

Monopolies can be beneficial to society under certain conditions. When there are economies of scale, a single firm may be able to serve the market more efficiently than several firms (*see* NATURAL MONOPOLY). Governments grant monopoly licenses to firms and individuals through patents in an effort to encourage innovation. In this case, rent-seeking behavior has socially desirable benefits which society promotes.

Bibliography

Arrow, K. J. (1962). Economic welfare and the allocation of resources for inventions. Nelson, R. *The Rate and Direction of Inventive Activity*. Princeton, NJ: Princeton University Press.

Leibenstein, H. (1966). Allocative efficiency vs. 'X-efficiency'. *American Economic Review*, 56, 392–415.

Martin, S. (1994). *Industrial Economics*. 2nd edn, New York: Macmillan.

Posner, R. (1975). The social costs of monopoly and regulation. *Journal of Political Economy*, 83, 807–27.

Shughart, W. F., Chappell, W. F. Cottle, R. L. (1994). *Modern Managerial Economics*. Cincinatti, OH: South-Western Publishing.

Tirole, J. (1988). *The Theory of Industrial Organization*. Cambridge, MA: MIT.

ROBERT E. MCAULIFFE

monopsony Monopsony exists when one firm is the only buyer of an input or product. The classic example of a monopsony is a one-company town where the only employer in the town is a textile mill or a coal mine. In purchases of inputs, the monopsonist can derive its power from other factors as well. For example, purchases of "house brand" goods where suppliers supply most of their output to a single retailer provide the buyer with a significant amount of monopsony power (also buyer power).

How many inputs should the monopsonist hire? What should be their pay? In a competitive labor market, each employer takes the wage rate as given, and the MARGINAL COST of hiring one more worker is simply the wage rate. In this case, the marginal cost of the input curve is horizontal and coincides with its supply curve. The supply curve facing the monopsonist is far different. A single buyer of labor in a textile mill town faces the entire labor supply of the town. While the competitive firm can hire all the labor it wants at the going wage, the monopsonist cannot. The monopsonist must pay successively higher wage rates to attract additional workers and the higher wage rate applies to all the workers previously hired. As a result, the marginal cost of input (labor) curve lies above its supply curve. A profit-maximizing monopsonist hires workers up to the point where the marginal revenue product as defined by the derived demand for labor of the last worker hired equals the marginal input cost. The wage rate is determined by the height of the labor supply curve at the level of employment. The monopsonist restricts hiring in order to pay a lower price for labor or other inputs. For example, in a monopsonistic labor market, the firm pays a lower wage rate than would prevail in the case of a competitive market, because workers lack alternative sources of employment and specialized inputs in general can be sold to one or at best a limited number of users. A gap between the derived demand of an input and the supply curve reflects the loss in EFFICIENCY in a monopsony.

A monopsony, like a monopoly, confronts the long-run problem of ENTRY and EXIT. If the single buyer succeeds in depressing the input price below the competitive price, it may not be feasible for a specialized input to exit immediately. However, in the long run, suppliers will not replace specialized equipment when it becomes obsolete and the incentive to produce inputs that are limited to one or a few uses will decrease. A producer that is concerned about the long-run relation with its supplier may be better off in not exercising its monopsony power in the short run (Carlton and Perloff, 1994).

Perry (1978) demonstrates that a powerful incentive for backward integration is provided by higher profits than can be earned if a monopsony integrates backward (see BACKWARD INTEGRATION). If the monopsonist purchases its supplier then it does not need to pay a higher input price on all the units used if it chooses to expand an input usage. The marginal input cost schedule becomes irrelevant and the integrated firm chooses to hire the input up to where the derived demand of input equals the market supply curve of the input. Complete backward integration in the input markets results in the allocatively efficient outcome of a competitive input market.

Bibliography

Carlton, D. W. Perloff, J. M. (1994). *Modern Industrial Organisation*. 2nd edn, New York: HarperCollins.

Perry, M. K. (1978). Vertical integration: the monopsony case. *American Economic Review*, **68**, 562–70.

LIDIJA POLUTNIK

moral hazard Moral hazard is an incentive problem that arises in cases where the actions of individuals cannot be observed and contracted upon, creating ASYMMETRIC INFORMATION among individual parties to a transaction. Moral hazard arises commonly in insurance markets, financial markets and labor markets. It arises in situations involving cooperative effort by two or more people, and in the context of principal–agent relationships (*see* PRINCIPAL-AGENT PROBLEM). In some cases of moral hazard, the actions of individuals are unobservable, but in many cases the problem is that the costs of observability are prohibitively high. Those costs are described as "monitoring costs." The nature of transactions characterized by moral hazard is such that individuals do not have incentives to behave in ways that lead to Pareto efficient outcomes (*see* PARETO OPTIMAL ALLOCATION). Solving the problem of moral hazard involves designing incentive contracts that reduce monitoring costs and combine risk sharing with the creation of appropriate incentives.

Insurance markets provide a good illustration of the moral hazard problem; if people can insure themselves against certain risks they are less likely to act with an appropriate level of care. Consider the example of auto theft. If the probability of a theft occurring depends on the actions of the car owner (e.g. where the individual parks, and whether or not they lock their car doors), then the insurance company faces an incentive problem; they want the car owner to take actions that minimize the probability of theft. In this case, full insurance will not be optimal since the insurance company will want the car owner's wealth to depend on her/his actions thus creating incentives for the car owner to take the proper amount of care (e.g. this can be used to explain deductibles). The amount of insurance an individual can purchase at actuarially fair rates is effectively rationed in the presence of moral hazard. An early article establishing these results is Spence and Zeckhauser (1971).

Holmstrom (1979) has shown that in the presence of moral hazard, Pareto optimal risk sharing in the context of a PRINCIPAL-AGENT PROBLEM is generally not possible because it will not induce the agents to take actions that are desired by the principal. A second-best solution to the problem is possible which trades off some risk sharing benefits for the provision of incentives for the desired behavior. One solution is to spend resources on monitoring agents' actions and use this information in the contract. Holmstrom shows that any additional information about the agent's actions, no matter how imperfect, can be used to improve the welfare of both the principal and the agent.

Shavell (1979) also explores what Pareto optimal fee schedules would look like in agency relationships characterized by moral hazard. He finds that the characteristics of these fee schedules are related to both the principal's and the agent's attitudes toward risk (*see* RISK AVERSION). He discusses the implications of his results for four examples of principal–agent relationships: strict liability versus negligence standards in the control of stochastic EXTERNALITIES, insurance, the lawyer–client relationship, and the relationship between STOCKHOLDERS and managers of a firm.

The analysis of moral hazard in the principal–agent context extends beyond the principal–single-agent to a multi-agent setting. Two features of a multi-agent setting that are not present in a single-agent setting are free-riding and competition. Holmstrom (1982) explores these as a way of better understanding the organizational design of firms. His focus is on "moral hazard in teams" where a team refers to a group of individuals who are organized in a way that productive inputs into the firm are related. He then examines the organization of production in this context when the agents' inputs are imperfectly observed. He finds that the free-rider problem can be resolved if ownership and labor are to some extent separated, and that relative performance evaluation, such as peer production averages, can reduce moral hazard costs. The latter finding is one explanation for executive incentive packages that base rewards on comparisons with peer firms (firms within the same industry).

Varian (1990) explores several issues related to group incentives in the context of a real world credit institution: the Grameen Bank in Bangladesh. One of the issues Varian explores is the use of groups of borrowers to reduce monitoring costs by the bank as a way of overcoming the moral hazard problem inherent in the credit relationship. The Grameen Bank creates incentives for borrowers to monitor one another by requiring them to form groups of five from among their peers and accept joint responsibility for repaying all group members' loans. Because their access to loans is tied to the repayment performance of the group, agents have an incentive to monitor their fellow group members to make sure they are taking actions that are consistent with repaying their loans. Stiglitz (1990) also models this use of "peer monitoring" as a solution to the moral hazard problem in credit markets.

In an early article on the relationship between agency costs and the ownership structure of the firm, Jensen and Meckling (1976) examine the problem of moral hazard in the context of the separation of ownership and control in the modern corporation. There is divergence between the interests of owners of the firm and managers. A moral hazard problem arises because of the difficulty owners have observing the actions of managers and thus writing complete contracts which require them to act in the owners' best interests. Real resources will therefore be allocated to monitoring activities by the owners (shareholders). In their definition of agency costs, Jensen and Meckling include the monitoring expenditures of shareholders: the costs associated with their attempts to measure and observe the actions of managers, as well as the costs of their efforts to control the actions of managers. Examples of these activities are audits, formal control systems, budget restrictions, and incentive compensation schemes.

Grossman and Hart (1980) examine the role of takeover bids in creating incentives for efficient management of the "stock market corporation." They assume significant costs in ensuring that managers and directors of corporations act in the interests of the shareholders. They model the stock market corporation as a common property resource (*see* PUBLIC-GOODS PROBLEM) and explain the deviation between potential benefits and actual benefits of collective action in terms of the problem of moral hazard. The extent of this deviation will depend upon the extent of the unpredictability associated with takeover bids. They argue that the higher the threat of a raid, the more efficient current management of a corporation will be. Shareholders will thus weigh the costs and benefits of creating the possible threat of a takeover bid as a way of monitoring the actions of managers.

The role of moral hazard in explaining the organization of production within firms has been an important area of research. Alchian and Demsetz (1972) examine information problems associated with the organization of production to explain how "team production" induces the contractual process of firms. Team production involves a cooperative activity, the essence of which is that the contribution of individual cooperating inputs to output cannot be identified. Their central question is one of incentives: How can members of a team be rewarded and induced to work efficiently? They conclude that monitoring to reduce shirking can be achieved more efficiently in a firm than through market bilateral negotiations among inputs. Mirrlees (1976) also explores issues of optimal payment schedules and organizational structure in cases where the performance of individuals in production can only be imperfectly observed. His conclusion that IMPERFECT INFORMATION binds the organization together is consistent with the conclusions of Alchian and Demsetz.

Attempts to study the effects of moral hazard in the labor market have been important for explaining disequilibrium phenomena such as involuntary unemployment. Firms may pay above market-clearing wages in order to prevent workers from shirking when their effort cannot

be directly observed. These "efficiency wages" may increase worker effort for two reasons. One is the threat of unemployment which is created by the above-market wages, and another is improved worker morale. The efficiency wage is the wage at which labor costs are minimized. Efficiency wage theory has also been used to explain the observed downward rigidity of wages, and layoffs. For a survey of efficiency wage models of the labor market, see Akerlof and Yellen (1986).

see also **imperfect information; asymmetric information; principal–agent problem**

Bibliography

Akerlof, G. A. Yellen, J. L. (eds) (1986). *Efficiency Wage Models of the Labor Market*. Cambridge, UK: CUP.

Alchian, A. Demsetz, H. (1972). Production, information costs, and economic organization. *American Economic Review*, 62, 777–95.

Grossman, S. Hart, O. (1980). Takeover bids, the free rider problem, and the theory of the corporation. *Bell Journal of Economics*, 11, 42–64.

Holmstrom, B. (1979). Moral hazard and observability. *Bell Journal of Economics*, 10, 74–91.

Holmstrom, B. (1982). Moral hazard in teams. *Bell Journal of Economics*, 13, 324–40.

Jensen, M. Meckling, W. (1976). Theory of the firm: managerial behavior, agency costs and ownership structure. *Journal of Financial Economics*, 3, 305–60.

Mirrlees, J. A. (1976). The optimal structure of incentives and authority within an organization. *Bell Journal of Economics*, 6, 105–31.

Shavell, S. (1979). Risk sharing and incentives in the principal and agent relationship. *Bell Journal of Economics*, 10, 55–73.

Spence, A. M. Zeckhauser, R. (1971). Insurance, information and individual action. *American Economic Review*, 61, 380–87.

Stiglitz, J. (1990). Peer monitoring and credit markets. *World Bank Economic Review*, 4, 351–66.

Varian, H. R. (1990). Monitoring agents with other agents. *Journal of Institutional and Theoretical Economics*, 146, 153–74.

ALEXANDRA BERNASEK

multicollinearity   Multicollinearity refers to the situation where the explanatory variables of a LINEAR REGRESSION are highly correlated with each other. This phenomenon is especially common in time-series data because of the presence of lagged variables and common time trends among explanatory variables. Perfect multicollinearity exists when an explanatory variable is an exact linear combination of other explanatory variables, making it mechanically impossible to calculate regression coefficients. This extreme case is unlikely unless the researcher has constructed a poorly specified model.

It is difficult to disentangle the separate effects of explanatory variables on the explained variable when multicollinearity is present. Coefficients may have the wrong sign or an implausible magnitude and small changes in the data can produce wide swings in the estimated coefficients. When combined with high VARIANCE in the error term and low variance in the explanatory variables, a high degree of multicollinearity will lead to high standard errors of the coefficients and low t-statistics (see STANDARD ERROR OF THE COEFFICIENT; T-STATISTIC). However, multicollinearity does not adversely affect the predictive power of the regression model as a whole.

One method of detecting multicollinearity is to examine the correlation matrix for high correlation among the explanatory variables. A signal that multicollinearity is problematic is a high R^2 and low t-statistics. More formal measures of the degree of multicollinearity are the condition number, the variance-inflation factor, and Theil's measure; see Maddala (1988).

A remedy is to increase the sample by adding more data which by providing additional information will help to lower variances. Since obtaining more data is usually difficult, researchers may resort to *ad hoc* techniques such as ridge regression, principal components regression, or omitting the offending variables. These *ad hoc* techniques have been criticized for producing biased or meaningless estimates. In such cases, it may be advisable to accept multicollinearity and interpret the regression coefficients with caution.

Bibliography

Greene, W. H. (1990). *Econometric Analysis*. 1st edn, New York: Macmillan.

Kennedy, P. (1985). *A Guide to Econometrics*. 2nd edn, Oxford, UK: Blackwell.

Maddala, G. S. (1988). *Introduction to Econometrics*. New York: Macmillan.

ALASTAIR MCFARLANE

—— N ——

natural monopoly A natural monopoly is defined by Sharkey (1982) and Panzar (1989) as a market which can be supplied more efficiently (at lower cost) by a single firm than by two or more firms. The conventional treatment in textbooks suggests that ECONOMIES OF SCALE are required for a natural monopoly but this need not be the case. For example, consider a single-product firm with a U-shaped average cost curve which has a minimum at 1 million units of output. If market demand were 1.1 million units and average costs did not rise too quickly, it would be more efficient for a single firm to produce this output than to have two firms in the market, and yet average costs would be rising for this single firm at an output level of 1.1 million units. Economies of scale are sufficient but not necessary for a single-product natural monopoly. It should also be noted that there could be economies at the firm level in a multiplant operation that could justify a natural monopoly even if economies of scale were exhausted at the level of the plant.

When a firm produces multiple products, economies of scale are no longer sufficient for a firm to be a natural monopoly. In the multiple product case, ECONOMIES OF SCOPE and of scale are necessary for a natural monopoly along with cost complementarities; see Sharkey (1982) and Panzar (1989). Even when a natural monopoly exists, Demsetz (1968) suggested that potential competitors should be willing to supply the market and this will constrain the monopolist's MARKET POWER so that regulation may not be necessary. Using Bell system data, Evans and Heckman (1984) tested to determine whether one firm could produce telecommunications output in the US at lower cost than two firms over the period 1958–77. They found that for qualifying data points, costs would be lower if two firms produced that output. In other words, the Bell system did not satisfy the necessary cost requirements to be classified as a natural monopoly. See also CONTESTABLE MARKETS and Baumol, Panzar and Willig (1982).

Bibliography

Baumol, W. J., Panzar, J. C. Willig, R. D. (1982). *Contestable Markets and the Theory of Industry Structure.* San Diego: Harcourt Brace Jovanovich.

Demsetz, H. (1968). Why regulate utilities? *Journal of Law and Economics*, 11, 55–65.

Evans, D. S. Heckman, J. J. (1984). A test for subadditivity of the cost function with application to the Bell system. *American Economic Review*, **74**, 615–23.

Panzar, J. C. (1989). Technological determinants of firm and industry structure. Schmalensee, R. Willig, R. D. *Handbook of Industrial Organization.* New York: North-Holland.

Sharkey, W. W. (1982). *The Theory of Natural Monopoly.* Cambridge: CUP.

ROBERT E. MCAULIFFE

net present value Used in CAPITAL BUDGETING decisions, a project's net present value (NPV) is the discounted CASH FLOW of benefits from that project. To calculate the NPV for a given investment, the net cash flow for each period must be calculated and discounted at the appropriate discount rate (the firm's COST OF CAPITAL is frequently used). Therefore, if an asset which costs P_0 today will generate cash flows of C in each period i for T periods in the future, then the net present value is

$$NPV = \sum_{i=0}^{T} \left[\frac{C_i}{(1 + r)^i} \right]$$

where C_0 will equal the cost of the asset, $- P_0$, representing a negative cash flow (an outlay) in the initial period. The cash flows from the investment must be calculated as after-tax values and all of the effects of the investment on the firm's cash flows must be considered. One feature of the NPV method of evaluating projects is that it assumes cash flows can be reinvested and earn the firm's cost of capital; Brigham and Gapenski (1993) argue this is more appropriate than the reinvestment assumption using the INTERNAL RATE OF RETURN method. The NPV approach also provides a more consistent ranking of alternative investment decisions for capital budgeting than other methods; see Brigham and Gapenski (1993) and Edwards, Kay and Mayer (1987).

Profit-maximizing firms will maximize the PRESENT VALUE of the firm by choosing those projects which have the highest NPV per dollar invested. In the example above, the cost of capital used to discount the cash flows from the investment is assumed to be constant over the life of the investment but this need not be the case and the NPV calculation can easily be modified to accommodate this change; see Brigham and Gapenski (1993), Edwards, Kay and Mayer (1987) and Shughart, Chappell and Cottle (1994).

If INFLATION is expected to occur during the life of the investment, then the estimated cash flows must be adjusted accordingly. The net present value above can be calculated using real (constant purchasing power) dollar values for both cash flows in the numerator and the discount rate in the denominator. Or managers can adjust estimated cash flows and the discount rate for expected inflation in their calculations. In either case, managers should be careful to note whether their firm's revenues adjust in the same manner as costs when inflation occurs.

see also **nominal income and prices; real prices**

Bibliography

Brigham, E. F. Gapenski, L. C. (1993). *Intermediate Financial Management*. New York: Dryden.

Edwards, J., Kay, J. Mayer, C. (1987). *The Economic Analysis of Accounting Profitability*. Oxford: OUP.

Shughart, W. F., Chappell, W. F. Cottle, R. L. (1994). *Modern Managerial Economics*. Cincinatti, OH: South-Western Publishing.

ROBERT E. MCAULIFFE

net present value criteria These rules for selecting value-maximizing projects follow from the discounted cash flow process known as net present value analysis (NPV). Conventionally stated, NPV analysis compares the present value of a project's initial investment (I_0) with the present value of project net CASH FLOW (NCF) over its life, all discounted at an appropriate risk-adjusted rate of return – essentially the opportunity cost of capital:

$$NPV = -I_0 + \sum_{t=1}^{n} \frac{NCF_t}{(1 + k)^t}.$$

The criteria lead to the adoption of projects that are worth more to the firm and its owners than the project's cost. The firm accepts all independent projects the NPV of which is greater than zero and rejects negative NPV projects. The NPV of a project represents the expected dollar addition to the market value of the firm adopting the project. In the case of interdependent projects, since NPV analysis compares present dollar values, value additivity holds and incremental analysis of project combinations is valid. In the extreme case of interdependent, mutually exclusive projects, one accepts that project with the highest NPV. With capital rationing – which is more often the case among divisions of a firm than external to the firm – NPV criteria can be used to select the set of projects that maximizes firm value subject to a budget constraint. Additionally, NPV criteria avoid all of the difficulties associated with other project selection methods, such as the INTERNAL RATE OF RETURN, the payback period and the accounting based average rate of return.

Sources of positive net present value projects lie in unexpected changes in product markets that affect the stream of income associated with projects, innovation, and market imperfections. The NPV rules, combined with capital market efficiency (*see* EFFICIENT MARKETS HYPOTHESIS), provide corporate managers with decision making criteria that maximize shareholder wealth, thereby facilitating separation of ownership from control without penalty.

MICHAEL CURLEY

nominal income and prices   Nominal values are simply current dollar values. Thus a consumer's nominal income is his or her current dollar income and the nominal price of a product is its current dollar price. Since economic decisions should be based on real values rather than nominal values, the distinction between nominal and REAL INCOME or nominal and REAL PRICES can matter in business decisions. This distinction becomes much more important as the rate of INFLATION increases because the difference between real and nominal measures will grow with the rate of inflation. For example, if an industry's costs rise by 10 percent and consumers' nominal incomes also rise by 10 percent, then if firms raise their prices by 10 percent, the nominal price of the product will be 10 percent higher but the real price of the industry's product will not have changed; see Douglas (1992).

Bibliography

Douglas, E. J. (1992). *Managerial Economics*. 4th edn, Englewood Cliffs, NJ: Prentice-Hall.

ROBERT E. MCAULIFFE

normal goods   A good is called normal if consumers choose to buy more of this good when their income increases. More precisely, a consumer chooses a level of consumption for each good which is determined by the consumer's preferences and budget constraint (which is, in turn, determined by the consumers' income and the goods' prices). When a consumer's REAL INCOME increases then she can afford to consume more of each good. However, whether she chooses to do this or not depends on her preferences. If the consumption of a good increases following an increase in the consumer's real income, then it is called normal (between the initial and the final income levels). If a good is not normal then it is called inferior (*see* INFERIOR GOODS). Of course, it is possible that a good is normal at some income levels and inferior at other levels. For example, as a consumer's income rises, the consumption of a given good may first increase and then decrease.

An important property of normal-goods is that their DEMAND CURVES have a negative slope. When the price of a normal good increases, both the INCOME EFFECT and the SUBSTITUTION EFFECT tend to decrease the quantity demanded.

NIKOLAOS VETTAS

O

objective of the firm Although it is normally assumed that firms pursue PROFIT MAXIMIZATION as their primary goal, a variety of alternative assumptions has appeared in the literature. Conventional theory treats the firm as a single homogeneous unit with the single goal of maximizing profits, but Nelson and Winter (1982) argue that even if firms did attempt to maximize profits, they could only do so in familiar, repetitive situations. When a firm produces a new product or faces a new environment, it lacks the information required to maximize profits and must learn and adapt to the new situation. Herbert Simon (1959) suggested that firms cannot maximize profits because of the inevitable compromises and UNCERTAINTY which arise in corporate decision-making and which lead to "satisficing" behavior rather than maximizing behavior. Under these circumstances, managers attempt to meet satisfactory goals for profits and sales rather than maximizing profits. But as Blaug (1992, p.159) has noted, the satisficing hypothesis does not yet provide specific predictions to challenge or replace profit maximization.

Since many managers are concerned with market share, another possible goal for a firm's managers could be sales maximization (Baumol, 1962) subject to a minimum profit constraint. Oliver Williamson (1964) questioned why the managers of the firm should pursue maximum profits for the owners instead of their own self interest. He proposed a theory of managerial discretion where managers could use the resources of the firm for personal objectives rather than maximize profits. The assumptions and predictions of these theories will be compared with the assumption of profit maximization below.

Sales maximization

Baumol (1962, 1977) investigated the consequences of assuming that firms maximize sales (*see* TOTAL REVENUE) subject to some minimum profit constraint. The minimum profit requirement is necessary because a firm could maximize sales but enter into BANKRUPTCY if profits were ignored. When the firm's goal is to maximize sales, Baumol found that the firm would spend more on advertising, service and other demand-increasing factors than would a profit-maximizing firm. In addition, changes in fixed costs or property taxes cause the sales-maximizing firm to raise prices and decrease output. This contradicts the predicted behavior of the profit-maximizing firm whose price and output are unchanged by a change in fixed costs, and businesses appear to raise their prices when fixed costs increase.

One interesting result discussed by Baumol (1977) is the multiproduct firm's choice of inputs and outputs under sales versus profit maximization. For a given level of costs, the sales-maximizing firm will use the same combination of inputs and produce the same combination of outputs as the profit-maximizing firm. This result occurs because profits are revenues minus costs and if the level of costs is fixed, maximizing profits must also maximize revenues. Therefore, Baumol concludes that the different predictions from sales maximization must be due to differences in the total level of costs and revenues rather than simply a reallocation of a given level of costs. Intuitively, the sales-maximizing firm reduces its profits from their maximum level to the minimum amount required, and this profit difference is a resource which is allocated to different products in order to maximize sales. To increase sales, the profit from a product is reduced (because the firm is producing beyond the point of maximum profits), so if sales are maximized, the firm must "spend" this reduction in profits where the sales increase will be highest. But just as profit-maximizing behavior requires the firm to hire inputs to the point where all are equally productive, sales-maximizing behavior requires the firm to increase output until the marginal increase in sales for one product (per dollar of profit sacrificed) is equal to the marginal increase in sales for another product (per dollar of profit lost).

Managerial discretion

Since economists assume that individuals act in their own self interest, it is natural to expect that the managers of the firm (who are normally not the owners) would do the same. Williamson (1964) suggested that managers have goals other than profit maximization which they would pursue using the firm's resources. This is an example of the PRINCIPAL–AGENT PROBLEM, where the interests of the managers (the agents) hired by the owners (the principals) conflict with the interests of the owners. Managers might prefer larger staffs, bigger offices and other cost-increasing expenditures than would be consistent with maximizing profits.

The managerial-discretion model predicts that the firm will vary the size of its staff and the level of perquisites directly with market conditions. Thus, if business conditions are poor the firm will reduce its staff and other non-essential expenses and will approximate the profit-maximizing level if market conditions worsen. In other circumstances, the level of staff employment will be greater than predicted for maximizing profits because of the managers' preference for staff. Furthermore, if fixed costs increase or a lump-sum tax is imposed, the firm will reduce its output, staff employment and its level of perquisites. In contrast, the profit-maximizing firm would not change its price or output levels. Williamson also observes that when a new manager with a lower preference for staff is installed, significant decreases in staff employment can occur without reducing performance, a result which is consistent with the managerial discretion theory.

Unfortunately, the satisficing, sales-maximizing and managerial discretion theories require knowledge about the decision-making process of each firm and the preferences of the firm's managers for specific predictions. In this respect, these hypotheses are less general than the profit-maximization assumption, although this does not mean that profit maximization is more accurate or appropriate. Rather, the alternatives must be better specified to replace the assumption of profit maximization in economic theory.

Bibliography

Baumol, W. J. (1962). On the theory of expansion of the firm. *American Economic Review*, 52, 1078–87.

Baumol, W. J. (1977). *Economic Theory and Operations Analysis*. Englewood Cliffs, NJ: Prentice-Hall.

Blaug, M. (1992). *The Methodology of Economics*. 2nd edn, New York: CUP.

Lesourne, J. (1992). *The Economics of Order and Disorder*. New York: OUP.

Nelson, R. R. Winter, S. G. (1982). *An Evolutionary Theory of Economic Change*. Cambridge, MA: Harvard University Press.

Simon, H. A. Theories of decision making in economics. *American Economic Review*, 49, 253–83.

Williamson, O. E. (1964). *The Economics of Discretionary Behavior: Managerial Objectives in a Theory of the Firm*. Englewood Cliffs, NJ: Prentice-Hall.

ROBERT E. MCAULIFFE

oligopoly This MARKET STRUCTURE is usually composed of a few firms with MARKET POWER and is characterized by strong and recognized interdependence among them. It is an important market structure and is frequently observed in industry.

Market characteristics

The major characteristics of an oligopolistic market structure are the following:

● The industry is composed of a few firms which are the major suppliers in the market.

● The number of firms in the industry does not change significantly through time because there are barriers to potential entrants in the market (*see* BARRIERS TO ENTRY).

- Companies produce either a relatively homogeneous product (as in the steel or the aluminum industry) or a differentiated product (as in the ready-to-eat cereal industry).

- Each firm takes into consideration its competitors' reaction to its own decisions.

- Due to the small number of companies in the industry, there are strong incentives for competition as well as cooperation among them.

- Both producers and consumers in the industry have IMPERFECT INFORMATION.

Since there are few companies in an oligopolistic industry, each firm has some market power. Economists have developed several measures to estimate the degree of economic concentration in the hands of few firms in an industry (see CONCENTRATION INDICES). The US Department of Commerce produces the Census of Manufacturers which reports concentration ratios for about 450 manufacturing industries in the US. In 1987, for six-tenths of these industries, the four-firm concentration ratio was below 40 percent, for three-tenths of them it was in the range of 41–70 percent, and for the remaining one-tenth it was over 70 percent. Apparently, sectors of the US manufacturing sector are significantly concentrated. Industries such as the motor vehicles and car bodies industry (SIC-3711) with a 90 percent concentration ratio, the aircraft industry (SIC-3721) with a 72 percent concentration ratio, and the cereal breakfast foods industry (SIC-2043) with an 87 percent concentration ratio, are just a few examples of industries with high levels of concentration in US manufacturing.

Models of oligopolistic behavior: homogeneous products

In this and the following sections, several theories of oligopoly are presented for markets with homogeneous (identical) products. For a discussion of differentiated products, see PRODUCT DIFFERENTIATION.

The extensive interaction and interdependence among companies in an oligopolistic industry makes the study of this market structure a rather complicated and challenging task. As early as 1838, economists began analyzing this particular market structure, and

especially after 1960, there has been a proliferation of models emphasizing different aspects of oligopoly. However, the variety of models could be seen as a virtue of the literature and not as a flaw, since the behavior of companies in this market structure depends on the particular characteristics of each industry and will vary across industries.

The crucial element of an oligopolistic industry is the fact that the outcome of a company's actions depends on the reaction of its competitors to its decisions. Consequently, the company must consider its competitors' reaction to its own decisions. In economic theory, this element is formalized by the company's *reaction function*. Economists frequently analyze oligopolistic competition by using GAME THEORY, since it allows them to study the interactions and strategies involved among companies in an oligopolistic market structure. Also, in studying oligopolistic industries, and due to the specific characteristics of this market structure, economists employ a special type of market equilibrium, called *Nash equilibrium*, due to the American mathematician J. Nash who defined it in 1951. In this equilibrium, each firm is doing the best it can, given what its competitors are doing, therefore, the company does not have an incentive to change its actions unilaterally (see EQUILIBRIUM).

Presented below, there is a brief discussion of the most important models of oligopolistic behavior in markets where firms produce identical products. The models are classified under three major families: *static models*, models of *two-stage competition*, and *dynamic models*.

Static models

These models analyze the strategic interactions among companies in an oligopolistic structure from a static, and therefore, *timeless* point of view. There are two major classifications of the models: *non-cooperative* models, and *cooperative* models; for a discussion of cooperative models of oligopoly, see CARTELS and COLLUSION.

Suggested by the French economist A. Cournot in 1838 (Carlton and Perloff, 1994), COURNOT COMPETITION is a non-cooperative model, where each firm simultaneously decides the level of its production and considers the output level of its competitors as given. After that, the prices are determined in the market, based on the industry's total output and the market demand. Thus each firm believes its competitors will not react to its output decision. If market demand for the product depends on price, given by $Q(P)$, the company's profit maximizing price markup is:

$$\frac{P(Q) - c}{P(Q)} = \frac{1}{ne_p}$$

where $P(Q)$ is the price the company receives (the inverse of the demand curve) based on the total output, Q, produced in the market by all of the firms, c is the firm's MARGINAL COST of production, n the number of firms in the industry, and e_p the price ELASTICITY of the industry demand. Notice that the market price depends on Q, the production of the entire industry.

This model has been criticized on the ground that it does not present any mechanism through which prices are determined because firms simply produce the amount they believe will maximize profits and the price is determined by the market. Also, the model is based on the assumption that companies compete in terms of output instead of prices, but many companies set their price for a product and allow the market to determine the level of their output (production).

Another non-cooperative model, suggested by the French economist J. Bertrand in 1883 (Carlton and Perloff, 1994), assumes that companies compete in prices instead of the level of their production. This is a crucial assumption, since it significantly alters the results of the model. Assuming that companies produce homogeneous products, consumers will buy from the company with the cheapest price. This means that each company has an incentive to lower its price to achieve higher sales. Consequently, firms continue to reduce their prices until they are equal to the per unit (marginal) cost of production. The Nash equilibrium occurs when $P = MC$, the same result as with PERFECT COMPETITION. Notice that this result does not depend on the number of companies in the market, and even in the case of a *duopoly* (two firms in the market) the result is preserved. Since Bertrand competition is very

intense, companies frequently prefer to compete with other means, other than prices (*see* PRODUCT DIFFERENTIATION).

This type of oligopolistic behavior is common in the airline industry. Various airline carriers offer routes connecting the same two cities in the country. Usually, their fares are very similar until one of them decides to lower its fares, in an effort to increase its sales. Immediately, all its competitors follow reducing their own fares, since if they do not do so they will lose sales. This price war continues until prices may even reach the marginal cost of production. This price competition is of course very devastating for the company's profits.

A cooperative model, collusion is based on the fact that some or all the companies in an industry decide jointly to maintain a certain level of prices (*price fixing*) or production, and thus reduce competition. Although illegal in US (*see* ANTITRUST POLICY), it exists in industries in other countries. Companies realize that price wars result in significant losses and through collusion, they agree to alleviate competition and keep their prices at a profitable level. However, the collusive agreements can be very fragile, not only because they are illegal in some countries, but mainly because there are strong incentives for individual companies to cheat on the agreement, to undercut their competitors, and increase their profits (*see* CARTELS).

If the participants in a collusive agreement detect a company cheating on the agreement, they might penalize it by increasing their own production and supply in the market and thus reduce the market price and profits. This type of punishment, if it is credible, results in a more stable collusive agreement. If the members of the colluding group are very quick in detecting defections from the agreement and are ready to "punish" any defector immediately, the collusive agreement will be more stable. On the other hand, if detection of defectors is difficult, and the "punishment" to defectors comes with a delay, then companies might have incentives to undercut their competitors and break the agreement. This may result in price wars until companies decide to comply with the agreement again.

Dominant firm models (two-stage competition)

In this family of models, it is assumed that there is usually one firm which dominates the industry

– the DOMINANT FIRM or *price leader* (*see* PRICE LEADERSHIP) – while the rest of the companies follow its behavior. The dominant company announces its decisions, and then the remaining firms in the industry (the *followers*) design their strategy based on this announcement.

This model gives rise to FIRST-MOVER ADVANTAGES and was introduced by von Stackelberg in 1934 (Carlton and Perloff, 1994). In the first stage of the game, the *dominant* firm sets its output by taking into consideration the way its competitors will react to its output decision. In the second stage of the game, the remaining companies set their profit maximizing output, given the dominant firm's production plans.

The dominant firm will earn higher profits because it sets its production at a high level (*see* FIRST-MOVER ADVANTAGES). The follower companies can either try to "get even" and also produce at high levels, which will depress prices and result in lower profits for the entire industry, or they can produce a profit-maximizing level of output and earn profits. It is optimal for them to choose the second policy, leaving the dominant firm with a large share of the market and high profits.

Intel and Microsoft are considered to be the leader companies in the computer industry (computer chips and software). They first announce the introduction of a new product in the market, and then the rest of the companies in the industry follow with their own.

Finally, there are some deviations from the Stackelberg model, such as the PRICE LEADERSHIP model, where the *leader* company announces the price of its product and the *follower* companies adjust their prices.

All the models discussed so far are based on the assumption that companies compete, either in terms of prices, or quantities. However, there are some other models, where it is assumed that firms compete in terms of advertising outlays, quality of their products, or product variety (*see* PRODUCT DIFFERENTIATION).

Dynamic models

These models bring the element of time in the analysis, by considering how a changing economic environment influences the company's strategic decisions. The economic environment changes over time either because of changes in the conditions of the entire economy or industry, or due to the particular decisions of the companies in the industry.

Every time a company takes an action in terms of its production, prices or investment, if it makes a commitment it forces its competitors to react. Because of this influence on its competitors, a company may use its decisions to deter the entry of new companies in the industry, or to make a "threat of punishment" credible in a collusive situation. For example, a company might decide to produce more than normally, or even to offer more varieties in the market to prevent entry of new companies in the industry by making entry unprofitable. Also, by building excess capacity or accumulating extra inventories, the company may convince its competitors that it can increase its market supply at any time. Consequently, in the case of COLLUSION it makes its threat of "punishing" any defectors more credible (*see* CREDIBLE STRATEGIES; LIMIT PRICING).

Empirical studies

Empirical research has flourished in the postwar period. Researchers are primarily interested in two questions. First, they have studied the degree of flexibility of prices in OLIGOPOLY and second the relation between market concentration, BARRIERS TO ENTRY and profitability. The studies are based upon data which come from different industries at the same point in time (*cross-section data*), or from one or more industries over time (*time-series data*).

Market concentration and price rigidity. In 1939, P. Sweezy presented a model of oligopolistic behavior, known now as the kinked demand model (*see* KINKED DEMAND CURVES), where he showed that, under certain conditions, prices in an oligopoly might not be very flexible over time (*rigid prices*). His work initiated an extensive discussion, theoretical and empirical, among economists, about the relation between market concentration and price rigidity.

The first empirical work was by G. Means (1935), who showed that prices were rather inflexible in US industry, and argued that in many industries prices did not obey the laws of demand and supply, but instead they were under the control of firms (i.e. prices were *administered*). Stigler and Kindahl (1970), collected US data on individual transactions between buyers and sellers and showed that prices were more flexible than Means found in his work. Carlton (1986) used a similar methodology. He calculated price rigidity as the average length of time during which prices were unchanged in different US industries. He found that price rigidity differed significantly across industries, from about 5.9 months in household appliances to 19.2 months in chemicals. Encaoua and Geroski (1984), using data from different countries, found that high industry concentration implied slow adjustment of prices to cost changes, and therefore high price rigidity.

Other researchers examined the behavior of price markups in manufacturing rather than prices themselves. Hall (1986) found that price markups were relatively high in a wide range of US manufacturing industries. Domowitz, Hubbard, and Petersen (1986), using data from US manufacturing during 1958–81, found that price markups were higher in more concentrated industries. Also, markups in concentrated industries tend to increase during economic booms and drop during economic recessions (*procyclical markups*), while in less concentrated industries they observed the exact opposite relation (*countercyclical markups*). Rotemberg and Saloner (1986) found that price markups were countercyclical. Overall, these studies point in the direction that there is some positive relation between market concentration and price rigidity.

Market concentration and profitability. This part of the economic literature explores the empirical relation between industry concentration, barriers to entry and profitability. In his path-breaking study, Bain (1951), collected data from 42 different US industries. He classified industries based on the 8-firm concentration ratio, and he split his data set in two samples: the high concentration sample, with concentration ratios above 70 percent, and the low concentration sample, with concentration ratios below 70 percent. He found that the rate of return (income per book value of the stockholders' equity) was 11.8 percent for the high concentration industries, versus 7.5 percent for the low concentration industries. He also found that high industry concentration was associated

with high barriers to entry and high profits. Bain's work initiated a number of empirical studies of a similar nature.

Mann (1966) reproduced Bain's results using data from the US economy and for 1950–1960. He found a 13.3 percent rate of return for the high concentration industries versus 9.0 percent for those with low concentration. Weiss (1974) surveyed a wide range of econometric studies in the area and concluded that there is a significant relation between market concentration, profits and barriers to entry (*see* STRUCTURE-CONDUCT-PERFORMANCE PARADIGM).

Most of the studies described above rely on cross-section data. Several researchers addressed the same questions by using TIME-SERIES DATA instead from particular industries. The airline industry has received considerable attention because of the rich data available. Although considered a *contestable market* by some, several studies concluded that concentration in a certain route connecting two cities does influence air fares (*see* CONTESTABLE MARKETS). Bailey, Graham and Kaplan (1985) and others found that if concentration doubled from 50 percent to 100 percent, fares would increase by 6 percent. Borenstein (1989) also found that concentration affected fares in city-pair markets. Overall, these studies show some modest positive relation between industry concentration and air fares. However, all these results must be interpreted with caution, since they are based on ACCOUNTING PROFIT data which might not be a good proxy for ECONOMIC PROFIT data.

Bibliography

Bailey, E. E., Graham, D. R. Kaplan, D. P. (1985). *Deregulating the Airlines.* Cambridge, MA: MIT.

Bain, J. S. (1951). Relation of profit rate to industry concentration: American manufacturing, 1936–1940. *Quarterly Journal of Economics*, 65, 293–324.

Borenstein, S. (1989). Hubs and fares: dominance and market power in the US airline industry. *Rand Journal of Economics*, 20, 344–65.

Carlton, D. (1986). The rigidity of prices. *American Economic Review*, 76, 637–58.

Carlton, D. W. Perloff, J. M. (1994). *Modern Industrial Organization.* 2nd edn, New York: HarperCollins.

Domowitz, I., Hubbard, R. G. Petersen, B. C. (1986). The intertemporal stability of the concentration-margins relationship. *Journal of Industrial Economics*, 17, 1–17.

Encaoua, D. Geroski, P. (1984). Price dynamics and competition in five countries. *University of Southampton Working Paper no. 8414*

Hall, R. (1986). Market structure and macroeconomic fluctuations. *Brookings Papers on Economic Activity*, 2, 285–322.

Mann, M. (1966). Seller concentration, barriers to entry, and rates of return in thirty industries, 1950–1960. *The Review of Economics and Statistics*, 48, 290–307.

Means, G. C. (1935). Industrial prices and their relative inflexibility. *Senate Document 13, 74th Congress, 1st session*. Washington, DC: US Government Printing Office.

Nash, J. F. (1950). Equilibrium points in N-person games. *Proceedings of the National Academy of Science*, 36, 48–9.

Rotemberg, J. Saloner, G. (1986). A supergame-theoretic model of price wars during booms. *American Economic Review*, 76, 390–407.

Stigler, G. J. Kindahl, J. K. (1970). *Behavior of Industrial Prices*. New York: National Bureau of Economic Research.

Sweezy, P. (1939). Demand under conditions of oligopoly. *Journal of Political Economy*, 47, 568–73.

Weiss, L. W. (1974). The concentration-profits relationship and antitrust. Goldschmid, J. *et al.* edn, *Industrial Concentration: The New Learning*. Boston: Little, Brown.

KOSTAS AXARLOGLOU

opportunity costs Opportunity costs are fundamental to economics, yet they are frequently overlooked in business practice. The opportunity cost of any decision or choice made by consumers or firms is the value of the next best choice which was sacrificed. For example, consider a division within a firm which produces computer chips which are used by another division to assemble computers. The computer-assembly division would prefer to obtain the chips at the production cost of the manufacturing division (say, $100 per chip) to increase its profits. However, if those chips can be sold in the market at $250 per chip, then every internal sale of chips to the assembly division has an opportunity cost of $250 to the company. Furthermore, if the company earns a 10 percent return on the capital it has invested in computer assembly but could earn 15 percent elsewhere, then this company should leave this industry in the long run; see Shughart, Chappell and Cottle (1994) for their discussion of internal transfer pricing between divisions.

The distinction between ECONOMIC PROFIT and ACCOUNTING PROFIT is based on the concept of opportunity costs. Suppose a company owns a building and does not pay rental expenses. Then accounting practices would not count those fees as costs to the firm. But if the building could be leased or rented, that represents the opportunity cost of using the building and should be considered in managerial decisions to maximize profits. If managers never consider alternative uses for the resources of the firm, how can they know that they have found the best use? The calculation of economic costs includes these opportunity costs and ensures that the scarce resources of the firm and of society are used where they are most needed (*see* EFFICIENCY).

Bibliography

Douglas, E. J. (1992). *Managerial Economics*. 4th edn, Englewood Cliffs, NJ: Prentice-Hall.

Shughart, W. F., Chappell, W. F. Cottle, R. L. (1994). *Modern Managerial Economics*. Cincinatti, OH: South-Western Publishing.

ROBERT E. MCAULIFFE

optimal variety To determine whether the variety offered in a market is optimal, the product variety produced in the market must be evaluated using social welfare considerations. A byproduct of the extensive research on PRODUCT VARIETY, optimal product variety is a welfare statement about the amount of product variety offered in the market, with respect to some level which is considered to be best from a social point of view. Obviously, the definition of the optimality criterion has a central role in the discussion, since the level of product variety provided in the market is evaluated with respect to this criterion.

When introducing a new variety in the market, a company has to compare the launching cost of the new product (usually costs related to research and development and necessary marketing costs for the new product) with the benefits from selling it. Also, by introducing a new variety, the company influences its competitors' and its own willingness to provide more variety in the future. In other words, a new brand creates an externality (*see*

EXTERNALITIES) for competitors. Specifically, there are three distinct externalities generated by the decision of the company to introduce a new product variety in the market. First, the company is not able to capture all the benefits from introducing a new product in the market (it does not capture the entire CONSUMER SURPLUS) unless it follows a special type of pricing policy called perfect PRICE DISCRIMINATION. Under these circumstances, firms have less incentive to offer new varieties, and the result might be an *underprovision* of product variety in the market. Second, by introducing a new variety in the market, a company "steals" sales from brands offered by its competitors which are close SUBSTITUTES to its own, and discourages them from introducing their own varieties in the market. This effect may lead to an *overprovision* of product variety in the market because consumers were already served by existing brands (so they are not much better off), yet the new brand imposes costs on the established firms which the new firm does not consider. Finally, in the case of a firm which produces more than one variety, if it prices its products with a price markup above the cost of production (*see* MARKUP PRICING), the company will allow some market share for additional varieties. Therefore, it makes it more profitable to offer more of these varieties in the market (*overprovision of product variety*).

Despite these factors, it is assumed that consumers value product variety since they can consume products which they prefer. Economists usually define the socially optimal level of product variety as the one which maximizes the sum of CONSUMER SURPLUS and PRODUCER SURPLUS. Based on this criterion, they evaluate the level of product variety actually offered in the market.

By emphasizing the various different aspects associated with the introduction of new varieties in the market, economists reach different conclusions regarding the optimal level of product variety provided in the market. In his study of MONOPOLISTIC COMPETITION Chamberlin (1933) concluded that the market produced more than the optimal level of product variety (overprovision). He obtained this result because he defined optimal product variety as that level which allowed companies to produce at the minimum of their average cost curve and therefore take full advantage of ECONOMIES OF SCALE. This conclusion was criticized by Dixit and Stiglitz (1977) who showed that the market could produce less than the optimal amount of product variety (underprovision) if the firms cannot capture all the benefits to consumers from introducing a new variety. Salop (1979) showed that market equilibrium may result in more variety than optimal, where the optimal variety is defined to minimize each firm's production costs and maximize consumer surplus while supplying every consumer in the market. Finally, Scherer (1979) attempted to test empirically whether the degree of product variety in the ready-to-eat breakfast cereals industry was socially optimal. He estimated the welfare gains from introducing a new variety and he compared them with the cost of launching a new variety in the market. He concluded that there was too much variety in the breakfast cereal product range.

Bibliography

Chamberlin, E. H. (1933). *The Theory of Monopolistic Competition*. Boston: Harvard University Press.

Dixit, A. K.   Stiglitz, J. E. (1977). Monopolistic competition and optimum product diversity. *American Economic Review*, **67**, 297–308.

Lancaster, K. (1990). *The economics of product variety: a survey*. Marketing Science, **9**, 89–206.

Salop, S. C. (1979). Monopolistic competition with outside goods. *Bell Journal of Economics*, **10**, 141–56.

Scherer, F. M. (1979). The welfare economics of product variety: an application to the ready-to-eat cereals industry. *Journal of Industrial Economics*, **28**, 113–34.

Tirole, J. (1988). *The Theory of Industrial Organization*. Cambridge, MA: MIT.

KOSTAS AXARLOGLOU

P

Pareto optimal allocation A "feasible allocation" is Pareto optimal (or Pareto efficient) if there is no other feasible allocation that makes at least one of the agents in an economy strictly better off without making someone else worse off. A feasible allocation is weakly Pareto optimal if there is no other feasible allocation that makes all the agents in an economy strictly better off. Clearly, if an allocation is Pareto optimal, then, it is weakly Pareto optimal as well, for if there is no allocation that can make at least one person better off without making someone else worse off, then, there should be no allocation that can make everybody better off. An "allocation" is a specification of how much of each good each agent will receive. An allocation is "feasible" if the total amount of each good assigned to agents does not exceed the total amount available in the economy.

The Pareto optimality concept is due to the 19th-century economist Vilfredo Pareto. Pareto optimality is a criterion of allocative EFFICIENCY, in that it can be a solution concept for the problem of using and allocating goods and resources in an efficient way. Thus, if an allocation is Pareto optimal, then goods are allocated in an efficient way; if it is not, then there is room for mutually advantageous trade.

The use of the Pareto optimality criterion can be demonstrated by an Edgeworth box diagram. The Edgeworth box is named after the 19th-century economist Francis Ysidro Edgeworth who invented the analytical tools of INDIFFERENCE CURVES and "contract curves." The Edgeworth box diagram is used to characterize efficient allocations when there are two agents and two goods. The dimensions of the box represent the total amounts of the two goods available in the economy. The lower left and the upper right corners are reserved as the origins

for the consumption spaces of the two agents. Thus, any point in the box shows how much each agent will receive of the two goods (measured horizontally and vertically from his origin).

The curve from the lower left to the upper right corner in the Edgeworth box shows the set of Pareto optimal allocations, and is called the "contract curve" because it shows the set of efficient allocations or "contracts." Along the contract curve, the indifference curves for the two agents are tangent to each other, so that their respective MARGINAL RATES OF SUBSTITUTION are equal. Any allocation on the contract curve of the diagram, such as allocation A, is Pareto optimal and weakly Pareto optimal because you cannot make either one of the agents better off without making the other worse off. Allocations outside the contract curve where the indifference curves are not tangent to each other, such as allocation B, are not Pareto optimal or weakly Pareto optimal because trade between the two agents can lead to allocations on the contract curve that either make at least one of the agents better off without making the other worse off, or make both agents better off. Thus, when the marginal rates of substitution are not equal, the allocation of resources is not efficient, and there is room for mutually beneficial trade. Finally, if point B represents the "initial endowment" (which is the endowment of goods that each agent has before any trade occurs), then the solid line is called the "core." The core is the subset of the weakly Pareto efficient allocations that are "individually rational," in the sense that each agent is better off by exchanging goods with the other agent than by simply consuming his endowment allocation.

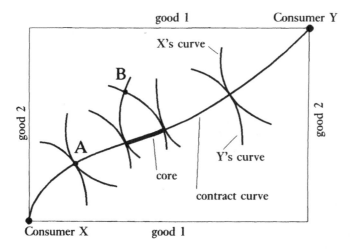

Figure 1   The Edgeworth box and the contract curve

see also **Coase Theorem**

Bibliography

Bator, F. M. (1957). The simple analytics of welfare maximization. *American Economic Review*, **47**, 22–59.

Edgeworth, F. Y. (1881). *Mathematical Physics*. London: Kegan Paul.

Pareto, V. (1906). *Manuale d'Economia Politica*. Milan: Societa Editrice.

THEOFANIS TSOULOUHAS

pecuniary economies   Pecuniary economies are cost savings resulting from large firm size which benefit the firm but not necessarily society as a whole. They are distinguished from real ECONOMIES OF SCALE in that the latter involves the reorganization of production in such a way that less of society's scarce resources are needed to produce a given level of output. As such, real economies not only benefit the firm by lowering its costs (and possibly raising its profits) but also enable society on the whole to produce more goods.

Pecuniary economies on the other hand typically are cost savings which are generated from MARKET POWER. For example, sometimes a manufacturer, due to its large size, is a large buyer of a raw material (or advertising services, retail shelf space, CAPITAL, etc.) and is thus able to purchase that material at a lower price than some of its smaller rivals. Its lower costs, even if passed on to consumers, are acquired at the expense of its suppliers. Here, no real resource saving occurs to society. Instead the end result of such economies is simply a wealth transfer from one firm (or group) to another.

Pecuniary economies can be beneficial to society when they reflect economies of scale in the supply of inputs. Thus if a firm grows larger and increases its orders from suppliers, the suppliers may now be able to enjoy lower costs through economies of scale which, if they lower the price to the purchasing firm, will create pecuniary economies for that firm. The purchasing firm does not have the economies in production itself, but enjoys pecuniary economies because larger orders allow suppliers to be more efficient and lower their costs.

Such economies should by no means be discounted by the managers of a firm. From a public policy point of view though, these gains should be treated differently. One example of this lies in the area of mergers. In evaluating the merits of a possible merger, the merging firms should consider both the real and pecuniary economies which may be achieved. Antitrust enforcement officials will consider only real economies in their evaluation, since in this case pecuniary economies do not benefit society as a whole.

Bibliography

Scherer, F. Ross, D. (1990). 3rd edn, *Industrial Market Structure and Economic Performance*. Boston: Houghton Mifflin.

GILBERT BECKER

perfect competition Perfect competition is one of the four BASIC MARKET STRUCTURES which exist in the economic classification system for markets. Although relatively few examples exist where markets completely fit the criteria for this market type, it is one of great focus in economics as it establishes a theoretical benchmark for the criteria needed to achieve socially optimal MARKET PERFORMANCE.

The criteria necessary for perfect competition are as follows:

(1) The market contains a large number of buyers and sellers, each of which is small relative to the size of the whole market.
(2) The product being produced by the rivals in this market is homogeneous and thereby lacking in features – ranging from product attributes (*see* PRODUCT ATTRIBUTES MODEL) to QUALITY differences to sales and service differences – by which each firm's product can be differentiated from its rival's in the eyes of consumers.
(3) Firms in the market have knowledge of and access to the same technology for producing the product, and both buyers and sellers have perfect information as to other conditions in the market.
(4) The ENTRY of new firms into the market may be described as being relatively easy to achieve in that no substantive BARRIERS TO ENTRY or exit deter new firms wishing to join the market.

Largely as a result of these criteria, managers of individual firms in this type of market find that they have no control over the price of their product as the combined forces of the market's supply and demand determine the market price for all firms. As such, perfectly competitive firms are said to be *price takers*. In addition, the ease of new entry, in theory, fosters a long run outcome in which price is high enough to cover all costs but does not offer any positive ECONOMIC PROFIT. Moreover, the threat of new entry promotes EFFICIENCY by forcing existing firms to minimize costs or be driven out of the market.

Markets most closely fitting the criteria for perfect competition often involve financial markets; commodities, such as agricultural goods; services, such as independent truckers; or the market for unskilled labor.

see also **oligopoly; monopolistic competition; monopoly**

Bibliography

Hirschey, M. Pappas, J. (1995). *Fundamentals of Managerial Economics*. 5th edn, Fort Worth: Dryden.

GILBERT BECKER

pioneering brands A pioneering brand is the first brand in a new market, or the first significantly different brand which creates a new market. When consumers have IMPERFECT INFORMATION about product quality, Schmalensee (1982) showed that the first brand in the market could enjoy significant advantages over later entrants if the product performs satisfactorily. This advantage arises because the pioneering brand is able to set the standard by which all subsequent brands will be judged, and this can have lasting effects. Firms entering the market in later periods find it more difficult to convince consumers to incur the SEARCH COSTS necessary to learn about their brands and this creates BARRIERS TO ENTRY.

In his study of the cigarette industry, Whitten (1979) found that the pioneering cigarette brands enjoyed substantially higher profits and market share relative to competing brands which followed. For example, the production of filter-tip cigarettes opened a new market for female smokers and the early entrants into the national market, Viceroy and Winston, enjoyed considerable leads over their competitors.

Bibliography

Schmalensee, R. (1982). Product differentiation advantages of pioneering brands. *American Economic Review*, **72**, 349–65.
Whitten, I. T. (1979). Brand performance in the cigarette industry and the advantages of early entry. *Staff report to the US Federal Trade Commission*.

ROBERT E. MCAULIFFE

predatory dumping Predatory dumping is the practice of international price discrimination (DUMPING) by an exporter with the intention or result of driving domestic producers in the targeted export market out of business. The predatory scenario is based on the assumption that an exporter charges a high price in his home market and then subsidizes export sales in a foreign market until local competition is driven out, after which the exporter monopolizes the market and raises prices. For the strategy to be successful, the exporter must have a sufficiently "deep pocket" to underprice any rivals in the target market for a time sufficient to drive them out of the market and then be able to prevent re-entry or new entry of rival firms (local or foreign) so that losses during the predatory stage can be recovered.

Strictly speaking, this predatory scenario, focusing on injury to competition itself, is extremely unlikely, since trade liberalization, reduced transportation costs and increased competition in world markets have reduced the ability of firms to pursue PRICE DISCRIMINATION and create worldwide monopolies, especially in undifferentiated intermediate product markets, which are the most likely targets for a dumping strategy. Often, however, the term "predatory" is used in a broader sense to describe injury to domestic producers in the importing country, who may lose market share or exit the market due to increased import competition. This concept of injury ignores any gains to consumers from the lower prices caused by dumping. Thus, antidumping laws treat all dumping as "predatory" if it results in injury to domestic import-competing firms.

KENT A. JONES

This practice, is considered to be one form of PRICE DISCRIMINATION and a restriction of free competition and typically faces a challenge in court under the antitrust laws (see ANTITRUST POLICY). The dissolution of Standard Oil Company in 1911 is a case in point. The company increased its market share to over 90 percent of the oil refining industry and was accused of achieving this through acquiring its rivals cheaply and attempting to drive away the rest through threats of selling below cost. The Supreme Court determined in its ruling that this behavior violated the antitrust laws because the objective of the company in undertaking this practice was to monopolize (see MONOPOLY) the market and thus, forced the break up of the company into 30 independent firms. One study (McGee, 1958) that looked at whether Standard Oil Company bought its competitors below their true value found that, in fact, Standard Oil had paid very handsomely for its acquisitions. Later decisions by the court, however, tended to also require proof that the company having obtained control over the market was likely to engage in acts that were detrimental to consumers.

Bibliography

McGee, J. (1958). Predatory price cutting: the Standard Oil (NJ) case. *Journal of Law and Economics*, 1, 137–69.

Petersen, H. C. (1993). *Business and Government*. New York: HarperCollins.

GOVIND HARIHARAN

predatory pricing Predatory pricing is the practice of pricing products, sometimes even lower than costs, in order to drive out or coerce competitors or to prevent ENTRY of new firms. Typically, credible threats are sufficient and need not be carried out except once in a while to convince competitors. Dumping (see DUMPING) products in a market with the purpose of driving out or acquiring rivals cheaply through lower prices is also considered to be a predatory pricing technique. Thus, larger firms and those with deeper pockets who also face potential gains from controlling the market (see MARKET POWER) are more likely to find it worthwhile to engage in such predatory pricing.

present value Cash flows which arrive at different times should not be compared until they are adjusted for the amount of time that elapses between each inflow (see CASH FLOW). For example, an immediate inflow of $1000 is not the same as ten annual inflows of $100 each, although each is nominally equal to $1000. The reasons they are not the same are:

(1) profitable investment opportunities exist, which means that the $1000 immediate inflow is better than the stream of ten $100 inflows (see OPPORTUNITY COSTS);

(2) inflation exists, so the purchasing power of the two alternatives is not the same (see INFLATION);

(3) time preference exists, i.e. individuals will choose to have current consumption in preference to consumption later, unless they are compensated for deferring consumption.

These three reasons are related but conceptually distinct. All three of them, and one more besides, which is the risk of the cash flows, are embedded in the opportunity discount rate (ODR), which is the rate used to discount the cash flows.

The amounts that are coming in later time periods need to be discounted in order to be commensurate with an amount that is now in hand. The process of discounting the cash flows that are to arrive in the future is called calculating the present value. A payment which is to arrive in one year's time, in order to be compared to a payment which is arriving today, must be divided by the amount $(1+r)$, where r is the annual opportunity discount rate. This discounting is required because funds which are in hand today could earn a return over the course of the year of r. A payment which is arriving in two years' time, in similar fashion, needs to be divided by the amount $(1+r)^2$, before it can be compared to a payment which is arriving today. The number which is calculated by adding the value of the payment arriving today, plus the discounted value of future payments, is called the present value.

In algebraic terms, if payments are CF_0, CF_1, CF_2, ..., CF_n arriving today, one year from today, two years from today, and yearly until year n, then the present value (PV) of this flow of funds is calculated as:

$$PV = CF_0 + \frac{CF_1}{(1+r)^1} + \frac{CF_2}{(1+r)^2} + \cdots + \frac{CF_n}{(1+r)^n} \quad (1)$$

Or, more generally, if payments are received once a year until year n:

$$PV = \sum_{i=0}^{n} \frac{CF_i}{(1+r)^i} \quad (2)$$

It should also be noted that in the present value calculations above, the interest rate used to discount the cash flows, r, is assumed to be the same over the n years. For investment decisions, managers may want to consider the effects that variations in the discount rate would have on their net present value calculations (*see* NET PRESENT VALUE).

Bibliography

Brigham, E. F. Gapenski, L. C. (1993). Intermediate Financial Management. New York: Dryden.
Edwards, J., Kay, J. Mayer, C. (1987). *The Economic Analysis of Accounting Profitability*. Oxford: OUP.

JOHN EDMUNDS AND ROBERTO BONIFAZ

price discrimination This is a specific pricing policy followed by companies with MARKET POWER, where different prices are charged for the same units of a product which are sold to different consumers, at the same or different periods of time. Companies use this pricing policy in an effort to increase their revenues and profits.

In market structures where companies have market power, the profit maximizing price for a product is given by the simple formula

$$P = \frac{1}{1 + \frac{1}{e_p}} MC$$

where P is the price of the product, MC is the MARGINAL COST, and e_p is the price ELASTICITY of market demand, i.e. the sensitivity of market demand with respect to price. The company determines its price by adding a *price markup* to its marginal cost (the company's per unit cost) which is inversely related to e_p (*see* MARKUP PRICING). This optimal price markup applies when the company charges the same price, P, for all the units it sells. On the other hand, since consumers value the same product differently, they are willing to pay different prices for it (each has a different RESERVATION PRICE). If possible, it is beneficial for the company to charge a higher price to those consumers with a higher reservation price instead of charging the same price to everybody. This way, it manages to increase its revenues without increasing its cost of production and overall profits are enhanced. In other words, the company has strong incentives to *price discriminate* across different consumers, and as will be discussed later, even across different units purchased by the same consumer. This idea is at the core of the concept of price discrimination. Actually, price discrimination across different consumers allows the company to extract some or all of the surplus consumers receive from purchasing the product (*see* CONSUMER SURPLUS) and adds it to its revenues and profits.

For successful price discrimination the following conditions are necessary:

- *Non-transferable products* – products must not be easily transferable across consumers, or groups of consumers, who pay different prices for the same product. In other words, the TRANSACTIONS COSTS of transferring units of the product between different consumers or groups of consumers, must be relatively high, so that the transaction is not profitable. On the contrary, if the transaction cost is low (*transferable commodities*), price discrimination is not effective, since those consumers who buy a product at a low price can sell (transfer) it to those who pay a higher price. In other words, the markets must be separate either geographically or by the identity of the consumers (*see* ARBITRAGE).

- Consumers, or groups of consumers, must have different reservation prices for the same product. If consumers had the same price elasticity of demand, then the profit maximizing price the company should charge each consumer would be the same.

- The company must be able either to receive some information or design a method to extract information about consumers' reservation prices and willingness to pay. However, this is not easy, since consumers do not have incentives to reveal their true reservation price.

Types of price discrimination

In economic literature, there is, traditionally, a distinction of three different types of price discrimination.

First degree price discrimination. Sometimes called *perfect price discrimination*, this is the pricing policy where each consumer is charged a price equal to his reservation price for the product. Since consumers have different reservation prices, they end up paying a different price for consuming the same product. It is very

difficult and costly for any company to accurately determine the reservation price of each of its consumers but this policy represents the maximum potential gain a company could extract. The service sector is the one where this pricing policy might possibly be found, since services are not easily transferable products. Also, companies are able to more accurately determine the reservation prices of their customers, although these estimates will be imprecise. For example, a law firm can charge different fees to different clients for the same type of legal advice, since it can extract some information about the willingness of its clients to pay the fees, based either on their income or, in case of a company, on its sales or profits.

Similarly, a consulting company can follow the same type of pricing, since the services it provides are client-specific, and therefore not transferable across clients.

Second degree price discrimination. In this case, the company charges different prices for the same product based upon the quantities purchased by consumers. Each consumer faces the same schedule of prices but will choose different quantities (and therefore pay different prices) based on their evaluation of the good. This form of price discrimination requires less information about each consumer's reservation price and the company simply separates consumers into different groups according to how much they are willing to buy. For example, companies may offer discounts to consumers who buy the product in larger quantities and by offering different quantities, the firm can separate consumers based on their willingness to buy the product; see BUNDLING.

Third degree price discrimination. This is the most extensive form of price discrimination in practice. Specifically, the company charges different prices to different groups of consumers who appear to have different reservation prices. Obviously, the firm tends to charge a higher price to the group of consumers with the lower price elasticity of demand.

There are many examples of this type of price discrimination. In the consumer goods industry, the use of coupons and rebates is widespread. A company charges the same price to all of its customers and then allows them to use discount coupons or rebates so they can buy its products at a lower price. The idea is that only those consumers who are sensitive to price (high price elasticity of demand) and therefore not willing to pay a lot, will clip, save and use the coupons in buying the product. Obviously, this is an indirect and effective way in revealing consumers' reservation prices. Also, senior citizen or student discounts in entertainment, or public transportation, are examples of a third degree price discrimination. Senior citizens and students usually have lower reservation price for many of the products they consume. Companies then charge them a lower price than the rest of the consumers who do not fall in these two categories.

In the airline industry, all tickets for the same flight with the same airline do not cost the same amount. The ticket for business class costs more than for economy, in part because business travelers have a more inelastic demand for travel and cannot always make arrangements in advance. Tourists are much more price sensitive and are willing to order their tickets early. In addition, the airline companies offer better services to passengers traveling first class and this gives some justification for those who are willing to pay a premium for the first class cabin. This type of price discrimination is sometimes called *quality discrimination*.

There are other types of price discrimination which cannot be easily classified under one of the above major types.

Intertemporal price discrimination. In this case, a company charges different prices to consumers who buy its product at different points in time. It is a pricing policy used extensively in the electronics industry when a new model is introduced in the market. The company initially sells the product at a rather high price for those consumers who are willing to pay the price and want to use it immediately, and later the price is decreased for those consumers with lower reservation prices (and as unit costs decline).

Finally, there are several other types of price discrimination. In the *two-part tariff* case, consumers pay an up-front fixed fee, which gives them the opportunity to consume a certain product, and then a per unit fee for the amount of units they actually purchase. Examples include amusement parks and various types of membership clubs. In the *peak-load* price discrimination policy, companies charge a higher price when their demand peaks up and a lower price during the off-peak period. Airline companies use it when they charge lower fares if passengers travel on Saturday evenings, or during off-peak seasons. Movie theaters use it when they charge more for the evening show than the matinee.

Bibliography

Hirschey, M., Pappas, J. (1995). *Fundamentals of Managerial Economics*. 5th edn, Orlando: Dryden.
Pashigian, P. (1995). *Price Theory and Applications*. New York: McGraw-Hill.
Pindyck, R. Rubinfeld, D. (1992). *Microeconomics*. 2nd edn, New York: Macmillan.
Tirole, J. (1988). *The Theory of Industrial Organization*. Cambridge, MA: MIT.
Varian, H. R. (1989). Price discrimination. Schmalensee, R. Willig, R. D. *Handbook of Industrial Organization*. New York: North-Holland.

KOSTAS AXARLOGLOU

price leadership As Stigler (1968) observed, this term has been used in the literature with different interpretations. In the case of a DOMINANT FIRM, the dominant firm determines the industry price while the smaller producers act as price-takers and sell at that price. However, the term has also been applied to those firms which are the first to announce their price changes and are typically followed by the other firms in the industry. In this case, the "price leader" is not necessarily a dominant firm in the industry with substantial market share and Stigler suggested that a firm might occupy this position if its prices correctly and rapidly reflected market conditions. Shugart (1990) argues that such a price leader may simply have better information or decision-making skills than rival firms who simply follow the price change. When the leading firm's price changes reflect changes in costs or market conditions, it is called **barometric price leadership** because the leader's price acts as a barometer of the market environment. This form of price leadership is consistent with competition in the market and does not necessarily indicate COLLUSION between the firms.

The crucial question in price leadership models is: why should other firms follow the price changes announced by the leading firm? When competing firms are price-takers, as in the dominant firm model, the other firms follow the price leader because they are so small relative to the size of the market that they believe their output will not affect industry price. With a barometric price leader, rival firms take advantage of what they recognize as the better information or decision-making of the leading firm. But in the case of a concentrated CARTELS, price leadership has been suggested as a method of tacit collusion (Markham, 1951) which helps firms to coordinate their pricing. Price leadership has been suspected in the cigarette industry (Stigler, 1968), steel, the ready-to-eat cereals industry (Scherer, 1980), gasoline and coal industries (Stigler, 1968), but alternative explanations of observed pricing behavior are also plausible, such as MARKUP PRICING; see Shugart (1990). Since collusive price leadership and barometric price leadership are difficult to distinguish empirically, Shugart (1990) argues that additional evidence is required to establish collusive behavior.

Bibliography

Markham, J. W. (1951). The nature and significance of price leadership. *American Economic Review*, 41, 891–905.

Scherer, F. M. (1980). *Industrial Market Structure and Economic Performance*. 2nd edn, Boston, MA: Houghton Mifflin.

Shughart, W. F. (1990). *The Organization of Industry*. Boston, MA: Irwin.

Stigler, G. J. (1968). *The Organization of Industry*. Chicago: University of Chicago Press.

ROBERT E. MCAULIFFE

principal–agent problem   The general problem of motivating one person or organization to act on behalf of another is known as the principal–agent problem. The principal–agent problem arises when the principal hires an agent to perform tasks on his behalf and the agent thereby influences the welfare of the principal. The principal–agent relationship provides a useful framework for analyzing situations in which there is ASYMMETRIC INFORMATION and when there is a need to design a contract or monitor the behavior of parties. MORAL HAZARD and ADVERSE SELECTION are also examples of the principal–agent problem.

For example, a typical firm is owned by shareholders (principals) who hire professional managers (agents) to run the company. The manager may be more interested in maximizing the firm's market share, size and growth in order to provide him and his subordinates greater opportunities for promotion. Furthermore, managers may prefer to make investments whose payoffs come earlier rather than later, avoid risks, shirk, and otherwise fail to maximize the profits of the firm. Although economists commonly assume PROFIT MAXIMIZATION when describing the decision making of a firm, the incentives of managers often differ from those of the shareholders and the efforts of the managers are impossible or too expensive to monitor. This would not be a problem if an enforceable contract could be drawn up that specified every duty of the manager and matched performance incentives to outcomes perfectly. Given that INCOMPLETE CONTRACTS occur frequently, due to bounded rationality, the firm's profit is less than the profit maximizing level and the difference is referred to as the residual loss.

Agency costs arise as principals try to ensure that the agents will act in the best interest of the principal. There are three types of agency costs: monitoring costs, bonding costs and the residual loss of a principal (Jensen and Meckling, 1976). The principal–agent framework is employed to analyze the role of monitoring and bonding activities in reducing the residual loss of the principal. Monitoring costs occur when the principal employs resources to observe the efforts of the agent or creates incentives for the agent to undertake actions that are more likely to assure efficient use of resources within the firm. For example, an employee receiving a fixed salary may be able to shirk on the job, thus the firm needs to develop a way of monitoring the performance, as well as, the honesty of the agent. Markets can also perform the monitoring function. In particular, the market for corporate control and the labor market for managers penalize managers who manage companies poorly. Thus, poor managers face a greater probability of unemployment and company takeovers, lower salaries, or a reputation for having brought a firm into bankruptcy (Fama, 1980).

In order to guarantee performance, the agent may be required to post a bond. If the agent does not fulfill the terms of their agreement, then he must forfeit the bond. Edward Lazear (1979) showed that for workers who expect to make a career within an organization, it may be to the advantage of both parties to align the incentives of the employee and the employer by paying the employee below his marginal product early in the career and above his marginal product later in the career. This rising wage pattern is similar to a worker posting a bond to be collected later in his career. In this compensation scheme it becomes efficient for the employee to work diligently in order to avoid being fired before the deferred rewards can be collected (i.e. or the bond is forfeited). For this scheme to be effective, employees must find the firm's promise to be credible and the employer must provide for mandatory retirement. Similarly, stock options and bonuses that can be exercised by the manager only when he retires or leaves in a mutually agreeable way create incentives for managers to maximize long-run profits of a firm. If the behavior of the manager is not acceptable to the owners of the firm, the manager faces reductions in the value of the deferred compensation.

Structuring the employee and managerial compensation packages is one of the ways in which the owners of a firm minimize the residual loss. In addition, owners of a firm who monitor the market price of their shares can thereby infer whether the agents are acting in their best interest; on the basis of that information alone they can buy and sell shares and limit the amount of residual losses imposed on them by the actions of the management. Hence, the power of stockholders to sell their stake in the firm promotes efficiency in the use of resources. In addition, a principal–agent problem is avoided when the owner of a firm also serves as the manager; in this case, the firm eliminates the agency costs and any residual loss.

Bibliography

Fama, E. F. (1980). Agency problems and the theory of the firm. *Journal of Political Economy*, **88**, 272–84.

Jensen, M. C. Meckling, W. H. (1976). Theory of the firm: managerial behavior, agency costs, and ownership structure. *Journal of Financial Economics*, 3, 305–60.

Lazear, E. (1979). Why is there mandatory retirement? *Journal of Political Economy*, 87, 1261–84.

Shughart, W. F., Chappell, W. F. Cottle, R. L. (1994). *Modern Managerial Economics*. Cincinatti, OH: South-Western Publishing.

LIDIJA POLUTNIK

prisoner's dilemma   The prisoner's dilemma is a classic illustration in GAME THEORY. Two suspects are arrested by the police and are charged with a minor crime. They are also suspected of a major crime but there is not enough evidence to convict them without a confession. The two prisoners are separated and are offered the following deal:

(1) If one prisoner confesses to the major crime and implicates the other, he will serve 6 months in jail while the other will serve 6 years in jail.

(2) If neither prisoner confesses to the major crime, each will be convicted of the minor offense and will serve 1 year in prison.

(3) If both prisoners confess to the major crime, they will both serve 3 years in prison.

The "payoffs" to the two prisoners, Al and Bill depend on the choice made by the other. These are shown in the matrix below where Al's payoff is shown in parentheses.

The interesting feature of these payoffs is that the best strategy for each suspect individually is to confess. Consider Al's payoffs from choosing to confess compared with the payoffs from choosing to be silent. Whether Bill chooses to confess or be silent, Al's best strategy is to confess, and the same result holds for Bill. Thus

		Bill	
		Confess	Be silent
	Confess	(–3) –3	(–.5) –6
Al			
	Be silent	(–6) –.5	(–1) –1

both prisoners are worse off pursuing their individual self interest than if they agreed to be silent.

The strategy pair (confess, confess) is a *Nash equilibrium* because it is the best response for each player given the strategy of the other (*see* EQUILIBRIUM), i.e. neither player can do better knowing the strategy chosen by the other. The prisoners would choose the same strategies if they used the minimax or MAXIMIN CRITERION to evaluate their decisions; see Rasmusen (1989).

If the players developed reputations to make the threat of punishment a credible threat, then the prisoner's dilemma can be avoided. Rasmusen notes that reputation can be important in a variety of repeated games such as duopoly (where the strategies are to maintain the current price or cut the price), employer–worker relations (where the worker chooses to work hard or slack off), product quality under IMPERFECT INFORMATION (where the firm chooses to produce a high quality product or a low quality product) and entry deterrence (where the incumbent firm may retaliate aggressively or accommodate (*see* ACCOMMODATION) an entrant).

see also **adverse selection; signaling**

Bibliography

Gibbons, R. (1992). *Game Theory for Applied Economists*. Princeton, NJ: Princeton University Press.
Rasmusen, E. (1989). *Games and Information*. Oxford, UK: Blackwell.

ROBERT E. MCAULIFFE

producer surplus   Producer surplus is the difference between the TOTAL REVENUE received by the producers of a product and the minimum amount they would require to produce and sell the product. Since the supply curve measures the minimum price required by suppliers to produce and sell the product, any price they receive above that amount would be the producer surplus. Thus the area above the market supply curve and below the market price measures the producer surplus in that market.

Producer surplus occurs because some factors of production are more productive than others, such as certain land in agriculture. If these resources are more productive over time, they are more valuable to the owners and should command a higher price which is an economic rent (*see* RENTS). Since these resources have a higher value, if the firm's managers properly accounted for the opportunity cost of these resources, the firm's costs would be higher (*see* OPPORTUNITY COSTS).

Producer surplus also plays a role in welfare analysis. Social welfare is frequently defined by economists as the gains from exchange and production by consumers and producers. Maximizing social welfare then requires maximization of the sum of producer surplus and CONSUMER SURPLUS. One of the significant achievements of modern welfare economics was the demonstration that perfectly competitive markets in general equilibrium will maximize social welfare; see Bator (1957), Baumol (1977) and EQUILIBRIUM.

Bibliography

Bator, F. M. (1957). The simple analytics of welfare maximization. *American Economic Review*, **47**, 22–59.
Baumol, W. J. (1977). *Economic Theory and Operations Analysis*. Englewood Cliffs, NJ: Prentice-Hall.
Pindyck, R. S.   Rubinfeld, D. L. (1995). *Microeconomics*. 3rd edn, Englewood Cliffs, NJ: Prentice-Hall.

ROBERT E. MCAULIFFE

product attributes model   Developed by Kelvin Lancaster (1971), the product attributes model sets out to explain consumer behavior as a process of choosing bundles of product characteristics or attributes inherent in goods and services, rather than simply choosing bundles of goods or services themselves. The basic assumption of the model is that the consumer's choice is based on maximizing utility from the product attributes subject to a budget constraint. The model is particularly useful in analyzing differentiated product markets, in which specific products that are substitutes for each other are distinguished by their embodiment of a specific set of characteristics.

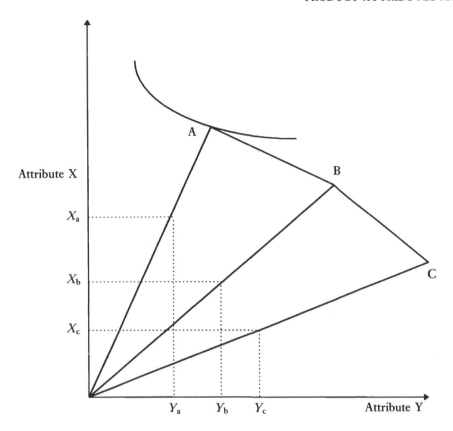

Figure 1   Product attributes and consumer choice

For purposes of exposition, a two-dimensional graph reveals the model's main features (see Douglas 1992 for textbook treatment and examples), and links it to the traditional BUDGET CONSTRAINT and indifference curve analysis of consumer behavior (*see* INDIFFERENCE CURVES). Figure 1 shows three specific products, each offering a specific amount of attribute X and attribute Y in constant proportions. Each unit of product A contains X_a of attribute X and Y_a of attribute Y, for example. Similarly, each unit of products B and C offers the attribute bundles (X_b, Y_b) and (X_c, Y_c), respectively. The attributes could represent calories (X) and vitamin content (Y) for competing brands of soups, for example. While some attributes can be measured objectively in this way, it may also be useful to consider more subjective attributes, such as "atmosphere" and "quality of food" in distinguishing among restaurants, for example. Sub-

jective attributes do, however, imply that the attribute content of a particular product may be determined largely by the perceptions of the individual consumer (see discussion of advertising below).

For a given budget constraint and set of prices for the products, the end points A, B, and C represent the limits of consumption along each attribute ray, and the line segment ABC defines the budget (or efficiency) frontier for the consumer. The consumer's choice is made by maximizing utility, as defined by the consumer's set of indifference curves, subject to the budget constraint. In this model, we interpret the slope of an indifference curve at a particular point (MARGINAL RATE OF SUBSTITUTION) as the rate at which the consumer is willing to trade off units of attribute Y for an additional unit of attribute X to remain at constant utility. Thus, the consumer's choice is influenced by his or her preference pattern in attribute space. As shown in figure 1, this consumer shows a strong preference for attribute Y and therefore chooses product A; a strong preference for attribute X would lead him or her to choose C. In this regard, the proliferation of differentiated products in a particular market can be explained as the result of the dispersion of tastes for various attributes among the population of consumers.

Note that the consumer will spend the entire budget on a single product A, B, or C if the highest indifference curve just touches the respective end point. If the highest indifference curve touches a point on the line segment between two attribute ray end points, then the consumer would choose to split consumption between the two adjacent products. If the product's consumption is indivisible (as in the case of an automobile or house), then such consumption splitting would be impossible, and the consumer's choice would be determined by the highest indifference curve that touches an end point; see Douglas (1992).

The product attributes model also allows an analysis of strategic behavior by firms and its effect on consumer choice. A decrease in the price of a product moves the end point further out along the ray, for example. Advertising can change the perception of the product in terms of attribute content and proportion (length and slope of the product ray) or the consumer's tastes for attributes (shape of individual consumers' indifference curves). Product positioning strategy may focus on opportunities based on "gaps" in the attribute space between rays, or may target existing products for direct competition.

Bibliography

Douglas, E. J. (1992). *Managerial Economics*. 4th edn, Englewood Cliffs, NJ: Prentice-Hall.

Lancaster, K. (1971). *Consumer Demand: A New Approach*. New York and London: Columbia University Press.

KENT A. JONES

product differentiation When firms in an industry sell products which are each distinct in the eyes of consumers, those products are said to be differentiated. Eaton and Lipsey (1989) suggested that differentiated products could be any set of closely related products in consumption and/or production. The degree of substitution between differentiated products varies and depends upon consumers' tastes in consumption, their information about other brands and upon ECONOMIES OF SCOPE in production. When firms produce differentiated products, each firm acquires some MARKET POWER and faces a downward-sloping demand curve for its brand. If consumers prefer particular brands relative to others, they have fewer substitutes in consumption and so product differentiation reduces the ELASTICITY of RESIDUAL DEMAND for the firm's product(s). Caves and Williamson (1985) noted that product differentiation requires two conditions: consumers must believe that differentiated goods within a product class are close substitutes for each other (relative to other products outside that class) and yet, consumers must find the differentiated brands to be imperfect substitutes so that each firm faces a downward-sloping demand curve. They found that IMPERFECT INFORMATION and complex product attributes combined with fixed costs were sufficient to explain product differentiation in US and Australian manufacturing industries.

Products may be differentiated *horizontally*, or *vertically*. **Horizontal differentiation** occurs when consumers have diverse preferences and do not agree on which product is best. **Vertical differentiation** exists when all consumers may agree which product is best in terms of QUALITY but purchase different brands because of differences in prices or in their incomes.

Theoretical analysis of product differentiation in economics has proceeded along two major lines: spatial or location models (sometimes referred to as address models) and representative consumer or Chamberlin models. Address models assume consumers have diverse preferences and that each consumer has a "most preferred" brand which he will purchase. In these models, consumers have preferences defined over the product attributes (*see* PRODUCT ATTRIBUTES MODEL) which are embodied in varying proportions in each good; see Lancaster (1966) and Archibald, Eaton and Lipsey (1986). In contrast, representative consumer models assume that consumers' prefer diversity and purchase each of the differentiated goods offered in the market (Dixit and Stiglitz, 1977). For example, people might enjoy eating dinner at different restaurants so if a new restaurant opened, it would share the market with the other establishments in the market. The address models treat the product space as continuous and provide insights into firms' product selection decisions while in representative consumer models consumers have preferences for goods and so the product space is discrete. In representative consumer models, each brand competes against all other brands in the market whereas competition between brands is localized in the address models because any firm will have at most two competing neighbors on either side in a one-dimensional market; see Archibald, Eaton and Lipsey (1986). Since most of the interesting issues concerning product differentiation can be illustrated with address models, the discussion will focus on that class.

Consider a market one mile in length with N identical consumers distributed uniformly over that distance who will purchase one unit of the good if the total cost of the purchase is less than their RESERVATION PRICE, R, or nothing otherwise. When consumers must travel from their location to purchase a product, it is costly for them. If their transportation costs are linear, the total purchase cost is given by:

$$p + t \times \theta \qquad (1)$$

where p is the price of the good, t is the transportation cost per unit of distance and θ is the "distance" between the consumer and the firm. All else equal, consumers will purchase from the firm which is closest to them to minimize their total costs. The transportation cost may reflect the time and other travel costs required to purchase the product (in physical space) or it could reflect the cost to the consumer of lost TOTAL UTILITY from purchasing a brand which is not exactly his most preferred brand (in product characteristics space). All else equal, a consumer would prefer to buy the brand closest to his ideal brand.

Where along this route would a firm want to locate? If the firm wants to be accessible to as many customers as possible, it should locate at the center of the market, half a mile from either end since this location will minimize the average transportation cost to consumers in the market. Now suppose a second firm wants to enter this market and, for the moment, assume that the price of the product in the market is fixed and will not change. In this case, the second firm would also choose to locate at the center of the market because this location provides the firm with the greatest potential market share. This result led Hotelling (1929) to conclude that, in the absence of price competition, market competition will lead to *minimal product differentiation* where firms offer virtually identical products to appeal to as many consumers as possible. Although this result is not always an EQUILIBRIUM configuration (see Ireland (1987) and Tirole (1988) and the sources cited there), it does explain the lack of diversity in broadcast television programming, political platforms and other cases where price competition does not occur.

If price competition does occur, the firms will want to increase product differentiation to reduce the intensity of price competition. To illustrate, consider two firms, each located at opposite ends of the mile-long market and assume that the prices they charge are sufficiently low (or that consumer reservation prices, R, are sufficiently high) so that all consumers purchase one unit of the product. A consumer at location θ^* will be indifferent purchasing from either firm 1 or firm 2 when the "full" prices paid are equal:

$$R - p_1 + t \times \theta^* = R - p_2 + t \times (1 - \theta^*) \quad (2)$$

where p_1 is the price charged by firm 1 and p_2 is the price charged by firm 2. This indifferent consumer at location θ^* determines the market share of each firm, which can be found by solving equation (2) for θ^*:

$$\theta^* = \frac{(p_2 - p_1 + t)}{2t} \qquad (3)$$

When the two firms charge identical prices, the indifferent consumer is at half the distance and the firms share the market equally. If both firms have the same, constant MARGINAL COST of production, c, it can be shown (Tirole, 1988) that the profit-maximizing price each firm will charge is equal to:

$$p_1 = p_2 = t + c \qquad (4)$$

As transportation cost (or, equivalently, product differentiation) increases, each firm has more local monopoly power and competes less for sales, so equilibrium prices will rise. In fact, firms have incentives to pursue *maximal* differentiation to reduce price competition and will choose to locate at the extremes of the market when transportation costs are quadratic; see Tirole (1988).

When firms compete in markets with differentiated products, there are forces which tend to increase the level of differentiation – and may possibly create a fragmented industry structure (*see* FRAGMENTED INDUSTRIES) – and forces that work in the opposite direction toward *minimal* differentiation. As previously discussed, firms would prefer to increase differentiation to avoid price competition, all else equal. But as Tirole observed, firms will also want to locate near consumers and this reduces product differentiation. For example, if consumers were clustered at the center of the one-mile market, we would expect firms to locate near the center of the market where the density of consumers was highest. This means that if consumers' tastes are not very different, the brands offered in the market should not be very different either. Another force reducing differentiation is positive EXTERNALITIES between firms which cause them to cluster together. These externalities arise when the costs of supplying firms in the industry fall when they share a common geographic location or when resources are more easily acquired (such as hiring computer professionals from nearby universities or competitors). Or, if firms share a geographic location, such as a shopping mall, they can reduce consumer SEARCH COSTS and raise their total demand even if price competition is intensified. Finally, Tirole notes that firms will tend to cluster when there is no price competition. It should also be noted that the amount of product differentiation supplied by a free market is unlikely to be the optimal level: unregulated markets may create too much or too little product variety (*see* OPTIMAL VARIETY). For example, in the one-mile market described above, if the two firms choose their locations and then compete in price, they will choose to locate at the extremes of the market. However, since consumer demand is inelastic, the optimal locations should be those which minimize transportation costs at one-quarter and three-quarter distance.

Salop (1979) developed a model where firms were located symmetrically around a circular market with free entry and would costlessly relocate when entry occurred. He found that an increase in the FIXED COSTS of production would lower the equilibrium number of brands and would cause prices to fall. If the size of the market increased or if consumer reservation prices rose, the equilibrium number of brands would increase.

Firms may also choose their locations strategically to create BARRIERS TO ENTRY in address models. Eaton and Lipsey (1989) show that firms could earn positive ECONOMIC PROFIT even when entry is "free" and Schmalensee (1978) argued that firms in the ready-to-eat breakfast cereals industry prevented entry through PRODUCT PROLIFERATION. Both conclusions arise from strategic product positioning by incumbent firms. Consider a product space which is circular to avoid problems with endpoints (Ireland, 1987; Tirole, 1988) and where consumers are uniformly distributed around the circle. If the firms in the industry chose their locations strategically, they could locate in such a way that each firm earned economic profits and yet any firm which tried to enter the industry would be unable to cover its fixed costs. For example, if there are product development costs which are SUNK COSTS once a firm enters the industry, then established firms could locate brands throughout the product space so that an entrant's best location would be between two existing brands. As long as the entrant's share of this area is less than its sunk costs, entry will be deterred, even though established firms earn economic profits. Schmalensee argued that there were brand-specific sunk costs of advertising in the ready-to-eat breakfast cereals industry and that the established firms offered so many brands that they literally crowded the product space and prevented entry. Eaton and Lipsey (1989) note that in these models there may be economic profits even with free entry, the free-entry industry equilibrium will not be unique, product variety will not be optimal and monopoly power may persist as established firms make strategic decisions to deter entry.

Bibliography

Archibald, G. C., Eaton, B. C. Lipsey, R. G. (1986). Address models of value theory. Stiglitz, J. E. and Mathewson, G. F. *New Developments in the Analysis of Market Structure*. Cambridge, MA: MIT.

Caves, R. E. Williamson, P. J. (1985). What is product differentiation, really? *Journal of Industrial Economics*, 34, 113–32.

Dixit, A. Stiglitz, J. E. (1977). Monopolistic competition and optimum product diversity. *American Economic Review*, 67, 297–308.

Eaton, B. C. Lipsey, R. G. (1989). Product differentiation. Schmalensee, R. Willig, R. D. *Handbook of Industrial Organization*. New York: North-Holland.

Hotelling, H. (1929). Stability in competition. *Economic Journal*, 39, 41–57.

Ireland, N. J. (1987). *Product Differentiation and Non Price Competition*. New York: Blackwell.

Lancaster, K. J. (1966). A new approach to consumer theory. *Journal of Political Economy*, 74, 132–57.

Salop, S. C. (1979). Monopolistic competition with outside goods. *Bell Journal of Economics*, 10, 141–56.

Schmalensee, R. (1978). Entry deterrence in the ready-to-eat breakfast cereal industry. *Bell Journal of Economics*, 9, 305–27.

Tirole, J. (1988). *The Theory of Industrial Organization*. Cambridge, MA: MIT.

ROBERT E. MCAULIFFE

product life cycle   From a variety of perspectives, researchers have hypothesized that products are characterized by patterns of evolution which have been called product life cycles. In most of these theories, new products evolve over time from "young" to "old", and the various stages of the cycle can be documented, because they are associated with certain observable characteristics; see INDUSTRY LIFE CYCLE and Clark (1985) for descriptions of the nature of the cycles. Thus, life cycle theory highlights the importance of product, in addition to process, innovation. Product innovation implies that technology is dispersed through the introduction of new products, whereas process innovation implies that technology is introduced through new production processes. The continuum of product life cycles, arising from product innovation, potentially has implications for patterns of trade, strategic behavior among firms, and even marketing strategies.

For example, Vernon (1966) suggests that international trade patterns are driven by the fact that new products are "born" in technologically superior developed countries, but when technology becomes standardized, production moves to less developed countries, where labor is cheaper. Based on the Schumpeterian notion of the innovative entrepreneur, other research investigates product life cycles in the context of strategic competition and innovation among firms. Recent marketing research simply tries to document the existence of product cycles using the implied observable characteristics of product cycle models. In practical terms, the existence of these product cycles can have implications for the speed at which manufacturers get new products on the market, the available recovery period for research and development, and the decision to innovate versus imitate. See Klepper (1992) for a full description and bibliography concerning product life cycles.

Bibliography

Clark, K. B. (1985). The interaction of design hierarchies and market concepts in technological evolution. *Research Policy*, 14, 235.

Klepper, S. (1992). Entry, exit, and innovation over the product life cycle. Presented at the 1992 Conference of the International Joseph A. Schumpeter Society, Kyoto, Japan.

Segerstrom, P. S., Anant, T. C. A., Dinopoulos, E. (1990). A Schumpeterian model of the product life cycle. *American Economic Review*, 80, 1077.

Vernon, R. (1966). International investment and international trade in the product cycle. *Quarterly Journal of Economics*, 80, 190.

LAURA POWER

product proliferation   When firms compete through PRODUCT DIFFERENTIATION, incumbent firms have incentives to offer many brands and "crowd the shelf." In 1972, the US ready-to-eat breakfast cereal manufacturers were charged with antitrust violations by the Federal Trade Commission. Among the charges was the claim that the cereal producers conspired to prevent entry through product proliferation. The alleged strategy of the cereal producers was to introduce a large number of brands to fill the market in such a way that existing brands could earn economic profits (*see* ECONOMIC PROFIT) and yet new entrants would not be able to enter the industry.

Schmalensee (1978) developed a theoretical model which showed how a product proliferation strategy might succeed. Scherer (1979) estimated the costs of introducing new cereal brands and compared those costs with the benefits to consumers of these brands to determine if the number of brands was excessive. He found that the benefits from the new brands were less than the costs and therefore the number of brands was not efficient (*see* OPTIMAL VARIETY).

Bibliography

Carlton, D. W. and Perloff, J. M. (1994). *Modern Industrial Organization*. 2nd edn, New York: HarperCollins.
Scherer, F. M. (1979). The welfare economics of product variety: an application to the ready-to-eat cereals industry. *Journal of Industrial Economics*, 28, 113–34.
Schmalensee, R. (1978). Entry deterrence in the ready-to-eat breakfasts cereal industry. *Bell Journal of Economics*, 9, 305–27.

ROBERT E. MCAULIFFE

product variety   These are the number of variants in a family of products with similar characteristics, usually referred to as brands or models of the product. Product varieties can differ from each other either in terms of quality, or in terms of other characteristics unrelated to quality (*see* PRODUCT DIFFERENTIATION).

As Eaton and Lipsey (1989) observed, several *stylized facts* are associated with product variety:

- Many industries offer a large number of similar but differentiated products.

- The number of different varieties offered in the market is a small subset of the set of all possible varieties.

- In most industries, companies produce more than one variety of the same product.

- Each consumer purchases only a small subset of the available varieties in the market.

- Consumers appear to have different preferences, since they consume different varieties, and this can not be explained solely by differences in their income.

The degree of product variety is determined by the interaction of consumers, firms (cost of production), and the MARKET STRUCTURE. Economists model consumer choice either through a representative consumer, who is assumed to have unlimited preference for different brands of the same product, or through many consumers, where each has a most preferred or "ideal" brand to consume. Companies offer product variety in order to increase their market share and revenues, but their costs of production also increase because of additional fixed costs associated with each brand and a more limited market which prevents firms from fully realizing ECONOMIES OF SCALE. Product varieties can also be used strategically to deter entry of competitors and protect market shares (*see* BARRIERS TO ENTRY; PRODUCT PROLIFERATION). Finally, market structure influences the degree of product variety in the market. In oligopolies and monopolistically competitive markets, companies introduce product varieties to compete with other firms.

Overall, product variety will be greater,

- the lower the fixed cost of introducing a variety in the market, since a new variety is more profitable the lower its fixed costs.

- the larger the market for the family of products in consideration, since large markets result in more revenues which can support the fixed costs of introducing more products.

- the weaker the degree of substitution between the different brands in the group, since the availability of substitutes increases the price ELASTICITY of market demand and lowers price markups (and profit margins); (*see* MARKUP PRICING).

Product variety is also a significant component in international trade. Countries with similar structures may engage in trade in similar industries (*intra-industry trade*), since they produce and trade different varieties in the same family of products; see Kierzkowski (1989). This is because consumers demand product variety due to differences in tastes, but firms prefer to produce few varieties (all else equal) when there are economies of scale. Therefore, countries may trade in different product varieties to satisfy consumers preferences while allowing companies to take advantage of economies of scale.

Product variety appears to have some impact on the long run growth of economies (Stokey, 1988; Grossman and Helpman, 1991). Finally, the amount of product variety in the market may be influenced by the business cycle: increasing during economic booms and decreasing during economic recessions. Consequently, firms are willing to adjust their pricing policies appropriately in response to these fluctuations in product variety over time; see Axarloglou (1993).

Bibliography

Axarloglou, K. (1993). Product variety, counter-cyclical price markups and short run macroeconomic fluctuations. *University of Michigan Working Paper*.

Eaton, B. C.   Lipsey, R. G. (1989). Product differentiation. Schamalensee, R.   Willig, R. D. *Handbook of Industrial Organization*. New York: North-Holland.

Grossman, G. M.   Helpman, E. (1991). *Innovation and Growth in the Global Economy*. Cambridge, MA: MIT.

Kierzkowski, H. (ed.) (1989). *Monopolistic Competition and International Trade*. New York: OUP.

Lancaster, K. J. (1990). The economics of product variety: a survey. *Marketing Science*, 9, 189–206.

Stokey, N. L. (1988). Learning by doing and the introduction of new goods. *Journal of Political Economy*, 96, 701–17.

Tirole, J. (1988). *The Theory of Industrial Organization*. Cambridge, MA: MIT.

KOSTAS AXARLOGLOU

production functions   The production function for a firm shows the maximum output which can be produced with specific levels of inputs, given the available technology. If the firm's output is denoted by q, and the inputs in production are capital, K, labor, L, and other inputs, R, then the production function can be written as:

$$q = F(K, L, R)$$

where the function $F(.)$ relates the levels of inputs to the level of output. Production functions have several properties; see Baumol (1977). The first property is the production function must exhibit diminishing returns. This means that if additional units of an input (such as labor) are added to production, holding the other inputs in production constant, eventually the increases in output will diminish (*see* LAW OF VARIABLE PROPORTIONS).

Another important property of production functions is returns to scale (or ECONOMIES OF SCALE). The issue here is the effect on output from increasing the amounts of all the inputs in production. For example, if all inputs in production are doubled, will output double or rise by a different amount? If doubling all inputs causes output to double, then there are CONSTANT RETURNS TO SCALE. If doubling all inputs causes output to more than double, then there are INCREASING RETURNS to scale. Finally, if doubling all inputs in production causes output to rise by less than double, there are decreasing returns to scale.

Production functions are also characterized by the degree of substitution between inputs in production (*see* SUBSTITUTION EFFECT). Some technologies require that inputs are used in fixed proportions, so that additional labor input cannot substitute for less capital input, for instance. The isoquant curves show the different combinations of inputs which are possible while keeping the output level constant (*see* ISOQUANT-ISOCOST CURVES). Normally, as the price rises for one input in production, firms will use less of that input and will substitute other inputs for the more expensive input.

see also **Cobb–Douglas production function**

Bibliography

Baumol, W. J. (1977). *Economic Theory and Operations Analysis*. Englewood Cliffs, NJ: Prentice-Hall.

Douglas, E. J. (1992). *Managerial Economics*. 4th edn, Englewood Cliffs, NJ: Prentice-Hall.

ROBERT E. MCAULIFFE

profit maximization   Although this goal is not always consistent with that of sales (revenue) maximization and other objectives of the firm (*see* OBJECTIVE OF THE FIRM), profit maximization is generally identified as one of the primary goals of most businesses. Since the level of profit is measured as the TOTAL REVENUE of the firm minus its TOTAL COSTS, profit maximization requires finding the level of output at which the difference between these two measures is a maximum. This level of output can be found by using marginal analysis where the MARGINAL REVENUE from one additional unit sold is compared with the MARGINAL COST of its production. The general rule for profit maximization requires that managers find that level of output where marginal revenue and marginal cost are equal, since at this level of output no extra profits could be earned by increasing or decreasing production. At output levels where the marginal revenue from an additional unit to be sold exceeds the cost of its production, additional profits can be made by increasing the level of output. Similarly, if the marginal cost of the last unit already produced was in excess of the additional revenue received from its sale, the marginal profit from that unit would be negative and its production and sale would have reduced total profits. In this case, the firm's output level should be decreased as this would increase total profits.

This method is universally applicable to firms regardless of the MARKET STRUCTURE in which they compete. Competitive firms, having no control over price, and monopolists, wherein management supply decisions may significantly influence price, may both use this technique to assure the highest level of profits possible. In addition, many alternative applications of this method may be used. For example, managers of retail shops who are considering extending their daily store hours or opening for business on weekends need to examine the marginal revenues and marginal costs of these additional hours to assure that the profit maximizing number of hours are chosen. Similarly, with respect to hiring decisions, choosing the optimal (profit maximizing) number of workers to hire requires the examination of the marginal gains and costs of additional workers.

see also economic profit

Bibliography

Hirschey, M. Pappas, J. (1995). *Fundamentals of Managerial Economics*. 5th edn, Fort Worth: Dryden.

Mansfield, E. (1993). *Managerial Economics*. 2nd edn, New York: Norton.

GILBERT BECKER

property rights   According to Armen Alchian (1987), "a property right is a socially enforced right to select uses of an economic good." Lawyers think of property as "bundles" of separate property rights that can be bought and sold, leased, mortgaged and partially divided. In recent, years the COASE THEOREM has encouraged economists to think about property more along the lines of the legal profession and thereby abandon or substantially modify older notions about production as combining factors of production (labor, capital and land) into output. All property rights systems are valuable to decision-makers when they are clearly defined and made secure with the assistance of infrastructures consisting of registrars, notaries, accountants, attorneys, sheriffs, and judges.

Property can take a myriad of forms in modern business situations and combinations of property in the form of a business corporation can be represented by shares of common stock or can be held in a trust in the form of trust shares. New combinations and new legal forms are conceivable as what Warren Samuels called the "legal-economic nexus" undergoes change. From the business point of view, property functions much as any typical business asset does (e.g. a machine) and its value is linked to the discounted presented value of its expected future flow of net benefits.

Well-defined property combinations, especially when owned by the modern limited liability corporation, have permitted the accumulation of vast amounts of financial capital from individuals who otherwise would not find it acceptable to hold their wealth in this way. By these institutional expedients, experimentation with new technologies and the creation of new business forms has resulted in the blossoming of new products and services that have become the hallmark of private property market systems.

The existence of property rights helps to avoid disputes, especially about incompatible uses of economic goods, such as with air and water rights. Property rights can provide incentives to others to mitigate the situation that originally led to the conflict about planned uses. When property rights help to mitigate disputes and align incentives we speak of the "efficiency enhancing" effects of property rights structures. For example, consider a small restaurant serving "fresh" fish to the public. The restaurant may impose side-effects (negative EXTERNALITIES) on its neighbors such as odors. Furthermore, the neighbors may protest and demand that the local licensing authorities shut it down. If the authorities were to make it clear to the neighbors that the restaurateur does indeed have a inviolable "property right" to sell cooked fish dinners at this location, then the neighbors are free to negotiate, perhaps to purchase that restaurant or, more creatively, give the owners a monthly cash stipend provided that they do not cook fish on certain days and/or between certain hours. Over time the neighbors may find it more economical to subsidize a better venting system for the restaurant or provide air conditioners to their homes thereby eliminating the odors altogether.

According to Ronald Coase, Harold Demsetz and other members of the law and economics school, such transactions, once property rights have been clearly defined and unhesitatingly enforced, will help to maximize the value of output and thereby make the markets more efficient (*see* EFFICIENCY). In such cases, the existence of clearly defined property rights is a precondition for the emergence of markets and the market processes associated with their presence.

As the market systems evolve, new forms of property emerge often with the assistance of government but sometimes without. Some property rights consist mostly of some person's promise to perform some act or acts at a future date. Buying and selling other people's promises, which was once restricted primarily to the banking and financial sector, has now expanded to create novel forms of property and new areas of entrepreneurial venturing. And so businesses are sold but always subject to conditions established by government agencies such as Federal, State, local officials and the courts. The buyer will not tender the purchase price for say, a restaurant, until the appropriate government agency has promised to issue a special license and that he also obtain the "air

rights" from the adjacent neighbor's property. In recent years, managers in different nations can avoid the risks of credit market conditions worsening and currency values falling by exchanging "swap promises" and an army of financial intermediaries has emerged to facilitate those trades. When one person's promise is made under certain conditions, then secondary markets may emerge in which these promises are salable thereby creating new forms of property and offering entrepreneurs new venturing opportunities. These opportunities include the creation of more valuable asset combinations and incentives to speculate about their future value.

Socialist economists raise poignant questions as to what should or should not be subject to one person's exclusive dominion and control. Human beings have a moral claim to be regarded as more than mere bundles of property rights. Exploring such insights, David P. Ellerman objected to well-entrenched factory systems in which workers sell their "labor services" to the owners of property for a predetermined price (wages and salaries) and where the owners of property contrive to keep the results of that labor activity along with any profits and/or capital gains. Ellerman suggested that it is more consonant with Western standards of morality and the meaning of language itself to have labor *hire* property and sell the outputs for their own account. In this way the traditional "employer–employee relation would have to be replaced by a system where each is self-employed and this is the parallel of political self-determination in democracy." To the extent that such radical thinking leads to a modification of the customs, norms and finally the legal system itself, the market system will assume a new shape and evolve in new directions.

One practical result of Ellerman's thinking is that modern managers may, in the future, become the agents of teams of employees who will need to find ways to protect their personal assets against the downside risks of business failure and tort liability. Under Ellerman's model, business organizations and factory-establishments will become more in the nature of massive tool and equipment rental operations. The workers become the lessees and the factory owners receive fixed prenegotiated rental prices. Regardless of how basic business institutions evolve and are restructured in the next millennium, it is reasonable to suppose that entrepreneurial venturing will continue to flourish even in a worker-style, capital-using economy because the search for new combinations of property and their purchase and sale remain indelible features of any market system.

Bibliography

Alchian, A. A. (1987). Property rights. Eatwell, J., Milgate, M. Newman P. *The New Palgrave: A Dictionary of Economics*. New York: Macmillan.

Demsetz, H. (1964). The exchange and enforcement of property rights. *Journal of Law and Economics*, 7, 11–26.

Dorn, J. A. (1994). The collapse of communism and post-communist reform. Boettke, P. J. *The Elgar Companion to Austrian Economics*. Aldershot, UK: Elgar Publishers.

Ellerman, D. P. (1992). *Property and Contract in Economics: The Case for Economic Democracy*. Cambridge, MA: Blackwell.

Rosenberg, N. Birdzell, L. E. Jr (1986). *How the West Grew Rich: The Economic Transformation of the Industrial World*. New York: Basic Books.

Samuels, W. J. (1989). The legal-economic nexus. *George Washington Law Review*, 57, 1556–78.

LAURENCE S. MOSS

public-goods problem Public goods have two properties that differentiate them from private goods. First, they are nonrival in consumption: once the good is provided, the additional resource cost of another person consuming the good is zero. In other words, these goods are used and not consumed. Second, public goods are nonexclusive: the consumption of a good is nonexcludable when it is either very costly or impossible to prevent others from consuming the good. Some examples of goods with this property are national defense, exploration of outer space, a television program, and street lighting. But, the definition of a public good is not absolute; it depends on market conditions, the state of technology and legal arrangements. For example, highway availability during rush hour traffic becomes rival in consumption and each driver creates a negative externality (*see* EXTERNALITIES). It is often possible to exclude consumers from consuming some public goods, for example, cable television.

Since public goods can be consumed by more than one consumer at the same time, the market demand for a public good is defined through the vertical summation of the demand curves of every consumer of a public good. Samuelson (1954) derived formal conditions for the efficient provision of public goods. If public goods are provided by private companies, then their level of production will be sub-optimal and correspondingly the incentives for overuse are greater. A free-rider problem occurs since consumers cannot be excluded from the consumption of a public good, they may try to avoid paying for their consumption of this good. In addition, it is difficult to determine the true market demand for public goods. At least since Samuelson, it has been known that financing schemes like those proposals where an individual's tax is set equal to his marginal benefit, provide perverse incentives for consumers to misrepresent their preferences. Consumers are reluctant to reveal high demand for public goods because they fear they will have to pay a higher tax. Schemes that are immune to such misrepresentations (in certain circumstances) have been developed in recent years (Clarke, 1971; Groves and Loeb, 1975).

The public-goods problem can be also improved upon by changing, assigning or creating PROPERTY RIGHTS. When property rights are secure and tradable and TRANSACTIONS COSTS are low, the COASE THEOREM suggests that people will trade rights until the new pattern of ownership is efficient. For example, if everyone is allowed to fish in a particular area then no one has property rights to the fish until they are caught. When property rights are unclear, markets are inefficient and in the case of fisheries substantial overfishing occurs. Unconstrained private fishing ignores the social costs of a smaller fish population in the future and fishermen make decisions with respect to their private benefits and costs of fishing today. The problem could be improved upon by giving exclusive fishing rights to one group in the fishery. In that case, the group would take into account the effect of current fishing on the future population of fish to avoid overfishing (also called the tragedy of the commons). This problem also arises in companies when individuals or departments have free access to a "common" resource, such as a secretarial pool or a copy machine. No one has an incentive to avoid overloading the pool (machine), so secretaries (and the machine) become overworked and the quality of service declines.

Bibliography

Carlton, D. W.   Perloff, J. M. (1994). *Modern Industrial Organization.* 2nd edn, New York: HarperCollins.

Clarke, E. H. (1971). Multipart pricing of public goods. *Public Choice*, 11, 17–33.

Groves, T. Loeb, M. (1975). Incentives and public inputs. *Journal of Public Economics*, 4, 211–26.

Samuelson, P. A. (1954). The pure theory of public expenditure. *Review of Economics and Statistics*, 36, 387–9.

LIDIJA POLUTNIK

Q

quality Variations in product quality introduce several issues concerning the performance of markets. When consumers cannot determine the level of quality of a good before purchase, their IMPERFECT INFORMATION can cause a *lemons problem* where the market breaks down. This problem arises because without additional information consumers expect a low level of quality and ultimately only low quality sellers will remain in the market (*see* LEMONS MARKET).

Quality improvement has been viewed in three different ways in the literature (Levhari and Peles, 1973; Beath and Katsoulacos, 1991). First, quality increases may increase the demand for the product (such as ADVERTISING expenditures and other promotional expenses). The second approach considers quality as a perfect substitute for quantity. In these models, consumers value the total level of services provided by the good (such as the total hours of light provided by a light bulb) and consider one 2-year light bulb as a perfect substitute for two 1-year light bulbs (*see* SUBSTITUTES). Finally, quality has been treated as an increase in the durability of a product.

Socially optimal quality levels

Will free markets provide the socially optimal level of quality? In the case of the single-product monopoly (where only one level of quality can be selected), the answer depends on how the marginal consumer in the market values quality. The socially optimal level of quality in a market is determined by consumers' willingness to pay for a quality increase on average. Therefore, an increase in quality is efficient if consumers in the market, on average, value that increase enough to pay the cost of providing it. However, for a profit-maximizing monopolist

the question is not whether on average consumers are willing to pay for an increase in quality, but whether the marginal consumer is willing to make that payment. So the level of quality in the market may be too high or too low depending on the marginal consumer's willingness to pay for quality; see Tirole (1988).

When firms compete in a market and can choose different levels of quality (there is *vertical* PRODUCT DIFFERENTIATION), firms have incentives to avoid price competition by choosing different quality levels. Thus when consumers in the market all rank the high-quality product above a low-quality product, but differ in their willingness to pay for high quality, firms will try to differentiate their products as much as possible. If one firm has positioned itself as the high-quality producer, then the next entrant will produce a low-quality product to avoid price competition, as long as consumer preferences are sufficiently diverse; see Tirole (1988). This incentive tends to create too much PRODUCT DIFFERENTIATION in the market.

When quality is a perfect substitute for quantity, will the level of quality provided in the market vary under different market structures (*see* MARKET STRUCTURE)? Since a monopolist is protected from competition, it had been thought that the level of product quality would be lower under MONOPOLY than under PERFECT COMPETITION (Schmalensee, 1970; Beath and Katsoulacos, 1991). But Swan (1970) found that a monopolist would provide the same level of quality (measured as durability) as perfectly competitive firms if there are CONSTANT RETURNS TO SCALE in production and when consumers are perfectly willing to substitute quality (durability) for quantity. Under these conditions, market structure does not affect the level of quality, although the result does not hold under different cost conditions or consumer preferences; see Liebowitz (1982).

Optimum durability and planned obsolescence

An interesting problem arises when a monopolist produces a durable good that lasts for several periods because once the product is sold, the monopolist faces competition in subsequent periods from its past production in the resale market. In addition, the monopolist is tempted to pursue intertemporal PRICE DISCRIMINATION by charging a high price to the early buyers who most want the product in the initial periods, then lowering the price in later periods to sell to consumers who value the product less. Since consumers expect the monopolist to decrease price in later periods (because that is its profit-maximizing choice) they are less willing to pay a high price today. Given this, Coase (1972) conjectured that monopoly profits would decrease as the length of time between price adjustments decreased and this limits monopoly power. To avoid this problem, a monopolist would prefer to lease a product rather than sell it and when this is possible, the monopolist will choose the socially optimal level of durability; see Tirole (1988). But when the monopolist cannot lease the product, it has incentives to plan obsolescence and decrease the durability of the good. This occurs because demand in the current period will be higher if fewer units of last period's production can be used this period; see Bulow (1986) and Tirole (1988).

Bibliography

Beath, J.   Katsoulacos, Y. (1991). *The Economic Theory of Product Differentiation.* Cambridge: CUP.

Bulow, J. (1986). An economic theory of planned obsolescence. *Quarterly Journal of Economics,* 51, 729–48.

Coase, R. (1972). Durability and monopoly. *Journal of Law and Economics,* 15, 143–9.

Levhari, D.   Peles, Y. (1973). Market structure, quality and durability. *Bell Journal of Economics,* 4, 235–48.

Liebowitz, S. (1982). Durability, market structure and new-used goods models. *American Economic Review,* 72, 816–24.

Schmalensee, R. (1970). Regulation and the durability of goods. *Bell Journal of Economics,* 1, 54–64.

Swan, P. L. (1970). Durability of consumer goods. *American Economic Review,* 60, 884–94.

Tirole, J. (1988). *The Theory of Industrial Organization.* Cambridge, MA: MIT.

ROBERT E. MCAULIFFE

R

R^2 R^2 denotes the coefficient of determination in LINEAR REGRESSION. The coefficient of determination is a measure of the goodness of fit of a regression to the data. The coefficient shows the proportion of the sample variation of the dependent variable that is explained by the regression of the dependent variable on the independent variables. For instance, an R^2 of 0.87 implies that the regression explains 87 percent of the variation in the dependent variable. In the context of a multiple regression, i. e. a regression with more than one independent variable, the coefficient is often called the "coefficient of multiple determination." Algebraically, R^2 is the ratio of the regression sum of squares (denoted by RSS) to the total sum of squares (denoted by TSS), i.e.

$$R^2 = \frac{RSS}{TSS}, RSS = \sum (\hat{Y}_i - \overline{Y})^2; \text{ and}$$

$$TSS = \sum (Y_i - \overline{Y})^2,$$

where RSS is the variation of the estimated values of the dependent variable, TSS is the sample variation of the dependent variable, and $\overline{Y}$ is the sample (arithmetic) mean of the dependent variable. Therefore, the variation in a variable is the sum of the squared deviations of the variable from its mean. Note that all summations are over the observations $i=1,2,...,T$, where T is the sample size. Because TSS=RSS+ESS, where

$$ESS = \sum \hat{v}_i^2$$

denotes the error sum of squares (which is the sum of the squared residuals of the regression), an alternative formula for R^2 is

$$R^2 = 1 - \frac{ESS}{TSS}.$$

R^2 is a unit-free measure and, by construction, its value is between 0 and 1. The closer R^2 is to 1 the better the explanatory power of the regression.

Although R^2 is a valuable measure of the goodness of fit, it requires careful use for a number of reasons. First, R^2 does not account for the "degrees of freedom" of the analysis, where the degrees of freedom are defined as the sample size used in the regression (denoted here by T) minus the number of independent variables in the regression (denoted by K) and minus 1 for the regression intercept. As a result:

(1) R^2 increases, or at least it does not decrease, even if variables which conceptually should not affect the dependent variable are included in the regression;

(2) when the sample size is not large enough compared to the number of independent variables, then, R^2 is likely to be high even when in truth the independent variables are not strongly related to the dependent variable.

Second, a high R^2 does not by itself imply that the regression model has been correctly specified (in the sense that no irrelevant variables have been included in the regression, and no significant variables have been omitted). For instance, a regression with TIME-SERIES DATA that exhibit significant upward growth may have a high R^2 even though some important explanatory variables have been omitted from the regression. Third, the interpretation of R^2 becomes difficult when the regression has no intercept. The reason is that without an intercept, the R^2 may not lie within the 0 to 1 range.

One way to correct some of the problems with R^2 is to modify the coefficient by adjusting for the degrees of freedom. The "adjusted" or "corrected" coefficient of determination, which is typically denoted by a "bar" on top of R^2, does just that. The adjusted coefficient is given by

$$\bar{R}^2 = 1 - \frac{\mathrm{ESS}/(T - K - 1)}{\mathrm{TSS}/(T - 1)}$$

where $T - K - 1$ is the number of degrees of freedom. Note that R^2 is always larger than or equal to the adjusted R^2, and also that the adjusted R^2 may even take negative values.

Bibliography

Maddala, G. S. (1992). *Introduction to Econometrics.* 2nd edn, New York: Macmillan.
Newbold, P. (1995). *Statistics for Business and Economics.* 4th edn, Englewood Cliffs, NJ: Prentice-Hall.
Pindyck, R. S. Rubinfeld, D. L. (1991). *Econometric Models and Economic Forecasts.* 3rd edn, New York: McGraw-Hill.

THEOFANIS TSOULOUHAS

real income   A consumer's real income is what that consumer can buy and it reflects that consumer's purchasing power or command over resources. Since INFLATION erodes the purchasing power of any amount of income, it is necessary to adjust nominal income (or current-dollar) figures for inflation to obtain real, inflation-adjusted income figures to determine the consumers' purchasing power (*see* NOMINAL INCOME AND PRICES). If the CONSUMER PRICE INDEX (CPI) reasonably measures changes in the cost of living for consumers in a given market, then the CPI can be used to adjust consumer income figures. Since the demand for many products is affected by changes in real income, adjusting nominal income figures for inflation can be important for forecasts and pricing decisions; see Douglas (1992).

When the price of a product changes, it affects demand through the INCOME EFFECT and the SUBSTITUTION EFFECT. The income effect reflects the change in the consumer's real income after the price change and will be stronger the greater the proportion of the consumer's income spent on the product. For example, a 10 percent price increase in the price of soda will have a negligible income effect, but a 10 percent increase in the price of housing will generate a significant income effect; see Shughart, Chappell and Cottle (1994).

Bibliography

Douglas, E. J. (1992). *Managerial Economics.* 4th edn, Englewood Cliffs, NJ: Prentice-Hall.
Shughart, W. F., Chappell, W. F. Cottle, R. L. (1994). *Modern Managerial Economics.* Cincinatti, OH: South-Western Publishing.

ROBERT E. MCAULIFFE

real prices   According to economic theory, the decisions made by consumers and firms are based on real or relative prices. The real price of a good is its cost in terms of other products: how much a consumer must sacrifice in other goods to obtain this product. To calculate real prices in dollars it is necessary to adjust for INFLATION using some deflator such as the CONSUMER PRICE INDEX or the producer price index. Dividing the current price by the appropriate deflator provides a measure of the real cost of the good in constant purchasing power base-year dollars. Such a calculation shows managers the real impact on consumers of a given change in the price of the product; see Douglas (1992).

Bibliography

Douglas, E. J. (1992). *Managerial Economics.* 4th edn, Englewood Cliffs, NJ: Prentice-Hall.

ROBERT E. MCAULIFFE

rent seeking   Broadly defined, rent seeking is an attempt by the owner or potential owner of an asset to secure excess returns on the asset by investing resources in influencing public policy. Krueger (1974) developed this concept originally in terms of the efforts by firms to capture monopoly profits by acquiring government-issued licenses on quotas that grant exclusive access to a market. One can extend this idea to the owner of a factor of production whose price is affected by government intervention in the market for the factor itself or for the final product in which the factor is an input. Bhagwati (1982) developed the broader definition of rent seeking to include what he termed "directly unproductive profit-seeking" (DUP) activities. To the extent that public policy can affect prices for assets or final products, the rent seeker has a strong incentive to invest resources to influence policy decisions in an attempt to alter market-driven prices or access to the market in his favor.

The problem of rent seeking stems from the general asymmetry in welfare effects of public policy: the benefits of government market intervention tend to be concentrated on small groups of identifiable beneficiaries, while its costs tend to be spread more thinly across the population. Trade policy provides the most salient examples of rent seeking in modern economies. Since a tariff or import quota can reduce import competition and allow domestic producers to raise prices and increase the returns on CAPITAL, labor or other factors of production, for example, firms and workers in a domestic import-competing industry are often motivated to lobby in favor of the trade restriction. In contrast, consumers, whose collective losses from the trade restriction are greater than the gains of the protected industry, are much more difficult to organize for the purposes of a counter-lobby.

If the government restricts trade through a quota arrangement, further opportunities for rent seeking arise as individuals invest resources to try to secure control over the quota rights, which give the holder the ability to raise the price of the imported product and thereby capture the scarcity premium associated with the trade restriction. Other examples include efforts by firms to acquire exclusive govern-ment-issued monopoly rights over an existing product and the expansion of productive capacity by firms in order to qualify for increased government allocations of inputs. In general, most government regulation of markets tends to create rent seeking activity in the broader sense.

Rent seeking has social costs, since it tends to dissipate above-market returns in the process of competition to get them (Friedman, 1990, p.476). Firms and individuals who can benefit from changes in government policies are often willing to divert real resources towards influen-cing policymakers. The OPPORTUNITY COSTS of such activities include not only the explicit financial outlays associated with lobbying (which presumably have their next best alter-native use in market-driven productive activities by the individual or firm), but also the implicit value of time and effort diverted from the "normal" activities of market participants towards the acquisition of political influence. Theoretically, the entire amount of excess returns associated with the government policy could be dissipated by rent seeking activity. This consideration suggests that the social cost of government regulation should include a measure of the wasted resources due to rent seeking.

see also **monopoly; deadweight loss**

Bibliography

Bhagwati, J. N. (1982). Directly unproductive, profit-seeking (DUP) activities. *Journal of Political Economy*, **90**, 988–1002.

Friedman, D. (1990). *Price Theory.* 2nd edn, Cincinnati: South-Western.

Krueger, A. O. (1974). The political economy of the rent-seeking society. *Journal of Political Economy*, **64**, 291–303.

KENT A. JONES

rents   Economic rents are defined as payments to entrepreneurs and owners of resources which are over and above the resource's opportunity cost (*see* OPPORTUNITY COSTS). For example, an economic rent is a portion of payment in excess of the minimum amount of profit necessary for a firm to enter a particular industry or a worker to accept a particular job. These excess payments are called economic rents because of the analogy to land rents: a given piece of land is fixed in supply, and whatever rent is received for it is by its nature a surplus over what is needed to keep the land in use. Often economic rents exist because of legal restrictions on entry into the industry. For example, the number of taxicab licenses and liquor licenses is often fixed by law, thus restricting entry to the industry and creating monopoly profits (economic rents). Occupational licensing laws which restrict labor supply and thereby increase the market wage also confer economic rents to licensees. In addition, economic profits (*see* ECONOMIC PROFIT) which may appear to exist in perfectly competitive markets in the long run are actually economic rents.

The existence of economic rents may lead to profit seeking and to RENT SEEKING behavior (Shughart, Chappell and Cottle, 1994). Entrepreneurs and owners of resources are selfishly motivated to reallocate their resources and find opportunities to put themselves in positions in which they would earn economic rents. Profit seekers are induced to enter the particular industry as a result of the existence of profits as well as to reallocate their scarce productive resources to their most highly valued uses. As a result of these decisions, output expands, prices decline, and in the long run economic profits are competed away and society's welfare is improved. However, rent-seeking refers to the firms who tend to spend money and exert effort to acquire and maintain the monopoly position or claims to resources that are in fixed supplies. In this case, resources may be used in an unproductive way from the society's point of view and its welfare may worsen.

Quasi rents are defined as short-run economic rents earned by the firm's fixed productive resources. Perfectly competitive firms in the short run are willing to produce as long as price is larger than average variable cost (*see* AVERAGE TOTAL COST). The difference between the price and average variable cost is called quasi rent, because it is similar to an economic rent in the short run but not in the long run. Whereas economic rents are defined in terms of decisions to enter a job or an industry, quasi-rents are defined in terms of a decision to exit (Milgrom and Roberts, 1992). These quasi rents are commonly created by costs associated with changing businesses, jobs, or careers, such as the cost of moving or specific on-the-job training. These costs cannot be recovered by the worker who chooses to change jobs because specialized human capital has been developed which cannot be used in another company. Quasi-rents represent a normal return on past investments and can continue to exist in long-term relationships given a proper contract design.

Bibliography

Milgrom, P. Roberts, J. (1992). *Economics, Organization and Management*. Englewood Cliffs, NJ: Prentice-Hall.
Shughart, W. F., Chappell, W. F. Cottle, R. L. (1994). *Modern Managerial Economics*. Cincinnati, OH: South-Western Publishing.

LIDIJA POLUTNIK

reservation price   A consumer's reservation price is the highest price that consumer would be willing to pay to purchase one unit of a product rather than forego the purchase. On the supply side of the market, the reservation price would reflect the minimum acceptable price at which a supplier would be willing to sell the product or service. The difference between the price a consumer pays for a product and the reservation price is the CONSUMER SURPLUS for that consumer while the difference between the price received by the supplier and its reservation price is the PRODUCER SURPLUS. Normally DEMAND CURVES measure the maximum quantity consumers will purchase at a specific price, but as Friedman (1976) has observed, this interpretation depends on the alternatives available to consumers. For example, conventional demand curves assume consumers are able to buy the specified quantity or less at the given price. However, the demand curve and the corresponding consumers' reservation prices will be different (and more likely, higher) if the choice is to purchase the specified amount or none. Similarly, the reservation price for suppliers will be different (and more likely, lower) if the purchase offer is an all-or-nothing bid.

Bibliography

Friedman, M. (1976). *Price Theory*. 2nd edn, Chicago: Aldine.

ROBERT E. MCAULIFFE

residual demand   The residual demand curve is the individual firm's demand curve which is that portion of market demand which is not supplied by other firms in the market. Thus it is the market demand curve minus the quantity supplied by other firms at each price (*see* DEMAND CURVES). If market demand is $D(p)$ and the supply of other firms is $S_o(p)$, then the residual demand for firm i is:

$$D_i(p) = D(p) - S_o(p)$$

The relationship between residual demand and market demand can also be expressed in terms of elasticities. For example, if there are n firms in an industry which are all identical, then the elasticity of residual demand facing firm i can be expressed as:

$$\varepsilon_i = \varepsilon_p \times n - \varepsilon_{so} \times (n - 1)$$

where ε_p is the price ELASTICITY of market demand, and ε_{so} is the elasticity of supply of the other firms in the market, which will be positive; see Carlton and Perloff (1994). As one might expect, the elasticity of residual demand facing a single firm is much higher than the elasticity of demand for the market, so a single firm will find its demand very sensitive to price changes. In addition, an individual firm's elasticity of demand will be higher (in absolute value) the greater the elasticity of supply of rival firms in the market, since there will be more substitutes available to firm i's customers when this supply elasticity is high.

When only one firm serves the market ($n = 1$), the firm is a MONOPOLY and the firm's demand is the same as market demand. For a DOMINANT FIRM facing a number of small, price-taking competitors, the elasticity of residual demand is

$$\varepsilon_d = \frac{Q}{Q_d} \times \varepsilon_p - \frac{Q_o}{Q_d} \times \varepsilon_{so}$$

where ε_d is the elasticity of residual demand for the dominant firm, Q_d is the output of the dominant firm, Q is industry output (which is the sum of the output produced by the dominant firm and its rivals) and Q_o is the output of the other, smaller firms in the market. Here, the MARKET POWER of the dominant firm falls the higher the elasticity of supply of the other firms in the market, and this forces the dominant firm to choose a lower price. The dominant firm will also have less market power the smaller the proportion of industry output it produces.

Bibliography

Carlton, D. W.   Perloff, J. M. (1994). *Modern Industrial Organization*. 2nd edn, New York: HarperCollins.
Stigler, G. J. (1968). *The Organization of Industry*. Chicago: University of Chicago Press.
Tirole, J. (1988). *The Theory of Industrial Organization*. Cambridge, MA: MIT Press.

ROBERT E. MCAULIFFE

risk aversion   Decisions involving risk are modeled as lotteries consisting of a set of possible outcomes and a probability distribution across these outcomes. In this environment, optimal decisions depend not only upon the outcomes and their associated probabilities, but also upon a decision-maker's attitude toward risk. An agent is said to be risk averse if he prefers the EXPECTED VALUE of a lottery to the lottery itself.

For example, consider a simple lottery of flipping a coin for which one receives $20 if the coin turns up "heads" and $0 if the coin is a "tails." The mathematical expectation or expected value of this lottery is $10. Facing a choice between the coin flip or accepting $10 with perfect certainty, a risk-averse agent will strictly prefer the certain $10. In fact, a risk-averse agent will accept some amount less that $10 rather than accepting the coin flip. The amount with which the agent is indifferent to the lottery is the CERTAINTY EQUIVALENT of the lottery.

In contrast, an agent who strictly prefers the coin flip to the certain $10 is said to be risk-preferring. A decision maker who is indifferent between the two prospects is said to demonstrate RISK NEUTRALITY.

The primary framework for the analysis of choices involving risk is the expected utility hypothesis associated with von Neumann and Morgenstern (1944). In their theory, if an agent meets certain rationality axioms, then his preferences over outcomes may be characterized by a continuous utility function. Then, an agent will evaluate lotteries in terms of expected utility rather than expected value. If an agent is risk averse, his utility function will be concave in income. In contrast, risk-preferring and risk-neutral agents have utility functions which are convex and linear respectively.

Since attitude toward risk is subjective, it is not surprising that agents may differ in the degree of risk aversion. Since risk-averse agents have concave utility functions, one might expect the curvature of the utility function to relate to the degree of risk aversion. Following Arrow (1971) and Pratt (1964), risk aversion may be measured by the following coefficient of absolute risk aversion, ARA:

$$ARA = -u''/u'$$

where u'' is the second derivative of the utility function with respect to income and u' is the first derivative. This coefficient is a measure of the concavity of the utility function that is scaled to be invariant to linear transformation of the utility function. Friedman and Savage (1948) argue that individuals may be risk-averse over some ranges of wealth while risk-preferring over other ranges. Empirical evidence suggests that most individuals become less risk averse as their income increases.

Risk aversion has a crucial role in the theory of both insurance and financial securities markets. Insurance markets exist so that risk-averse agents may spread their risk among market participants. That insurance purchasers are willing to pay premiums in excess of the expected value of their losses demonstrates their risk aversion. In financial markets, investors require a higher return from risky securities. The latter example shows that risk aversion does not imply that an individual will not accept risky propositions, but rather that they will require additional compensation to do so.

Bibliography

Arrow, K. J. (1971). *Essays in the Theory of Risk-Bearing.* Amsterdam: North-Holland.

Friedman, M. Savage L. J. (1948). The utility analysis of choices involving risk. *Journal of Political Economy*, **56**, 279–304.

Pratt, J. (1964). Risk aversion in the small and in the large. *Econometrica*, **32** , 122–36.

von Neumann, J. Morgenstern, O. (1944). *Theory of Games and Economic Behavior.* Princeton: Princeton University Press.

ROGER TUTTEROW

risk neutrality   In choices involving risk, optimal decisions depend upon the set of possible outcomes, the probability of their occurrence and the decision maker's attitude toward risk. A decision maker is said to be "risk neutral" if he evaluates decisions in terms of the EXPECTED VALUE of the outcomes. For a risk neutral agent, the expected value and CERTAINTY EQUIVALENT of a lottery are equal.

There is little reason to expect that an individual should display risk neutrality. However, Arrow and Lind (1970) showed that if returns on an investment are spread over a large population and are distributed independently of any aggregate risk, then one may evaluate the investment as if risk-neutral. A variant of this risk-spreading argument is frequently used to defend risk neutrality in firms owned by a large number of stockholders.

Bibliography

Arrow, K. Lind, R. (1970). Uncertainty and the evaluation of public investment decisions. *American Economic Review*, **60**, 364–78.

ROGER TUTTEROW

risk premium   In the theory of choice under risk, a risk premium is defined as the difference between the EXPECTED VALUE and the CERTAINTY EQUIVALENT of a lottery. One may consider the risk premium as the compensation necessary to entice a risk-averse agent to accept a risky proposition. Pratt (1964) demonstrated that for "small" gambles, the risk premium is proportionate to the VARIANCE of the outcomes, the proportion varying with the decision maker's degree of RISK AVERSION. Further, it can be shown that the more risk-averse the agent, the larger the risk premium associated with a given lottery.

In financial markets, risk premiums exist as the additional return necessary to entice investors to accept risky investments. In debt markets, yields include premiums for default and interest rate risk. The returns on equity securities includes premiums for uncertainty about residual cash flows.

Bibliography

Pratt, J. (1964). Risk aversion in the small and in the large. *Econometrica*, **32**, 122–36.

ROGER TUTTEROW

S

search costs These are the costs incurred by consumers as they try to find those products which best satisfy their needs. Search costs include the time spent looking for a product, finding the best price and the costs of purchasing brands which failed to meet the consumer's expectations. These costs will be higher:

(1) the greater consumers' real incomes (*see* REAL INCOME), because the opportunity cost of lost time is higher,
(2) the more dispersed prices are in the market, because more effort would be required to find the best price,
(3) the more geographically dispersed sellers are in the market, and
(4) the less information consumers have initially.

Since search costs may reduce sales, institutions exist in markets to reduce those costs to potential buyers. Shopping malls reduce search costs by providing a central location for consumers to find sellers, firms may reduce search costs through ADVERTISING expenditures, establishing reputations for quality or providing free samples to consumers. Consumers also receive information from independent sources such as Consumer Reports and Underwriters' Laboratories that help to overcome IMPERFECT INFORMATION in the market.

see also **search goods; transactions costs**

ROBERT E. MCAULIFFE

search goods Search goods are those products whose quality can be determined by inspection before purchase. The distinction between search goods and EXPERIENCE GOODS was developed by Nelson (1970, 1974) who suggested that ADVERTISING played an important role in providing information to consumers in markets where information may be imperfect. Since consumers can verify the truthfulness of advertising claims for search goods before purchasing the product, Nelson suggested that the information provided by advertising for search goods was more likely to be truthful. In addition, the content of advertising messages for search goods was likely to be more factual and direct than for experience goods, and this implied that search goods would be more heavily advertised in the print media (newspapers and magazines) rather than in broadcast media and that local media outlets would be used in greater proportion than national media outlets since local media would provide more directly relevant information to consumers.

Nelson found that his classification of products into search and experience categories allowed him to explain differences in advertising–sales ratios between products and in the media used by different products. Ehrlich and Fisher (1982) extended the model of advertising in the market for information and weighed the costs and benefits of different methods of providing information to the market. For example, the potential buyers of producer goods tend to be small in number, very knowledgeable and benefit more from information provided through trade shows and salespeople. But the potential buyers of consumer products are more numerous, less knowledgeable and more heterogeneous, so broadcast media may be the most cost-effective means to provide information to this audience. Since information can be efficiently supplied through a variety of channels in the producer goods industries, Ehrlich and Fisher also predicted that advertising for these products would be less intensive than for consumer goods.

Bibliography

Ehrlich, I. Fisher, L. (1982). The derived demand for advertising: a theoretical and empirical investigation. *American Economic Review*, 72, 366–88.

Nelson, P. (1970). Information and consumer behavior. *Journal of Political Economy*, 78, 311–29.

Nelson, P. (1974). Advertising as information. *Journal of Political Economy*, 81, 729–54.

ROBERT E. MCAULIFFE

Sherman Act   The Sherman Act of 1890 is the first major US antitrust law (*see* CLAYTON ACT; FEDERAL TRADE COMMISSION ACT; ANTITRUST POLICY). Written in an era of increasing industrialization, the Sherman Act was in part an effort to quell the attempts to, and consequences of, increasing MARKET POWER. Section 1 of the Act proscribes: "Every contract, combination in the form of trust or otherwise, or conspiracy, in restraint of trade or commerce"; see Stelzer (1986, pp.594–8) for a more complete statement of this Statute. Although debate continues as to the meaning of this phrase, managers should be aware of certain definitive interpretations which the courts have consistently maintained. The first is that horizontal price fixing, i.e. any agreement between rival firms to coordinate prices, is in violation of the Act. Beginning with US v Trenton Potteries Company in 1927, the court has strictly held the position that price fixing is *per se* illegal, meaning that the behavior is in and of itself a violation of the law. Thus, defenses of the fairness of the fixed prices, the need for price fixing during an economically unstable period for the industry, and other arguments have consistently been struck down. The court has insisted that market forces shall determine what constitutes reasonable prices.

Evidence of illegal price fixing includes sharing price lists, discussing prices through trade associations, and more recently signalling price information through computer networks as was alleged to have occurred in the airline industry. Controversy still exists concerning pricing in OLIGOPOLY markets where differing forms of PRICE LEADERSHIP are common and where conscious awareness of parallel pricing behavior among rivals is often routine. The difficulty herein lies with the recognition that quite often a firm has no choice but to follow a parallel pricing strategy – in reaction, for example, to a rival's price decrease – in order to avoid losses. Thus, what may appear to be a conspiracy is not necessarily one. To date the courts have typically required hard evidence beyond parallel pricing in order to infer a price fixing conspiracy.

Resale price maintenance, sometimes known as vertical price fixing, is an entirely different pricing agreement whereby a manufacturer establishes minimum prices at which retailers can resell its products. Prior to 1975, this type of price fixing was exempt from the Sherman Act. Allowing the institution of a minimum resale price was seen as a method to protect small retailers from the growth of large discount outlets which would otherwise have been able to offer lower prices than their smaller rivals. With the repeal of the laws protecting resale price maintenance, vertical price fixing currently is illegal, perhaps to the benefit of consumers who are able to find lower prices.

Enforcement of the Sherman Act concerning vertical price fixing has varied in the past two decades. During the 1980s, the federal government showed little interest in initiating cases against vertical price fixers. In 1995 though, a case was brought against Reebok International Corp., concerning the resale of its athletic footwear. Reebok agreed in a consent decree to not impose required minimum prices on retailers, nor to threaten retailers with termination of the supply of its footwear in instances where the retailer does not conform with the manufacturer's suggested minimum resale price. Thus, managers should be aware that a manufacturer's policy of identifying a resale price is not illegal as long as it is merely suggested and not imposed upon the retailer as a condition of the contractual agreement.

In addition to horizontal price fixing, market sharing agreements among rivals have also been proscribed by the courts in their interpretation of Section 1 of the Sherman Act. These arrangements, whereby would-be rivals agree to serve only certain customers, or avoid each other's geographic territories, are also *per se* illegal. This type of activity is often a significant component of the behavior of CARTELS which are also illegal under US antitrust law.

Section 2 of the Sherman Act indicates that "every person who shall monopolize, or attempt to monopolize, or combine or conspire ... to monopolize any part of the trade or commerce ..." is in violation of the law. Here again managers should be aware of several important and long-standing interpretations of this Section by the US courts. First, the law identifies the act of *monopolizing*, rather than the mere existence of MONOPOLY, as being proscribed. Beginning perhaps with the 1914 case of Standard Oil Company of New Jersey v US, the Supreme Court has recognized and maintained this distinction. In that case, the court found that the firm had intended by its actions to dominate the market by driving out existing competitors and excluding other potential competitors from the industry. By contrast, the court also indicated in that case that the achievement of a monopoly position through procompetitive business practices such as the production of a superior product would not be a violation of the law.

Second, the courts have indicated that having a pure monopoly position (i.e. a 100 percent market share) is not a necessary requirement for finding a violation. While the trusts in the major early cases involving the oil and tobacco industries were found to have approximately 90 percent market shares, in the 1945 case of US v ALCOA, the firm was found to be in violation of Section 2 even though, by some measures, it held only 60 percent of the market. By contrast, in 1920, the US Steel Corp., found to have held slightly more than 50 percent of the national market, was considered by the courts not to have achieved sufficient market power, and in part for this reason was found not to be in violation of the law.

As a result, the courts appear to have created a two-part test for establishing a violation of Section 2 of the Act. First, *prima facie* evidence of the existence of market power through holding a significant share of the relevant market (seemingly in excess of 60 percent) must be present. Second, evidence of anticompetitive attempts to monopolize must be demonstrated.

A third important interpretation also evolved from the US Steel case. The court made clear the distinction between the absolute size of a firm and its size relative to the market. It held

that absolute size does not necessarily convey market power and thus is not by itself an offense.

The enforcement of the Sherman Act, as revised in 1974, allows for criminal penalties to be imposed by the courts, including fines of up to $1 million dollars for a corporation or $100,000 for an individual, along with imprisonment for up to three years for violations. The Act also allows for civil proceedings in which the courts may, and often have, issued injunctions against the continuation of anticompetitive behavior. In addition, the courts can find the MARKET STRUCTURE to be the source of the offense and can require remedial action. This may include the dissolution of a company into several smaller rivals, as was the case in US v Standard Oil of New Jersey in 1914, or the divestiture of some assets and the creation of separate firms, as was the result of the court-approved settlement between the government and the AT&T Corporation in 1982.

As Howard (1983) points out, defendants in antitrust cases brought by the government may choose to plead *nolo contendere*, not contending the charge brought against them. This strategy, which does not require admission of any wrongdoing, results in no *prima facie* evidence being established against the firm. Here, the court may administer whatever remedy it sees as being necessary and appropriate. One possible benefit to the firm from such a plea, along with avoiding lengthy and costly court proceedings, concerns additional private antitrust suits (allowed by Section 4 of the Act) which may be brought against the firm by injured parties. As a result of the plea, injured parties would have to develop their own evidence establishing that a violation of the Act had in fact occurred. The cost of the case development may deter some injured parties from initiating action. None the less, the vast majority of antitrust cases filed in court are private suits, perhaps in large part because treble damages are awarded when injury is discovered in these cases. The benefits and potential abuses of the treble damages system, and the incentives of the antitrust law penalty system in general, have recently come under heightened scrutiny by Breit and Elzinga (1986), Werden and Simon (1987), Grippando (1989) and others.

Bibliography

Breit, W.   Elzinga, K. (1986). *Antitrust Penalty Reform*. Washington, DC: American Enterprise Institute.

Greer, D. (1992). *Industrial Organization and Public Policy*. 3rd edn, New York: Macmillan.

Grippando, J. (1989). Caught in the non-act: expanding criminal antitrust liability for corporate officials. *Antitrust Bulletin*, 34, 713–57.

Howard, M. (1983). *Antitrust and Trade Regulation*. Englewood Cliffs, NJ: Prentice-Hall.

Martin, S. (1994). *Industrial Economics*. 2nd edn, New York: Macmillan.

Neale, A. (1977). *The Antitrust Laws of the U.S.A.* 2nd edn, Cambridge: CUP.

Stelzer, I. (1986). *Selected Antitrust Cases: Landmark Decisions*. 7th edn, Homewood: Irwin.

Werden, G.   Simon, M. (1987). Why price fixers should go to jail. *Antitrust Bulletin*, 32, 913–37.

GILBERT BECKER

short run   The short run is defined as that period of time during which at least one input in production is fixed and cannot be changed. Frequently capital, such as plant and equipment, is treated as fixed in the short run while labor and materials are considered to be variable, but long term labor contracts or unions may make some labor costs fixed. Given that at least one input is fixed in the short run, DIMINISHING RETURNS will apply to production.

As Stigler (1966) and De Alessi (1967) have noted, the language distinguishing the short run from the long run is ambiguous. For very short periods of time, all factors of production are fixed. For slightly longer periods of time, all factors of production are variable if no expense were spared. De Alessi argues that firms will adjust different inputs in the short run depending on the relative costs and benefits for a particular change given the production technologies available. The costs of adjusting factors of production should be higher the shorter the time interval under consideration, and for some inputs those costs will increase much more rapidly than for others. Therefore it may be more appropriate to think of the short

run as the period of time when the firm cannot change some factors of production without significantly affecting the costs of those factors relative to the expected benefits.

Bibliography

De Alessi, L. (1967). The short run revisited. *American Economic Review*, 57, 460–61.

Stigler, G. J. (1966). *The Theory of Price*. 3rd edn, New York: MacMillan.

ROBERT E. MCAULIFFE

short run cost curves   The SHORT RUN is defined as that period of time during which at least one input in production is fixed and cannot be changed. Frequently capital, such as plant and equipment, is treated as fixed in the short run while labor and materials are considered to be variable, but long-term labor contracts or unions may make some labor costs fixed as well. Given that at least one input is fixed in the short run, DIMINISHING RETURNS will apply to production.

Following convention and to simplify the discussion, consider a firm using only two inputs in production where capital will be treated as the fixed factor of production and labor will be considered variable. This means that, in the short run, the amount of capital the firm has available cannot be altered from its fixed level K_0 and the short run production function (*see* PRODUCTION FUNCTIONS) for the firm is then:

$$q = F(L, K_0) \qquad (1)$$

where q is the quantity of output produced and L is the quantity of labor employed. Total production costs for the firm will be equal to the wage rate (w) times the amount of labor employed (assuming labor can be hired at a constant wage) plus the fixed amount of capital times the economic cost of capital (r). Total costs are then:

$$\text{TC} = w \times L + r \times K_0 \qquad (2)$$

The first term on the right-hand side of equation (2) is the total labor cost for the firm and these are the firm's total variable costs in this example (*see* TOTAL VARIABLE COST). The second term on the right is the firm's economic cost of capital which is a fixed cost and does not vary with output (*see* FIXED COSTS). The firm's short run cost curves can then be derived by observing the changes in total costs (or the changes in total variable costs) as output changes. Since capital inputs are fixed in the short run, the firm must adjust labor inputs to change output, and the output which will be produced is determined by the production function in equation (1). In this example, total variable costs are just the labor costs in equation (2), so marginal costs (*see* MARGINAL COST) are then equal to

$$MC = \frac{\Delta TVC}{\Delta q} = \frac{w \times \Delta L}{\Delta q}$$

$$= w \times \left\{\frac{\Delta L}{\Delta q}\right\} = \frac{w}{MPL} \qquad (3)$$

where ΔTVC is the change in total variable costs, Δq is the change in output, and the term in braces on the right is the inverse of the MARGINAL PRODUCT of labor (MP_L). The marginal cost curve is the slope of the total variable cost curve at different output levels and since the wage rate is assumed to be constant, marginal costs will vary with changes in the marginal product of labor. Variable and marginal costs will be zero if no labor is hired and no output is produced. If one worker were hired, the variable and marginal costs of producing the first few units of output would be high (because the marginal product of a single worker would be low), but as additional workers are hired, the marginal product of labor increases which causes marginal costs to decrease. Eventually, the marginal product of labor will reach a maximum value which, in this example, corresponds to the minimum value of the marginal cost curve. After this (point A in figure 1), the marginal product of labor decreases and the marginal cost of production increases.

The corresponding short run average cost curves can also be derived from the underlying production function and prices of inputs (see equations (1) and (2)). There are three short run average cost curves: average total costs (SRATC), average variable costs (SRAVC), and average fixed costs (SRAFC). These average cost curves are given by:

$$SRATC = \frac{TC}{q} = \frac{(w \times L + r \times K_0)}{q} \qquad (4)$$

$$SRAVC = \frac{TVC}{q} = \frac{w \times L}{q} \qquad (5)$$

$$SRAFC = \frac{TFC}{q} = \frac{r \times K_0}{q} \qquad (6)$$

where TC is the firm's total costs in equation (1) (including the OPPORTUNITY COSTS of capital), TVC the firm's total variable costs and TFC the total fixed costs of the firm. Of these average cost curves, average fixed cost is the least important in economics because fixed costs do not affect short run decisions. The short run marginal, average and average variable cost curves are depicted in figure 1.

The marginal cost curve intersects both average cost curves at their respective minimum points (B and C), and as marginal costs continue to increase, the average cost curves rise but at a slower rate. As long as the marginal cost curve lies below the average variable and average total cost curves, the average cost curves must be falling because the cost of producing the last unit (the marginal cost) is less than the average cost of all the preceding units produced, and this pulls the average cost curves down. Similarly, when the marginal cost curve lies above the average variable and average total cost curves, it pulls them up since the cost of the last unit exceeds the average of the previous units produced and adding any number to an average which exceeds the average must force the average value to rise.

The average variable cost curve plays a role in short run decisions because the firm does not have to incur these costs and can choose to produce no output. Therefore, if the price the firm will receive for its output is too low, the revenues earned will not cover the firm's variable costs and the firm should shut down and produce nothing. Since fixed costs must be paid whether or not the firm produces output, these costs should have no effect on a manager's decision to produce in the current period. But the firm must pay variable costs only when output is produced, and if those variable costs cannot be paid from the revenues generated from production, there is no reason to incur

Costs

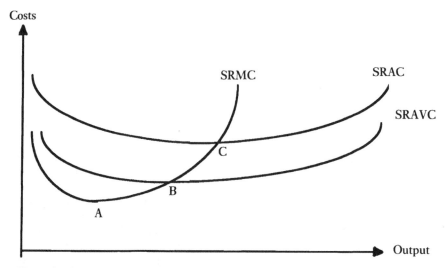

Figure 1   Short run cost curves

them. If the revenues can cover variable costs, then any additional earnings can be applied to fixed costs and reduce the firm's short run losses. A perfectly competitive firm will maximize profits by producing output where price equals marginal cost for those points where marginal cost lies above the short run average variable cost curve (the marginal cost curve above point B in figure 1).

Theoretically, the short run average total cost curve, ATC, serves as a benchmark to predict industry trends. As mentioned above, the ATC curve includes the opportunity cost of capital, which is the normal, risk-adjusted rate of return which could be earned if the firm's capital were employed in its next best use. When the firm's total revenues exceed its total costs (which include the normal return on capital), the firm is earning an ECONOMIC PROFIT. This occurs when the price of the product (which is average revenue) lies above the ATC curve at the firm's profit-maximizing output level (*see* PROFIT MAXIMIZATION). Therefore, when the product's price lies above the ATC curve, firms can earn higher returns in this industry than elsewhere and, if there are no BARRIERS TO ENTRY, entry should occur in the long run. Similarly, if the price is below the firm's ATC curve, firms in this industry are earning less than they could earn elsewhere and there should be EXIT from this industry in the long run.

Unfortunately, as Stigler (1966) and Friedman (1976) have observed, average total costs (which include the opportunity cost of capital) will change as industry demand changes. For example, an increase demand will cause profits to rise and increases the value of the firm's assets. Or a firm might have access to better resources or a better location which lower its costs of production and allow the firm to enjoy a return apparently above the normal, competitive rate. However, in both cases, these resources could be sold for a capital gain and this is an opportunity cost to the firm. Therefore, if the firm valued its assets at this higher (market) value, its true long run average costs would be higher and its rate of return would be lower (*see* RENTS). What appears to be above normal profits may occur because of the failure to properly capitalize the value of the firm's assets.

Bibliography

Douglas, E. J. (1992). *Managerial Economics*. 4th edn, Englewood Cliffs, NJ: Prentice-Hall.

Friedman, M. (1976). *Price Theory*. 2nd edn, Chicago: Aldine.

Stigler, G. J. (1966). *The Theory of Price*. 3rd edn, New York: Macmillan.

Shughart, W. F., Chappell, W. F. Cottle, R. L. (1994). *Modern Managerial Economics*. Cincinatti, OH: South-Western Publishing.

ROBERT E. MCAULIFFE

signaling When information is not readily available, individuals can take the initiative to produce signals that reveal their attributes. Spence (1974) provided a systematic explanation of investment in education as a means of signaling productivity to the market. Suppose there are two types of workers: those with high ability whose marginal product of labor is 2 and those with low ability whose marginal product of labor is 1. Workers may invest in education or a degree at positive cost but by assumption, education does not increase on-the-job productivity. If information about each individual's productivity were available to the employer, workers would be paid their respective MARGINAL PRODUCT. When there is ASYMMETRIC INFORMATION, where employers do not know their prospective workers' marginal products and workers do, the employer pays everyone the same wage. That wage would be equal to the expected productivity of a randomly chosen worker. High-ability workers in pursuit of higher wages would want to signal employers about their greater productivity. Also, employers would benefit from such a signal by selecting more productive workers and avoiding the cost of hiring and training workers that may potentially be fired. Education might be a credible signal if high ability workers can complete education with less effort (lower cost) than low ability workers. If education is used as a signal of differentiating high ability workers from low ability workers, employers and employees benefit from this information; however, in this model there is no other benefit from public spending on education. Even when there is a positive relationship between workers' productivity and spending on education, we find some overinvestment in education (Milgrom and Roberts, 1992).

Signaling has been used to explain a variety of other strategic decisions. The quality of the product that is known to the producer but not to the potential customer can be signaled by using price, advertising, guaranties or warranties, and so on. For example, a high quality producer may use a low price or uninformative advertising to signal high quality if his cost of using this signal is lower than that of a low quality producer (Nelson, 1974). Milgrom and Roberts (1982) show that when a firm that is entering the market does not know the costs of the established firm in the market, the established firm may be able to deter entry by charging a lower price because the reduced price signals to potential entrants that the costs of the established firm are so low that as entry occurs the entrant will experience a loss (*see* LIMIT PRICING). Milgrom and Roberts (1986) show that for goods which are purchased often, both price and advertising could be employed to provide signals to customers. For these goods, high quality firms have an incentive to set a low price expecting to earn profits on future purchases. On the other hand, durable goods should enter the market at a high price and as Bagwell and Riordan (1991) show, the price should decrease with time as information about the quality of the good spreads. In financial markets, managers have significantly more information about their company's performance and prospects than their investors. Signaling has been employed to analyze financial decisions which have the ability to influence what investors believe about the firm's prospects. For example, Ross (1977) showed that a choice of a company to increase its debt–equity ratio provided a signal for investors that its equity shares were more valuable.

see also **adverse selection; firm financial structure**

Bibliography

Bagwell, K. Riordan, M. K. (1991). High and declining prices signal product quality. *American Economic Review*, 81, 224–39.

Milgrom, P. Roberts, J. (1982). Limit pricing and entry under incomplete information: an equilibrium analysis. *Econometrica*, 50, 443–59.

Milgrom, P. Roberts, J. (1986). Price and advertising signals of product quality. *Journal of Political Economy*, 94, 796–821.

Milgrom, P. Roberts, J. (1992). *Economics, Organization and Management*. Englewood Cliffs, NJ: Prentice-Hall.

Nelson, P. (1974). Advertising as information. *Journal of Political Economy*, 84, 729–54.

Ross, S. (1977). The determination of financial structure: the incentive signaling approach. *Bell Journal of Economics*, 8, 23–40.

Spence, A. M. (1974). *Market Signaling: Informa-tional Transfer in Hiring and Related Screening Processes*. Cambridge, MA: Harvard University Press.

LIDIJA POLUTNIK

simultaneous equations bias   This refers to the bias from using LINEAR REGRESSION to estimate the parameters of an equation that is part of a system of simultaneous equations. For example, when market prices and quantities sold are determined by both supply and demand, direct estimates of the demand or supply curves by linear regression will be biased, because one of the basic assumptions regarding the ERROR TERMS IN REGRESSION is violated.

To see this, consider the supply and demand for any good below:

$$Q_t^d = \alpha_1 + \alpha_2 P + \varepsilon_t^d, \tag{1}$$

$$Q_t^s = \beta_1 + \beta_2 P + \varepsilon_t^s, \tag{2}$$

$$Q_t^d = Q_t^s, \tag{3}$$

where Q is the quantity supplied or demanded, P is the price of the product, and the ε_t^i are random disturbances to demand and supply. Equations (1)–(3) are referred to as *structural equations*, which reflect specific features of the market. These equations are mutually dependent, so random variations in demand or supply will cause random variations in price. But if demand is randomly high (or low) in a given period the price will be higher (lower) in that period as well, and this means there is a correlation between one of the right-hand side variables in the regression (price) and the error term which biases linear regression estimates. The same problem occurs with estimates of the supply curve, or with estimates of any simultaneous relationship in which variables on the right-hand side of the regression are not exogenous.

To see why the estimates from linear regression are biased, substitute equations (1) and (2) into equation (3) above and solve for price:

$$P = \frac{(\beta_1 + \varepsilon_t^s - \alpha_1 - \varepsilon_t^d)}{\beta_2 - \alpha_2}. \tag{4}$$

The linear regression estimator for the slope of the demand curve, α_2, α_2^L, is calculated as follows:

$$\alpha_2^L = \frac{\text{Cov}(Q^d, P)}{\text{Var}(P)}, \tag{5}$$

where $\text{Cov}(Q^d, P)$ is the COVARIANCE between the quantity demanded and price, and $\text{Var}(P)$ is the VARIANCE of the price data. For the linear regression estimator to be unbiased, there must be no correlation (or covariance) between the right-hand side variables in the regression (P in this example) and the error term, ε_t^d. To check this assumption, take the covariance of the demand curve (equation (1) above) with respect to P. This yields

$$\text{Cov}(Q^d, P) = \alpha_2 \text{Var}(P) + \text{Cov}(P, \varepsilon_t^d). \tag{6}$$

Dividing both sides by the variance of P and solving for α_2 provides the linear regression estimator of α_2.

$$\alpha_2^L = \frac{\text{Cov}(Q^d, P)}{\text{Var}(P)} - \frac{\text{Cov}(P, \varepsilon_t^d)}{\text{Var}(P)}. \tag{7}$$

The first term on the right in equation (7) is the correct estimator of α_2, but the second term – which represents the covariance between the error term and the price variable – must be zero for the linear regression estimator to be unbiased. Since the solution for price in equation (4) shows that variations in the error term will cause variations in price, the covariance between P and ε_t^d will not be zero as needed, and thus the estimator is biased. The degree to which the linear regression estimator is biased will depend on the size of the covariance between price and the error term, the last term in equation (7).

There are several methods for obtaining unbiased estimators of the parameters in simultaneous equations systems (see Greene (1993), Maddala (1992), and ESTIMATING DEMAND), but it is important for researchers to know that linear regression methods cannot be used in general to estimate demand or supply equations directly.

Bibliography

Greene, W. H. (1993). *Econometric analysis* (2nd edn). New York: Macmillan.

Maddala, G. S. (1992). *Introduction to econometrics* (2nd edn). New York: Macmillan.

ROBERT E. MCAULIFFE

standard deviation   The standard deviation of a random variable is the square root of its VARIANCE and it measures dispersion around the EXPECTED VALUE, or mean of that random variable. For a discrete random variable, X, which has specific outcomes denoted by X_i and where the probability distribution of the values of X is given by $f(x)$, then the standard deviation of X, σ, is calculated as

$$\sigma = \sqrt{\sum f(x) \times (X_i - E(X))^2}$$

where $E(X)$ is the expected value of the random variable, X, and denotes the summation over all possible values of X. Each squared deviation of the outcome, X, from the expected value, $E(X)$, is weighted by its probability, $f(x)$.

A manager who wishes to calculate the standard deviation for a sample of T observations would estimate the standard deviation using

$$s = \sqrt{\sum \frac{1}{T-1} \times (X_i - \overline{X})^2}$$

where $\overline{X}$ is the sample mean. Note that the squared deviations are divided by $T-1$ and not by T because a *degree of freedom* has been lost. Some of the sample information has already been used to calculate the sample mean, and given this calculation only $T-1$ of the observations are independent; see Maddala (1992) or Greene (1993). Most numerical software programs and spreadsheets will calculate the sample standard deviation for a set of observations.

Since more risk is associated with greater dispersion in the possible outcomes, the standard deviation can be used as a measure of risk. The COEFFICIENT OF VARIATION, one measure of risk per dollar of expected return, uses the standard deviation as a measure of risk. The standard error of an estimated coefficient can be used for hypothesis testing to determine if an explanatory variable in a LINEAR REGRESSION

has a significant effect on the dependent variable. Such a test would be useful to managers who may wish to determine if a recent change in policy (advertising, pricing, etc.) had significant effects on sales, profits, or some other variable of interest.

see also **t-statistic**

Bibliography

Douglas, E. J. (1992). *Managerial Economics*. 4th edn, Englewood Cliffs, NJ: Prentice-Hall.

Greene, W. H. (1993). *Econometric Analysis*. 2nd edn, New York: Macmillan.

Maddala, G. S. (1992). *Introduction to Econometrics*. 2nd edn, New York: Macmillan.

ROBERT E. MCAULIFFE

standard error of estimate   The standard error of estimate (SEE) is the square root of the VARIANCE of the residuals from a LINEAR REGRESSION. This information is crucial because no standard errors or CONFIDENCE INTERVALS can be calculated without it. For a simple linear regression with T observations and one explanatory variable, X, the population relation between the dependent variable, Y, and X would be

$$Y_i = \beta_0 + \beta_1 \times X_i + \nu_i$$

where the Y are observations on the *dependent* variable, the X are observations on the *independent* or *explanatory* variable, and the ν are the population error terms. The population error terms are assumed to have zero mean and variance σ^2. Since the true population values of β_0, β_1 and ν are not known, they must be estimated. If $\hat{\beta}_0$ and $\hat{\beta}_1$ are the estimators of the population values, then the estimated residuals are given by:

$$\hat{\nu}_i = Y_i - \hat{\beta}_0 - \hat{\beta}_1 \times X_i$$

The estimator for the population variance, σ^2 is S^2 and is calculated as:

$$s^2 = \frac{1}{T-2} \sum_{i-1}^{t} \hat{\nu}_i^2$$

and the SEE for the regression is simply the square root of s. Note that the sum of the squared residuals is divided by $T-2$ rather than by T because two degrees of freedom are lost estimating β_0 and β_1; see Maddala (1992) or Greene (1993). In a multiple regression with T observations, k explanatory variables and a constant term, the estimated variance, s^2 would be divided by $T - k - 1$.

The SEE is also useful as a guide in forecasting. Larger values of the SEE imply larger forecasting errors, all else equal, and the SEE can be compared to the size of the dependent variable to gauge the likely size of forecast errors.

Bibliography

Douglas, E. J. (1992). *Managerial Economics*. 4th edn, Englewood Cliffs, NJ: Prentice-Hall.
Greene, W. H. (1993). *Econometric Analysis*. 2nd edn, New York: Macmillan.
Maddala, G. S. (1992). *Introduction to Econometrics*. 2nd edn, New York: Macmillan.

ROBERT E. MCAULIFFE

standard error of the coefficient In a LINEAR REGRESSION this is the estimated standard error which is used to test hypotheses regarding the estimated coefficients. In a simple linear regression with T observations and one explanatory variable, the population regression relation is:

$$Y_i = \beta_0 + \beta_1 \times X_i + \nu_i \qquad (1)$$

where the Y are observations on the *dependent* variable, the X are observations on the *independent* or *explanatory* variable, and the ν are population error terms. It can be shown that the variance of the ordinary least squares estimator of β_1, $\hat{\beta}_1$, is

$$\text{var}(\hat{\beta}_1) = \frac{\sigma^2}{\sum(X_i - \overline{X})^2} \qquad (2)$$

where σ^2 is the population variance; see Maddala (1992) or Greene (1993). Since the population variance is generally unknown, it is replaced by the estimator, s^2, which is calculated as:

$$s^2 = \frac{1}{T-2}\sum_{i=1}^{T} \hat{\nu}_i^2 \qquad (3)$$

(*see* STANDARD ERROR OF ESTIMATE). The estimated standard error for the coefficient $\hat{\beta}_1$ is then:

$$S_{\hat{\beta}_1} = \sqrt{\frac{s^2}{\sum(X_i - X)^2}} \qquad (4)$$

This value is reported by most statistical software programs as part of the standard regression output, often with the appropriate t-statistics to test the null hypothesis that the coefficient is not significantly different from zero (*see* T-STATISTIC). Note that the standard error for the coefficient above depends on the estimated variance of the error terms, the variance of the explanatory variable, and the number of observations corrected for degrees of freedom. Intuitively this means that an estimated coefficient is more reliable the greater the range (variance) of X values in the sample because the data has more information. In a multiple regression with k explanatory variables, a constant term and T observations, the X in equation (4) would be matrices and the sum of squared residuals in equation (3) would be divided by $T - k - 1$; see Maddala (1992) or Greene (1993).

Bibliography

Douglas, E. J. (1992). *Managerial Economics*. 4th edn, Englewood Cliffs, NJ: Prentice-Hall.
Greene, W. H. (1993). *Econometric Analysis*. 2nd edn, New York: Macmillan.
Maddala, G. S. (1992). *Introduction to Econometrics*. 2nd edn, New York: Macmillan.

ROBERT E. MCAULIFFE

stochastic dominance Situations involving risk are often modeled as a probability distribution across a set of possible outcomes. In this environment, optimal decisions depend upon not only the outcomes and their associated probabilities, but also upon the decision maker's attitude toward risk.

Early work on choice under uncertainty centered upon characterizing agents' preferences over statistical moments of a probability distribution. In particular, portfolio theory and asset valuation models frequently assume preferences over the first two moments, mean (*see* EXPECTED VALUE) and VARIANCE. Generally, one distribution is said to be preferred to another distribution if the former has either the same mean and lower variance or a higher mean and the same variance. Markowitz (1950) is a standard reference on the application of this framework to portfolio theory.

While the mean–variance framework is intuitively appealing, it is generally inconsistent with the premier theoretical paradigm for choice under uncertainty – von Neumann and Morgenstern's expected utility hypothesis. In expected utility theory, a rational agent's preferences over uncertain outcomes may be represented by a continuous utility function such that the agent will evaluate lotteries in terms of expected utility. Characterizing an agent's preference in terms of mean and variance is only consistent with expected utility for a few restrictive cases; those in which the utility function is quadratic or the outcomes are normally distributed. In contrast, the stochastic dominance ordering is always consistent with expected UTILITY MAXIMIZATION. Furthermore, it incorporates the entire probability distribution rather than a few statistical moments.

Let $F(z)$ and $G(z)$ denote two cumulative distribution functions over the set of outcomes z. Intuitively, $F(z^*)$ denotes the probability of obtaining an outcome at least as large as z^*. Then we say that $F(z)$ first-degree stochastic dominates $G(z)$ if $F(z)$ $G(z)$ for all z, with the inequality holding strictly for some z. Quirk & Saposnik (1962) showed that the stochastic dominating distribution will be preferred by all expected utility maximizing agents who prefer more income to less. Thus, first-degree stochastic dominance makes no assumption about the decision maker's attitude toward risk.

By making further assumptions about the agent's preference, the stochastic dominance ordering may be generalized to higher degrees. Hadar Russell (1969) and Hanoch Levy (1969)

introduced the notion of second-degree stochastic dominance. Formally, $F(z)$ second-degree stochastic dominates $G(z)$ if

$$\int_{-\infty}^{z} F(x)\, dx \leq \int_{-\infty}^{z} G(x)\, dx$$

for all z, with the inequality holding strictly for some z. Second-degree stochastic dominance is equivalent to expected utility maximization for all agents with increasing, concave utility functions; that is, those agents who display RISK AVERSION.

Stochastic dominance may be extended to an nth degree ordering. For a review of these extensions, as well as the application of stochastic dominance to financial valuation models, the reader is referred to Ingersoll (1987) and the citations contained therein.

Bibliography

Hadar, J. Russell, W. R. (1969). Rules for ordering uncertain prospects. *American Economic Review*, 59, 25–34.
Hanoch, G. Levy, C. (1969). Efficiency analysis of choices involving risk. *Review of Economic Studies*, 36, 335–46.
Ingersoll, J. E., Jr. (1987). *Theory of financial decision making*. Ottowa: Rowman Littlefield.
Markowitz, H. M. (1950). *Portfolio selection*. Cowles Foundation Monograph 16. New Haven: Yale University Press.
Quirk, J. P. Saposnik, R. (1962). Admissibility and measurable utility functions. *Review of Economic Studies*, 29, 140–6.
von Neumann, J. Morgenstern, O. (1944). *Theory of games and economic behavior*. Princeton, NJ: Princeton University Press.

ROGER TUTTEROW

stockholders Financial resources for the firm come from lenders and stockholders. Lenders put money into the firm for stated periods of time, and require to be paid stipulated amounts of interest. When the terms of the loan agreement call for repayment to occur, they can legally demand to be repaid. Stockholders put money into the firm without any expectation or legal right to be repaid at any particular time in the future. They expect to earn dividends on the money they invest, but the money is permanently invested in the business, so stockholders can only realize a lump-sum recovery of their investment by selling their shares to other investors. The firm does not have a legal obligation to redeem the shares which the founding stockholders bought at the time the firm was created. The stockholders, therefore, are residual claimants on the income stream of the firm. Senior claimants are employees, trade creditors, tax authorities, and lenders, including banks and bondholders. The stockholders are in the most junior position, and consequently face the greatest risk of being wiped out of the firm fails.

Stockholders have control, in theory at least, over the firm. As long as the firm is in compliance with the terms of its agreements with senior claimants, the stockholders have the right to name the Board of Directors, which in turn names the line managers who run the day-to-day affairs of the firm. They can benefit if the firm is very profitable, or if another firm tries to buy enough shares to acquire control. At the same time, however, the interests of the stockholders may not be the same as those of the firm's managers (see PRINCIPAL-AGENT PROBLEM).

It is important to note that the firm's managers may develop goals distinctly different from those of the stockholders (because of the principal-agent problem). Herbert Simon (1959) has emphasized that managers tend to behave in ways that are "satisfactory" to the stockholders rather than profit maximizing. Instead of managers maximizing long-run profits, they maximize individual goals subject to the constraint of satisfying stockholders.

Stockholders can benefit if the firm's managers optimize its capital structure, by repurchasing shares in the market and subsequently holding them in the treasury, or by borrowing money and paying a large one-time cash dividend. Stockholders are also better served by managers when contracts and managerial rewards align the managers' interests with the stockholders. For example, when managers' rewards are in the form of stock options, they have greater incentives to maximize profits and raise the value of their shares, which is in the stockholders' interest as well.

Bibliography

Hogendorn, J. (1995). *Modern Economics*. Englewood Cliffs, NJ: Prentice-Hall.

Milgrom, P. Roberts, J. (1992). *Economics, Organization and Management*. Englewood Cliffs, NJ: Prentice-Hall.

Simon, H. A. (1959). Theories of decision making in economics. *American Economic Review*, **49**, 253–83.

JOHN EDMUNDS AND ROBERTO BONIFAZ

strategic behavior Firms behave strategically when they engage in activities intended to change their rivals' expectations. A firm may reduce prices or significantly increase ADVERTISING expenditures when threatened by ENTRY in an attempt to prevent entry. If these are CREDIBLE STRATEGIES, then entry may be deterred. In addition, the firm may establish a reputation for aggressive behavior to send a signal to other potential entrants.

A variety of strategic options are available to firms, such as investing in excess capacity, engaging in research and development, pricing decisions, PRODUCT DIFFERENTIATION, QUALITY choice and PRODUCT PROLIFERATION. When the US Federal Trade Commission charged the ready-to-eat breakfast cereals firms of antitrust violations, one of the allegations made was that the existing firms introduced new brands to prevent entry. By saturating the market with new brands, there was no room left for new entry despite the high profits earned by the existing firms; see Schmalensee (1978).

Bibliography

Carlton, D. W. Perloff, J. M. (1994). *Modern Industrial Organization*. 2nd edn, New York: HarperCollins.

Schmalensee, R. (1978). Entry deterrence in the ready-to-eat breakfast cereal industry. *Bell Journal of Economics*, **9**, 305–27.

ROBERT E. MCAULIFFE

structure-conduct-performance paradigm This basic model from the field of Industrial Organization economics is used both as a vehicle for industry analysis and to provide a framework for public policy discussion. By examining the three elements of the paradigm as they pertain to a specific industry, a firm's managers are better able to evaluate the competitive nature and process of that industry. Knowledge of the elements of MARKET STRUCTURE such as the condition of ENTRY into the market and the number of firms already within, as well as the prevailing forms of strategic rivalry, is shown by Porter (1980) and others as being essential to building a successful long-term business strategy. Researchers have explored numerous industries in the manufacturing, retail, service and other sectors using this paradigm; see Adams and Brock (1995) and Deutsch (1993).

Historically, the paradigm has primarily been used by economists and public policy officials for the study of industrial policy questions. Considerable controversy has evolved as a result of the two distinct views which the paradigm supports. The early development of the paradigm by Bain (1951, 1956) and others presented the traditional view that market structure was causally responsible for market conduct and ultimately for MARKET PERFORMANCE. This position, known as the **structuralist view**, maintains that non competitive (e.g. MONO-POLY and OLIGOPOLY) market structures lead to undesirable forms of rivalry and poor market performance relative to their more competitive counterparts (*see* MONOPOLISTIC COMPETI-TION; PERFECT COMPETITION). Bain's argument that markets having high CONCEN-TRATION INDICES were environments which were conducive to price fixing and other forms of COLLUSION has come to be called the **concentration–collusion hypothesis**. In addition, the structuralist view holds that high BARRIERS TO ENTRY foster excess ECONOMIC PROFIT, and that these structural conditions result in technical inefficiency by producers and a misallocation of society's resources (*see* EFFICIENCY).

The economic analysis resulting from this view yields several conclusions which may assist managers in evaluating a market in which they wish to compete. First, the level of interdependence in rivals' conduct is related to the number of rivals and their size. Pricing strategies are more interdependent in markets with fewer rivals and high concentration levels. For example, in some markets PRICE LEADERSHIP may be in effect. Also, price SIGNALING, overt collusion, and even tacit awareness of acceptable forms of rivalry are more likely since fewness in numbers facilitates communication and

diminishes cheating on commonly accepted industry goals. A lack of PRODUCT DIFFEREN-TIATION and a similarity of cost conditions across rivals are two other structural conditions which are conducive to greater uniformity in pricing strategies among the rivals. Finally, strategies including ADVERTISING expenditures, brand proliferation (*see* PRODUCT PRO-LIFERATION), control of shelf space, and the creation of excess industry capacity have been cited as forms of conduct which evolve in highly concentrated industries in an effort to forestall entry (*see* LIMIT PRICING).

Considerable empirical investigation of these arguments has been performed. Bain (1956) demonstrated that both high industry concentration and high entry barriers were associated with significantly higher profit rates. Following Bain, a number of empirical investigations using LINEAR REGRESSION were performed over the next two decades. A variety of market CON-CENTRATION INDICES were examined for their effect on performance variables such as price cost margins and rates of return on owner's equity. The theoretical underpinning of many of these studies was fortified by Cowling and Waterson (1976). Their work showed that a strong theoretical link exists between the HERFINDAHL-HIRSCHMAN INDEX (HHI), which measures industry concentration, and the LERNER INDEX (L), which measures performance. Specifically, it was demonstrated that

$$L = \frac{\text{HHI}}{\varepsilon_p}$$

where ε_p is the absolute value of the price ELASTICITY of demand. Weiss (1974), in a summary of over 40 of the early studies, concludes that this evidence shows support for the concentration–collusion hypothesis. Several of these studies also included measures of barriers to entry arising from advertising expenditures, capital requirements and ECONO-MIES OF SCALE. These studies found additional support for the structure causes performance model. Taken as a whole, these studies have been used to support ANTITRUST POLICY which calls for careful scrutiny of monopoly and oligopoly behavior and governmental action to break up those industries having highly concentrated market structures. In addition, the use of HORIZONTAL MERGER GUIDELINES to prevent the occurrence of increasing concentration has also been justified by this analysis.

Controversy about the traditional view arises from a competing version of the paradigm which argues that the causal linkage between structure, conduct and performance is much more complex, especially in that market structure is not exogenously determined. TECHNICAL EFFICIENCY, profitability and other market performance variables, coupled with business strategy, can and do alter market structure. At the center of this view is the **efficiency hypothesis** which holds that market structure is determined by a competitive process which forces firms to achieve MINIMUM EFFICIENT SCALE (MES) in order to survive. As such, minimum firm size, relative to overall market demand dictates that some industries be more concentrated than others if society is to achieve maximum benefits from cost efficient production.

In one early but important empirical study in support of this alternative view, Demsetz (1973) examines the impact of industry concentration on the profit rates of firms of different sizes. If the collusion hypothesis was correct, small firms would also be expected to benefit by following their larger rivals to the new higher prices. His findings demonstrated that as industry concentration rose, the profit rates for large firms also tended to rise, but that no such tendency was exhibited for smaller firms. The concentration-collusion hypothesis was thus rejected in favor of the explanation that the greater profits of the larger firms in concentrated industries were due to their efficiency.

Numerous measurement problems (*see* MARKET PERFORMANCE) have also led to criticism of the early studies of the structuralist view. Notably, these studies did not examine the impact of concentration and barriers on performance in the long run. Some studies now show that the high profits of concentrated industries tend to decline over time. In a broad survey of the more recent literature, Schmalensee (1989) finds that the support for the concentration-profits link is weak. In addition, he finds some support for the efficiency hypothesis in recent studies which show that concentration is positively related to various measures of efficient scale.

Some of the recent literature, in the spirit of the structuralist view, has turned to econometric modelling of specific industries in an effort to establish the extent of market power existing in an industry. These models investigate the effects of structure and conduct upon prices and other market outcomes. Bresnahan's survey (1989) of this literature concludes that the evidence indicates that some concentrated markets hold considerable market power. Since other studies have also shown that industry concentration levels cannot be fully explained by the existing technology, the controversy between the two views of the paradigm continues.

see also **market power**

Bibliography

Adams, W.   Brock, J. (1995). *The Structure of American Industry*. 9th edn, Englewood Cliffs, NJ: Prentice-Hall.

Bain, J. (1951). Relation of profit rate to industry concentration: American manufacturing, 1936-1940. *Quarterly Journal of Economics*, **65**, 293-324.

Bain, J. (1956). *Barriers to New Competition*. Cambridge: Harvard University Press.

Bresnahan, T. (1989). Industries with market power. Schmalensee, R.   Willig, R. *Handbook of Industrial Organization*. Amsterdam: Elsevier Science.

Cowling, K.   Waterson, M. (1976). Price-cost margins and market structure. *Economica*, **43**, 267-74.

Demsetz, H. (1973). Industry structure, market rivalry and public policy. *Journal of Law and Economics*, **16**, 1-9.

Duetsch, L. (1993). *Industry Studies*. Englewood Cliffs, NJ: Prentice-Hall.

Porter, M. E. (1980). *Competitive Strategy*. New York: Free Press.

Schmalensee, R. (1989). Interindustry studies of structure and performance. Schmalensee, R. Willig, R. *Handbook of Industrial Organization*. Amsterdam: Elsevier Science.

Weiss, L. (1974). The concentration-profits relationship and antitrust. Goldschmid, H., Mann, H. Weston, J. *Industrial Concentration: The New Learning*. Boston: Little, Brown.

GILBERT BECKER

substitutes   When products or inputs are substitutes, one may be used instead of the other(s) to satisfy demand or meet production requirements. Products which are substitutes in consumption should have a large, positive cross elasticity of demand (*see* CROSS ELASTICITIES), where if the price of butter rises, for example, it causes an increase in the quantity demanded of margarine. Inputs in production may also be substitutes depending on the technology of production employed. A rise in the cost of skilled labor may increase the demand for unskilled labor or for labor-saving machinery if technology permits.

ROBERT E. MCAULIFFE

substitution effect A change in the price of a product affects consumer demand through the INCOME EFFECT and substitution effect. If the price of a product rises, the real price of the product increases (*see* REAL PRICES) and the consumer's BUDGET CONSTRAINT is more binding. The increase in the relative price of butter, for example, will cause the consumer to substitute other products, such as margarine, for butter and the consumer will move along her indifference curve (if possible) substituting margarine for butter (*see* INDIFFERENCE CURVES). The substitution effect refers to this movement along the consumer's indifference curve. The income effect from the price change may force the consumer to a new indifference curve if consumers spend a significant portion of their income on this good. This occurs because a price increase reduces the consumer's REAL INCOME and leaves the consumer worse off; see Douglas (1992) and Shughart, Chappell and Cottle (1994).

Bibliography

Douglas, E. J. (1992). *Managerial Economics*. 4th edn, Englewood Cliffs, NJ: Prentice-Hall.
Shughart, W. F., Chappell, W. F. Cottle, R. L. (1994). *Modern Managerial Economics*. Cincinatti, OH: South-Western Publishing.

ROBERT E. MCAULIFFE

sunk costs Sunk costs are those costs which cannot be recovered by the firm. As with FIXED COSTS, these costs do not vary with output produced and, as Tirole (1988) suggests, the differences between the two are matters of degree. Consider a firm which rents a machine for $100,000 per month which has an economic life of two years and costs $2 million to purchase. The $100,000 monthly rental fee is a fixed cost each month to the firm. Suppose instead that the firm decided to purchase the machine and, once purchased, the resale value of the machine was zero. Now the $2 million purchase price is a sunk cost to the firm because the asset has no alternative uses – its opportunity cost is zero (*see* OPPORTUNITY COSTS). If the firm could sell the machine for $1 million, then the sunk cost would be only $1 million, that portion of the original price which is not recoverable. The portion of any asset's purchase cost which is sunk will depend upon the resale market for that asset. Assets which are very specialized and unique to an industry or for which resale markets do not exist or are "thin" will have a greater percentage of their purchase cost "sunk" (*see* ASSET SPECIFICITY).

Sunk costs play an important role in determining MARKET STRUCTURE because they represent a barrier to entry (*see* BARRIERS TO ENTRY) to new firms. Once incurred, sunk costs should have no effect on the pricing and output decisions of established firms and, if necessary, established firms would produce output as long as AVERAGE VARIABLE COSTS were covered. This is not the case for a potential entrant who must pay these costs to enter the industry and must expect to cover them if entry is to succeed. An asymmetry is thus created between the established firms, for whom these costs are irrelevant, and potential entrants who must include them in the entry decision. Sunk costs act as a barrier to EXIT once firms are in an industry and may affect the intensity of competition between established firms, particularly if the industry is declining (*see* DECLINING INDUSTRY; INDUSTRY LIFE CYCLE).

Baumol, Panzar and Willig (1982) argued that when entry and exit were absolutely free and costless the market was perfectly contestable (*see* CONTESTABLE MARKETS). Free, costless entry and exit require that entrants have no sunk costs (even if there are fixed costs), enabling them to quickly enter the industry, undercut the established firms, and exit before the incumbents could retaliate. In these markets, the threat of entry would discipline established firms (even a natural monopolist) to the point where they earned no ECONOMIC PROFIT. But Weitzman (1983) argued that there are no purely fixed costs and theoretically, economies of scale cannot exist without sunk costs. Both fixed costs and sunk costs imply some commitment by the firm for some period of time. For fixed costs, the commitment lasts for the duration of the SHORT RUN, while sunk costs commit the firm for a longer period of time; see Tirole (1988). In replying to their critics, Baumol, Panzar and Willig usefully distinguished economic sunk costs from technological sunk costs. Although a firm might need a period of time to physically produce the goods or services for the market, an entrant could enter into conditional CONTRACTS with buyers and sell its output before actually producing the product. In such a case, the entrant would not incur the sunk costs of production unless enough contracts were sold and, once sold, the existing firm(s) would be subject to hit-and-run entry.

Sutton (1991) extended the notion of sunk costs by suggesting that there may be endogenous sunk costs in an industry in addition to exogenous sunk costs. He developed a two-stage model where in the first stage, if a firm chose to enter the industry, it would incur fixed setup costs to produce output, such as acquiring a MINIMUM EFFICIENT SCALE (MES) (MES) plant and incurring advertising and research and development expenses to establish the product(s). In the second stage, those firms in the industry would compete for profits through price or quantity competition. Sutton considered the fixed costs of acquiring an MES plant as exogenous sunk costs while the advertising and research and development expenditures were endogenous sunk costs because firms could adjust these costs in stage 1 to improve their competitive position in stage 2. In industries where exogenous sunk costs were most significant, the industry structure would become less concentrated as the market grew, but in those industries where endogenous sunk costs were more important, a concentrated industry structure arose even as market size increased. He found that industries with high concentration and high advertising and research and development expenditures in one country were also highly concentrated in other countries. He attributed this result to a competitive

escalation of these endogenous sunk expenditures which kept industry concentration levels high and prevented entry from having a significant effect on industry structure.

Bibliography

Baumol, W. J., Panzar, J. C. Willig, R. D. (1982). *Contestable Markets and the Theory of Industry Structure*. San Diego: Harcourt Brace Jovanovich.

Baumol, W. J., Panzar, J. C. Willig, R. D. (1983). Contestable markets: an uprising in the theory of industry structure: reply. *American Economic Review*, 73, 491–6.

Schwartz, M. Reynolds, R. J. (1983). Contestable markets: an uprising in the theory of industry structure: comment. *American Economic Review*, 73, 488–90.

Shepherd, W. G. (1984). 'Contestability' vs. competition. *American Economic Review*, 74, 572–87.

Sutton, J. (1991). *Sunk Costs and Market Structure*. Cambridge, MA: MIT.

Tirole, J. (1988). *The Theory of Industrial Organization*. Cambridge, MA: MIT.

Weitzman, M. L. (1983). Contestable markets: an uprising in the theory of industry structure: comment. *American Economic Review*, 73, 486–7.

ROBERT E. MCAULIFFE

survivor principle   In order to determine the ability of any firm in an industry to successfully compete in the market, cost functions are typically estimated. However, for quick and easy casual information on the structure of cost and ECONOMIES OF SCALE in an industry, a popular approach is to look at firms of different scales or sizes over time to see which sizes survived. If it is observed that small firms in one industry tended to go out of business or were taken over while medium and large firms continued to survive, it leads to the possibility that in this industry the small firms had higher per unit costs (*see* AVERAGE TOTAL COST) and hence, could not compete with the medium and large size firms. In this example, the smallest size or scale of operations at which firms become competitive in this industry and have the potential to survive is then the medium sized firm. In order to survive smaller firms must either merge or increase their scale of operation. Such an analysis based on survival trends in an industry was made popular by a Nobel economist, George Stigler (1958), and is referred to as survivor principle/analysis. All that is needed for such an analysis is to break up the firms in an industry into different size classes and observe which size class or classes seem to be growing and which are declining. In the physician medical practice industry, for example, it was found that between the period of 1965 and 1980, practices with one or two physicians had the largest market share but their share was declining throughout the period (Mardel and Zuckerman, 1985). This suggests that in this industry small group practices may no longer be very efficient and one would expect a gradual movement toward larger sized practices. In another study, Blair and Vogel (1978) looked at the health insurance industry between 1958 and 1973 and observed that the larger size firms seemed to be surviving and hence, were likely to be more efficient. In many of these studies, including a study on manufacturing (Weiss, 1964), a wide range of sizes were found to be able to survive suggesting that a large number of relatively smaller firms could survive providing some semblance of a competitive market (*see* PERFECT COMPETITION; MINIMUM EFFICIENT SCALE).

Bibliography

Blair, R. D. Vogel, R. J. (1978). A survivor analysis of commercial health insurers. *Journal of Business*, **51**, 521–30.

Mardel, W. D. Zuckerman, S. (1985). Competition and medical groups: a survivor analysis. *Journal of Health Economics*, **4**, 167.

Stigler, G. J. (1958). The economies of scale. *Journal of Law and Economics*, **1**, 54–71.

Weiss, L. (1964). The survivor techniques and the extent of suboptimal capacity. *Journal of Political Economy*, **72**, 246–61.

GOVIND HARIHARAN

T

t-statistic Most statistical software programs report the t-statistic along with other summary information as part of the routine output from a LINEAR REGRESSION. The t-statistic is used for hypothesis testing when the true population variance is unknown and is replaced by the estimated sample variance. For example, suppose a firm has TIME-SERIES DATA on its sales and a manager wants to determine if there is a significant relationship between its sales and GROSS DOMESTIC PRODUCT (GDP). The regression might be specified as:

$$\text{sales}_t = \beta_0 + \beta_1 \times \text{GDP}_t + \nu_t \qquad (1)$$

where ν_t is a random error term. If there is no statistically significant relationship between sales and GDP, the estimated value for β_1 should be zero. But since β_1 is itself a random variable, even if its true value were zero we would observe a range of values for β_1 around zero. Given that any estimated value for β_1 is not likely to equal zero exactly, the t-statistic is used to determine whether the estimated value is sufficiently different from zero so that random chance is unlikely to be the cause and more likely that the true relationship is nonzero. For a regression with T observations, the t-statistic is calculated as:

$$\frac{\beta_1 - \mu}{s_\beta} \qquad (2)$$

where μ is the hypothesized value for β_1 (the null hypothesis) and s_β is the estimated STANDARD ERROR OF THE COEFFICIENT β_1, from the regression. The statistic above has a t distribution with T - 2 degrees of freedom because sample information has been used to determine two coefficients, β_0 and β_1; see Maddala (1992) or Greene (1993). In the example here, the null hypothesis is that $\beta_1 = 0$, so the t-statistic would then be

$$\frac{\beta_1}{s_\beta} \qquad (3)$$

which is simply the estimated value for the coefficient divided by its standard error. If the sample size is large, a 95 percent confidence interval is approximately β_1 plus or minus 2 standard deviations (*see* CONFIDENCE INTERVALS), so if the value in equation (3) is greater than 2 in absolute value, then we would reject the null hypothesis that β_1 is equal to zero. In samples with fewer than 30 observations (or 30 degrees of freedom), critical values of the t-distribution can be found in statistical tables; see Kmenta (1986) or Maddala (1992). For example, if the estimated value of $\beta1$ were 8 and its standard error were 2, then the value of the t-statistic in equation (3) would be 4. When software programs provide t-statistics as part of their standard regression output, the calculated values are based on equation (3) where the null hypothesis is that the coefficient equals zero.

In the context of a multiple regression, a degree of freedom is lost for every coefficient which is estimated, including the constant term. Therefore if there are T observations, k explanatory variables and a constant term, the test statistic will have $T - k - 1$ degrees of freedom.

Bibliography

Greene, W. H. (1993). *Econometric Analysis*. 2nd edn, New York: Macmillan.

Kmenta, J. (1986). *Elements of Econometrics*. 2nd edn, New York: Macmillan.

Maddala, G. S. (1992). *Introduction to Econometrics.* 2nd edn, New York: Macmillan.

ROBERT E. MCAULIFFE

technical efficiency   In physics, efficiency is the ratio of useful work done to total energy expended and the same general idea is associated with the term in production. Economists simply replace "useful work" by "outputs" and "energy" by "inputs." Technical efficiency means the adequate use of the available resources in order to obtain the maximum product. A productive activity is inefficient whenever it is possible to reduce the amount of some of its inputs without reducing the level of output, or whenever the output can be increased without using more inputs. Note that there is no reference to prices in this definition of efficiency, as opposed to allocative or economic efficiency.

Bibliography

Färe, R., Grosskopf, S. Lovell, C. A. K. (1985). *The Measurement of Efficiency of Production.* Boston: Kluwer-Nijhoff.

EDUARDO LEY

time-series data   Time-series data is information gathered for specific variables which are observed over a period of time. For example, a firm might have quarterly pricing and sales data available for ten years which could be used to estimate the future demand for its product. But a manager could also estimate demand if the firm had pricing and sales data available from 40 branches located across the country. The data in this second example is cross-section data and is obtained by gathering information from different locations at the same point in time. It is also possible to combine cross-section and time-series data (a *pooled sample*) to examine how demand varied across locations and over time. Each data source raises different estimation problems for analysts and requires different econometric methods.

Since economic theory specifies relationships between variables holding all else constant (the CETERIS PARIBUS assumption), researchers must be careful to ensure that the LINEAR REGRESSION is properly specified. For example, when using time-series data, changes in INFLATION are likely, so variables must be adjusted to reflect real values. This problem is not likely to be significant in CROSS-SECTION ANALYSIS.

see also **consumer price index; real income; real prices**

ROBERT E. MCAULIFFE

time-series forecasting models   Time-series forecasting models are techniques used to explain changes in economic variables over time. As with other statistical methods, an underlying assumption is that the variable being modeled is stochastic, i. e. it contains a random component. Since data observations are realized over time, time series models differ from other statistical techniques in that the order in which the data are observed is of primary importance.

Time-series models are classified as time domain or frequency domain models. In a frequency domain model, the time series is decomposed into a sum of its cyclical components. This method, also known as spectral analysis, is beyond the scope of this essay. For a discussion of spectral analysis, see Granger and Newbold (1986).

If a single variable is to be explained in terms of its own past and future values, then the model is said to be *univariate*. For example, a model which forecasts an interest rate by using only the past values of the interest rate is a univariate model. In contrast, *multivariate* models consider how a set of variables interact over time. A model which explains the relationship between the interest rate, money supply, and GROSS DOMESTIC PRODUCT is a multivariate model.

An important requirement for most time-series models is that the variable under consideration follows a stationary process. A process is said to be *weakly stationary* if its mean and variance are constant over time, i.e. they exhibit no trend. The combination of weak stationarity and a normal distribution is sufficient to meet a stricter stationarity condition. While many economic and financial variables are not stationary, one can usually transform them into variables which are stationary. In subsequent discussions, we assume that the variable being forecast is either stationary or has been transformed into a stationary process.

The most basic methods for forecasting time-series data are *moving average* and *exponential smoothing* models. These techniques range from simple models, in which the forecast value for a given period is the average of its past values, to more sophisticated models which contain error-correcting components. The latter models include various exponential smoothing methods in which forecasts are corrected for past forecasting errors.

A second approach to forecasting is time-series *decomposition*. In this technique, variations in the data are separated into trend, seasonal, cyclical and random components. The interaction of these components may be either additive or multiplicative. A time series is decomposed through a series of iterations in which the individual components are extracted from the overall series. For example, by calculating a moving average of length longer than the seasonal component, one may separate the trend and cyclical components from the seasonal and random components. Similar procedures allow the remaining individual components to be identified. Finally, the systematic components (trend, cyclical, and seasonal) are combined to generate a forecast.

The selection of an appropriate forecasting technique requires consideration of data availability as well as time and resource constraints. Although the methods described above may be outperformed by more sophisticated models, they remain popular among managers due to their intuitive appeal and ease of use. Makridakis, Wheelwright and McGee (1983) provide an excellent critical survey of these techniques.

Perhaps the most important class of forecasting models are *autoregressive moving-average (ARMA)* models. In ARMA models, the forecast for a variable is based upon the past values of that variable, past forecasting errors and a contemporaneous error term. By autoregressive, we mean that the current value of the variable depends upon its own past observations. For example, if the current inflation rate depends upon the p most recent inflation rates, then one says that inflation follows an auto-

regressive model of order p. Letting x_t denote the inflation rate at time t, this model is written as:

$$x_t = \Phi_i x_{t-1} + \ldots + \Phi_p x_{t-p} + u_t \qquad (1)$$

where Φ_i denotes the autoregressive parameters.

Alternatively, a variable may be generated as the weighted average of previous random disturbances. If the variable is generated by the q most recent disturbances, then we say that it follows a moving-average process of order q and may be written as:

$$x_t = u_t - \theta_1 u_{t-1} - \ldots - \theta_q u_{t-q}, \qquad (2)$$

where $u_{t-1},\ldots,u_{t-q}$ are serially independent random terms (the error terms have no AUTO-CORRELATION) and the θ_i are the moving average coefficients.

Time-series variables may contain both autoregressive and moving-average components. For example, a variable may follow a process which is pth order autoregressive and qth order moving-average. This model, denoted ARMA(p,q), is written as

$$x_t = \Phi_1 x_{t-1} + \ldots + \Phi_p x_{t-p}$$

$$+ u_t - \theta_1 u_{t-1} - \ldots - \theta_q u_{t-q}$$

It is common to represent ARMA models with "backshift" or "lag" notation. Define B as the operator which lags (moves) an observation back one period such that $Bx_t = x_{t-1}$. For example, if x_t is the unemployment rate for the current period, then Bx_t denotes the unemployment rate for last period. In general, $B^d x_t$ denotes the unemployment rate d periods ago. Using backshift notation, the ARMA(p,q) model may be rewritten as

$$x_t(1 - \Phi_1 B - \ldots - \Phi_p B^p)$$

$$= u_t(1 - \theta_1 B - \ldots - \theta_q B^q)$$

As previously noted, most times-series models, including ARMA models, require that the underlying process is stationary. While many economic variables are not stationary, they often may be transformed into a stationary process. The most common such transformation is differencing. Let x_t denote the observation on variable x at time t. Then, $x_t - x_{t-1}$ or $x_t - Bx_t$ is then called the first difference of the variable. Differencing is a particularly useful transformation for time series which include a time trend and thus are non-stationary. In this case, a first difference is frequently sufficient to remove the trend. In other cases, it may take repeated differencing to obtain a stationary process. Formally, if one must difference a series d times to render it stationary, then it is written as $x_t (1 - B)^d$ and the series is said to integrated of order d. Thus, the ARMA(p,q) model generalizes to an ARIMA(p,d,q) where p, d, and q refer to the order of the autoregressive component, the degree of differencing required to make the process stationary and the order of the moving-average process respectively. The ARIMA(p,d,q) model is written as

$$x_t (1 - B)^d (1 - \Phi_1 B - \ldots - \Phi_p B^p)$$

$$= u_t (1 - \theta_1 B - \ldots - \theta_q B^q)$$

Perhaps the most challenging aspect of using ARIMA models is the specification of the model, i.e. the selection of autoregressive, integration and moving-average orders. The most widely accepted methodology for model specification is that suggested by Box and Jenkins (1970).

Following Box and Jenkins, models are developed in three steps: identification, estimation, and diagnostic testing. During the identification phase, one inspects the plot of correlation coefficients between data observations and their lagged values. Specifically, one calculates both the simple and partial correlation coefficients between x_t, x_{t-1}, x_t and x_{t-2}, x_t and x_{t-3} etc. By inspecting the plots of these coefficients, also known as correlograms, one may infer the likely structure of the model. Specifying a model by inspecting the correlograms is not a mechanical process but rather requires experience.

After a model structure is selected, the parameters of the model, $\Phi_1, \ldots, \Phi_p, \theta_1, \ldots, \theta_q$, are estimated simultaneously by the maximum likelihood method. Finally, the residuals of the model are subject to diagnostic tests. If these tests are passed, the residuals are considered "white noise" (random) and the model is

deemed suitable for forecasting use. Failure of these tests suggests that the model is incorrectly specified and must be revised.

In some instances, it may be of interest to generate forecasting models which utilize information contained in other economic variables. For example, a manager may wish to incorporate information on advertising expenditures into a sales forecast. This is a simple example of a multivariate times-series model. One should note that for multivariate times series, the concept of a stationary process is complicated by the possibility of cointegration, i.e. linear combinations of variables may be stationary even if the individual variables are not. In such cases, failing to recognize cointegration may lead to misleading results.

A popular multivariate extension of the univariate ARIMA model is the *transfer function model*. This model extends the Box–Jenkins methodology to allow changes in an exogenous "input" variable to induce changes in an endogenous "output" variable. By inspecting a plot of the correlation coefficients between the output variable and previous values of the input variable, one may infer the temporal relationship between the variables. For example, one might find that the inflation rate is highly correlated with changes in the money supply which occurred three months prior. To assist with identification, it is common to filter or "prewhiten" both variables with an ARIMA model before estimating the correlation coefficients. Having identified the temporal relationship between the variables, the transfer function is estimated. Finally, an ARIMA model is fit to the residuals of the transfer function and diagnostic test are performed.

Another useful multivariate time-series model is *vector autoregression (VAR)*. This technique, popularized by Sims (1980), explains changes in a vector (or set) of variables in terms of past observations on those variables. Unlike transfer function models, VAR does not impose restrictions upon the exogeniety of a specific variable, but rather, it allows changes in variables to "feedback" into the other variables in the model. Advocates of VAR argue that the technique is useful since it imposes few *a priori* restrictions upon the structure of the model. One disadvantage of VAR models is that they sometimes require estimation of a large number of parameters. In practical application, if data sets are small, the parameter requirements of a VAR model may be prohibitive. While most early applications of VAR were to macroeconomic models, applications in microeconomics and financial economics are becoming more common.

Recent advances in time-series forecasting model include tests for cointegration of time series, analysis of models in which the variance of the error term varies over time (ARCH) and the development of unit root test. These topics are beyond the scope of this essay. Interested readers are referred to Enders (1995) and the citations contained therein.

Bibliography

Box, G. Jenkins, G. (1970). *Time Series Analysis: Forecasting and Control.* San Francisco: Holden-Day.

Enders, W. (1995). *Applied Econometric Time Series.* New York: Wiley.

Granger, C. Newbold, P. (1986). *Forecasting Economic Time Series.* San Diego: Academic Press.

Makridakis, S., Wheelwright, S. McGee, V. (1983). *Forecasting: Methods and Applications.* 2nd edn, New York: Wiley.

Sims, C. (1980). Macroeconomics and reality. *Econometrica,* 48, 1–49.

ROGER TUTTEROW

total costs   The total costs facing any business are the sum of two distinct categories of costs:

(1) total variable costs and
(2) total FIXED COSTS.

The total cost function is the relation between the total dollar expenditures, for resources, by a firm and the level of output and sales achieved by the firm. The total costs of a firm naturally tend to increase with the level of output and sales effort as more resources are needed to achieve this growth. In the SHORT RUN, the total costs eventually tend to increase at an increasing rate due to the declining marginal productivity of additional units of variable inputs being combined with fixed inputs (*see* DIMINISHING RETURNS). In the long run, where the size of fixed inputs can be adjusted, the total cost of production may initially increase at a decreasing rate as output grows

due to ECONOMIES OF SCALE. Ordinarily, at some higher rate of output, total costs will tend to increase at a constant rate (*see* MINIMUM EFFICIENT SCALE).

The total costs of a firm are important in determining the firm's profit. Since profit is measured as TOTAL REVENUE minus total cost, efforts which reduce total cost without decreasing revenues will enhance profits. Economists distinguish between ECONOMIC PROFIT and ACCOUNTING PROFIT. This distinction is based entirely on the differing methods which the two disciplines employ in measuring costs. The difference lies in the inclusion of OPPORTUNITY COSTS in the measure of total economic costs.

see also **long run cost curves; short run cost curves**

Bibliography

Mansfield, E. (1993). *Managerial Economics Theory, Applications and Cases.* 2nd edn, New York: Norton.

GILBERT BECKER

total product   Total product refers to the output produced by varying the level of one input, holding the level of other inputs constant. Thus the total product of labor is the total output produced by changing labor input while the other factors of production are not changed (including the level of technology). The total product curve can be derived from the production function in the SHORT RUN (*see* PRODUCTION FUNCTIONS). The typical total product curve is S-shaped where the first units of labor, for example, are very productive and output increases rapidly. But as more workers are added to the fixed amount of capital, diminishing marginal returns occur and the increases in output from additional workers diminish. The total product curve is the foundation for the firm's SHORT RUN COST CURVES.

see also **marginal product; marginal cost**

Bibliography

Douglas, E. J. (1992). *Managerial Economics.* 4th edn, Englewood Cliffs, NJ: Prentice-Hall.

Shughart, W. F., Chappell, W. F. Cottle, R. L. (1994). *Modern Managerial Economics.* Cincinatti, OH: South-Western Publishing.

ROBERT E. MCAULIFFE

total revenue Total revenue is the total amount of dollars received by a firm or an industry from the sale of its product in a given time period. Often known as sales revenue or sales receipts, its measure is equivalent in value to the total dollar expenditures which are made by the consumers of a given product. These revenues are determined by the price (*P*) of the product and the quantity (*Q*) demanded at that price, and are calculated as

$$TR = P \times Q$$

The quantity demanded depends upon consumer tastes, income, and other factors (*see* DEMAND FUNCTION), while price is determined by market supply forces as well.

Under PERFECT COMPETITION, total revenue increases in proportion with unit sales by the firm since price is fixed. For imperfectly competitive markets, for example OLIGOPOLY, firms maintain some control over the price of their product. As such, managers must be aware of the LAW OF DEMAND which indicates that any price change for a good will typically induce an opposite change in its quantity demanded and thus the change in the total revenue of the firm is uncertain. Here, as consumer demand for a good typically declines with an increase in the price of the good, the size of the consumer reaction is critical to the overall impact on total revenue. Alternative strategies, such as increasing advertising or improving product quality, may raise unit sales without requiring a reduction in price and thus would increase total revenue.

Total revenue is also important in the calculation of the firm's profits, since profit is measured as total revenue minus TOTAL COSTS. Maximizing total revenue is sometimes a goal of managers although this goal, by itself, is not equivalent to that of PROFIT MAXIMIZATION as it ignores costs. For a firm selling to two or more well defined sets of consumers, maximizing total revenues requires that the MARGINAL REVENUE from each group be equal (*see* PRICE DISCRIMINATION).

see also **elasticity; inelastic demand**

Bibliography

Pashigian, P. (1995). *Price Theory and Applications.* New York: McGraw-Hill.

GILBERT BECKER

total utility Total utility is the total benefit or satisfaction an individual receives by consuming goods or taking part in an activity. For example, consumers acquire utility from the product attributes in the goods and services which they purchase (*see* PRODUCT ATTRIBUTES MODEL). These items fulfill various physical and psychic needs. Similarly, workers gain utility from their jobs, through the satisfaction of accomplishment and also from the income which is generated. While consumer utility arises from the goods themselves, giving to others (e.g. gifts, charity) also generates utility as can the actual purchase of the good (e.g. "finding a real bargain"). An individual's preferences toward risk can also be identified, through an examination of the level of utility generated from different levels of income (*see* RISK AVERSION).

In the economic theory of consumer behavior, total utility is typically assumed to increase with an increase in the number of units of any one good, and with an increase in the total number of all goods, which an individual acquires. In other words, for most goods, more is preferred to less. As the rate of consumption of any one good grows, the total utility tends to increase at a decreasing rate though, as the first units of the good provide the highest utility and additional units eventually generate less utility (*see* DIMINISHING MARGINAL UTILITY).

Although some models of economic behavior examine the situation where the individual's goal is to achieve a satisfactory level of utility, it is generally assumed that UTILITY MAXIMIZATION is the objective. Here, INDIFFERENCE CURVES are useful. This analytical tool measures utility ordinally, and thus only requires that the individual be able to rank any available choice as yielding more, less, or the same amount of total utility as other alternatives. Earlier consumer models, which measured utility cardinally, were weaker in that they assumed that the exact amount by which MARGINAL UTILITY differs across choices could be specified. Identifying, and perhaps altering (e.g. through ADVERTISING), the underlying sources of consumer utility is central to understanding and generating consumer demand for a product.

Bibliography

Hirschey, M. Pappas, J. (1995). *Fundamentals of Managerial Economics*. 5th edn, Fort Worth: Dryden.
Hyman, D. (1993). *Modern Microeconomics*. 3rd edn, Homewood: Irwin.
Varian, H. (1978). *Microeconomic Analysis*. New York: Norton.

GILBERT BECKER

total variable cost Measures the total variable costs of production in the short run. Total variable costs are those costs which vary with the output level produced such as workers' wages, material inputs, etc. Total variable cost depends on the quantity of output produced and is equal to zero when no output is produced. In addition to the per unit input cost, the MARGINAL PRODUCT of inputs and the technology employed by the company influence the level of total variable cost (*see* SHORT RUN COST CURVES).

The curvature of a total variable cost curve is determined by the impact of successive increases in output on total variable cost. Typically, total variable costs will increase initially at a decreasing rate but will eventually increase at an increasing rate because of DIMINISHING RETURNS in production (*see* TOTAL COSTS; AVERAGE VARIABLE COSTS; MARGINAL PRODUCT).

Labor costs are usually considered as variable in nature, i.e. they can be reduced if the worker works fewer hours and vice versa. However, there are many examples of labor costs which are not strictly related to the number of hours of work and can be defined as quasi-fixed. Examples are employee benefits such as health insurance, pension plans, costs of hiring and training new employees, and the costs of legally required social insurance programs. The company pays for these costs on a per worker rather than per labor hour worked basis. A company's

decision about the optimal combination of inputs in its production process will be influenced by the amount of these quasi-fixed costs per worker. For example, part-time employees are less likely to be covered by the company's health insurance policy and are usually given fewer fringe benefits in general making them a relatively cheaper input in production than a full-time worker (Ehrenberg and Smith, 1994).

Bibliography

Carlton, D. W. Perloff, J. M. (1994). *Modern Industrial Organization*. 2nd edn, New York: HarperCollins.
Douglas, E. J. (1992). *Managerial Economics*. 4th edn, Englewood Cliffs, NJ: Prentice-Hall.
Ehrenberg, R. G. Smith, R. S. (1994). *Modern Labor Economics*. 5th edn, New York: HarperCollins.

LIDIJA POLUTNIK

transactions costs Transactions costs are the expenses in time and resources that are associated with the process of buying and selling other than the price. The level of these costs depends on the type of transaction conducted as well as its organizational form. According to Coase (1937), a firm emerges as an organization of economic activity when it can economize on the transaction costs by performing activities within its boundaries rather than having these activities performed by the market. Some examples of transactions cost when the firm uses the market are: searching for the best price, best quality and delivery terms, the costs of writing a contract, monitoring and enforcing the agreement as well as bargaining costs. If the firm decides to conduct activities itself, it faces a different set of transaction costs. Some examples of these are the costs of coordinating purchases and production activities and the costs of motivating and monitoring the workforce to ensure best behavior for the firm.

According to Williamson (1979), the advantages of organizing activities within a firm and for firms to integrate (*see* VERTICAL INTEGRATION) are greater when transactions have certain characteristics. ASSET SPECIFICITY creates incentives for opportunistic behavior where a contract or practice is needed to protect the participant against premature renegotiation or cancellation of a contract. Vertical integration may also enable a firm to economize on transactions costs when the degree of competition in supplying industries is low and there is a possibility of a supplier holding up production. Managers may not be able to enumerate and articulate all the contingencies of a contract due to bounded rationality which present possibilities for opportunistic behavior as well (*see* INCOMPLETE CONTRACTS). When transactions occur frequently and over a long period of time, it may be more efficient to conduct these transactions within a firm. Transactions costs increase as the complexity of a transaction increases and as the predictability of the market for an activity decreases. The higher the transactions costs, the more likely the firm will choose to organize that activity within its organization.

Transactions-cost economics can be employed to analyze the structure, conduct, and performance across industries; it enables us to evaluate contractual relations among and within firms as a result of organizations economizing on transactions costs when information is incomplete and enforcement problems exist.

see also **Coase theorem; principal–agent problem**

Bibliography

Carlton, D. W. Perloff, J. M. (1994). *Modern Industrial Organization.* 2nd edn, New York: HarperCollins.

Coase, R. H. (1937). The nature of the firm. *Economica,* **4,** 386–405.

Milgrom, P. Roberts, J. (1992). *Economics, Organization and Management.* Englewood Cliffs, NJ: Prentice-Hall.

Williamson, O. E. (1979). Transaction-cost economics: the governance of contractual relations. *Journal of Law and Economics,* **22,** 233–61.

LIDIJA POLUTNIK

transfer pricing A transfer price is an internal price that is charged for a product or service by a selling division to a buying division within the same corporation (see Hirshleifer, 1956, 1957; Copithorne, 1971; Horst, 1971, 1977). The prime goal of a transfer pricing

mechanism is to maximize global firm value. Specifically, transfer pricing can affect firm value in two prime areas: tax minimization and optimal resource allocation.

The minimization of global taxes can be achieved when a company with operations in countries with different tax bases shifts profits from high- to low-tax areas. One way to do this is to charge a high transfer price by a producing division in a low-tax country to a consuming division in a high-tax country. Similar strategies can also be implemented to minimize tariff charges and the effects of exchange controls. However, since a country's tax revenue is affected by a company's transfer pricing mechanisms, international tax treaties and local laws constrain the methods by which a transfer price for tax purposes may be set.

Transfer pricing also affects how the divisions within a firm allocate their resources. Since firm value is maximized when its limited resources are allocated optimally, by implication transfer pricing affects firm value. For example, if at one extreme a firm were to charge an excessive price for a facility, potential users would shun the facility and it would have excess capacity. At the other extreme, if its use is permitted free of charge, there is little incentive for the consumers to use it in a cost-effective manner. Thus, on the one hand, an appropriate transfer price would avoid excess capacity, while on the other it would not precipitate additional value-decreasing investment outlays.

Transfer pricing affects optimal resource allocation when a company has two or more decentralized divisions, the profit or cost performance of which is independently measured, and the incentive schemes of which are tied to these performance measures. To maximize firm value, the transfer price between the two divisions should be the OPPORTUNITY COST of the good or service transferred. The opportunity cost of the transferred unit is defined as the value that the producing division could have received had the unit been employed in its next best alternative use. Unfortunately, an accurate opportunity cost is difficult to ascertain. In part, this is because division managers may jealously guard the information necessary to calculate an opportunity cost which has a direct impact on performance evaluation by their superiors. In addition, even in the presence of perfect information, cost classification issues make an opportunity cost very difficult or costly to assess. Nevertheless, three common methods of transfer pricing methods have emerged: market-based, cost-based, and negotiated price.

In a market-based approach, the opportunity cost is proxied by the price that prevails for a like good or service in a competitive open market (*see* PERFECT COMPETITION). An advantage of this system is that the price is externally observable and price distortion between the two divisions is minimized. This method is also favored by tax authorities, since they are able to use information that is external to the firm to determine whether they have received fair tax revenues. A disadvantage is that a market price for a similar good in a competitive market is not always available. Furthermore, even if an external market does exist for the intermediate good, the assumption of a competitive market is likely to be erroneous. This is because the preference for internal production implies BARRIERS TO ENTRY and/or EXIT which render the assumption of a competitive market fallacious. This is highlighted by ECONOMIES OF SCALE and/or ECONOMIES OF SCOPE, as well as quality control standards or other synergies which may exist when the intermediate good is produced internally. In the final analysis, once the unrealistic premise of competitive markets is removed, PREDATORY PRICING practices and the like cannot be ruled out and an exclusive focus on market price is unlikely to be the optimal transfer price for the firm (see Deschamps Mehta, 1989).

In the absence of an external market for the intermediate good, a company will often resort to setting a transfer price based on costs. In principle, the MARGINAL COST of the transferred good may closely represent its opportunity cost. However, the selling division has an incentive to exaggerate its classification of costs as marginal. Another problem is that even if marginal costs are classified fairly, the selling division may not show a profit, since no contribution toward fixed costs is incorporated in the price. Some companies resolve this problem by pricing at marginal cost plus a premium. At the extreme, many companies permit a transfer price at full cost, representing the sum of marginal and FIXED COSTS (see

Brickley, Smith, Zimmerman, 1995). Such a system, however, removes the incentive by the selling division to provide the good or service in the most cost-effective manner.

A severe disadvantage inherent in any cost based transfer price method is that most firms rely on accounting data. This approach is erroneous, since identifying the opportunity cost and hence the transfer price is an economic as opposed to an accounting issue. For example, large differences in costs can emerge when fixed costs are depreciated over an accounting life as opposed to an economic life (*see* ECONOMIC DEPRECIATION). In practice, however, because of the availability, many firms resort to accounting data when establishing a transfer price.

One solution to the conflict of interests which exists between producing and consuming divisions is to have a system of negotiation when setting transfer prices. In such a system, the selling and buying divisions negotiate both a price and quantity of transferred goods or services. The problem with this is that the transfer price may not represent the opportunity cost, and hence firm value is not maximized. Part of the reason is that the transfer price depends on the negotiating skills of the two divisions. Another disadvantage to price negotiation is that it can entail significant time and effort on the part of the negotiators.

In summary, transfer pricing affects firm value in two major ways. The first is the role that it plays in taking advantage of global market imperfections, such as differences in tax structures and other regulations among countries. The second is the effect that it has on the optimal allocation of a firm's resources. In theory, a firm's resources are optimally allocated when the transfer price is set at the opportunity cost of the good or service transferred. If an external competitive market exists for the intermediate good, then the opportunity cost can be proxied at this external market price. However, an external market price does not necessarily represent opportunity cost, as it does not incorporate internal synergies which may exist with internal transfers. These differences and the preference for an internal market make the assumption of a competitive market structure fallacious. In this case, firms may resort to cost or negotiation methods of transfer pricing, which also have their weaknesses. Irrespective of the discussed methods, there ultimately exists an inherent conflict of interest within decentralized organizations between setting a transfer price which maximizes division profitability and a transfer price which maximizes total firm value.

Bibliography

Brickley, J., Smith, C. Zimmerman, J. (1995). Transfer pricing and the control of internal corporate transactions. *Journal of Applied Corporate Finance*, **8**, 60–7.

Copithorne, L. W. (1971). International corporate transfer prices and government policy. *Canadian Journal of Economics*, **4**, 324–41.

Deschamps, B. Mehta, D. (1989). *Chief financial officer: Strategy formulation and implementation.* New York: John Wiley.

Hirshleifer, J. (1956). On the economics of transfer pricing. *Journal of Business*, **29**, 172–84.

Hirshleifer, J. (1957). Economics of the divisionalized firm. *Journal of Business*, **30**, 96–108.

Horst, T. (1971). Theory of the multinational firm: optimal behavior under differing tariff and tax rates. *Journal of Political Economy*, **79**, 1059–72.

Horst, T. (1977). American taxation of multinational firms. *American Economic Review*, **67**, 376–89.

DILEEP R. MEHTA and JAMES G. TOMPKINS

tying   Tying occurs when the sale or lease of one good is made conditional on the purchase of a second good (or service). The first good is identified as the *tying* good while the second good is the *tied* good. For example, when Loews Inc., holding the movie rights to a number of hit movies, required TV networks to buy some less desirable movies in order to be able to acquire the hits, it tied the lesser movies (the tied goods) to the hits (the tying goods).

These types of arrangements, which come in many forms, have the potential to cause economic harm to COMPETITION. As such, they may violate Section 3 of the CLAYTON ACT, or, in cases of ties between goods and services (and other special cases), Section 1 of the SHERMAN ACT. The possible adverse effects include:

(1) the extension of MARKET POWER from the market for the tying good into the market for the tied good,
(2) the reduction of freedom of choice by consumers, and
(3) the foreclosure of rivals from access to markets.

This last consequence may be especially true of exclusive deals contracts which, in some respects, parallel the act of tying (*see* CLAYTON ACT).

Tying contracts have also been shown to offer economic benefits in some circumstances. These include:

(1) production and distribution ECONOMIES OF SCALE and
(2) the protection of product QUALITY, for example, by tying a service contract to the sale of a product.

Both of these benefits offer potential advantages to consumers and producers. Consumers stand to gain from lower prices due to the lower costs if the market is competitive. They also gain from their greater certainty of the product's performance. Producers may gain greater profits from lower costs and also gain in their greater ability to protect their reputation. In addition, producers in imperfectly competitive markets may gain from the extension of market power or simply from the additional sales achieved. As such, tying is only illegal where it "substantially lessens competition," and where the existence of some market power in the tying good's market has been demonstrated (*see* CLAYTON ACT).

Bibliography

Blair, R. Kasserman, D. (1985). *Antitrust Economics*. Homewood: Irwin.

Greer, D. (1992). *Industrial Organization and Public Policy*. 3rd edn, New York: Macmillan.

GILBERT BECKER

— U —

uncertainty Frank Knight (1971) emphasized the distinction between risk and uncertainty. He defined risk as measurable or quantifiable, such as when a life assurance firm calculates the probabilities of paying benefits to survivors. The term "risk" applies to known probabilities and outcomes. However, in many business situations, managers cannot reasonably calculate probabilities and may not know the possible outcomes in the future. In these cases, where risk cannot be quantified, Knight argued there is uncertainty. Situations involving uncertainty as defined by Knight are much more difficult for decision making and this is why profits are awarded to business people: as a reward and a return for significant risk bearing.

Bibliography

Douglas, E. J. (1992). *Managerial Economics*. 4th edn, Englewood Cliffs, NJ: Prentice-Hall.

Knight, F. H. (1971). *Risk, Uncertainty and Profit*. Chicago: The University of Chicago Press.

ROBERT E. MCAULIFFE

utility maximization In most economic models, it is assumed that individuals attempt to maximize their TOTAL UTILITY. Ordinarily, these individuals must choose between alternatives and are faced with constraints. For example, consumers purchase a set of goods or product attributes which give them the most satisfaction (*see* PRODUCT ATTRIBUTES MODEL), given their limited income. Workers select a number of hours to work based on their preferences between work and leisure, subject to a time constraint and market constraints including the wage rate being offered. Managers and owners maximize their satisfaction by making investment decisions based on their preferences toward risk and rates of return, often subject to a constraint of limited funds. These and other decisions can be examined using INDIFFERENCE CURVES.

The model of consumer behavior typically describes the choice between two goods, for example, X and Y, or between one good and a composite good (the remaining funds for all other goods). The indifference curves of any individual show that consumer's tastes toward these two items. The slope of these indifference curves shows the rate at which the consumer is willing to trade one good for another, which depends on the ratio of the MARGINAL UTILITY (MU) of one good, X, to that of the other good, Y (*see* MARGINAL RATE OF SUBSTITUTION). The consumer is limited by a BUDGET CONSTRAINT which identifies the set of choices actually available given his income and the prices of the goods. The consumer's goal is to choose from this obtainable set that bundle which gives the most satisfaction.

The condition for utility maximization can be formally written as:

$$\frac{\text{MU}_x}{\text{MU}_y} = \frac{P_x}{P_y} \qquad (1)$$

where the ratio on the left-hand side of the equation shows the rate at which the consumer is willing to trade the two goods. The right-hand side of the equation measures the ratio of the prices (P) of the two goods, which indicates the market rate at which the consumer must trade the two goods. For example, assume that the consumer was willing to trade three units of good Y for one extra unit of X (since his MU_x was three times that of Y). Here, the ratio of the marginal utilities would be 3:1. If the market

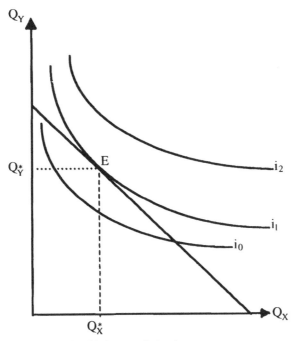

Figure 1   Utility maximization

price of X was only twice that of Y the consumer would only have to give up two units of Y to obtain the additional unit of X desired. Greater utility would be achieved by making this trade and by continuing to sacrifice more units of Y for additional X until the equality as stated in equation (1) is achieved.

Formally, this is described in the figure below. The consumer chooses a combination of goods Y and X whose quantities (Q) are measured on the vertical and horizontal axes. The indifference curves are marked $i_0, i_1, i_2, ...$, with higher numbers indicating greater total utility. The budget line, typically linear, has a slope which is determined by the ratio of the market determined prices. Point E represents utility maximization for the consumer. This is the tangency point between the budget line and the highest indifference curve within the budget constraint. Points on higher indifference curves, while more desirable, are unachievable given current prices and the consumer's income. Points below the budget line, while obtainable, offer less total utility than E as they fall on lower indifference curves. The tangency at E indicates that the slopes of the indifference curve and the budget line are equal, and as such the quantity

of good Y which the consumer is willing to trade for additional units of good X is equal to the amount he has to trade. The combination of Q^*y and Q^*x will be chosen by the utility maximizing consumer.

From the diagram, a strategy of lowering the price of X, Px, can be shown to alter the budget line in such a way that a higher indifference curve can be achieved. The new utility maximization point typically holds a greater quantity of good X, which is consistent with the LAW OF DEMAND. Moreover, the size of the INCOME EFFECT and SUBSTITUTION EFFECT of the price change can be derived from this model. Alternatively, it can be demonstrated that a change in consumer tastes, perhaps resulting from ADVERTISING or other promotion of good X, would increase the steepness of the slopes of all of the curves in the indifference map by altering the marginal rates of substitution. Once again, a new utility maximization point would be found. While remaining on the initial budget line, the consumer again will typically purchase more of good X.

Numerous other applications of this utility maximization model have been generated. Lancaster (1971) analyzes consumer demand for products by developing indifference curves for product attributes. Hyman (1993) and others demonstrate the conditions under which frequent flyer plans are profitable, food stamps and other programs are effective, and cost of living adjustments for recipients of government assistance are justifiable.

Bibliography

Douglas, E. (1992). *Managerial Economics: Analysis and Strategy*. 4th edn, Englewood Cliffs, NJ: Prentice-Hall.

Hirschey, M. Pappas, J. (1995). *Fundamentals of Managerial Economics*. 5th edn, Fort Worth: Dryden.

Hyman, D. (1993). *Modern Microeconomics*. 3rd edn, Homewood: Irwin.

Lancaster, K. (1971). *Consumer Demand: A New Approach*. New York: Columbia University Press.

GILBERT BECKER

V

variance The variance, or second moment, of a random variable measures the dispersion of outcomes around that variable's EXPECTED VALUE. For a discrete random variable, X, which has specific outcomes denoted by X_i and where the probability distribution of the values of X is given by $f(x_i)$, then the variance of X, σ^2, is calculated as

$$\text{var}(X) = \sigma^2 = \sum_x f(x_i) \times (X_i - E(X))^2$$

where $E(X)$ is the expected value of the random variable, X, and $\sum_X$ denotes the summation over all possible values of X. Each squared deviation of the outcome, X, from the expected value, $E(X)$, is weighted by its probability, $f(x_i)$.

For a given sample with T observations, an unbiased estimator of the variance of a random variable is s^2 which is calculated as

$$s^2 = \frac{1}{T-1} \times \sum_{i=1}^{T} (X_i - \overline{X})^2$$

where $\overline{X}$ is the sample mean. Note that the squared deviations are divided by $T-1$ and not by T because sample information has already been used to calculate the sample mean, so only $T-1$ of the observations are independent; see Maddala (1992) or Greene (1993). Most numerical software programs and spreadsheets will calculate the sample variance for a set of observations.

Normally, the greater the variance (or dispersion) of possible outcomes around the mean, the greater the risk to a manager or investor. The variance may thus be used to measure risk (or the square root of the variance, the STANDARD DEVIATION).

Bibliography

Douglas, E. J. (1992). *Managerial Economics*. 4th edn, Englewood Cliffs, NJ: Prentice-Hall.
Greene, W. H. (1993). *Econometric Analysis*. 2nd edn, New York: Macmillan.
Maddala, G. S. (1992). *Introduction to Econometrics*. 2nd edn, New York: Macmillan.

ROBERT E. MCAULIFFE

vertical integration Vertical integration refers to the expansion of a firm into earlier or later stages in the production process. For example, when General Motors decides to manufacture car radiators in its own plants instead of purchasing them from external sources they are vertically integrating.

There are two types of integration. Forward ("upstream") integration occurs when a firm decides to produce a product or service that uses its own product or service as an input (e.g. GM starts selling cars at company owned dealerships). Backward ("downstream") integration occurs when one firm decides to produce the inputs itself rather than purchasing them from outside sources (e.g. GM producing radiators) (*see* BACKWARD INTEGRATION). The distinguishing feature of any vertical integration is the replacement of a market purchase by an internal transfer. This could occur as a result of the acquisition of other firms or just an expansion within a firm. Assuming that firms are organized for the purposes of earning profits, a primary reason for replacing a market exchange with an internal transfer must be that, for that particular input, the latter mechanism is less expensive than the former.

Nobel economist Ronald Coase was interested in finding out why people organize production activities in the hierarchical (*see* HIERARCHY) structure of the firm and coordinate their decisions through a central authority rather relying on market exchange (Coase, 1937) (*see* COASE THEOREM). His explanation was that organizing activities through the hierarchy of a firm is often more efficient than market exchange because production requires the coordination of many transactions among many resource owners. According to Coase, the costs of transacting business through market relations are often higher than those of undertaking the same activities within the firm. Coase's major insight was that economic activity is most easily understood in terms of the transaction costs (*see* TRANSACTIONS COSTS) involved in any system of exchange between individuals.

Coase's analysis of transaction costs and vertical integration provides a good starting point for understanding the organizational decisions of the firm, but it falls somewhat short of a complete treatment in two important aspects (Schupack, 1977). First, Coase provides little detail concerning the underlying sources of transaction costs. This void limits the predictive use of the analysis. Moreover, Coase implicitly assumes that a competitive intermediate product markets exist, so that MARKET STRUCTURE influences on and consequences of vertical integration simply do not arise.

Although Coase mentions SEARCH COSTS and the problems of long-term CONTRACTS, the most extensive treatment of the determinants of transaction costs has been carried out by Williamson (1974). He identified two sets of factors whose elements interact to increase the costs of market exchange. The first set of factors, which Williamson referred to as "transactional factors" (market uncertainty and trading partners) are concerned with the environmental characteristics of the relevant intermediate product market. According to Williamson, market uncertainty increases transaction costs since a greater degree of uncertainty in a market will result in the negotiation of more lengthy and complex contracts between buyers and sellers of the intermediate product. Such complexity is required to guard the trading parties against changes in the market that might alter the precontract incentives to perform in the agreed manner. Market uncertainty increases transaction costs. In addition, reductions in the number of trading partners available to the firm is likely to increase the costs of market exchange. The second set of factors are referred to as human factors (e.g. opportunism). Opportunism refers to situations where the use of deception can be expected to increase profits; in such situations, honesty in trading is not as likely.

Where the intermediate product is produced by the same firm that employs it, a considerable degree of flexibility to adapt to changing market conditions is realized. In addition, internal transfers are likely to reduce the opportunistic tendencies of the parties to the exchange. This results from the fact that "internal divisions (*see* INTERNAL ORGANIZATION OF THE FIRM) do not have preemptive claims on profit streams" (Williamson, 1974). The information flows between related stages of production are also likely to improve when these stages are combined within a single firm for several reasons:

(1) there is a reduction in the incentive to behave opportunistically,
(2) common experiences tend to facilitate the overall flow of information within the firm, and
(3) the firm has much greater access to the relevant performance data of its internal divisions.

The key inquiry is whether vertical integration will result in increased profits. There are several factors which determine the answer to this query:

(1) managerial capacity
(2) easily observable quality
(3) number of suppliers
(4) monitoring
(5) contractual alternatives and
(6) legal limits on vertical integration.

Managerial capacity

As the firm takes on more and more activities, the manager starts losing track of things and the quality of managerial decisions suffers. The larger the firm, the longer the lines of communication between the manager and the production worker who must implement the decision. The capability of management limits the amount of information the manager can comprehend about the firm's operations. When the firm takes on additional functions, it can experience diseconomies (*see* DISECONOMIES OF SCALE) similar to those it experiences when it expands output beyond the efficient scale of production.

Easily observable quality

If an input is well defined and its quality is easily determined at the time of purchase, it is more apt to be purchased in the market than produced internally, other things constant (*see* QUALITY). For example, a flour mill will typically buy its wheat in the market while the manufacturer of a sensitive measuring instrument which requires a crucial gauge may produce it so it can monitor quality. Another reason why producers sometimes integrate backward is so they can make guarantees to their customers about the quality of the components or ingredients in a product (e.g. Frank Perdue raises his own chickens).

Number of suppliers

A firm wants an uninterrupted source of component parts. When there are many interchangeable suppliers of a particular input, a firm is more likely to purchase that input in the market rather than produce it internally, other things constant. If the resource market is so unstable that the firm cannot rely on a consistent supply of the component, the firm may produce the item to insulate itself from the unstable market. In addition, the existence of a large number of potential suppliers increases the likelihood of COMPETITION between those firms driving down prices.

Monitoring

The cost and ability to monitor production is another important factor. The more costly or difficult it is to monitor different production activities within a firm, the more efficient it may be to purchase components from external sources. This is related to some of the other factors mentioned above.

Contractual alternatives

Various contractual arrangements exist that will result in a firm receiving some of the features exhibited by the vertically integrated firm. For example, a long-term contract can resolve supply or demand reliability problems.

Legal limits on vertical integration

Courts often scrutinize cases in which they feel a firm has vertically integrated to acquire MARKET POWER (Blair and Kaserman, 1983). The major objection of the courts involves vertical market foreclosure (or BARRIERS TO ENTRY), which allegedly occurs when a supplier acquires one of its customers and this results in the supplier's rivals being prevented from competing for the acquired firm's business (Bork, 1969; Williamson, 1979). Both the SHERMAN ACT and the CLAYTON ACT have been used to challenge instances of vertical integration (*see* ANTITRUST POLICY). The Department of Justice (DOJ) and courts are starting to focus their analysis of vertical integration cases on more than simply market foreclosure (Burns, 1993). The three competitive problems which can result from vertical integration that the DOJ has identified are: increased entry barriers, possibility of COLLUSION, and the possible evasion of price regulation.

In summary, whether vertical integration will increase profitability for a firm is not always obvious and depends on a slew of institutional, legal and structural factors.

Bibliography

Blair, R. D. Kaserman, D. L. (1983). *Law and Economics of Vertical Integration and Control.* Orlando: Academic Press.

Bork, R. (1969). *Public Policy Toward Mergers.* Pacific Palisades: Goodyear.

Burns, J. W. (1993). Vertical restraints, efficiency, and the real world. *Fordham Law Review*, **62**, 597.

Coase, R. (1937). The nature of the firm. *Economica*, **4**, 386–405.

Schupack, M. B. (1977). The theory of vertical integration: a survey. *Working Paper No. 77–31.*

Williamson, O. E. (1974). The economics of antitrust: transactions cost considerations. *University of Pennsylvania Law Review*, **122**, 1439–96.

Williamson, O. E. (1979). Assessing vertical market restrictions: antitrust ramifications of the transaction cost approach. *University of Pennsylvania Law Review*, 127, 953.

GOVIND HARIHARAN and SEAN HOPKINS

X

X-efficiency X-efficiency is a state of production in which, for a given level of input usage, there is no way of increasing the output. The output process is thus also said to be production efficient (Friedman, 1990, p. 436). In contrast, **X-inefficiency** represents the failure to obtain maximum output from a given combination of inputs. Leibenstein (1966) developed the idea of X-inefficiency as a way of describing the results of a weakened incentive structure for cost-conscious, efficient management, especially in the absence of competitive market forces. For example, a state-run monopoly that does not incorporate the goal of profit maximization tends to create an incentive structure among managers in the firm discouraging aggressive cost-efficiency. In general, government bureaucracies driven by the goal of maximizing their operating budgets offer the most salient examples of X-inefficiency (Niskanen, 1971). Such managerial lassitude is based on the assumption that the market environment determines incentives for effort on the part of managers. Application of this concept to private monopolies or to firms enjoying government protection from competition is problematical, however (Stigler, 1976). Critics of the concept of X-efficiency claim that the existence of a monopoly or beneficial government intervention may not reduce managerial effort itself, but rather may merely re-direct managerial efforts towards RENT SEEKING, for example. Nonetheless, to the extent that a weakening of the market discipline of competition reduces the incentive of managers to maximize the productive potential of inputs, technology, and research and development, the concept of X-efficiency has some explanatory power.

Bibliography

Friedman, D. (1990). *Price Theory*. 2nd edn, Cincinnati, OH: South-Western Publishing.
Leibenstein, H. (1966). Allocative efficiency vs. X-efficiency. *American Economic Review*, 56, 342–415.
Niskanen, W. (1971). *Bureaucracy and Representative Government*. Chicago: Aldine-Atherton.
Stigler, G. J. (1976). The Xistence of X-efficiency. *American Economic Review*, 66, 212–16.

KENT A. JONES

INDEX

Compiled by Meg Davies (Registered Indexer)

Printed and bound in the UK by
CPI Antony Rowe, Eastbourne

Printed and bound by CPI Group (UK) Ltd, Croydon, CR0 4YY

16/04/2025

14658833-0003